MAC
WISEMAN

All My Memories
Fit For Print

"Mac Wiseman: All My Memories Fit For Print"
. . . As Told To Walt Trott

Catalog data:
Wiseman, Malcolm and Trott, Walt
Foreword by Daniels, Charlie

ISBN # 978 0-9632684-5-7 (cloth : alk. paper)
ISBN # 978-0-9908105-0-6 (Soft cover)
ISBN # 978 0-9908105-1-3 (e-book)
p.cm ~ (American Arts Culture series)

NOVA
B O O K S

Nova titles published in its American Arts Culture Series:

"Kitty Wells: The Honky Tonk Angels" by Walt Trott, 1993
"Sister Sunshine: Martha Carson" by Walt Trott, 1998
"Flight Of The MoonBirds" by Faye Partee, 2004
"The Original Goober – The Life & Times of James Buchanan" by Ruth White, 2004
"Number One Country Hits, 1944-2004" by Arnold Rogers & Jerry Langley, 2005
"Many Tears Ago: The Life & Times of Jenny Lou Carson" by Arnold Rogers & Jerry Langley, 2005
"Little Known Facts About Country Music" by Jack Selover, 2009
"A Place Called Paradise" by Shirley Hutchins, 2009
"My Memories of Jim Reeves… And Other Celebrities" by Joyce Jackson, 2010
"Every Highway Out Of Nashville, Vol. 2" by Ruth White, 2014

Dedication:

"At my farewell party, please only smiles, no tears!!! In every way, I've had a wonderful, happy life. Therefore, this book "the story of my life," I respectfully dedicate to God, my Mom and Dad. See you later, Love Mac."

A FAMILY AFFAIR — Entertainer Mac Wiseman has a word with his parents, Mr. and Mrs. Howard Wiseman of Route 1, Crimora, during a reception yesterday in honor of the internationally-known singer and guitarist. Yesterday was designated "Mac Wiseman Day" in conjunction with Waynesboro's Fall Foliage Festival.

Mac Wiseman following a performance in Waynesboro, Va., October 21, 1973.

Mac Wiseman pickin' and singin' for fans.

Foreword by Charlie Daniels

I discovered Mac Wiseman in the early 1950s, when as a fledgling bluegrass musician, I would buy his new records as soon as I could get my hands on them after they came out.

To say I was a huge fan would be an understatement and in those days we only got single 78rpm records. Albums were rare, so there were no album covers to give you a look at the artist and tell you a little about them. Even a picture was hard to come by.

I never even knew what Mac looked like until I had become a dyed-in-the-wool fan, but it made no difference what he looked like. It was the way he sang and played guitar that made me want to learn every song he released.

If I could have, I would have probably imitated Mac's voice, but the truth is that nobody can imitate Mac's voice. He's one of a kind and he only has to sing three notes before every bluegrass fan in the room knows who it is.

It would have been hard for me to handle at that age to think that many years later I would have the honor of becoming friends with this gentle and talented man.

Now all of us Mac Wiseman fans have a chance to learn about a career that spans many decades, and ride along as Mac carves out his unique place in musical history and in the hearts of us, his fans.

Wiseman's Words

Let me think about the highlights of my life and the many hats I've worn in this business of music, just to see if we can get you intrigued enough to want to read this book that delves into one man's journey on the road of life. Believe me, I'm thankful for all those who took the time to jog their memories that helped make this possible.

Now I ponder how best to approach this preface? Do I hit on some of the more negative aspects of my life recalled in the pages that follow, to entice readers as the tabloids do? That could include busting my butt to show fellow farm hands my bout with infantile paralysis didn't deter me from doing hard labor in loading hay bales or whatever; the hard-scrabble existence my first wife and I experienced while trying to carve out a career for myself; noting how a banjo got me forever typecast in bluegrass, when I felt as country as Carl Smith; explaining why some players grew disgruntled, due to my decision to go it alone; sharing the sheer frustration felt after years in the business of not getting any firm offers from major labels; and coping with a resentful crew after beating out their choice at the union ballot box, thanks in part to endorsements by Bill Anderson and Chet Atkins.

Probably upfront, I should cite my recollections of a legal skirmish resulting from a riotous gate-crasher's shooting at a music festival I ran; or yanking Jimmy Martin off-stage, after the "King of Bluegrass" overstayed his welcome; and disclosing how I almost shot "McHale's Navy" co-star Bobby Wright, mistaking him for a prowler. I also confide that an unprovoked Little Jimmy Dickens slapped my face, but bolted before I could take him over my one good knee to blister his butt; and point out John Hartford woke me from a sound sleep to come to the studio, only to find myself singing an ode to marijuana (way before it was being legalized).

Sure there are some things best left unsaid, including the time I stole a kiss from sweet Connie Smith, or the pleasure derived from relieving myself on the grave of a late musical nemesis, and perhaps even some of the episodes I actually do write about: Like how Cowboy Jack Clement went too far with his philosophical piffle "If you're not having fun, you're not doing your job," while producing my records; or how much I enjoyed after hours' partying with pals like Tex Ritter, Mother Maybelle Carter, Hank Snow and Johnnie Wright, as well as Earl and Louise Scruggs; or having Marty Robbins come to my financial rescue during my draining divorce case.

Among my sweeter memories, however, are working in tandem with such pioneering legends as Molly O'Day, Flatt & Scruggs, Bill Monroe, Hank Williams, Uncle Dave Macon and Merle Travis; also narrating a critically-acclaimed film documentary; performing for a crowd by lantern light; pickin' and singin' atop a projection booth at drive-in movies; and having the last laugh on a duo forcing my resignation by a salary cut, then lost a lucrative broadcast offer, contingent on having me in their troupe.

I also enjoyed touring with my good buddy Johnny Cash, notably at the Hollywood Bowl, Carnegie Hall and Newport Folk Festivals, and I'll add John invited me to record his final session just prior to his passing. I treasured that and our friendship.

Not all my choices have been right on, whether in my career or personal life. Even though a new form of surgery resulted in my losing over one hundred and fifty pounds, I regret that decision, as it was pure torture. I'm not sorry I departed Capitol Records when I did, along with Tex Ritter and Faron Young, although some saw it as a career-killing move. Instead, I moved on to record for RCA, and additional labels, notably CMH.

I wish I could tell you "and he lived happily ever after," but some of those deals didn't work out as well as I hoped. Nonetheless, I'm pleased that there were still good opportunities in store for me in days that followed. I've shared the scene with such iconic entertainers as Bob Hope, Lucille Ball, Arthur Godfrey, Dean Martin and even Old Blue Eyes' heir, little green-eyed vocalist Frank Sinatra, Jr.

I've also been blessed to work with a wide variety of artists, some of whom come to mind are Woody Herman, David Grisman, Jeff Foxworthy, Jim & Jesse, The Osborne Brothers, Grandpa Jones and Johnny Gimble, who assembled original Bob Wills sidemen for my Western Swing album "Songs That Made the Jukebox Play." No one was more surprised than I when the National Academy of Recording Arts & Sciences bestowed a Grammy nomination on my 1989 CMH album "From Grass Roots To Bluegrass."

During the 1990s, Scott Rouse threw a life line, calling on me, Doc Watson, Del McCoury and R&B bassist Bootsy Collins to be GrooveGrass Boyz, recording a hit single "Country Macarena" plus subsequent albums. Scott also produced Charlie Daniels' "Songs From the Longleaf Pines," inviting me to sing and play on several tracks, as well as on Scott's all-star "Christmas On the Mountain" CD, for which I wrote "Christmas Memories."

I must give an appreciative nod to my old friend and former neighbor Charlie Daniels, who graciously wrote the Foreword for me, after having beat the devil himself, down in Georgia. Maybe I didn't beat the devil, but we've sure gone a few rounds and I'm still standing on at least one good foot. Seriously, I give praise to the one above for gifting me with a pleasant-enough voice, and as another friend, George Jones, once proclaimed, letting me live long enough to tell it all.

In turn, I also appreciate both John Prine and Merle Haggard inviting me to do duet albums with them in my twilight years, as well as recent guest vocals for CDs of Leona Williams, Peter Cooper, April Verch, Jett Williams and now my own Wrinkled Records album "Songs From My Mother's Hand," which also honors my parents.

Who would've thought a country boy from the foothills of the Blue Ridge Mountains, would be honored one day by the Bluegrass Preservation Hall of Greats, Bluegrass Hall of Honor, Virginia's Music Hall of Fame, Country Music Hall of Fame, and presented the national Presidential Medal of the Arts (with an accompanying $20,000 cash prize, a nice plus)!

We hope you'll enjoy reading about my career climb, travels, travails and occasional misadventures, as much as I have living them. Now I look forward to future endeavors, and indeed, I'll confide, it's still so sweet to be remembered!

- Mac

Preface

$\mathbf{M}$ac Wiseman's career has spanned several decades. Although from infancy he suffered polio, he is not "a man of constant sorrow." Instead, he turned adversity into triumph. A survivor, Mac succeeded on and off stage, thanks to his disciplined career course.

Being invited to write with Mac, a man who prompted a lyric to Hank Williams, is an honor in itself. Immediately there's the challenge of getting it right for a man who apprenticed with pioneers Buddy Starcher and Molly O'Day, became one of Flatt & Scruggs' original Foggy Mountain Boys, and busted a nut hitting high notes beside Father of Bluegrass himself, Bill Monroe! Yes, Mac's shared the stage with numerous icons, including Uncle Dave Macon, Roy Acuff, Slim Whitman, Webb Pierce, Lefty Frizzell, Kitty Wells, Marty Robbins, Patsy Cline, Jim Reeves, and Johnny Cash, on an amazing journey to his ninth decade.

Mac's contribution has been significant. Apart from being an entertainer of note and an influence to younger artists, he's championed the revival of songs from a bygone era, bringing them back into mainstream favor. Among those he left an indelible stamp on are "'Tis Sweet To Be Remembered," "Love Letters In the Sand," "I Wonder How the Old Folks Are At Home" and "Jimmy Brown The Newsboy."

Mac's preference for ballads boasting a pleasing melody and powerful lyrics made him an early hero of mine. Among artists Mac's influenced are Charlie Daniels, Ronnie Milsap and Del McCoury, willing captives of his wide-ranging vocals and distinctive performing style. Fortunately, they're among artists and colleagues sharing their thoughts on Mac in the interviews compiled herein.

Literally the last of a dying breed, Mac hit coal-mine camps, honky-tonks, radio barn dances, outdoor festivals, and onward to national TV, film and wide-ranging concerts at prestigious venues like Madison Square Garden, The Hollywood Bowl, Carnegie Hall, Newport Folk Festival, and abroad to London's Wembley Stadium. Attesting to his innovative musicianship, Mac added drums to his country recordings and introduced twin fiddles on bluegrass discs. His diversity is reflected in sessions with Art Satherley, Jack Clement, John Prine, Charlie Daniels and big band icon Woody Herman.

A natural rangy tenor, Mac defied categories and critics by simply defining his own performing persona, whether preserving beautiful melodic creations or introducing new material. Nobody puts any more depth of feeling into a ballad than Wiseman, whose warm vocals have a calming affect on audiences, though in equally fine fashion he delivers uptempo tunes like "Davy Crockett" or "Johnny's Cash and Charley's Pride." In addition to being called the best tenor voice in bluegrass, he's also earned praise for his flat-top pickin' style and rhythm guitar playing.

In retrospect, Wiseman's bigger handicap was the label heads, unable to get a handle on how to guide him musically. Chet Atkins wanted Mac on RCA, yet proved hesitant on how to record him, and though Ken Nelson thought to launch him as a Capitol folk artist, failed to follow through. Mac's mentor-of-sorts Randy

Wood at Dot, couldn't make up his mind on which side of the microphone to put him, finding him equally adept as artist or producer.

As a result, Wiseman stretched musical boundaries, being the first active artist producing discs as A&R honcho on such memorable acts as Reno & Smiley, Cowboy Copas, Bonnie Guitar and Jimmy C. Newman, switching easily from bluegrass to country. Sole surviving founding father of the Country Music Association today, Mac also helped promote other trade organizations like the Gospel Music Association, International Bluegrass Music Association and ROPE (The Reunion Of Professional Entertainers). Managing the WWVA *Wheeling Jamboree* in West Virginia, he rescued it from drowning in red ink during the late 1960s, then kicked off Kentucky's *Renfro Valley Barn Dance Festival* in the 1970s and still going strong. As an officer and board member in the American Federation of Musicians, Mac championed fellow musicians.

Wiseman's own relevance has been proven time and again. Consider he became in-demand on the college concert circuit in the late 1950s, helped pioneer bluegrass festivals in the 1960s, and toured Canada and Europe in subsequent decades. By the mid-1990s, a series of Groovegrass Boyz recordings with Doc Watson, Del McCoury, Bootsy Collins and Scott Rouse, returned him to the charts. Mac's since recorded with Johnny Cash, Charlie Daniels, John Prine, Leona Williams, April Verch, Jett Williams and Merle Haggard. That's a compelling endorsement for an Octogenarian.

At long last, the Country Music Hall of Fame in 2014, acknowledged Wiseman's various contributions via induction into the Country Music Hall of Fame, and we're pleased that the man himself is around to enjoy the ultimate accolade.

Mac's awesome accomplishments are detailed on the pages that follow. Though off the road, he's still tackling new tasks close to home. Besides having cut more albums than many of his peers during decades of recording, he's stunned us by delivering a solo studio effort, based on his mother's hand-written notebooks of songs she compiled for him in his youth: "Songs From My Mother's Hand." Among his supporting players is twenty-something mandolin virtuoso Sierra Hull, which is rather remarkable, as well. Mac's is a rich legacy for aspiring artists and fans alike to absorb.

Having interviewed Mac through the years, I was quite familiar with his career, and while editor of the AFM union newspaper, *The Nashville Musician,* then Secretary-Treasurer Wiseman co-signed my checks for a year-and-a-half. I've enjoyed unprecedented access to him at home, as well as numerous telephone chats, not only with him, but many friends and colleagues. I can only hope we've done justice to a unique career, and again I'll say another *thank you* to an American musical treasure, for making it all happen!

- Walt Trott

Prelude...

"Well, this one is like nothing else," proclaimed Peter Cooper, co-producer of a then-forthcoming folk album with Mac Wiseman. The daily *Tennessean* newspaper reporter was introducing a broadcast with the artist to discuss their disc, in Nashville's SiriusXM Studios, June 25, 2014.

"Maybe someone will do another one like this – like Mac Wiseman's *'Songs From My Mother's Hand'* – one day. To do so, they'll need to have a mother who writes the words to songs she hears on the radio into composition books that serve as the family songbook. In those books, they'll need to find passion and inspiration that fuel a monumental, Hall of Fame-caliber life in music. They'll need to cherish those books throughout their life, then take them into a recording studio at age eighty-nine and sing the songs their mother wrote down, in a voice of weathered, heartening beauty. Well, this one is like nothing else."

Acknowledgments:

This book began many years back, at least in the idea stage, while Mac was AFM Nashville's Local 257 Musicians Union's Secretary-Treasurer and Walt was editor for the union publication - *The Nashville Musician* – as the veteran vocalist first suggested doing his biography. Of course, he figured it would take two volumes, though that would not be a feasible plan. Many years later, when Mac revisited his idea of a book, it developed that both Mac and Walt had time to devote to such a project. Thanks to many hours of interviews, reflections and research, the book began to take shape, and for that much appreciation goes to an assortment of friends, family and fans, who willingly gave their support in one way or another, notably Charlie Daniels for his sincere Foreword. Among so many others are Eddie Adcock, Bill Anderson, Larry Black, Donnie Bryant, Laura Weber Cash, Jack Clement, Peter Cooper, Charlie Dick, Leslie Elliott, David Ferguson, Tillman Franks, Katie Gillon, Billy Grammer, Katie Haas, Merle Haggard, Dan Hays, John Rice Irwin, Ramona Jones, Thomm Jutz, Sandy Knox, Charlie Lamb, Doyle Lawson, Don Light, Jo Walker Meador, Del McCoury, Jesse McReynolds, Ronnie Milsap, Ken Nelson, Jimmy C. Newman, Bobby Osborne, Patricia Presley, John Prine, Ronnie Reno, George Riddle, Scott Rouse, Dave (Mudcat) Saunders, Jim Shumate, Pete Stamper, Eddie Stubbs, April Verch, Lyle West, Leona Williams, Bobby & Johnnie Wright, and, of course, family members like Randy, Maxine & Scott Wiseman. A valued behind-the-scenes contributor is Nova Books' Tom Barkoukis, who designed the covers, assisted with illustrations and formats. There's also a very patient UK discographer Dick Grant, deserving of recognition, along with Ruth White, here in the good ol' USA. A special nod goes to Craig W. Gill at the University Press of Mississippi in Jackson, for his initial interest and encouragement.

"Mac is one of the heroes. Having Mac cut 'Me & Bobby McGee' was one of the highlights of my life. When I was young, he had a hit song on 'Love Letters in the Sand' and I just loved that. Maybe someone tried to put him in that bluegrass box, but he is so much more than that. Mac's is a great, great voice," so stated Country Music Hall of Famer and Nashville Songwriters Hall of Famer, Kris Kristofferson, in *The Tennessean*.

Contents

Crimora

Mac's kin Janie Sampson and husband surrounded by residents at their early 20th century whistle-stop store that doubled as a post office, near Crimora.

The Old Mill where Mac's dad worked; adjacent to the South River lake in Crimora.

The old Wiseman homestead near Crimora, as it looks today.

1 Beginnings...
'Danger Heartbreak Ahead'

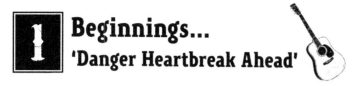

"Danger, heartbreak ahead
Be sure little heart, for you know
Yes, you know what happened to you before
There's danger, travel slow..."

Mac Wiseman's salad days saw him featured on the bandstand with Bill Monroe, and Flatt & Scruggs, acts credited with pioneering "bluegrass" music. While acknowledging their tall talents, Mac isn't so sure that bluegrass began with them, feeling it's simply another term applied to his beloved acoustical mountain music.

Hailing from the heart of Appalachia, Wiseman asserts it's the raw, down-home, "shit-kicking" music he grew up listening to as a youth: "It's hoedowns and reels, the same music J. E. Mainer of Mainer's Mountaineers and Pop Stoneman played way back when, without instrumental breaks and bluesy solos."

Going against accepted ideology, Mac's view is rather than being its "inventor," Monroe merely defined a certain style that helped popularize it in the postwar years, 1945-'46, "though indeed Bill was a master." Without a doubt, Monroe assembled a quite magical acoustic band in that time. To complement his own chop-chord mandolin pickin' style, Bill settled on lead guitarist Lester Flatt, noted for his near-trademark G-run, to provide backup and rhythm; banjoist Earl Scruggs' unique three-finger pickin' style; melded to Chubby Wise's blues-tinged fiddling, ably switching from lead to melodic fills; rhythmically underscored by bass-fiddler Howard Watts (a.k.a. Cedric Rainwater).

Bill Monroe & his Blue Grass Band (from left) Jack Thompson,
Chubby Wise, Monroe, Mac and Rudy Lyles.

1

As Monroe created the beat, Scruggs' banjo amplified it. They led a contingent that raised the bar, set the modern standard and helped define the so-called bluegrass genre. Bluegrass boasts a tight backbeat, solid rhythms and high lonesome vocals like Bill's, muses Mac, adding, eyes a'twinkling, "You can 'grass anything... I think if Monroe had called his band the Green Mountain Boys, we'd be calling it Green Mountain music instead of Bluegrass music."

Mac suggests succinctly what Bill created was a word or title, while stressing such reasoning does no disservice to Monroe, hailed as "Father of Bluegrass." Wiseman merely believes there's more history to it than that specific style formulated in the mid-1940s by Bill's Blue Grass Boys, which amounted to a fusion of acoustic string sounds its members learned from boyhood and simply improved upon.

That assertion creates something of a paradox regarding Mac's career, considering he's a welcome member of the bluegrass family, and as such has benefitted handsomely, playing a wide network of bluegrass festivals. This coming at a time when rock and roll threatened the livelihood of acoustic country acts. Ultimately, Mac's connection with the genre won him induction into both the Society For the Preservation of Bluegrass Music in America's Bluegrass Hall of Greats (1987), and the International Bluegrass Music Association's Bluegrass Hall of Honor (1993).

The mark of Mac Wiseman, whatever his characterization of bluegrass, is that in his 70th year as a professional performer, he still stands for something after many of his peers have left the scene. In April 2010, Mac hit number twelve on *Billboard's* Bluegrass album chart with his Rural Rhythm retrospective "Mac Wiseman Bluegrass, 1971." On June 24, 2013, he concluded his final studio session for a duets album with Merle Haggard in Madison's Hilltop Studio, featuring backup vocals furnished by The Isaacs and Vince Gill.

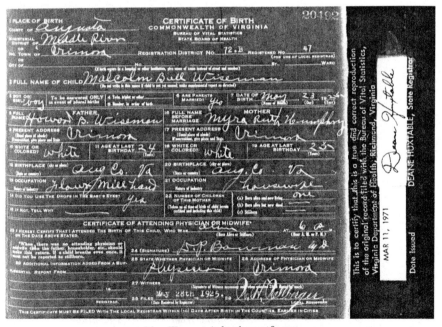

Mac Wiseman's birth certificate.

2

The fact is Mac loves the music, its practitioners and various forms, but resists what he calls the media-led hype to apply labels to anything not the norm, trying to pigeonhole or categorize it in a format made easier to critique or review. Similarly, he feels country DJs kept bluegrass subordinate in airplay to commercial country recordings for decades.

Prior to the time that radio differentiated country from bluegrass, Mac's pure country vocals had competed along with the likes of Faron Young or Carl Smith: "I got country airplay as much as those guys before the terminology 'bluegrass' came along and because we had a banjo on my first records, they lumped me into that category. It was almost a dirty word and country stations stopped playing bluegrass. I really think they misinterpreted what bluegrass was and decided it didn't fit their country club crowd."

Malcolm, age three months.

To Mac, it was all country music and he feels each recording should speak for itself; his obvious riposte being one of resentment. Reportedly, Earl Scruggs shared Mac's feelings about being pigeonholed, pointing out that his major hits were country successes, notably the number one "The Ballad of Jed Clampett." Classifying their product as primarily bluegrass, meant they were unable to compete with mainstream country peers on a level playing field.

Long regarded as somewhat of a musical maverick, Mac didn't even enter this world in a usual way, literally being born with a bang! No doubt first-time mom Ruth Wiseman counted on a smooth delivery, but as her contractions came closer, there was no drowning out dynamite blasting from a nearby stone quarry. Indeed six p.m., the hour of birth, seemed a late hour to set off explosions. Finally "Doc" Bowman assured her harried husband Howard their first baby was a boy, and both mother and son seemed just fine. That marked Malcolm Bell Wiseman's noisy debut on the scene, Saturday, May 23, 1925. According to his birth certificate, Mac's bow occurred in the Commonwealth State of Virginia's Augusta County.

"I was born in 1925 in a small house on the banks of the South River in Crimora, which is now a hole in the hillside," explained Mac. "My dad was a miller in the nearby mill, and I was raised in a sparsely settled community."

If the former Myra Ruth Humphreys shuddered at the sound of the blasts unexpectedly trumpeting her baby's birth, it was far more devastating six months later, discovering he suffered a debilitating disease. She'd suspected something was amiss when he whimpered in discomfort while she bathed his legs, and soon had

3

her suspicions confirmed by the MD's: The baby had contracted an acute infection to his right leg, an affliction usually resulting in muscular paralysis. It was a viral inflammation within the spinal cord, medically termed poliomyelitis, and since it seemed to affect very young victims, was labeled infantile paralysis.

Like most farm wives, Ruth was pleased their first-born was a boy, who could grow up to help work the farm and maybe one day inherit the fruits of their labors. She winced upon hearing of the spread of this noxious disease nationally, even as the medical profession struggled to contain it by quarantining whole communities. Mac's parents prayed for a miracle, but found in years to come he had more backbone than to lay back and let a withered leg keep him down.

Mac pointed out, "At age two, my family had moved into a bigger house on the Rockfish Road that runs north and south through the Shenandoah Valley, then parallel to State Route 11 (now Interstate-81). We lived there four years and I turned six during the Great Depression, when we moved into my mother's family homestead, including some sixty-five acres where we raised nearly everything we ate."

Howard B. Wiseman, in his earlier days.

Infant Mac at the Humphreys' home (his grandparents).

This indention in the countryside today marks the site of the house Mac was born in. (On the hilltop is the Barger barn.)

4

2 'Empty Cot In The Bunkhouse'... Breakthrough

"There's a range for every cowboy
Where the foreman takes care of his own
There'll be an empty saddle tonight
But he's happy up there I know..."

Quite honestly, Mac Wiseman never cared for his middle name: Bell. Mac reasons he may have been named for Malcolm Coiner, an area service station owner and friend, while Bell was a family name: "It was my father's middle name, and why I chose not to reveal it in interviews was that I thought it might be a distraction, and thinking about the characters in books by that name, including Belle in 'Beauty & The Beast,' Belle (Watling) in 'Gone With The Wind' and, of course, Belle Starr, all seemed too feminine to me.

"Coiner's was the place where I first heard a banjo played in person. Late at night when it was too hot to sleep, my dad took Mom, my sister Virginia and me there to buy Eskimo Pies (a chocolate-covered vanilla ice cream bar) to cool off. That guy who played banjo was Joe Sandy, a big, heavy-set fellow, who knocked me out with his playing. Though years later, I didn't relish using it on my records, as the banjoist plays the melody, which can throw a ballad singer off."

In Wiseman's birth year, Calvin Coolidge was President, the mighty Pittsburgh Pirates won the World Series' pennant, and WSM-Nashville first signed on the air, showcasing country fiddle soloist Uncle Jimmy Thompson. Soon that slot evolved into a barn dance program that a few seasons later morphed into the *Grand Ole Opry*, both hosted by WSM's first program director, known as the Solemn Ol' Judge, George D. Hay.

Mac's birth certificate simply stated that Ruth was twenty-five, Howard twenty-four, and his attending physician was D. P. Bowman. Ruth and Howard, a miller by trade, were then farming "on the fringes of Crimora," a whistle-stop at the foot of the Appalachian Mountain Trail. The mill they resided near was known as Deraunders.

Youngsters today may find it difficult to comprehend that all the days of Mac's boyhood, the Wisemans had no electricity, indoor plumbing or telephone in any of the three houses Mac was raised in, not unusual then for those raised in rural areas. Yet thankfully, he says the family did boast one of the first battery-operated radios in the community.

Mac remembers fellow entertainer Raymond Fairchild, who grew up in the Maggie Valley (North Carolina) area of the Great Smoky Mountains, telling him of his own youth: "He always plays that Appalachian Homecoming in Norris, Tennessee. Well, he said growing up, he learned to play banjo in the dark. His hardworking dad turned off all the lamps when he went to bed, because he had to rise at dawn, so Ray had to learn and practice in the dark."

After Howard Wiseman went to work for the flour mill, he created a little wheat crop backup, a storage "wheat bank," to draw out as needed: "So we could swap our eggs and such for store-bought sugar and coffee when needed."

The Barger blockhouse.

One item not purchased in the Wiseman household was liquor, as both of Mac's parents were teetotalers: "I never could get up the courage to ask my mom if her father had been a drinker, thinking maybe that was the reason she was so against it."

Mac was born in the fifth year of the passing of the national Prohibition Act, which forbade making or selling of alcoholic beverages, though it ran rampant in cities or out in the countryside, where rural "stills" helped supply city "speakeasies" (not to mention "bathtub gin" made by city dwellers).

"I remember years later when we had family get-togethers, occasionally my brother Kennie and I would have a beer. But when we saw how uneasy it made our mother to see us sipping these, we just did away with them altogether."

Mac's siblings are Virginia, Kenneth and Naomi; fortunately, none suffered the dreaded polio Mac had to endure.

"I don't remember it, of course, being so young, but I heard later there was quite an epidemic. There were so many cases of polio breaking out, they had to quarantine a whole town in Virginia. They didn't know why," Mac explains. "It was much worse then. Some physicians they say couldn't even agree on how to cope with it," much like the HIV/AIDS pandemic that erupted in the 1980s.

Shortly after Mac started school, the nation voted in a new President, former New York Governor Franklin Delano Roosevelt, who had contracted polio in 1921. Oddly enough, FDR was thirty-nine, whereas most of the disease's victims were babies or young children. In 1840, European physician Jakob Heine first detected the disease itself, and by the early twentieth century most of those diagnosed with it in the U.S. were youngsters.

Mac learned that his mother would regularly massage his polio leg from the hip down with olive oil: "Since I would whimper - not cry - every time she bathed me, my mom and dad took me to Staunton (the county seat) to see what the trouble

6

was… After learning of the problem, she had no idea what to do, but knowing her baby was in pain, thought it would help some massaging the leg.

"Later, that procedure would become known worldwide as the Elizabeth Kenny Treatment (she, a valiant Australian bush nurse, pioneered a similar treatment for infantile paralysis - and Cerebral Palsy - Down Under from 1929). A number of doctors later told me that had she not done that, my leg might have become withered and paralyzed like President Roosevelt's did. So it was a miracle or at least divine inspiration that my mother did that for me."

Yet another artist suffering the affliction was Western singer Tex Williams, who overcame polio at an early age, and went on to become a mid-1940s' hit maker. The burly balladeer boasted number one songs such as "Smoke! Smoke! Smoke! (That Cigarette)."

Ruth and Howard Wiseman's 1924 wedding shot.

"While we were at the *Town Hall Party* in 1957, Tex told me he was a victim of polio, and I said, 'I'm glad you're able to wear cowboy boots,' something I had wished I could do." Wiseman saw Tex walked with a bit of a limp, and Williams confided that he suffered similar shortness of leg, but compensated by wearing a built-up, custom-made boot with a zipper inside to accommodate the withered leg.

"I ordered me some boots custom-made, too, after that," grins Wiseman. Tex, who died in 1985, was so proud of his cowboy image that he wore his western wear on and off stage.

Mac claims Howard, his father, was another innovative person: "Dad only had schooling up to the third or fourth grade, but Mom finished up grade school, and they always encouraged me to get an education. One time my dad worked for a big land owner who had a number of farms, and when I was two, we moved onto one of his tenant farms where my sister Virginia was born."

"I had to wait until I was seven to attend school, as my birthday fell in May. My first year at an elementary school in Harriston, I'd walk about a half mile to a little country store, where we bought things like coffee and sugar with our egg money, in order to catch a ride in a covered wagon for my first two years of school, three-and-a-half miles away. More than eighty years later, the school is still standing.

"Following my sixth year of grade school, I had my first corrective surgeries for my polio leg during summer break. Unable to work the farm while convalescing, I learned to play my three dollar and ninety-nine cent Sears & Roebuck guitar ordered from a catalog. While attending the seventh grade, I wore a cast all the way up to my hip. To enable me to attend school during that period, my mother drove me to the store to catch the covered wagon, which the county soon replaced with a bus."

Despite a slight age difference - Ruth was born August 18, 1899, and Howard on May 15, 1901 – the Wisemans were well suited as a couple. Where he might let things slide a bit, she was a stickler for details, and skillfully managed their meager finances, while maintaining faith in him as a breadwinner.

"My dad had a passion about getting seed catalogs each spring real early. Anything that was different, he wanted to be the first to try it in his garden. There was one for banana cantaloupes, which look like a large banana... After people took a taste, they found they were really good, like an original banana. Dad raised vegetables and such to peddle from his horse-drawn wagon and had a route he'd follow, stopping along the way to chat and he was quite a joker, too. One spring Dad was looking thru his seed catalogs and saw an advertisement for yellow-meat watermelons, though they tasted like the red-meat ones. So he was going to play a joke on his regular customers, and the first time he made his rounds with the ripe melons, dropped off a few of these yellow-meat watermelons, as a surprise. It backfired on him. His customers never saw yellow-meat ones and thought they were like still 'green' and without tasting, threw them away, and so he had to replace them.

"Another time, just as the watermelons were ripening, Dad would go check his patch to find that a number of melons had been busted open, and they had the heart of the melon scooped out, leaving the seeds. He couldn't figure out how this was happening, so he built a little lean-to next to the melon patch, the lean-to was much like brush arbors... this was done by cutting the small trees about head-high and folding the tops into the middle, protecting them from the sun and rain. Dad took refuge in his arbor, where he could see the patch and wait for the ones a-bustin' his watermelons. Incidentally, he had his shotgun with him. Sure enough, after a few days - on Sunday - three neighbor boys came into the patch to help themselves again. Then Dad stepped out with his gun and said, 'Can I help you boys?' The kids didn't know whether to run or have a bowel-movement."

Mac's father also invented his own method of planting seed in order to finish faster and reap a greater abundance, a system known in the family as "laying-off plow."

"Dad did pretty well back then and even had a Model-T Ford automobile and a Model-T truck with solid rubber tires. They were building highways through the area and Dad with his truck worked for nine dollars a day - that was big money then - hauling for a major road project from Waynesboro to Winchester on the Rockfish Highway. Dad also worked constructing the Skyline Drive from Buena Vista to Luray, Virginia (on the upper part of the Blue Ridge Mountain)."

Despite having only a fourth grade education, Howard attended barber school in Richmond, then set up his own business in the fittingly-named New Hope, Virginia, a shop Mac says still stands.

"My Dad later took a course in welding. That was after I left home and I felt that took a lot of initiative on his part. It got so folks in the area used to call on Dad to fix things for them."

Mac's maternal grandfather Thomas Humphreys was a horticulturist, who planted lots of fruit trees, including a cherry tree which stands out in Mac's mind, and yet another memorable tree, an apple tree they called "Maiden's Blush" because he says, "It would produce a yellow apple with reddish spots like a lady would blush." Granddad also had the only gooseberry tree for miles around, which Mac and other kids picked clean.

Regarding the cherry tree, Mac recalls it as sort of a centerpiece of the orchard, and its size allowed a boy to walk out on the limb or branch, reaching up even higher to get more cherries. He adds, "The gooseberry thing was really only a bush about as high as our garden fence. Mom made us pies from the gooseberries. Oh God, they were so great! - You know, one of Bradley Kincaid's most popular records was 'Gooseberry Pie' - but wasn't enough there for her to can them.

"Right outside the back door where we lived was an old apple-dumpling tree. We called it that because Mom would make apple dumplings from its huge apples. She'd core it, wrap it in dough, and bake it; it was a rather soft-meat apple. They were really delicious."

Mac remembers as a wee lad when salesmen on the road tossed out promotional cans of snuff to farmers; limp and all, he scoured the grounds to retrieve them, knowing that two aunts who "dipped" would pay him a nickel a can. No doubt the hard-pressed companies in those dire times were anxious to distribute and promote their product amongst the rural population.

"The Great Depression put my dad's barbershop out of business, but he kept his barber tools, including razors and such, and as word got around, people would come to our house to have him cut their hair. He might charge twenty-five-cents a head. Lots of his customers were rather untimely. For instance, one old gentleman often came on Sunday mornings and he'd sit on the woodpile until he saw someone was up, before coming into the house to have his haircut. He was a mountain man who lived nearby. His name was Mr. Will Hoy, and he didn't have much to say. I thought it unusual when he was leaving that he said, 'Good mornin' to y'all,' which to him was like saying goodbye (though most folks said it upon arrival)."

Ruthie also learned to cut hair: "She got to where she could cut hair pretty good, doing our heads and her sister Esther's ten kids... Back then we didn't have much, but we got our hair cut. We didn't have a lot of clothes in the closet. You'd have school clothes, work clothes and probably one dress-up outfit."

With the infamous Black Monday and Tuesday, October 28-29, 1929, the Wall Street stock market "crashed," sending America's economy spiraling into a severe slump prompting devastating financial losses, business bankruptcies, farm foreclosures, along with unprecedented unemployment, suicides and national bank closings. Like other grassroots Americans, the Wiseman family felt its terrible repercussions.

"My dad was out of work for a time during the Depression, and that's why we moved onto the Humphreys' family farm. It got so my father couldn't even afford to buy licenses for his car or truck. They sat up there by the barn shed, rusting into the ground. That broke him, both financially and spiritually, as I remember it. So he hired out on different jobs."

An imaginative boy, Mac would sit in the vehicles and pretend he was driving them: "I must've put a million miles on them." There were times when the small fry would mimic his mom, making mud cakes, but cracking a real egg onto them - obviously a no-no - and adding a flower petal or two for decoration.

"Whenever she felt I needed some discipline, she would send me to get a switch for her to punish me; of course, I'd come back with the smallest one I could find. Invariably she'd say that wasn't big enough for the wrong done, and send me back out for a bigger switch (to better suit the misdeed)."

Apparently Little Mac had an inner voice to urge him on. It refused to accept that he was different from the neighbor boys, having a handicap that could've held him back:

"I guess I had a lot of will-power and determination. I was four years old and carrying in the wood for our stove, even though I was clumsy with that bad foot of mine. Carrying in those big pieces with limbs and such, I would trip and one time cut my face and I still have that scar. I was very analytical about it, but was damn fortunate I didn't put out an eye."

Memories Mac holds dear today include times spent singing at the Pleasant Hill Church of the Brethren, which is still open and where he attends services when visiting family members. Just down the road today on state road Three Forty is Crimora's only restaurant, The 340 Snack Bar, operated by Nellie Gochenour, an attractive widow who also owns the trailer park across the road, where Mac's niece Debbie lives.

"I was baptized in the usual way in the South River - three times forward instead of backwards, as the congregation believes 'we are baptized into His death,' for at the moment of passing, Jesus' head fell forward," explains Mac. This ceremony conducted by the local Church, some one hundred and fifty years old, prompted their nickname, the "Dunkers." Brethren clergy had a rotating system; that is, four different

Crimora's Pleasant Hill Church, note cemetery on right.

preachers would come by once a month, taking turns conducting services and baptisms. Baptisms would usually follow the conclusion of a revival or prayer meeting."

In later years, Wiseman learned that Church of the Brethren had churches elsewhere: "I met another musician who told me he was also a member of the Church of The Brethren, his church being in Indiana... I was originally on our church's Cradle Roll, baptized at age twelve, and remain a member of Pleasant Hill Church until this day (to which he quietly makes monetary donations)."

The Church of the Brethren began in Schwarzenau, Germany in 1708, organized by Alexander Mack during the Protestant Reformation. It believes entirely in the New Testament with heavy emphasis on The Sermon On the Mount. Their first location in the U.S. occurred in 1723, in Germantown, Pennsylvania and now (despite some withdrawals over doctrinal differences) boasts more than a thousand congregations in the states and Puerto Rico, with membership numbering nearly one hundred and twenty-three thousand believers. Meanwhile, a branch of the Brethren established in Nigeria currently outnumbers (with one hundred and twenty-eight thousand) membership in the States.

"I was always pleased when I heard somebody say to me, 'I turned my life around when I found God.' After doing a lot of thinking and pondering, while doing this book, it dawned on me there was never a time that I didn't know God. Oh, I've stumbled and fell many times, but God was always there to pick me up and point me back in the right direction.

"In 1957, while working with Dot Records, I joined a Baptist church in Santa Fe Springs, about twenty miles from Hollywood, a new township at the time. It was next door to Whittier, California, home of former President Nixon (then vice president). This was the first time in years that I was off the road and able to attend church regularly, and its teachings were similar."

As with most youngsters, Mac's mother was his initial inspiration for regularly attending church. At one time, she encouraged her son to be the church secretary to write about congregational happenings. Despite chores and hard work as a farm boy, Mac was always eager to go to church and attend school.

Smiling, Mac offers the name of his primary school teacher, Miss Engleman: "She was very thoughtful and went out of her way to help us. I was sick a lot as a child and she let me stay in at recess time, and would literally tutor me, so I could keep up with the class."

Due to having had polio, Mac was always very susceptible to many other diseases, including having pneumonia six times, measles, whooping cough and mumps.

At twelve, Mac bought his first guitar, that Gene Autry model: "That took a lot of nickels working for somebody else. It came in by mail in a cardboard box and it's a wonder it didn't get crushed. I used that box as my guitar case to protect it. It was a year before I could get the damned thing in tune. Nobody around

Miss Engleman

11

there knew how to do it... Then an old guy, Preacher Maiden, came along to hold a revival. At the time, different parishioners would take him in for a night to help out. He stayed at our place one night and I had the guitar. 'Let me see that,' he said.

Preacher Maiden visited.

"It wasn't worth a damn, really, but he tuned it for me," Mac continues. "It was probably out of tune by the time he went down the road, but I'd watched him. I kinda wish I had it today as a childhood memento."

Mac's game leg gave him a lot of pain during his boyhood: "Oh yes, especially while working the farm. I had that weakened ankle... and whenever I put my weight on it, it was quite painful. So it wasn't easy. When I reached the age of thirteen, after completing the sixth grade, I had a couple corrective surgeries on it. The doctors had felt they should hold off until my body was nearly full-grown. I'm grateful they did. Now I only feel a little weakness. The one leg didn't develop as rapidly as the other, so it's a little shorter and a lot smaller."

During his thirteenth summer, Mac's surgeries were accomplished separately after school let out, at the University of Virginia-Charlottesville's campus hospital, laying him up for nearly a year: "Actually while I completed the seventh grade, I was still on crutches; nonetheless, they voted me Valedictorian."

He also remembers that his folks weren't immediately sold on letting him go to Charlottesville: "At first they were very reluctant until I insisted on it. Then they became very supportive. I had two corrective surgeries at that time. Back before they built the interstates through the mountains, it was a hard ride over to Charlottesville (driving on a two-lane road). To show you how green I was, at thirteen years old, I was just old enough to get a bed in the adult section. I lay there a couple days not knowing where to go to the bathroom. Then this big black orderly named Banks saved my bladder, when he asked, 'Don't you ever take a leak?'... I was just grateful to be in a room because it was so crowded, while others had beds in the hallway.

"While I was wearing the cast, my mother told me later that my dad didn't really want me to go on to the seventh grade, for fear I would fall and break that leg. My mother's comment regarding the situation was she believed if I skipped or stayed home a year, I would be behind my schoolmates and might not finish school. Since I was walking on crutches and had the cast, it was impossible for me to walk that half-mile to catch the school bus; consequently, mom would harness the horse, hitch it to a buckboard and took me to meet the school bus herself. She did that the entire winter, which made it possible for me to go to school.

12

"Mom was never one to beat us children with her hand, she used switches. One afternoon, when she picked me up at the bus, she was a little bit late and I was quite disturbed because there was a radio show coming on from Richmond called The Caro-Ginians, and by her being late, I missed their program. So all the way home I griped about missing that show because she was late. We got almost home and I was still being critical, and without saying a word, she backhanded me across the mouth. So I sure didn't say any more."

By the following Easter, for the first time in Mac's life, he was able to walk with his polio foot flat on the ground, thanks to a specially-designed shoe: "I needed it built-up, as the leg is still about an inch-and-a-half shorter. I remember the first time I had a shoe on was the following April, which meant it was a good ten months that I couldn't really walk on that foot."

During convalescence, Mac perfected his guitar playing: "I had time to mess with it, as I couldn't do anything physically," initially learning how to chord to accompany his youthful vocals. "That was the greatest frustration. I'll never forget the night that I was able to get that coordination down, so I could do the changes along with the songs I was singing. I sat at that old table of Mom's [which he still has] and can visualize it so clearly now. She'd be washing dishes and I'd be sitting there with my songbooks she'd written in for me, pickin' and singin' along in the kerosene light, and I'd know I had to go from G to C, but by the time I got to C, I was already singing in D. I can still remember the song when I finally got that coordination down - 'There's An Empty Cot In The Bunkhouse Tonight' - and Lord'a mighty once I got that coordination going on that song, they had to whip me to go to bed that night. I went through those books like there was no tomorrow."

Gene Autry, the movies' premier singing cowboy, had recorded Mac's vocal "breakthrough" song, and Mac used a store-bought Autry model guitar at that, rather fittingly: *"There's a cot unused in the bunkhouse tonight/There's a pinto's head bending low/His spurs and chaps hang on the wall/Limpy's gone where the good cowboys go... There's a range for every cowboy/Where the foreman takes care of his own/There'll be an empty saddle tonight/But he's happy up there I know."*

3 'Wonder How The Old Folks Are'... Recall

"You could hear the cattle lowing in the lane
You could see the fields of bluegrass where I've grown
You could almost hear them cry, as they kissed their boy goodbye
Well, I wonder how the old folks are at home..."

"I've seen snow as high as the hood of a car," says Wiseman in recalling the harsh Virginia winters. "It was about a half-mile then to the main road where you could catch a school bus. But the first two years, I went to school in a damn wagon pulled by mules. I swear to you I did. It was covered-in and not exposed to the elements, and kind of resembled an Amish hearse, but it was cold riding. It would pull into an old country store where most of us could walk to; it was about three miles to Harriston, where I went to school."

Mac shared his thoughts about washday, and how his mom coped in cold weather: "Washday saw my mother hunched over a galvanized wash-tub, scrubbing dirty clothes on a washboard. Then she had a folding ironing board on which she would iron the clothes, after drying them on a clothesline outdoors. It was a hard job. In those days, we had our school clothes and soon as we'd get home, we'd change into work clothes - you'd be careful not to dirty too many clothes, knowing how she had to wash them. When winter came, sometimes the sheets and such would freeze as stiff as boards and she'd have to wait until the sun come out to thaw them out. It wasn't easy on her hands. My part in washday was drawing water from our sixty-six-foot well on a windlass (its handle)... Another chore I had was to draw water for our three cows, and I swear they drank more than camels!"

Coming home from school, there was nothing like hot soup to warm one up: "My mother canned what she called succotash, and made a lot of soups and stews, in which she put a layer of corn, a layer of lima beans and a layer of stewed tomatoes. Then when she was ready to cook up soup or stews, she would get this mix, add some potatoes and onions to it and we had stew!" He remembers it as both tasty and warming.

As a result of his lame leg, Mac missed out on some sport programs his classmates took for granted. Mac fondly recalls the Principal - Mr. Kiser - who also taught the fifth, sixth and seventh grades, as well as coaching sports. He recognized Mac's pitching skills, and arranged for him to play ball, while another boy ran all but first base for him: "Mr. Kiser became a friend of our family actually. We were just poor country folk. I remember we raised peanuts in our garden for our own use, and we'd give him a bag of peanuts. He enjoyed that."

Coach Kiser obviously admired Mac's spunk and positive spirit, as well.

"I always liked school because I wanted to make something out of myself in spite of my handicap. I remember getting up at daybreak to do the plowing until it was time to go catch the school bus. Then when I got home from school, I'd change clothes and plow until dark, so I wouldn't have to miss school."

Mac had a three-mile walk to catch that bus, and often he and Dad walked together a half-mile, before Howard veered off in another direction to the mill. Eyes misting over, Mac shares a tender moment between father and son: "Years later, when he was an old man, my father told me, 'I used to see you hopping up the road to catch a ride to work, and wished there was more I could do for you.' I was quite moved by his recollection. That was also the only time he ever told me that he loved me."

Mac pauses, reflecting on that long-ago scene. A parent, of course, wants to do what he can for a child, but being a struggling farmer, who also had to work away from home to make ends meet, Howard's resources were limited. He was keenly aware of his boy's fortitude, having to do chores before going to school, then finishing his chores when he got home, so he could continue to go to school. Then in high school, Howard's son worked into the evening at a factory, saving his earnings for an uncertain future.

Poignantly, Mac adds that he never doubted his dad's love for him, noting Howard had shown that in so many ways. The point he was trying to make was men of Howard's generation and situation in life, didn't openly express their feelings and love as much as maybe mothers did.

Sharing yet another morsel of family history, Mac continues, "My dad was doing pretty well in a barbershop when he and my mother married (June 18, 1924). Imagine if you will the condition of roads then, mostly dirt roads that were often muddy, but my mom and dad drove to their honeymoon in Washington, D.C., about a hundred miles away. They were determined to go there and indeed saw the U.S. Mint, where they make money, and actually walked to the top of the Washington Monument, which had no elevator back then."

Although Mac grew up through the Great Depression, he doesn't ever recall going hungry: "My mother was very resourceful and, though there weren't any jobs available, Dad would go out and stand on the road where they were doing construction, or go to the railroad and wait for somebody to not show up or to fall out sick, and get in a few hours work for fifty- to seventy-five cents an hour before he got that regular job at the mill. They always had a big garden, milk-cows, chickens, pigs and a couple of horses. My mother was great about canning and baked bread and rolls twice a week. She had dried beans and dried apples and made the best dried apple pie."

Mac remembers, too, she would place a clean cloth on the roof where she spread kernels of corn and long green beans, which is where the terminology shuck beans came from: "Overnight they soaked in water, and that reconstituted them until they had texture to them like a fresh bean, though it made them turn a bit brown. They were like snap beans without the texture. Slices of apple she'd dry up there, adding those made the most delicious dried apple fried pies. The apples were enclosed in the pie crust or pastry… "

Regarding their third residence, Mac points out, "We moved into her parents' old home (1931) and it was a hundred years old then (and is still standing). It was a big old house, so open, but we heated it with wood. We had mounds of wood piled as high as the house. That old house had a lot of cracks around the windows and the doors, letting cold or hot air in whatever the season. In the winter, we had the wood-burning stove in our living room, so my folks would drag three beds out into the living room for us all to sleep in there to keep warm. We'd stick clothes and other things into the cracks, trying to keep out the blowing cold air. Something that gave me great peace of mind, while sleeping in that crowded living room, was each night before going to sleep, my mom and dad would read to us from the Bible, and hold prayer. That was very comforting indeed.

"We had a dug-out cellar we called the dairy because we kept our dairy products in there. My mom canned and stored those in there in the summer and that got us through the winter. As soon as the weather started getting cold, however, we had to carry what was left back upstairs or it would freeze. It was an existence, I'll tell you. But, hell, I didn't know any different. Everybody else around there was poor. I wasn't ashamed at all. We even went barefoot part of the year. I wore overalls a long time, went to school in overalls and sometimes to church in overalls with patches, but they were clean. I never went to bed with an empty tummy."

Although Virginia winters could be hard, especially for those whose houses might not be as insulated as the richer folks' residences, Mac also recalls how the other seasons brought problems as well. The South River, where he was baptized, snaked up behind the Red Flour Mill, where they also made cider. He remembers, "A swinging bridge crossing the river was anchored on each side and would have a walkway with short boards across a heavy cable that spanned the South River, for pedestrians to use to get across. Since it was a swinging bridge, it had a tendency to go up and down. Anyone who jumped up and down might scare someone else trying to walk across.

"There was no bridge that cars could cross and it was a long drive around it, probably three or four miles. When the river was in its normal banks, it had some deep places and also had some sandbars you could walk across or perhaps drive a car across by zigzagging from sandbar to sandbar - and there were some pretty deep waters. We would stop on the riverbank before fording the river and take the fan belt off, so the fan wouldn't run and throw water back over the engine and short it out. After crossing the river, we stopped to put the fan belt back on so the fan could cool the radiator water. Dad, being a mechanic, knew that, so Lord, I crossed it many times going to work. That saved a lot of mileage over winding, dirt roads. In width, it was nearly three hundred to four hundred yards."

Mention of the seasons sparks still another memory: "Years later, when touring Canada in the winter, I saw it was really tough on people way up north. I recall being in New Brunswick in the late 1950s or maybe early '60s, especially up in Moncton, when I was working with a guy who had an early morning weekday TV show. We were booked for ten days, and it was snowing like crazy every day we were up there. I mean the snow was so deep and crusted over that people were coming out of upstairs windows. The only way you knew where a road was is when you saw three or four feet of a light-pole sticking up out of the snow. Well, I didn't think we'd get but two or three turn out for our shows, but apparently they suffered 'cabin fever,' for we had good crowds everywhere we went. Those were hardy souls, hungry for entertainment."

That's equally true for folks back then who lived in rural or farm communities in the States, who also yearned for live entertainment. In Mac's youth, music was free for the listening, for those who had access to a battery-operated radio, that is, as did the Wisemans. Mac emphasizes, "Bradley Kincaid, Charlie Poole, Riley Puckett, Clayton McMichen, Fiddlin' John Carson, Uncle Dave Macon, all were among the pioneers that helped influence me, for they were there at the beginning of the recording era. Bradley Kincaid and his story-songs, well I was very much impressed by them. You know I've got Charlie Poole's box set. One time down in Atlanta, I was riding the elevator and Bill Carlisle pointed out Fiddlin' John Carson to me (he was the operator running it)."

Bradley Kincaid, Mac's boyhood hero.

Uncle Dave Macon and his Opry troupers were characters: "I first met Uncle Dave in early 1946, when working with Juanita and Lee Moore out of WSVA-Harrisonburg, and we were booked in Hagerstown, Maryland, at an outdoor park run by Bud Messner, who had an all-girl band. Mary Klick was one and Rose Lee (real name Doris Schetrompf, who would wed Joe Maphis) was another player; there were five girls in the band, but I don't know the others. We had both Uncle Dave, Curly Fox & Texas Ruby, and this was Sunday afternoon. Curly and Ruby were a little late getting there, having worked the Saturday night Opry. So we did a second set before they arrived. Curly was dressed so impressively in a snow-white suit, a blood-red shirt that set off his curly hair, seems like he was redheaded. His band consisted of some younger guys like Grady Martin and Jabbo Arrington, who played twin guitars and later worked with Jimmy Dickens.

"I had first heard Curly Fox as a youngster working our farm in Virginia. I'd get up early to do the chores such as milking and feeding the horses and hogs, to be back at the house by 7:15 a.m. to listen to Curly and a flattop guitar player (on WLW-Cincinnati). He never mentioned what the guitar player's name was, but I found out he was Red Phillips, who later ran a car lot in Dallas or Houston, somewhere down in Texas. He was probably the best picker I ever heard. Curly played mostly novelty tunes on fiddle and with that guy backing him up, that's all they needed."

Not much got by Ruth. She caught on to her son's growing passion for music and looked for ways to nurture that interest: "Yes, my mother was a great inspiration. We'd go to every little old concert that came to our local school. Entertainers including the Leary Family, whose daughter Wilma Lee later wed their bandsman Stoney Cooper and they became a famous duo. The Learys played a lot of schools back then," beams Mac, confiding he had a boyhood crush on Wilma Lee, which years later he good-naturedly told her backstage. [He would also record with the Coopers' daughter Carol Lee.]

Among Mac's more treasured memories are the hand-written notebooks of traditional songs, compiled and presented him by his mom, who read shaped notes: "My mother was such an avid fan of down-home music, she used to sit and listen to the radio, particularly in the winter while making quilts and crocheting. In her compositional books, held together by spiral rings, she'd write down whatever they sang. If she couldn't catch it all at first, a few days or even weeks later they sang the same song, so she'd jot down the rest of it.

"Back then, radio announcers weren't DJ's and stations weren't serviced by record companies. It was all broadcast live. I've got thirteen of those books in Mom's handwriting - and she numbered them. She would cut her page numbers off of Raymon (Almanac) Calendars to paste on the books. What a priceless collection!"

Perusing their titles recalls music history, among them "Bye To Baby Buntin'," "The Old Wooden Rocker," "My Mother's Old Sun-Bonnet," "The Belle of the Mohawk Valley," "Branded Wherever I Go," "The Little Mohee," "Gentle Nettie Moore," "Little Pal," "Brother Take Warning," "The Wreck On the Highway" on up to 1942's "Let's Remember Pearl Harbor."

Mac says he was about thirteen when she began doing this, "and without knowing it, she provided me a map that I'd follow for the rest of my life. Oh, how she encouraged me, simply by going to the trouble of writing down these songs."

It was about age eight that Mac really began working the family farm, which covered some sixty-five acres: "Mom and I ran the farm, which my mom and her sister owned. Later, they bought out my aunt's interest. We had chickens, pigs and cows. We also had two workhorses, which I worked with from a tender age. My dad would have to help put on their harnesses, when I was too small to reach up high enough to do it."

Mac and siblings Virginia and Kennie.

Mac remembers their field crops were primarily corn, wheat and hay: "We observed a four-year rotation on crops. One year it was corn, the next wheat, and we'd sow the grass seed in with the wheat, so that when we harvested wheat, the seed would still be there, and we'd get two years from it, one of wheat, the other two of haymaking, then in the fifth year, we'd go back to corn again. Today, this would be known as organic farming. That means it was free of that extra bullshit found in today's plantings; that is no insecticide sprays or modernized fertilizer. My dad raised buckwheat... Dad put the wheat in the mill, so he'd have that 'banked' to draw on in the winter to get flour for bread, until the next crop came in. Corn and hay were not money crops, but were used to feed the hogs, chickens, cows and horses... Farmers rely a lot on luck, but can get better odds in Las Vegas."

From an early age, Mac became adept at bringing in firewood: "We went in the woods with an old crosscut saw. Because I was so small, Dad had to kneel down on the other side of the log, so that the saw could run level. And we carried water from the spring. I was busy that's for certain, getting wood for the fires, hauling water for cooking, drinking and bathing on Saturday night - whether you needed it or not - plus tending and feeding the livestock and, of course, turning the fields with the plows."

One year, they got some seed wheat and when it came up there was a lot of rye mixed in, recalls Mac: "Rye grows about six inches higher than wheat. So in order to have wheat to bank, my mother and I each walked a five-acre field, cutting the tops off the rye, so the rye seeds wouldn't be in there when thrashed. We'd do that for hours.

"Our barn wasn't large enough to accommodate our wheat after we cut it. Consequently, it was in shocks and had to stay in shocks until The Thrasher - there was only one thrasher in the community - came around to us. You can imagine that the larger farms got preference before they came to our place. If you had rain, then the wheat would sprout within the shock, turning black, making it un-bankable. We couldn't separate it, so it all went to chicken feed.

"I'd see my mother stand there and cry, saying, 'What are we going to do about wheat for flour?' That was for her homemade breads. Using a wood stove, she made six loaves of bread and twelve rolls twice a week, in addition to pies, cakes, donuts, dried apple fried pies, and that's the main reason we needed that flour. It used to break my heart to see her cry over that, as we broke our ass working in that field to get the wheat."

Back then the wheat Thrasher went to the bigger farms first, explains Mac, "Because they paid by the bushel, so us smaller farmers were last. Each machine had a counter and based on that the operator would charge the going rate at the time. At thrashing time, we would take the wheat straw and fill our mattress with it, too, and that had to last until the next thrashing. As you slept on it, the damn straw would grind up and eventually got pretty damned lumpy.

"One thing you had to watch out for was bedbugs - these were carried about by birds usually - and I recall seeing mother in the spring putting the mattresses on the clothes-line, and she'd pour kerosene over it to try and kill any bugs, then leave it out there to air out. Mom would also hang her quilts and carpets out in the spring, beat them with a broom or whatever to drive the winter's dust out.

"From start to finish, we did our own butchering. At daylight, we'd shoot the first hog, slit his throat, and hang it up so that the body would drain clear of blood, then take it to the scalding pan (filled with hot water); heating the water was an art unto itself. If you heated it too much, that would make the hair set up, then you'd have to shave the damn hog and end up with bristles in the meat. You'd test the temperature on your wrist, as you do a baby's milk-bottle. We would make our own sausage and made bacon from the slabs.

"The way we cured it was in a big wooden salt box that could hold up to three hogs. We would put a layer of salt, then a layer of meat, then a layer of salt… and after six weeks, the salt would have drawn all the moisture out of the meat, so we'd take it out of the box of salt and hang it in the smokehouse. You know that could keep for years. You'd just go to the smokehouse and cut off whatever part you wanted to cook.

"I remember my dad would make the sausage, mixing it in a galvanized wash tub, and he'd add the sage, the pepper, whatever, then fry a little patty to taste and see if his seasoning was right. In order to preserve the meat, my mother would can

19

it and it would have a layer of lard on top and that sealed in the meat and its flavor. She would store it in 'the dairy.' Mmmm, she baked some hellacious sausage and eggs and flapjacks!"

Explaining their sweet 'n sour, apple-butter and sauerkraut mixes, he says: "Another annual chore was making sauerkraut from the cabbage we grew. That we'd make in a five-gallon earthenware crock. You'd cut the cabbage real fine, and put salted water in the crock. The way you'd test the strength of the salt water mixture is be sure it was capable of floating a raw egg; that practice was passed on down from generation to generation. It actually pickles the cabbage, turning it into sauerkraut."

Another big observance came in the fall, making apple-butter. "This was a neighborhood event. To get the brown color into the apple - otherwise, it would look like applesauce - you had to cook it in a copper kettle. Since there was only one copper apple-butter kettle in the community, neighbors would gather the night before after doing their chores, and we'd peel and slice a huge flour barrel full of apples, which we called Apple Snits.

"Starting early the next morning, we'd build a fire under this big copper-kettle, put the snits in the water, add whatever seasoning desired, and all day long stir this mixture until it reached the consistency needed. Cooking these apple snits gave the apple-butter its color. And you'd have to book that kettle, as it was the only one available. As a result, you learned to ask a neighbor when he planned to make his apple-butter, then you'd usually try for the next day."

Mac says besides the barnyard chickens, another source for eggs were "Guinea hens." Finding them wasn't easy though. Following Guinea hens to locate their nests became one of Mac's quests, "Guineas are like sentinels. They won't roost in anything like a hen house - they roost in trees, and it was my job to locate their nests, usually well hidden, as they were very smart. If they knew we were following, they would stay away for hours. When they disappeared, I guessed that they were gone to their nests. So I'd search around that area and most of the time I could find the nests."

Guinea fowl are actually great hunters of insects and especially ticks that can cause Lyme disease, so farmers generally welcome their presence. Further, the meat of a young Guinea is both tender and flavorful.

"My mother would use their eggs for cooking, leaving our hen eggs for bartering. They were actually a bit richer tasting eggs than the barnyard hens', and the egg itself appeared in the shape of a (child's toy) top, that is they weren't completely oval like a regular hen's, as the one end came to a point. Yes, the Guineas themselves were good eating, but were more of a dark meat."

Mac also points out, "It's amazing, too, how smart crows are. If a flock came in, they would have a sentinel posted, so if we tried to slip up on them to try and kill them, the sentinel would warn them before we could get close enough. Crows would pull up the young stalks (about three or four-inches high), just to get a grain of corn off it. Then, of course, we'd have to replant again."

Hot beds were set out, consisting of tomatoes, cabbage and sweet potato slits, by Ruth and her son, potted in about two or three inches: "We would dig the ground in an area the size of a grave, putting in two layers for seeding, first came the cow manure, followed by a second layer of dirt. We'd place a window over the plantings to protect them in bad weather and when the sun shone on the glass, it made the ground warmer.

Once the seeds sprouted, they were transplanted into our regular garden."

Wiseman recalls even pine trees that grew in their mountainous region were valued for their resin, a sticky substance cut out of the bark by a knife, machete or hatchet. Although called evergreens, the sap or resin runs faster during spring or fall. The pine resin or pitch gives the tree its resilience to extreme weather, insect infestation, fungus, mold or cancerous growths, as it's nature's healing system for trees. This resin also helps heal dry or cracked skin, caused by farm chores, washing dishes or hanging out clothes in cold weather. Some say it's also helpful as a home remedy for cancer wounds. Incidentally, the pine needles provide vitamin C, which can be brewed into a tea, chewed or prepared as vinegar.

Yet another "home remedy" utilized by Indians and farmers, also was indigenous to Wiseman's part of the country: "Burdock or Dock plants we used as a poultice like when we had a lame horse. These are plants that grew wild. We didn't cultivate them. The plain Dock had a leaf with a sort of fuzzy side, while the Burdock's big leaves were slick. We put them in vinegar, before wrapping them around the horse's leg. We'd put a rope around the hoof or injured leg and bring it up over the horse and tie it, so the animal couldn't put any pressure on it.

"Actually they moved about like a three-legged horse," says Wiseman. "You know back in the old West if a horse sprained a leg, they might shoot it. We just had work horses you see, so we doctored them, trying to make them well again."

Huckleberries, a succulent treat, grew wild in the mountain region where Mac grew up: "My dad and I would pick them and as a matter of self-preservation, you did that rather quietly in order not to spread the word you'd found a good picking patch. They made good preserves, jellies and pies, so my mom would can them, and we'd gather them by the bushel. One time when dad and I found a good patch and tried to keep quiet, this big black fellow came running down the mountain, somersaulting and losing his berries, as he had run into a rattlesnake up there.

"I have fond memories of those times, of berrying with Dad. We would stroll along mountain streams and find fox grapes, which are about a third larger than an average grape, and Mom also canned them. It was so much fun for us, because you'd wade in the cool streams, then reach up and pluck the grapes off their vines. This being summertime, it was refreshing; you see, these vines would grow across the stream like in a grape arbor.

"On our trip up into the mountains, we'd put little jellies and jams on a shingle on the ground, usually by a mountain trail; then on the way back, we'd find that the bees would've found this, and so we followed the bees back to their trees where they had their hives. Then we'd chop down the whole tree, to dig into the section where they made their honey. We'd burn a torch or some rags to make smoke that drove them away, then we'd get the honey to take home. We used honey to cook with, or as seasoning, for Mom would put it on fruit pies and such."

4 'Will There Be Any Stars In My Crown'... Predestined

"O what joy it will be when His face I behold,
Living gems at His feet to lay down!
It would sweeten my bliss in the city of gold,
Should there be any stars in my crown..."

"Ever heard the phrase 'a cat could charm the birds out of a tree?' Well, I've seen them do it," grins Wiseman. "That is, the cat would make eye contact with a bird in a tree, and before you knew it the bird would tumble to the ground. It was like it had been hypnotized."

Another phenomenon Mac encountered on the farm: "Blue Jays and Black Crows were like sentinels because they'd sit up in the trees while the rest of them were feeding on our crop. Once they spotted a human coming, they would squawk until the others would fly away before we could shoot them."

According to Mac, Howard was raised as a farmer's son, but was not keen on farming the rest of his life: "He was kind of a jack-of-all-trades, a good mechanic and had worked in a creamery, but primarily he was a miller. He ran a mill and ground wheat, and a cider mill. I've seen wagons lined up as many as fifteen-to-twenty in a caravan waiting to get in there to get their apples ground up... they'd put the pressure to them and that's how they made the cider that turned into vinegar. My father was quite inventive. He liked to make buckwheat flour there (at the Red Mill)... Dad was probably about five-foot, seven or five-foot eight inches and not a real sturdy guy, but I seen him toting a hundred-pound sack of flour on his back to carry all the way home. Although he loved music, I never saw him have an inclination to play, but he did like to sing bass at the church."

Howard saw to it the family had a hand-wound phonograph and radio: "Incidentally, I have them both. The name of the radio was Freed-Eismann, I remember, because it sounded like Wiseman. It was a monster of a thing with three dials on it like a combination safe. It had both a volume control and a tone control on it... We bought our records through mail-order catalogs from Sears or Montgomery-Ward's (rural chain stores). These were usually the music of Vernon Dalhart, Gene Austin, Bing Crosby, Gene Autry and the Carter Family, artists who were popular in that time period."

Aside from these influences, Mac enjoyed radio singers such as Bradley Kincaid. "He sang a lot of story songs, and they were my favorites. The old songs just blew me away," continues Mac, who still collects treasured tunes of yesteryear. "We listened to a lot of radio, especially Saturday nights. Besides WSM's Opry then, there were also barn dance shows from Jacksonville, Florida, and from Hopkinsville, Kentucky, the few stations that were mostly all clear-channel, so you could hear them all over the country. We'd stay up listening to programs until the wee hours of the morning... often neighbors would gather 'round just to listen to our radio, as they didn't have one. Sometimes my mom would cook them breakfast before they'd go home early Sunday morning.

In those days before FDR's Social Security support took hold, a lot of family's elderly moved in with their children to stay out of the proverbial Poor House. In order to give the immediate family some relief, seniors often spent several weeks at a time with other family members, including nieces and nephews.

The Wisemans, a music-loving family, enjoyed sing-a-longs. Mac recalls, "I remember an old English ballad 'Granny's Rockin' Chair,' and the songs like Bradley Kincaid did including 'Barbara Allen' that told a story. We had one record [Mac still has it] that my grandmother (Naomi) on my dad's side loved. She was a tall, red-haired, dignified lady who lived with us awhile. She was crippled with arthritis and used a stool to get around the house with, insisting on washing dishes and helping out. My mom would often help her get ready for bed and when she settled in she would say, 'Now Ruthie, play my song.' It was on a large over-sized disc, bigger than the 78-rpm album, and the song was 'Will There Be Any Stars in My Crown' [a 19th century hymn by Eliza Hewitt and John R. Sweney]. She wanted to hear it every night."

Mac would one day record Grandma's favorite: *"Will there be any stars, any stars in my crown/When at evening the sun goeth down?/When I wake with the blest in the mansions of rest/Will there be any stars in my crown?... "* (He recently re-recorded it.)

"When I was a little boy you know I had red hair, but it darkened as I grew older. Virginia had brown hair like mine, but both Kennie and Naomi grew up as redheads," he chuckles.

Mac can't recall his mother's parents, as his maternal grandfather Thomas Humphreys died in May 1925, the month he was born. "I have only a dim memory of my grandmother (Susan), who died when I was about four years old. Although they've told me about little things I would do with my dad's father (Kenneth), I can't really recall him."

"My mother didn't have any brothers growing up, so she worked a lot with her dad. She would rather work outside than do housework. As I said, she and I ran that little scratch farm. I mean, there was a lot of it I could do alone, but when it came to things like hauling wheat into the barn, she would give me a hand."

Mama Ruth became a champion of her son's love of music. "She played the old pump organ, then later the piano in church. She was that good. Stamps-Baxter (sheet music publishers) would come into the community and hold singing schools. They'd be there three or four weeks once people signed up. They were out of Texas and their motive was to sell sheet music, so my mother could read the shaped notes she learned at their singing school." [Shaped notation derives from a system of ear training once used in Britain and Colonial America, starting in the late 17th and early 18th centuries, a concept based on the syllables of *fa so la ti do.* It presents notes as a series of shapes - circle, square, triangle - corresponding to the musical diatonic scale. This makes it possible for a group to come together and quickly master four-part harmony singing.]

A visiting show that left a lasting impression on the adolescent Mac was one headlined by the *Grand Ole Opry's* Pee Wee King & His Golden West Cowboys, at the time featuring newcomer Eddy Arnold as lead singer. Mac especially remembers Eddy singing "How Can You Forget So Soon," which he later recorded and recalls its writer Joe L. Frank was Pee Wee's father-in-law. "Hearing Eddy sing that song was a turning point for me. I thought maybe I could become a singer like that… "

At a later DJ convention, Mac was surprised when J. L.'s widow walked up to thank him for recording the song, which had been written with her in mind.

"When I was about eight or nine and out pulling weeds in the garden or doing a variety of chores, working hard, my mom, bless her heart, would say, 'Don't you think it's about time to come in and take a little rest and get you a cold drink of water?' Well, there was a Red Network and a Blue Network and they actually followed each other on the radio along about mid-morning in the early 1930s. There'd be fifteen minutes of Bing Crosby singing and fifteen minutes of Canadian Wilf Carter. Their shows were broadcast back-to-back out of New York. She knew damn well I wanted to hear those programs. I'd sit there under an apple tree and she'd turn the radio up real loud. So for a half hour, I heard those and then got back to my work."

Crooner Crosby and troubadour Carter, also known as Montana Slim, were quite different musically. As time would tell, Mac's tastes were indeed versatile. Apart from music, Mac the boy especially enjoyed hunting and trapping. One humorous remembrance brought a twinkle to his eye: "I used box traps to catch rabbits, possum and even skunks, selling their fur. I would hunt at night with a neighbor kid, Junior Parr, tracking possum and polecats (skunks), sometimes capturing them live. We'd sneak up and flash a light on them. They were startled enough that we could grab 'em by the tail and drop 'em in a bag the other would hold. Now a polecat can't spray you as long as he can't brace his front feet. But one night Junior wasn't holding the sack wide enough, and I got a face full of spray! That piss blinded me temporarily, but to this day, I've had no trouble with cataracts."

Customers for their skins included a service station owner near school who paid fifteen-cents each per pelt or let them trade-out for some of the goodies he sold; and an older gentleman, a Mr. Workman, who specialized in animal skins. After Mac tried skinning the animals for Mr. Workman, he suggested bringing them intact, carcass and all, "because I botched up the skinning process and he could earn more if he skinned them himself."

Mac warmly reminisces about childhood Saturday nights: "That's when my dad got paid and he would stop at the little country store to buy three Milky Way candy bars and three Pepsi Colas, and bring them home to us. He'd cut them up six ways, so we would all get a piece. That was also bath night, when they got out the old galvanized tub. I was pretty lucky, as I had seniority. Time it got around to bathing the youngest, that water was pretty potent."

Then there were the Sunday mornings, when he woke up to some enticing smells: "Mom would be getting breakfast for us, often consisting of mackerel cakes, as salmon was too expensive, scrambled eggs, and at the same time, she would be frying chicken for our Sunday dinner. It was quite customary for other families to come home with us from church with all their children, and we'd have dinner together. We also at times went to their houses."

For the most part, Mac's grades in school were good. He still has a number of his report cards to back this up: "I remember Miss Engleman was my teacher in grades one and two, then Miss Cline taught third and fourth grades. Teachers had to double up on classes in our schools."

One of the Bible school teachers, Mrs. Driver, stayed at the Wiseman home while Bible school was going on, being customary thereabouts: "She drove a Model A Ford. We were all gathered around the cistern pump, a huge concrete tank to catch rain that ran off into the church's gutters and into pipes from the roof. The cistern was full of rainwater. We were all anxious to get a drink of water, and the teacher slapped me in the face, thinking I was crowding some other kids out. Normally, I would ride home with her in the Model A, but this time I didn't, knowing my mother would ask why, so I'd get a chance to tell her what had happened."

In service to the community, Mac would mow the graveyard with a push mower on an old field they used for a cemetery, which was really uneven and rocky: "The only rewarding thing about doing the mowing was the field boasted the biggest and best strawberries in that area. That was my pay, and I feasted on them."

Another inspiration to Mac, with his game leg, was a Biblical teaching from 2 Corinthians 12:6 that reads in part: "Even if I should choose to boast, I would not be a fool, because I would be speaking the truth. But I refrain, so no one will think more of me than is warranted by what I do or say. 7: To keep me from becoming conceited because of these surpassingly great revelations, there was given me a thorn in my flesh, a messenger of Satan, to torment me. 8: Three times I pleaded with the Lord to take it away from me. 9: But he said to me, 'My grace is sufficient for you, for my power is made perfect in weakness.' Therefore I will boast all the more gladly about my weaknesses, so that Christ's power may rest on me. 10: That is why, for Christ's sake, I delight in weaknesses, in insults, in hardships, in persecutions, in difficulties. For when I am weak, then I am strong."

Regarding church and community service, Mac's mother did her part, too.

"My mother's mite box, actually known as a widow's mite box, was really an empty baking soda can. Now this was Depression times, and the ladies of the community would put spare change in there and once a year, at a meeting of the Ladies' Aid Society, they'd all open their mite boxes and collectively donate their change to aid the needy families in the neighborhood."

Mac felt his mom was also a with-it lady, who loved to go to country music shows locally at "venues" like the schoolhouse, and could be quite brave, as well: "Being the oldest, she took me. She and I would walk a half-mile to the little country store to catch the school bus to take us to the concerts (four miles away). I recall one night she and I were walking home about ten o'clock. It was a cold, winter night, with a bit of snow on the ground, not unlike the night in Bethlehem when baby Jesus was born. As we were walking up the road, we heard a sound like a baby crying. We stopped to listen, then the sound stopped. Soon as we started walking, we heard it again. There was a barbwire fence along the road with a field on the other side, so my mother wasn't about to hurry home until she saw what that was all about. She crawled through that barbwire fence - and she was a good-sized lady - to check it out, and left me standing out in the road. When she got over into the field, she found an old cat (making the eerie sound), and both of us were very relieved to find out what it was."

All of the family were amazed and astounded the day that Ruth had encountered a poisonous rattlesnake in the upstairs bedroom when she went up to make the bed: "We had an old Civil War musket that stood in the corner, but wouldn't fire. Well, my mother took the gun and beat the snake to death with it. That took a lot of courage on her part."

Ruth's mother Susan had only two daughters, so Ruth became her father's "son" and wasn't hesitant about working in the fields. Come spring, she and Mac would plant potatoes.

"When they were mature, rather than take up the whole plant, because there would be a lot of small immature potatoes, she would take a table fork and put it in the ground and groveling around with it, she could determine if a potato was big enough, then jab it and bring it up and that way didn't kill the plant itself, allowing those small potatoes to mature.

"We always had a 'hot bed' in early spring in which we planted tomato seeds, then raised tomato plants and cabbage plants, as well, in that hot bed. In the hot bed, we would put sweet potatoes, so they would sprout... we called sweet potato plant 'slips,' and it's a mystery to me why they called it that. We would plant the sweet potato slips in the tops of ridges, so the potato would grow above ground. The interesting thing about that was in the fall we very carefully watched the weather, because at the first frost, we had to get out there before the sun came up and cut those sweet potato vines off, for if the sun hit frosted plants, it would blacken the potato, which then wouldn't be worth a hoot. They learned this through experience."

The Wisemans also grew Sorghum cane in their garden, planting eight to ten rows, explains Mac: "In the fall when it reached maturity, we'd cut it down and use the main stalk. Then there was this old guy in the community who traveled throughout the countryside, and with his mill process would run the stalks through it to collect its clear juice in a big pan.

"You'd build a fire under the container and cook that off, to make blackstrap molasses. His pay would be a portion of the molasses to sell to those who didn't grow it. While cooking it down, you'd skim the foam off it as it cooked. Us kids used to enjoy that and we'd play games while it was being cooked."

Mac remembers his mom possessed ingenuity, as well: "In the spring after we had jelly sandwiches all winter for lunches, for a change my mother would put chocolate icing between two saltine crackers like a sandwich, and that was a real treat when we opened our lunch at school. Another thing she did in the spring, when lettuce was ready for like salads or sandwiches, she would take that lettuce and put hardboiled eggs inside, and that gave us even more variety at lunch time.

"This reminds me, one time I went to get my lunch and got hold of the wrong bag, and it felt really heavy, so I thought there must've been something good in there! Took it outside and opened it up, and there was a claw hammer and six hickory nuts," Mac chuckles.

Howard used to buy his cigars in cans and upon finishing his smokes, converted it into a lunchbox, by adding a handle on it. Even though there weren't a lot of extras for them growing up, the Wiseman children were contented, enjoying their home life. Mac continues, "I recall we used to get one pair of shoes a year that usually we wore to school or church. I'd go to get the milk cows in the morning barefoot and my feet would get cold, so where the cows had been resting, I'd stand where they'd been laying to warm my feet a bit before running them up to the barn. Then at daylight, I'd have to do the milking."

Mac also recalls some of Ruth's home remedies: "As a kid, naturally we couldn't drink coffee, but when we were ill, Mom would make a sort of coffee soup served over toasted bread or such, which she knew would appeal to us, as we'd lost our appetites. My Mom would toast bread on a fork, which she held over an open flame to brown on the stove or firebox... Wolf iron.

"When I did get old enough to drink coffee, I did enjoy it. If we got sick, my Mom would give us cod liver oil; so I thought I'd put a stop to that. When it came time for me, I put it in my cup of coffee, thinking it would go down easier. As a result, I couldn't drink coffee for a couple years, because it made me think of that cod liver oil, which, of course, would float on top of the coffee, giving you an awful flavor."

Mac talks, too, about Sassafras tea: "It was what folks considered a blood cleanser; in the spring time, they would dig up the roots and make their tea from the bark. If you drank excessive amounts, it would make you weak as could be."

Then there was the time he was running an errand for his principal Mr. Kiser, who asked him to bring back a bar of soap: "We used homemade Lye soap at home, but he said to bring him a bar of Palmolive Soap. I remember wondering what was that?"

Mac's wondering took many forms. Like many rural youths, he suffered pangs of wanderlust: "We lived approximately a half-mile from the railroad and in the evenings while doing my chores, quite often it would be dusk dark, and I'd see a passenger train traveling down the tracks. From the light inside the passenger train, I'd see the people, and would wonder where they might've come from and where they were going... I was probably about twelve or thirteen and even at that young age, I had the urge to go somewhere."

Movies have long been a form of escapism, and also served as a means of learning for a farm boy unfamiliar with life outside his little corner of the world. Mac says the first movie he ever saw was on a field trip with his grade school class, to a Grottoes, Virginia, theater: D.W. Griffith's 1915 silent epic, "Birth Of a Nation" (with Lillian Gish) and now out of favor due to its racial overtones amid depiction of the KKK.

"I'll never forget it, I was goggle-eyed, as it was the first film I'd ever seen. At the same theater, later, I saw the Sons of the Pioneers in person (probably consisting then of Bob Nolan, Shug Fisher, Hugh Farr, his brother Karl, and Lloyd Perryman)."

While playing Branson, Mo., in 1992, however, Mac met the succeeding generation Sons Of the Pioneers, who were performing at a nearby theater. Although he didn't know the current players, Mac knew he would enjoy hearing their repertory of cowboy songs once again. As a nostalgia act, they pretty much stuck to the group's original Western hits.

"I went to see them and they treated me like a star. The then-current leader Dale Warren was married to Fiddlin' Kate (a.k.a. Marge Warren) - once staff fiddler on the *Town Hall Party* show I did - and I asked Dale how she was doing now? He said, 'She's fine; in fact, she's home cooking my supper. Come on home and see her'."

Mac remembers his Great-Uncle Henry McCausland took him to see his first color film "Drums Along the Mohawk" (starring Henry Fonda and Claudette Colbert) in 1939. On a couple occasions, Uncle Henry also took a teen-aged Mac to see a black minstrel tent show advertised as "Silas Green from New Orleans," featuring a bevy of beauties backing the fictional character of Silas Green, singing and dancing, during an appearance in nearby Waynesboro.

27

Decades later, a comic named Nipsey Russell whom Mac would meet, said he got his start with a Silas show. In 1940, however, here's how a *Time* magazine music reviewer described the Green touring troupe: "This year their troubles start when they go to a hospital with suitcases labeled M.D. (Mule Drivers), are mistaken for two medicos, (and) end in jail. The show is garnished with such slapstick as putting a patient to sleep by letting him smell an old shoe, such gags as 'Your head sets on one end of your spine and you sit on the other.' Silas gets broad at times, but never really dirty. What keeps it moving are its dances and specialty acts, its gold-toothed but good-looking chorus."

Mac adds, "It was a show that came by once a year. He took me there a second time. My mother didn't object. As we just told her it was a tent show, and she never questioned Henry, him being her uncle."

The youngster thought his uncle knew all there was to know about hunting and fishing, and a few other things that mattered to an adolescent boy: "Actually, he was a renowned area surveyor, a school teacher... and always seemed to find time for me. He used to take me fishing and quail hunting. Incidentally, the first time I shot a quail, I was caught by the game warden. Uncle Henry was there. I had been following dad through the fields on the hunt and they wouldn't even let me carry a gun. Well, we went into this old gentleman's house for lunch. Anyway, his name was McGee and when I told him about not being able to carry a gun (at age twelve), he said,

Great Uncle Henry McCausland.

'Why that boy's big enough to carry a gun,' and gave me his gun to carry that afternoon.

"While standing in the yard, contemplating where we'd hunt next, the dogs ran across this little dirt road and got on point in an old orchard (that's when a trained dog is at a steady-to-wing-shot-and-kill position after spotting its quarry). We weren't about to pass that up, so hurried across to the orchard, flushed out the birds and we all shot at them. It just so happened the game warden was driving down that little dirt road at the time. Now Uncle Henry had a license, but Dad and I didn't. Actually you could hunt on your own land without a license, but that warden wrote a ticket to both Dad and I, summoning us to the county seat (in Staunton) to pay a fine. Dad didn't know how to tell my mom about the citations, without letting her know I was carrying a gun. Anyway, Dad got sick and couldn't go to pay the fines at Staunton, so Uncle Henry and I went instead."

Uncle Henry would stay with Mac and his family, until he moved into a nursing home when he required constant care: "He liked his little drink, and kept a jug out on the back porch. He'd step out now and then to have a little snort from his jug. I remember, too, we used to go night fishing in South River a lot, at a little island which we'd row out to before dark. Uncle Henry and my dad put out trotlines in the fall, and we'd have to build a little fire as it got cold in the evening. We'd shoot blackbirds, cut them up for bait and then put trotlines along the riverbank. The fish we caught mostly were called 'suckers,' and though very bony, were quite tasty. We'd catch turtles and it seems to me like they had thirteen kinds of meat in them, some flavored like chickens or Guineas. We also caught a lot of eels. They didn't have a strong taste and they were all meat. Dad would dry their skins and make bootlaces out of the hides. Those were tough laces.

"Yeah, we'd fish on into the night, checkin' the trotlines periodically with lanterns, take off any fish, bait the lines again and set them back out. Then we'd sit at the campfire for another hour or so… that meant fishing on into the night. I liked tagging along with them though they smoked and chewed, which sometimes became pretty boring to a kid, sitting by the fire with nothing to do."

When it came to earning extra income for himself, even as a youngster, Mac could be quite entrepreneurial, and had a clear vision of how to handle business: "I used to take a double-shovel plow, and I'd harness my one-eyed horse Nellie, get on and pull the plow up in front of me, resting on the harness, and go through the community, plowing people's gardens. They'd see me coming and flag me down, because they knew I did a good job. Nellie was the perfect horse to plow gardens with, as she would not step on the plants (despite having only one eye). One afternoon, I came by this old country store, and a rainstorm came up. I tied my horse to the hitching rail and went inside to wait out the storm.

"After the storm, I went to untie my horse and head down the road, and noticed the horse was getting kinda fidgety. When I caught hold of her bridle to calm her down, she pulled back strongly and I reached over to get hold of a woven wire fence and when I did, the electric current running through that fence, caused by a short from a nearby gas pump, hit me hard! My hand, coming into contact with the electric current, stuck to that fence. Feeling that on her metal bit, the horse just took off… I took one hand to pull the other off the fence, but when I got it off, the other stuck to it; luckily for me, there was a fellow at the store who got a broom with a wooden handle, and told me to grab onto it! Not being metal, it didn't shock him, so he was able to pull me away from the fence. It was a strong enough shock that I was almost home, a half mile away, before I realized where I was. It had shocked the hell out of me, you know."

Mac also worked a bit at his father's work place: "My Dad's working in the flour mill became somewhat of a family operation, as his brother Luther - whom I called Uncle Lute - was a salesman who went down into North Carolina to sell flour and wheat to little country stores that served their local people. Another uncle, Sam Black, would take the order my Uncle Lute turned in, load his truck with the flour and feed to fill the orders. One of my favorite things was to go on the route with Uncle Lute to take orders, and later with Uncle Sam to deliver them. I was able to do this because my high school had a rule that you could be exempt from exams, if you had a B average. So I could take those three days off from exams and go with the uncles."

29

5 'A Fire In My Heart'...
Musically Speaking

"You started a flame
A fire in my heart,
I thought you'd be true
That we'd never part. . . "

"Let me tell you about Lady," Mac mischievously volunteers. "Our farm horse, Lady, used to plow or pull a buggy, and was good anywhere you wanted to work her. With my bad polio leg, I often rode her and she was great under a saddle. I recall when I had rode to Crimora to get a five-gallon can of kerosene (for lamps, etc.) and the road we were riding ran parallel to the Norfolk & Western Railroad. Well, the wind was blowing in our face and a train was traveling in the same direction we were, and no doubt the engineer could see us and then blew the whistle! This startled Lady so, and I didn't have hold of the reins, as I was carrying the kerosene, which was like gold to us. Well, that horse just took off a-running down the road! But I hung on - while holding onto the kerosene as well - all the time knowing she was very obedient to commands...

"After about a mile, I'd calmed her, talking her into slowing down. Believe me, that was scary as hell, and in those times that kerosene cost a lot of money, so I held onto it for dear life. Incidentally, that old gray mare lived to be twenty years old, rather a substantial age for a horse."

Mac remembers riding Lady over to the blacksmith's shop under Dad's orders: "Adam Shaner, the blacksmith, kept sheep and as they got older, he'd slaughter them to sell parts off to neighbors. My dad usually bought a quarter, a hind quarter. Ironically, he lived in my great-grandfather's house. For me, it was always fascinating to watch Adam, when I would ride over to pick up that quarter of mutton."

Yet another boyhood fondness carried over to the present day, is his feeling about a tin roof: "I had a tin roof built on my sun-deck here (Nashville), because as a boy I slept upstairs in the house we lived in, which didn't have a ceiling or anything, just a tin roof.

"A tin roof on my sun-deck brings back a million memories. When a boy, I'd go to sleep during a thunderstorm, and I'd hear the rain beating on our roof, and that would lull me into a restful sleep. Still, at night now, I turn off the TV and listen to the rain falling on that tin roof. I love it. You know in the hot part of summer, it also drew heat, making it sometimes unbearably hot. If it didn't cool down enough by opening the windows for a breeze, we'd go downstairs, usually my Dad and me, to lay on the cool linoleum carpet with our pillows and then we'd drift off to sleep."

As Mac reached adolescence, he hired himself out to work for area farmers, like Will Bruce, who got a bit more than they bargained for. These were non-mechanized farms: "I would work twice as hard as the others, just to show them I could.

I was fourteen and making a dollar and a half for a ten-hour workday. So for six days, I earned nine dollars. Mr. Bruce had a pair of horses that were huge. I was a scrawny kid and at the corners of the field, I couldn't lift and turn the plow, so I had to make a complete circle to get the plow back in the furrow, and get a-going again."

Crimora's huge Barger farm; and (right) teen-aged Mac loaded hay here.

Another farmer Mac worked for was Russell (Doc) Barger: "He had a huge estate, with three or four big farms. Barger's Block House was a big industry in Crimora. It being a fertilizer plant… There was no summer break for me. The day after school was out in high school, I'd be working the next day, and continue right up until the day before school started."

While Mac always wanted to play music, he never nurtured a desire to follow it as a career, and in fact thought he might like to be a CPA: "In high school, I took subjects such as typing and bookkeeping. You see when I got out of high school, I had no intention of going into music full-time, as much as I loved it. Nor was it considered the most reputable thing to do for a career. Understand there were a lot of 'drifters' who came into towns to pick and sing a while and then take off in the middle of the night, leaving unpaid bills. So it didn't enter my mind to pursue it (as a vocation). Foremost, I felt that I owed my folks more than that, because they deprived themselves to put me through high school.

"Some weekends, however, I participated in amateur shows and played at lawn parties from age twelve, and though I loved the music, and as I said, I had no idea of pursuing it professionally at that time."

Mac made his first radio appearance at thirteen on WSVA-Harrisonburg, the biggest station in the area at the time: "It had to do with the Future Farmers of America (FFA), which I really wanted no part of, as I just came off a scratch farm. But when it was their turn to do fifteen minutes at the local station, they had a band

but no singer. I went with them for their time period. I was FFA for a day. But at that early age, that was uptown for me! I welcomed the opportunity to sing on the radio in Harrisonburg."

Station WSVA had first signed on the air in 1935, and was a one thousand-watt station that the Wisemans regularly tuned into, especially Ruth, who copied

WSVA-Harrisonburg station building. down a lot of the songs she heard and

31

compiled, and later presented her elder son, derived from such broadcasts. Its call letters, WSVA, stood for "We Serve Virginia Agriculture." WSVA's biggest star was Buddy Starcher, whose songs included "Fire In My Heart," a title rather descriptive of young Mac's burning desire to succeed.

During Mac's sophomore year at New Hope, he was elected Beta Club president. At fourteen, Mac entered a talent contest near Mt. Jackson, Virginia, at McClanahan's Grove, and won first place in the vocal division. His prize money was a dollar and fifty cents. Incidentally, fiddler Buck Ryan from Mt. Jackson, who later played with Jimmy Dean's Texas Wildcats on his Washington, D.C. TV show, won the day's fiddling contest.

"That talent contest was hosted by Frank Salt (real name Kurtz), who earlier performed on radio [and on Broadway with ukulele player Jack Pepper, who would wed future movie star Ginger Rogers] as Salt & Pepper. I remember he was with his wife then, though I don't recall her name [Margaret McConnell] just now, but she was an elegant lady, who had been a stage dancer in New York. They were known as Salt & Peanuts. When I was younger they hosted an open mic show for amateurs. I'd go up and sing sometimes, and I remember he said I reminded him of a young Bradley Kincaid. Hearing that I walked on air… Frank only knew me as Malcolm. Years later, he booked me as Mac Wiseman at his Oak Grove Park near Bluefield, West Virginia, and when he saw me come in, called out, 'My God, it's Malcolm!,' and we had a wonderful reunion. "

Whenever young Mac's parents would go to Harrisonburg to shop, the lad would go off on his own and "hang out" at WSVA, never dreaming how his association with that station would later set him on his life's path as an artist. Initially, the pre-teen Mac linked up with a couple young musicians, fiddler Homer Crickenberger, and mandolinist David Sullivan.

David Sullivan and Mac.

"We were in the formative stages. We played what were called pie suppers and lawn parties. These were fund-raisers for church, as well as schools, and the ladies sold baked goods and knick-knacks they made. They gave us our dinner for free to perform. We also played in church quite a bit."

As a New Hope High School freshman, Wiseman got another break: "That's when the Hungry Five came together, and I stepped right into that. They were two or three years ahead of me and had up-to-date instruments - a steel guitar, lead guitar, bass, accordion and fiddle."

The players were Harry Kerr on bass; Kelly Chapman on Hawaiian steel guitar; Boyd Thompson on accordion; Glenn Gochenour on lead guitar; and fiddlin' friend Crickenberger, who no doubt recommended Mac.

"There again, they were good musicians but had no singer. I mean, I could barely keep up with them on my guitar, but I learned a ton from them, and they treated me as an equal… no, we didn't become the Hungry Six."

Smiling at the memory, Mac points out, "Incidentally, a promoter in Waynesboro, the closest town to Crimora of any size, threw a seventieth birthday bash for me and unbeknownst to me, rounded up all those old musicians, and when I finished my set, the emcee encouraged an encore, saying to me, 'There's some folks who want to pick with you, OK?' I looked around, and like to have fainted! It was the whole damned bunch together, the Hungry Five! - except one. You know, most of those guys had been drafted into World War II immediately when they got out of high school; however, they all went to work for DuPont (chemical factory) the place to work. The one fellow, who played bass, Harry Kerr, my favorite, had died. I remember we would rehearse at his house once a week, and his mom would feed and encourage us."

In his sophomore year, Mac was president of the Beta Club. "I recall the Beta Clubs of Virginia had a convention in Roanoke, about a hundred miles south of my high school. One year, the school sent me and my friend Warren Drumheller, and two female students, Marguerite Foley and Reba Crickenberger (Homer's sister), to the convention. The tricky part was when Warren and I would send the girls to the meetings, while he and I would go shoot pool. They would take notes and fill us in, so we could make our reports back at school."

During summer's school break, Mac sought work in the local textile factory - Duplan - shortly after obtaining his first Social Security card: "You had to be sixteen then to get one. I had just finished my junior year, but they were skeptical

Mac and Homer Crickenberger.

about hiring students and training them, because, of course, they would quit come September to go back to school. So I fibbed and told them I was through with school. Otherwise, they wouldn't have hired me. I had to ride the work-bus, as you couldn't get gasoline due to its being war-time when even tires were rationed. Then when school started again, I had to face them and tell them I'd changed my mind and was going back to school. Though they didn't like that, they were so short-handed, they offered me a foreman's job full-time.

"I wasn't ready for that sort of responsibility, but I did agree to work their third shift from 11 p.m. until 7 a.m. the next morning. I worked that shift through much of my senior year. Well, the guy who was our fiddler lived right at the end of the road where I could get off the work bus there at my buddy's house, change into my school-clothes, and go to school. Then I'd reverse the procedure after going home and getting about four or five hours sleep. That nearly did me in."

Nonetheless, Mac made enough money that he could put some savings aside, which would hopefully serve him well after graduation. But he also relieved his parents of some costs, by buying his own school-clothes, books and incidentals.

Mac says his paternal name Wiseman is probably of German derivation, and the family follows the religious doctrine of the Church of The Brethren, founded in Germany.

"I think the German spelling would be a bit different, probably W-e-i-s-m-a-n-n," notes the vocalist, who feels his mother's people were from England. "Now when I was touring in Europe, I found there were a lot of Wiseman names in Switzerland, as well. Tex Ritter (whose surname is German) once told me he thought that it was an English name."

None of Mac's siblings pursued music, "but everybody's alive and in good health. Isn't that fabulous!" he proclaims. His whole family's been very supportive of his long musical journey, and proud of his personal mission to preserve and promote America's roots music, closely mirroring its customs and culture.

Growing up, Mac remembers appreciatively how the town-folk rallied behind him: "Because of the polio leg, everybody in the community, bless their hearts, was with me. Very openly it would be their comment, 'Follow your music, it will get you out of these rocky fields.' There was such encouragement there."

Little did Mac imagine that one day he would be cited as Crimora's Favorite Son. Nor was he aware that African-American athlete and educator Maven Huffman ranks right behind Mac as the most-celebrated name in an official listing of Zip Code 24431's famous former residents. Huffman became a big draw on the World Wrestling Entertainment circuit before retiring in 2005, and was last heard on cable television's *Home Shopping Network* as a fitness consultant.

Mac says there weren't a lot of blacks in the community, little more than two percent of the population in that segregated era, but as he recalls there was seemingly good rapport between the races. He recalls a memorable meal he had at a black farmer's house during thrashing time: "There was a huge bridle wreath bush and a large lilac bush that was on the way to our little country store. The building was gone, but the shrubbery was still there all through my boyhood. It had been occupied years past by some blacks, which as far as I know no one in our community discriminated against. We were swamped with farm work in the community when our grain was being thrashed and it was customary wherever you were come meal time, the people who lived there were supposed to furnish your meal.

"I distinctly remember helping this old black gentleman thrash his wheat, and, thank you, I had one of the best dinners I ever ate in my life. He was a bachelor, who had his sister come in to prepare the meal. Voluntarily he wouldn't eat with us inside the house, but took his meal outside to eat on the porch. Old habits die hard, but no one seemed to discriminate against the blacks in our community, and we'd even swap work and go fishing with them."

'A Star-Spangled Banner'...
Home of the Brave

"Though I realize I'm crippled, that is true, sir,
Please don't judge my courage by my twisted leg.
Let me show my Uncle Sam what I can do, sir,
Let me help to bring the Axis down a peg.
If I do some great deed I will be a hero,
And a hero brave is what I want to be.
There's a Star-Spangled Banner waving somewhere,
In that Heaven there should be a place for me."

While in high school, Mac decided there was one sport he might be able to master: "In part, I tried tennis, hoping to get closer to the girls, but in the end, I was too fumbly to be any good," determining finally "that dog won't hunt."

By the late 1930s, having survived the Great Depression, things appeared to be looking up for Mac and his peers. Even as war clouds loomed to threaten the horizon, it was an era of Andy Hardy movies and souped-up cars, Big Bands and jitterbug dancers, comic books and singing cowboys. Still, it was also a time of uncertainty and confusion for teen-agers like Mac, when the morning newspaper affirmed the September 1940 Congressional passage of the Selective Training and Service Bill, a.k.a. "The Draft," the nation's first ever in peacetime for those eighteen and up. In those days, work, school and music took such worldly matters off Mac's mind for the most part. Mac had just turned fifteen when that historic Bill passed through Congress.

"Ours is a great country to live in," maintains Mac, who would have gladly fought for it, if given the chance. "I guess my mother's prayers kept me out of service."

Meanwhile, helping to launch a 1940s' shift to the honky-tonk music

Mac's high school picture.

sounds that Jimmie Davis and Tex Ritter helped spearhead, was Texas newcomer Ernest Tubb, who grabbed the musical merry-go-round's gold ring with his love gone wrong creation "Walkin' the Floor Over You." Proving a great heart-healer for E.T. was the fact that his career-making song topped the million-selling mark, rare for country, and covered by no less than cinematic crooner Bing Crosby.

Draft or no draft, following the December 7, 1941 Japanese sneak attack on Pearl Harbor, Hawaii, the music scene aroused Americans to rally to the cause via such songs as "Praise the Lord, And Pass the Ammunition!" (Kay Kyser, 1942), "(Let's) Remember Pearl Harbor!" (Sammy Kaye, 1942), and a country disc "There's a Star-Spangled Banner Waving Somewhere" (Elton Britt, 1942), all multi-million-selling singles.

According to publisher Bob Miller, the man behind Elton Britt's gold record "There's a Star-Spangled Banner Waving Somewhere" (written by Paul Roberts, with Shelby Darnell nee Miller credited as co-writer), the general population embraced this song in part because of the fervor for fighting back, and their preference for a good rootsy song with its cultural simplicity. Because of his belief that the song should remain pure to its intended market, Miller raised a ruckus - and received some ridicule - by placing a notice in *Variety*, the showbiz Bible, warning big bands not to record or release a version of this patriotic paean. Since it was meant for hillbilly audiences, Miller feared it would lose the common touch that made the song so popular (it generated some three million in music sales).

Nonetheless, Decca pop star Dick Haymes and The Song Spinners did release a cover in 1943. Of course, Capitol's country artist Jimmy Wakely covered it first, their version released in July '42, two months after Britt's hit radio.

True, the song's lyrics were especially meaningful to Draft-exempt country boy Wiseman, whose own damaged leg kept him from following school buddies into battle, much as the fictional mountain boy in the song was denied doing what he felt was his duty: *Though I realize I'm crippled that is true, Sir/Please don't judge my courage by my twisted leg/Let me show my Uncle Sam what I can do, Sir/Let me help to bring the Axis down a peg..."* (The "Axis" being the combined German-Italian-Japanese forces determined to defeat America and its allies.)

Mac adds, " I think a big reason for the rise in popularity of country music was because the servicemen (and women) from all parts of the South mixed with their northern brothers, and by intermingling, began hearing one another's songs. So World War II was a melting pot of American music, which soon made it universally popular.

"It was the true beginning of traditional country music's great popularity boom thanks in part to those Southerners, who quite often took their guitars with them, to entertain their buddies with songs they knew. Prior to that the music had for the most part stayed as segregated as in the Civil War period. As an example, (Kentuckians) Bradley Kincaid and a young Grandpa Jones took their music to New England, performing on WBZ-Boston radio, where it was well received. I used to listen to Bradley Kincaid down in Virginia, and that's how I learned a lot of those old songs like 'Barbara Allen' (many of which Mac would record)."

With America deep into the war, Ernest Tubb's bar room ballads kept the jukebox playing, thanks to titles like "Try Me One More Time," and "The Soldier's Last Letter." Then there were fellow country stars like Texan Al Dexter, whose "Pistol Packin' Mama" hit number one country *and* pop, and was equally covered by Crosby, as well. WLS-Chicago alumnus Red Foley, who could croon with the best of the pop boys, crossed over, too, initially hitting number one with "Smoke On the Water."

In retrospect, the war brought together people from all corners of the country, creating friendships, romances and a new musical awareness, whether hillbilly, Dixieland jazz, boogie-woogie, folk or big band sounds. This new amalgamation also helped produce greater understanding and appreciation of various musical genres, as well as customs and traditions.

Even before the war started, the Great Depression encouraged sons of the south to head north, finding steady employment in the automobile industry and other factories, which went into higher gear during World War II, as the labor demand increased, especially to produce airplanes, jeeps, tanks, ships and other essential war-time equipment.

During their off-duty hours, workers liked to sit back, drink a cool brew, listen and dance to musical favorites on the jukeboxes, peppering the countryside in honky-tonks, truck stops, drugstores, restaurants, lounges and hotels. At the time, a tune would play for a nickel. Some of the itinerants also played live music, often just for tips or free food and drinks.

Mac points out that the jukebox phenomenon really started up strong during the war years, until it became a thriving business across the nation, numbering an estimated seventy-five thousand jukeboxes playing the evolving music of America. Attesting to their growing popularity, *Billboard* added a jukebox chart, and soon jukebox play alone could create a hit record. Mac's first label boss, Randy Wood at Dot, was well aware of this fact.

As singer-songwriter John Prine affirms, Mac was something of an oldies' music scholar, noting they joined forces for their 2007 CD "Standard Songs For Average People," dusting off chestnuts like "Pistol Packin' Mama," "I Love You Because," "Old Cape Cod" and The Death of Floyd Collins."

Wiseman made no secret of his love for vintage songs, especially those seemingly forgotten by others, hoping to introduce them to new generations by recording them anew. Mac did his homework on the golden oldies, notably the artists of yesteryear who helped popularize the songs. Some of the earlier ballads he's revived date back to the nineteenth century.

Another affecting song dealing with wartime was Kate Smith's recording "(There'll Be Bluebirds Over) The White Cliffs of Dover," which was popularized originally by British diva Vera Lynn. who sang so poignantly, *"There'll be bluebirds over/The white cliffs of Dover/Tomorrow, just you wait and see..."*

According to Mac, that song made quite an impact on him: "It told of the RAF pilots returning from missions over Germany, and quite often they would run out of fuel and were flying so low, some would crash into the cliffs. Years later, while touring in Europe, after playing Wembley, they gave me a plane ticket to take me to our shows in Denmark, Germany, Belgium, but I had always wanted to visit the site of the White Cliffs of Dover that Kate Smith had sung about, and always wanted to cross the (English) Channel by boat (prompting him to cash in his tickets).

"So I hired a cab to take me there to see the cliffs. I saw the bluebirds flying in and out of their nests... and just traveled back in my mind reflecting on that song and its lyrics. Then I glanced to the right and what did I see but a Holiday Inn! Then

I boarded the ferry, a huge one, and we landed at Calais, France. (Pre-arranged, the European promoter met Mac at Calais.)"

By the mid-1920s, country music was already spreading its wings in popularity among the masses, though its folk-flavored predecessors had always been there, especially among mountain or hill people, whose forebears brought beloved ballads, lullabies and traditional tunes along, sealed within their hearts, while emigrating from Europe.

Historically, the first bona fide commercial country recording reportedly was Eck Robertson's fiddling rendition of "Sally Gooden," recorded in New York City on July 1, 1922, for the Victor Talking Machine Company. That acoustical performance was nearly a year ahead of Fiddlin' John Carson's 1923 Atlanta, Georgia, recording "Little Old Log Cabin In the Lane," as captured by pioneer producer Ralph Peer on portable equipment. Carson accompanied himself vocally, as well, and the disc found favor among young and old alike.

One of the more interesting 1920s' trends musically was the popularity of story-songs that told of tragic events. The late 1925 Vernon Dalhart record "The Death of Floyd Collins," paid homage to a February 1925 passing of a man trapped in a Kentucky cave, just a few months before Mac's birth. It was one of the first records of a factual incident of recent occurrence, triggering further topical tunes by Dalhart and others.

"O come all ye young people, and listen while I tell/The fate of Floyd Collins, a lad we all knew well/His face was fair and handsome/His heart was true and brave/His body now lies sleeping/In a lonely sandstone grave..."

Earlier, Henry Whitter's May 1924 release "The Wreck Of the Southern Old 97," and Ernest Stoneman's "The Titanic," released a year later on the same Okeh label, reflected on real-life tragedies of the past. Whitter's song recalled the September 27, 1903 wreck of the Old 97 train near Danville, Virginia. Stoneman sang about the "unsinkable" British luxury liner *RMS Titanic*, struck by an iceberg in the Atlantic Ocean, April 14, 1912, and subsequently sank to the bottom of the sea.

Former opera singer Marion Try Slaughter, who performed professionally under the *nom de guerre* Vernon Dalhart and other names when "moonlighting" for rival recording companies, was undoubtedly country's biggest single star of the 1920s, thanks in large part to his ultra-successful "The Prisoner's Song," recorded August 13, 1924, also in New York City. "The Prisoner's... " plea to his sweetheart appealed to audiences of all stripes, making it the biggest sheet music and seller for the first half of the twentieth century, hitting its peak popularity in the spring, returning at year's end with a vengeance, to become big all over again for several more weeks. Through the years many other artists, including Mac, have recorded this classic song, while Dalhart's version enjoyed the additional status of being the first two-sided country success, seemingly backed with his popular version of "The Wreck of the Old 97."

"The Death of Floyd Collins" hit in December 1925, less than a year following Collins' tragic death in a Kentucky cave. That and other Dalhart successes Wiseman revived include "The Baggage Coach Ahead" and "The Letter Edged in Black."

Like so many of us, Mac heard these gems in later years on the radio. Mention of radio reminds us that reportedly by the late 1920s, there were six hundred and eighteen stations throughout the U.S.A. and networks were regularly broadcasting from coast to coast. By 1929, radio sales had boomed, becoming a six hundred million dollar business.

A 1930s' headline in *Variety*, proclaimed: "Radio kills sheet music & discs." Nobody publicly theorized then that radio and records could form an unofficial partnership that ensured both airplay and sales for artists and their recordings. One of radio's earliest vocal stars, Gene Autry - who enjoyed the mega-hit "That Silver-Haired Daddy of Mine" - used it as a stepping-stone to movie stardom, becoming Hollywood's first singing cowboy. He was, of course, followed by Tex Ritter, Roy Rogers and later, the likes of Monte Hale and Rex Allen.

By the late 1930s, Depression era artists were again scoring hit singles, a la Jimmie Davis on songs like "Be Nobody's Darlin' But Mine," "It Makes No Difference Now" and "You Are My Sunshine." The Sons Of the Pioneers, like Autry, chalked up cowboy hits such as "Tumbling Tumbleweeds" and "Cool Water," both penned by Pioneers' co-founder Bob Nolan, featuring unknown vocalist Leonard Sly. Sly soon became King of the Cowboys, under the screen name Roy Rogers. Ritter, who co-starred with young Rita Hayworth, and married another co-star, Dorothy Fay, also enjoyed a successful recording career that kicked into high gear in the 1940s, via classic cuts "There's a New Moon Over My Shoulder," "You Two-Timed Me One Time Too Often" and "Jealous Heart."

Two of the strongest exponents of early country music were radio station WLS-Chicago's *National Barn Dance*, boasting such celebrated music-makers as Autry, Bradley Kincaid, Patsy Montana, Lulu Belle & Scotty, George Gobel, Pat Buttram and the Hoosier Hotshots; while WSM-Nashville's *Grand Ole Opry* headlined major acts, including Uncle Dave Macon, Dr. Humphrey Bate, DeFord Bailey, and a decade later Fiddlin' Arthur Smith, Sam & Kirk McGee and The Delmore Brothers.

As the 1940s' began, two non-pop bandleaders who became household names were Bob Wills and Roy Acuff. Wills' Western Swing songs, augmented by twin fiddles, like "San Antonio Rose," "Worried Mind" and "Sugar Moon," proved highly popular, as did Acuff's mix of parlor tunes - "Great Speckled Bird" - and upbeat train tributes - "Wabash Cannonball" - representing Appalachian styles of rarin' back and letting go vocally. These appealed to fans both at home and abroad.

Attesting to Acuff's popularity, Japanese snipers tried to anger American fighting forces by yelling negatively about their respective icons: "To hell with Roosevelt!, To hell with Babe Ruth!, And to hell with Roy Acuff!"

Roy Acuff and Mac backstage.

39

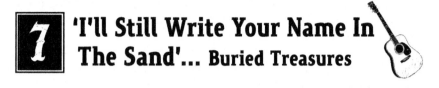

'I'll Still Write Your Name In The Sand'... Buried Treasures

"It's been many years since we were childhood sweethearts
Blissful days that I never can forget
And you know I still love you little darlin'
Though the years bring me only regret...
If I talk, will you try to understand
No matter how you treat me, I love you
And I still write your name in the sand..."

Following graduation in 1943, Mac made application for employment with one of the area's major chemical firms, Merck & Company, still a major pharmaceutical employer locally: "A lot of my relatives and friends worked there, so I filled out the paperwork and took the physical, but due to my disability, they turned me down. Talk about a pity party! I felt so depressed I went into Harrisonburg and was sitting in a bank feeling sorry for myself, when Woody Williams, a local entertainer, saw me through the window.

"Woody was on his way to radio station WSVA, just around the corner, and he stopped in to see why I looked so downcast. I told him my sad story, and he said something like, 'Aw, it's not the end of the world. Why don't you come up to the station and sing a song with me,' adding, 'If you want to work with me a few weeks while you figure out what it is you want to do, well, we'll work that out, too.' So I did.

"But remember the war was on and it wasn't an easy time for acts, what with gas rationing making it nearly impossible to make show-dates, or for the fans to drive to your gigs. That's why I went to work in a manganese mine as a chemist's lab assistant. My Granddad had worked there in the mine below, as did my Dad. [Crimora's Manganese Mine started in 1866.] But when I was hired, it was an open-pit type operation due to the new equipment, which enabled them to dig from the top down for the manganese and iron they sought. I worked hard there.

"It was an indoor job, but really my main deal was to go out in the field where they were drilling and get ore samples, bring them in and prepare them for him (the chemist) to test. We'd put them in a beaker and put them over that little lamp to see if the iron content was there, and make sure it was worthwhile to drill there. He was older and he'd sit there and doze, but I got so I could do most anything he could do."

Meanwhile, Mac was saving money off that job and the occasional shows he would play: "When I was a teen, about seventeen, I was real buddies with a guy on a farm who would get us all the gas ration stamps we needed, as these were tractor-related stamps (reserved for farmers who supplied food for the war effort). Everything back then was rationed, including coffee, meat, shoes and rubber (items being diverted to the military)."

Never afraid of work, Mac did whatever was necessary to build up his savings: "Coming out of the Depression, I didn't trust banks too much. I even worked on Sundays - which my mother didn't appreciate - as a guard at the mining company. There wasn't any gate or anything, but curiosity seekers might come by," Mac explains, adding, "It was late afternoon one fall day in late 1943, as I was heading for home when this gentleman I didn't know, asked if he could give me a lift home? I told him I had a ride, but thanked him. He persisted, telling me he had something important to talk about with me. As we drove, he said I had been recommended by the Infantile Paralysis Foundation, and explained that they would match my money, buck-for-buck, if I wanted to attend college. I sure did.

"That answered why I'd been saving my money all that time and so I selected the Shenandoah Conservatory of Music in Dayton, just outside Harrisonburg, as my school of choice. I took a bookkeeping course and music-related classes including piano and voice, but not enough that would change my singing style.

"The main reason I went there is the local radio station program director in Harrisonburg - Dick Johnson - was teaching a radio course. Part of the training included doing hands-on work at the station, after it had signed off for the evening. We were taught script-writing and running the control board, whatever, and I was enjoying this when after about six months of attendance, the instructor said he thought I was doing well enough that he offered me a full-time job. This, after one of his mainstay workers had been drafted, so figuring that's why I was going to the Conservatory in the first place to prepare myself to work in radio, I accepted his offer. You know Patsy Cline later told me she had uncles and aunts who attended the conservatory."

Mac found himself working some seventy-hour weeks: starting up the station early in the a.m., writing scripts, delivering news, reading commercials, signing off at sunset, and continuing on into the weekend, when he found often he was the only person aboard. Despite the long hours and heavy workload, Mac was making only about twenty dollars weekly at WSVA.

"You never heard the news like I reported it. I never learned French, so you can imagine when the allied troops invaded France to drive the Nazis out, well, I renamed every one of those towns listed, having no idea of the proper pronunciation, but I called them something I thought was close... "

Besides running the board, the youthful announcer enjoyed singing on radio, "but there wasn't any money in it. You worked for nothing, but got to promote your shows booked. It was swap time, barter time, on the radio."

Thus he was agreeable when a noted artist like Buddy Starcher, who hosted regular shows, invited him to accompany his group on personal appearances: "We'd drive out that evening and come back in and he'd give me five dollars, and I needed that extra income."

Buddy Starcher.

Starcher, one of Ruthie's favorite singers, proved to be a true mentor to Mac, who later would revive Starcher's hit "I'll Still Write Your Name In the Sand." In 1932, Starcher had chosen to entertain the war veterans camped along the Potomoc River in Washington, D.C., who were protesting the delay in issuing their World War I bonuses by then-President Herbert Hoover. To disperse the veterans or "Bonus Army," General Douglas MacArthur ordered the infamous charge by some six hundred-strong troopers, led by cavalry Major George Patton. Starcher's may have been an unpopular decision with politicians, but not among GIs at the encampment, burned and broken down.

From spring 1944, Wiseman worked at WSVA and learned everything from the ground up, including writing ads for station sponsors: "I mean copywriting, to announcing news, doing disc jockey-type shows and such. Back then it was transcription shows for the big bands. I got to be as well-versed in big bands, as I was in country. We had recordings of Glen Gray, the Dorsey Brothers (Tommy and Jimmy), Harry James, Woody Herman, whom he would later meet – playing all of them. Anyhow, it was just a great training period for me."

In that era, radio staffers playing records were not known as DJs; however, Mac was playing a four-hour block of pop songs at WSVA, which helped familiarize him with pop sounds as well as country.

Locally based artists like Buddy and Lee Moore, would be in the studio doing their live shows, and often would motion for Mac in the control room to come in and do a song or two. Starcher called his show *All-Star Round Up*.

"They would take me out on their gigs and give me some change. God, it was all good training. Buddy and I became the greatest friends, staying in touch up to his death. Yes, I recorded some of

Lee and Juanita Moore's band (from left): Leslie Keith, Juanita, Lee, Roger Lee, Mac and Buster Puffenbarger.

Buddy's songs. He had some good ones, though I think he got beat out of them. But what a showman he was. If it weren't for Buddy, I might have starved to death. Five or six years before he died, I had an opportunity to sit with him and pick his head so-to-speak, asking him some pertinent questions, things that I never asked him before."

Mac recalls that Buddy met and married singer Mary Ann, who had been performing on WBAL-Baltimore with Happy Johnny, hailed as the Arthur Godfrey of that area. As singer-songwriter-musician, Buddy Starcher had the right combination to become a major name on the country music horizon - and did achieve some passing fame worth noting.

While he never made it into the international realm of such contemporaries as Roy Acuff or Pee Wee King, Starcher scored a pair of *Billboard* hits, self-penned, that showed he had the goods: "I'll Still Write Your Name In the Sand" (Top Ten, 1949) and "History Repeats Itself" (Top Five, 1966). Starcher's latter song, citing the uncanny similarities concerning the assassinations of Presidents Abraham Lincoln and John Kennedy, crossed over into the pop Top Forty chart.

West Virginia native Obey Edgar Starcher was nearly twenty years Mac's senior. He developed a life-long love affair with broadcasting, and when radio was king, worked at such stations as WFBR-Baltimore, WSVA-Harrisonburg, WCAU-Philadelphia and WIBG-Philadelphia. He stayed long enough to play out an area by making personal appearances within listening distance of his shows.

Starcher's refusal to settle in Nashville may have resulted in his lack of lasting name recognition. Nonetheless, Starcher charted his Starday album "History Repeats Itself," which had been picked up by major label Decca Records, and made the trade's Top Forty pop chart. Starcher and his singer-wife also cut a 1961 duets album for Four Star: "Buddy & Mary Ann Starcher."

From 1960-'66, Buddy hosted his own WCHS-TV program in Charleston, West Virginia. Mac remembers: "Mary Ann told me that they had taken out a life insurance policy on Buddy, thinking it would help cover funeral services, but learned later that at age eighty, it was cut off. Mary Ann said that the insurance company kept accepting the premiums they paid, five years after they said it had expired." [Buddy died November 2, 2001, in Harrisonburg, at age ninety-five.]

Mac was pleased to learn that Buddy had played his music as the closing theme during Starcher's radio shows in Philadelphia and Miami: "He liked my recording of 'Sundown,' as it had a sort of rhumba beat to it. You know, back then a lot of stations signed off at sundown."

Romantically speaking, Mac seemingly had little time left for dating classmates in high school. Yet, the teen did develop a crush on Dorothy Drummond, to whom he once presented a pendant as a Christmas gift, much to his mother's displeasure. Many years later, Mac encountered Dorothy - who still had his pendant - and her husband Harold (Duck) Riddle at a class reunion, confiding to her that because of his shyness, he hadn't pursued her properly. Whereupon she smiled and replied, "Apparently you got over that rather quickly!"

Actually, Mac and Duck had been best friends. "I never knew that he had an interest in her. He was one helluva basketball player, not that he was tall, but he could maneuver in and out around those other players."

Although Mac had been fully focused on

High School date Dorothy Drummond.

getting an education and advancing himself career-wise, he did indeed date girls at school, that is, until he hooked up with a pretty student a couple grades behind him, Alberta Forbus. She soon commanded full attention, though at eighteen he had a plan for the future: "When I first came out of high school, I had put in an application to work for Merck, but they'd turned me down due to my physical affliction from polio. This was 1943, right at the height of the war, and I tried every branch I could to get into the service, including the SeaBees, but they wouldn't take me either, all due to the polio. Bless my mother's soul, for my sake she was broken-hearted each time I was rejected."

Mac, who had been a couple years younger than his Hungry Five band mates, watched them march off to war shortly after the Japanese made their December 7, 1941 sneak attack on Hawaii, as they were of draft age. (He was only sixteen then.)

Alberta and Mac became quite involved as a couple. Finally on May 4, 1944, he and Alberta, who was two years younger, made it official, becoming man and wife. Mac was still working for that WSVA pittance, but building a steady following among those tuning in the various broadcasts he was featured on. One particular show Mac sang on regularly was WSVA's *Kitchen Frolic*.

Alberta and Malcolm Wiseman's wedding day.

Artists were paid mainly by sponsors, based on a "per inquiry" (P.I.) system, wherein an advertiser shelled out a percentage of pay according to the number of orders that the announcer or singer generated among their listening audience, be it furniture, baby chicks, cure-alls or garden seed.

"So you had to be a good salesman, as well as singer and apart from the live shows you played after hours, it was the only source of income you got. Of course, the harder you pitched the product, the more you sold and the bigger your paycheck."

Mac grew up with a handicap, but never let it hold him back: "I did what had to be done and moved on to the next job when I was working on farms. Most of the time I'd finished my work before the other (able-bodied) boys. That work ethic has stayed with me throughout my whole life."

Both a hero and role model to Mac was America's President, a man of wealth who could have wallowed in self-pity upon discovering he was paralyzed from polio in the early 1920s; instead, went on to serve as Governor of New York and then President. Mac was especially saddened by the announcement of his death on April 12, 1945, feeling as though he had lost a member of the family.

"He was our savior you know, having pulled us through the Great Depression and most of World War II," muses Mac. "I was able to identify with him because he had the paralysis. I can't pinpoint in any way when I discovered that he had suffered from polio, as we didn't see many pictures of him, and most of what we heard from him was on radio (via periodic *Fireside Chats*). I know when he died, this whole country was at half-mast, because he forced himself to stay active right up until the very end [dying just three weeks prior to Germany's surrender].

"In the last couple of years, there was a therapist who came here to assist me two or three times a week, and she had worked at that Georgia facility in Warm

Springs. She was quite knowledgeable and it was interesting that she told me about some of the conditions created to make it more comfortable for him, you see."

Incidentally, Mac never had an opportunity to vote for his favorite president, as he was not quite twenty at the time of FDR's death, because back then the minimum voting age was twenty-one.

As Wiseman developed his own radio skills, he began looking for better situations around the area or nearby states. A plus was his pleasing personality: "One thing I noticed was the station managers and program directors were driving Fords and Chevrolets, while the 'hillbillies' were driving Cadillacs. I thought, 'Damn, this needs a little looking into'..."

Mac found that his education and experience gave him a leg-up on other country boys seeking jobs in radio: "It really did. It gave me the vocabulary that I could talk to the bosses and wasn't just another hillbilly performer."

In spring 1945, Mac accepted an offer to work at WMFD-Frederick, Maryland, where he would also organize his first country band: "I knew a guy in Frederick (Joe Johnson), who had been on our station and asked him if there was any chance of getting a band together there. He said yeah, and that led to my first little band (including Denver Dan Spurrier on accordion, Rusty Harp on rhythm and Mac on bass and vocals). Rusty Harp sang similar to Gene Autry. So we did western songs like that, including those of The Sons Of The Pioneers and Bob Wills. We didn't have 'bluegrass' as it is today back then. We had to give ourselves time from singing on the station to get out to our gigs. For the carnivals we played, you had to get there at least by 6 o'clock to draw the crowds in for the 7 p.m. show. Thanks to our radio promotion, we had good crowds.

"We did well in the summer, because every little town had a firemen's carnival and they'd hire us and then we could advertise it on radio. We also played a lot of grange halls in Virginia and Maryland in those days. The Eagles Clubs were big back then. In fact, I joined the Eagles while I was in Frederick, mainly because you could get a drink there on Sundays."

Mac also put one of the lessons he learned from Buddy Starcher to work for him. He began handling all the booking for his new group: "Right away we got bookings at all those holiday events. Every little town had like a county fair and firemen's carnival. So we did all right revenue-wise, up until bad weather set in."

Still, times could be tough in Frederick, just as it had been in Harrisonburg. It was wartime and the boys had to pay double for gasoline and tires, necessities for playing gigs, many in outlying towns. The situation had prompted more-experienced groups to disband, hoping for better times. One fellow he met in Frederick who became a good friend was Doc Williams, newly discharged from the military, but a mainstay at WWVA's *Wheeling Jamboree*. Mac and his boys were fired up by their own positive reception on radio.

One of their more lucrative bookings totaled three hundred dollars a week, which went a long way for band members in those days. That was a gig at the Oyster Roast: "It was right down on the beach on the Maryland shore, where they harvested the oysters. They'd cook the oysters every which way, fried, stewed or roasted. They actually approached me, apparently having heard us on the radio. I didn't have to solicit that gig, as it was a fund-raiser for the local town. I liked to have fainted when they offered me three hundred dollars for three days. You see we had been working shows for fifty dollars, and I split it with the boys. I mean you could buy a damn good car for seven or eight hundred dollars in those days."

Unfortunately, the Oyster Roast proved a booking exception. Meantime, Mac remained a fan of the Opry stars of the era, and lit up when his band found themselves opening for WSM acts: "My first encounter with any Opry-connected act was when I did a show in Hagerstown, Maryland. It was Texas Ruby and Curly Fox - whose backup band [his Fox Hunters] included Grady Martin and Jabbo Arrington - headlining.

"I was working out of Harrisonburg and Bud Messner, who owned a radio station, was emcee. I remember Ruby and Curly were late getting there, so they hit the stage running from their car, along with Jabbo and Grady. Ruby sang a couple songs then went backstage, leaving Curly out on stage. I overheard him chewing her out, saying, 'Get back out there and help me.' Bud and his Skyline Boys worked out of WJEJ-Hagerstown nearly five years, before moving on to WCHA-Chambersburg, Pennsylvania. He would also operate a music store there (with wife Molly, an heiress to the R. J. Reynolds tobacco family of Winston-Salem, North Carolina.)."

It was on the road that Mac first encountered some of the musicians who would become regulars on the later Nashville recording scene, many of whom would work with him. Grady Martin became one of the most-in-demand session players during the evolution of the Nashville Sound, but Jabbo Arrington died at a young age in the early 1950s. Before that, Jabbo and Grady became members of Little Jimmy Dickens' Country Boys band and adapted a double-guitar playing solo that proved popular with crowds.

Although it occurred sooner than either anticipated, but once Alberta announced her pregnancy, Mac had further incentive to bring home a bigger paycheck. His parents were delighted, too, as it would be their first grandchild.

"In the fall, when the carnivals dried up, we'd starve. Buck Ryan was with another group (Uncle Joe Johnson's) when we lived across the street from each other in little old rat-infested apartments. They literally were. It was a damn shame to have to live like that. Like myself, Buck had married quite young and both our wives were pregnant. We'd each go out with the groups we were with and get up the next morning to compare how much we made last night. Then we'd pool our money to get enough to eat breakfast for all four of us.

"I could see that wasn't going anywhere for the winter, so Alberta and I came back down to the valley. I went to work with Lee Moore at WSVA. I made a deal with my father-in-law (Charles Richard Forbus) in Waynesboro, so we could stay there until after the baby was born in January. He was to keep account of it, and I would pay him. It was twenty-five or thirty miles to Harrisonburg and regardless of the weather, I got up early in the morning and drove that distance. Then we'd go out at night and do our shows."

Lee's mid-1940s band included Moore, wife Juanita on guitar, Leslie Keith on fiddle, Buster Puffenbarger on accordion and Mac, whose itinerary only allowed him about six hours' sleep nightly - if he were lucky: "Buster went on to work with Sunshine Sue (at WRVA's *Old Dominion Barn Dance*). He and his sisters performed like the Harden Trio (of later 'Tippy Toeing' fame)."

How much easier life would've been for the troupe if there had been super-highways such as today's I-64, which connects west to Charleston and east to Norfolk; or I-81 which starts in Tennessee, continues through Bristol, Roanoke, and into Pennsylvania and points north. Instead, the boys had to pack themselves into sedans not built with instruments or sound systems in mind, drive over two-lane roads that often wound through twisting mountainous terrain, especially treacherous in winter.

Upon the arrival of baby Randolph Carson Wiseman, nicknamed "Randy," on January 25, 1946, it proved even harder getting a full night's rest. Mac remembers it well: "At night we would play schoolhouses and halls, but I was never late for that radio program at 8 o'clock in the morning, if the roads were at all passable, and not slick from ice or sleet. Usually, I would leave about 7 or 7:30 to get there on time."

Alberta and baby son Randy.

Hired as their featured vocalist, Lee and Juanita paid Mac thirty-five dollars a week. Mom's homemade songbooks came in handy when Mac needed songs to sing. For a time after the baby was born, he and Alberta shared accommodations with them: "We lived in a house they called the Hillbilly Mansion. He and Juanita had the downstairs, while me, my wife and our new baby had the upstairs. Lee let me sell my program books and mail-order candy, which I ordered from Chicago in boxes similar to Cracker Jacks, but containing six or seven pieces of salt-water taffy. I sold them for like a quarter a box. Some of the boxes would have a 'prize' in them. That was a good gimmick and I sold a ton of that stuff."

One of his favorite get-away-from-it-all pastimes was fishing, and somehow Mac fit it into his schedule: "Lee and I fished a lot and we didn't use regular worms as bait, we used night-crawlers, which were three or four times the size of the other worms. We'd just use rod and reel and didn't use any plugs. Sometimes we'd go over to Raleigh Springs, West Virginia, on Route 33, to trout fish. I enjoyed that."

8 'Tramp On The Street'...
Payback's Hell!

"He was some mother's darlin',
He was some mother's son
Once he was fair,
And once he was young.
Some mother rocked him,
Her darlin' to sleep,
But they left him to die,
Like a tramp on the street."

"I loved Molly to death, but her husband Lynn was something else. To me, if the world were a cow, he'd be the asshole," joshes Mac, recalling time spent in pioneer country and gospel vocalist Molly O'Day's troupe.

Fate it seems had a whole lot to do with Wiseman's career course. During July 1946, Lee Moore's deal with WSVA, ended with the expiration of his contract, so he decided to move back to performing in West Virginia. That prospect did not appeal to Mac and Alberta.

Lee's fiddler Leslie Keith, whose claim to fame would be as co-composer of "The Black Mountain (Blues) Rag," put Mac wise to the fact that mountain songbird Molly and husband Lynn had an opening in their Cumberland Mountain Folks band. While discussing their front man Slim Sweet's upcoming departure, Keith told the couple, "I know who you need."

Slim left to join Archie Campbell and Red Kirk in a new vocal trio. At the time, Molly's troupe was booked regularly on WNOX-Knoxville, home to the *Mid-Day Merry-Go-'Round* and the weekend *Tennessee Barn Dance* programs. Under the guiding hand of Lowell Blanchard, the ten thousand-watt WNOX became a proving ground for such talents as Roy Acuff, Pee Wee King, Charlie Monroe, Homer & Jethro, Cliff & Bill Carlisle, Martha Carson, Mother Maybelle & The Carter Sisters, Carl Story and Johnnie & Jack featuring Kitty Wells.

Meanwhile, singer-musician Molly O'Day caught the ear of Acuff-Rose music publisher Fred Rose in Nashville. Lynn also sang and played guitar in their band, while Molly's brother Cecil "Skeets" Williamson played fiddle and George "Speedy" Krise, dobro. Publisher Rose supplied O'Day some of her best songs, including "Tramp On the Street" (by Hazel & Grady Cole), a favorite of newcomer Hank Williams, and she sang Hank's self-penned songs like "The Singing Waterfall." Coincidentally, Mac described her as "a female Hank Williams," citing her raw, robust vocal style: "She had that same kind of presence on stage and boasted a plaintive, simple sincerity to her vocals."

Recalling his notification to report to WNOX, Mac smiles, "I had never worked on WNOX, but was quite familiar with a station in St. Louis, Missouri, with the call letters KMOX. It was a fifty thousand watt station where Happy Cheshire had a big country show, and I remember *Rock Creek Park* was a popular St. Louis venue.

Well, Lynn Davis sent a telegram to let me know I should come over to WNOX to audition. Mistakenly, I called KMOX to ask for Lynn Davis, and they never heard of him, and then suggested I look at his telegram more closely. So I called WNOX-Knoxville and got an audition. They hired me right away. It was the fall of 1946. All I did was open shows for them, until we went to Chicago to record her tracks for Columbia Records... and then I played bass."

Competition was a bit fiercer now, as many of the GIs were returning home to resume their pre-war lives and jobs, including musicians. Leslie Keith, who would later tell Mac about another opening at WCYB-Bristol, Virginia; had also

Recording in Chicago (from left) Molly O'Day, Skeets Williamson, Lynn Davis, Speedy Krise and Mac.

heeded Uncle Sam's call: "That was unusual because he was already about forty-some years old."

Keith knew Molly when she was Lois Laverne Williamson in Beckley, West Virginia, although actually born in Paintsville, Kentucky, daughter of a coal-miner. She and brothers Skeets and "Duke" (Joe, a banjoist) worked in the Happy Valley Boys band led by Johnnie Bailes. She joined Leonard "Lynn" Davis' Forty Niners Band in Bluefield, and in 1941, while at WHAS-Louisville, she adopted the stage name Molly O'Day. Earlier names she used were Mountain Fern and Dixie Lee Williamson.

As noted, Fred Rose became an O'Day champion, convincing Columbia A&R chief Art Satherley to sign and record her. Fortunately, Mac had joined her troupe by the time she was told to record her debut session at a WBBM-Chicago studio, situated at 410 North Michigan Avenue.

"A highlight for me was during the drive up there, we stopped in the heart of the Renfro Valley where we spent the night," adds Wiseman. "I remember having listened to the *Renfro Valley Barn Dance* radio show, and it was a real treat to see the folks in the Valley there dressed in their costumes. They were having a turkey shoot, using real turkeys, as it was near Thanksgiving. There were five of us driving up to Chicago that time."

On Saturday, December 14, 1946, Mac was in the Windy City with O'Day recording "The Tramp On The Street," "When God Comes and Gathers His Jewels," "The Black Sheep Returned To the Fold" and "Put My Rubber Doll Away." During that initial afternoon session, they also recorded four more Acuff-Rose copyrights: "That Tear-Stained Letter," "Drunken Driver," "Six More Miles To the Graveyard" and originally written by Jim Anglin "The Lonely Mound of Clay," which Roy

Acuff purchased from Anglin, as Jim marched off to war. The other eight songs, recorded December 16, likely were: "The Singing Waterfall," "At the First Fall of Snow," "Matthew 24," "I Don't Care If Tomorrow Never Comes," "A Hero's Death," "I'll Never See Sunshine Again," "Too Late, Too Late" and "Why Do You Weep, Dear Willow?"

Their acoustic sessions featured Molly's emotional lead vocals, while accompanying herself on either guitar or banjo, alongside Lynn, Skeets, Speedy and Mac. The latter was well aware of the importance of their producer, British-born Arthur Edward Satherley, warmly hailed as "Uncle Art."

"Even back then I was very familiar with him being connected with Columbia and knew that he had first recorded such greats as Gene Autry and Roy Acuff, and was a legendary man in music," muses Wiseman. Satherley, who initially recorded such black legends as Blind Lemon Jefferson, Ma Rainey and Josh White, indeed went on to produce country greats Bob Wills, Bill Monroe, Al Dexter, Red Foley and Little Jimmy Dickens. Mac points out that Uncle Art lived to be ninety-six years old (having died February 10, 1986, fifteen years after induction into the Country Music Hall of Fame).

Producing O'Day's 1946 Chicago session was Art Satherley (left) with Mac, Molly and Lynn Davis.

O'Day was one of the few women Satherley cut country, and had high hopes for her commercial success. Wiseman shared his respect for her talents: "Yes, to me, Molly had that kind of charisma that came across on the radio. I'd go out with their full band and, though I played stand-up bass on her records, I never played bass on their shows. I really didn't know how to play bass well and Molly really didn't use bass in her band - nor did I originally. I had filled in before on bass, always on a borrowed instrument."

Though only two years his senior, Molly made quite an impression on Mac. Among songs she helped popularize were "Teardrops Falling In the Snow," "On the Evening Train," "Heaven's Radio" and "Poor Ellen Smith."

"I remember the first thing we'd do when we got to a venue, whether it was a school or a courthouse, whatever, the entire band started moving the chairs as close to the stage and closer together as we could, because we knew we were gonna need that standing room. We would do as high as two or three shows until midnight. Do one show, empty that place out and fill that mother up again. That's how popular she was. And they didn't have any records out at that time. I didn't realize it at the time, but she had quite an influence on me with her pure mountain style singing. A number of songs she sang, I'd use later in my repertoire (like 'Poor Ellen Smith').

"Molly played a lot of schoolhouses up in the mountain region. I remember one occasion when we pulled up as close to the school as you could get, but we had to cross a small drawbridge on a path that wound around the mountain. We saw the school lights were on. Well, we had a bulky sound system that was in a suitcase-sort-of-deal that fit in the trunk. It was just too heavy for one guy, so me and Skeets carried it together. There was an adjustable microphone stand, which we put through the handles on the speaker to tote it. Now him and me with my puny leg had to struggle to get it carried up there to the school. We got inside there and found the 'lights' we saw were only kerosene lamps. There was no electricity! We looked at each other and it was either chuckle or cry, so we just laughed at the situation. You know we were mostly only playing those gigs for seventy per cent of the 'door' (paid admissions, probably fifteen-cents or a quarter)."

According to Mac, he would usually open their shows: "I had the 'featured' spot on her program, like the warm-up act does today. I'd come out and sing for about fifteen or twenty minutes, usually performing other artists' songs, not having any records out myself. I did numbers like 'Roly Poly,' 'Big Rock in the Road,' whatever was current at the time."

What triggered the friction between Mac and Lynn was a money matter: "The reason I left was he lied to me. They were paying me fifty dollars a week, but he said I could sell my songbooks on the show. Well, I was selling Stamps-Baxter songbooks with my picture on the front and singing the songs out of it. They printed them up for me in Texas. I had just ordered two thousand songbooks and they were great and I was selling the heck out of those books. But, after a couple months, just before Christmas, that S.O.B. came to me and stopped me from selling because he said it was cutting into his sales."

Based on Lynn's promise, Mac had an order for a couple thousand songbooks printed up and thus couldn't pay for them. So he wrote the company and explained the situation, vowing to pay them eventually for the order. Mercifully, the firm agreed, and Mac did indeed pay up - and saved the correspondence they exchanged to this day.

Later, Molly left Acuff-Rose and recorded her final Columbia tracks in 1951, never having attained the heights envisioned for her by either Rose or Satherley. Lynn entered the ministry and thereafter Molly devoted herself to performing gospel music. After suffering from lung cancer, she lost her battle on December 5, 1987, at age sixty-four, while residing in Huntington, West Virginia. Surprisingly, O'Day only recorded thirty-six songs for Columbia between 1946-1951, but *New York Times'* folk music critic Robert Shelton nonetheless described her as "One of the greatest, if not the greatest, woman singer in country music."

She had worked the periodic Cherokee Indian Fair, site of an early bluegrass-style festival, as Mac remembers: "They held it twice a year. I played it in 1946, with Molly. In later years, I was playing the festival and would talk about how it brought back memories, but folks would always look a bit skeptical. Then one day, an old Indian with lines on his face like three miles of bad road came up and said, 'I saw you years ago at the Indian Fair...' Well, I was so glad to see him, I even sat him on my knee for a picture, feeling like he was the sole survivor, my only proof that I had played there."

Following his departure from the O'Day-Davis troupe, Mac received another fruitful call from pal Leslie Keith (then with the Stanley Brothers) in the spring of 1947. Keith wanted Wiseman to know of an opening on WCYB-Bristol's noontime program called *Farm & Fun Time*.

As Mac recalls it, "Leslie said, 'The program director asked me if I knew of another group, so if you want to put a band together, you would be it.' That just thrilled me to death. So I got an audition disc cut and, dig this, I had Tex Isley on a Merle Travis-style guitar, the Louvin Brothers - Charlie, guitar and Ira, mandolin - and L. E. White (later a hit songwriter), who was a helluva fiddler at the time. They made that audition disc with me and I told them what the deal would be, a split and the whole plan. Everybody was set to go... and we had a great sound.

"I took it to the P.D (Program Director), who played just a little bit of it and said, 'You're just what we're looking for,' and told me to come in on a certain day. Well, opening day the only one that showed up was Tex Isley (who, despite his nickname, was really from North Carolina). The other three didn't call or nothing. Now I know that P.D. thought I was a damned liar, that the audition was a made-up thing to get the job. I was standing there with egg all over my face, so I explained to him I didn't know where they were and said if they were dead and I wanted to send flowers, I wouldn't know where to send them.

"I told him I could get a few more guys if he'd give me a few days. He said, *'We're buying you. You put a band together.'* That's when Curly Seckler came to work with me. In fact, I hired the old Charlie Monroe band, that's what I did. Curly came out of that group, and fiddler Paul Prince and even Isley had been in the Monroe band.

"You know in the early 1970s, when I ran that festival in Renfro Valley, Kentucky, L. E. White (who wrote Conway's 'After The Fire Is Gone' and 'To See My Angel Cry') was there. He came to me and said, 'I'd like to talk to you.' He sat there with tears in his eyes and apologized to me, saying he was just a kid, but should've known better. But I want you to know, to this day, those damn Louvin brothers have never mentioned it. It's unreal. All they had to do was say, 'We didn't think we could make that,' you know." Incidentally, the Stanley Brothers (Carter and Ralph) were also getting their start at WCYB at that time. Behind the scenes their father Lee Stanley, a wannabe country singer who had worked in the sawmill, was assisting with their bookings.

Occasionally, Mac and his new band, which he dubbed The Country Boys, would share the stage with the Stanleys. Performing around the tri-state area, Mac lined up the bookings, as he was more familiar with the territory. Although Ralph and Mac never had a cross word between them, he and Carter had a falling out.

"I was doing the *Farm & Fun Time* program in 1947. That was a two-hour show and we'd rotate twice, getting fifteen minutes apiece, and they also had something on farm and news. Not having records or anything, and as inconvenient as it was, I always was a big believer in early morning shows. I thought it was the best time to reach the people. That's when the housewife was up and getting everyone off to work and school. It's the time that she could be listening to the radio and doing work as well, prepping for lunch.

"Since the band wouldn't show up half the time, I'd do an hour at 6 o'clock by myself, just me and my guitar, and sell items such as my songbooks, which I didn't have to split (proceeds) with them," explains Mac, grinning as he notes, "I added my wife and our first baby's picture on the back and sold the same book (he designed earlier)."

The Country Boys worked schoolhouses and such on a percentage basis: "Generally, the school got thirty per cent, we got seventy per cent, but we also sold our pictures and songbooks, and 'pretty girl' cakes (as a promotional gimmick); that is, we'd pick out a pretty local girl and I'd stop, pick up a cake from the store, and then we'd raffle her and the cake off for a date. We also played a lot of courthouses in the Bristol area, because they were big enough to hold a crowd."

Fortunately, there were no repercussions regarding the date raffles; however, the troupers' gigs for rugged coalminers, who'd been cooped up in the mines, could get a bit over-exuberant on occasion.

"Yeah, sometimes they'd get a bit rowdy. Actually, I never had any real trouble in the coal camps. Some of 'em came right out of the mines to see our shows (soot and all). If they got loud, Carter Stanley would stop their performances and reprimand them. I'd just giggle and say, 'If you want to talk, you'll have to get your own show.' Yeah, they got liquored up a little sometimes, and the Stanleys might go out and find their car turned upside down or something (no doubt due to Carter scolding the crowd)."

There were other factors Mac faced that were more pressing: "Money-wise, it was nip and tuck, I'll tell you. We'd deduct car expenses, any posters ordered, then split the money equally. I couldn't pay a salary because I didn't get a salary from the radio station, and didn't have the money. But, I always split evenly with the band after our shows. I also used to feature them and part of my indoctrination speech was, 'You don't have to be as good as Merle Travis, but give me everything you got,' and in doing my vocals, I tried to make them sound good, and I wanted them to play good in their spots."

Yet another familiar face on WCYB was A. P. Carter, patriarch of the pioneering Carter Family: "Now old Mr. Carter, A.P., was on every day, doing a five-minute slot, during which he sang and sold pocket Testaments. You know, he'd drive over to Bristol from his home in Hiltons, riding on those old country roads, just to sing one or two songs, and to give his pitch for those li'l Testament Bibles.

"The station was in the Shelby Hotel, with the studio itself half a story down in the basement, which had concrete windowsills almost even to the street, just high enough to sit on, and I can see it now, that old gentleman coming out in good weather and sitting down there with me. I'd talk to him and pick his brain so-to-speak. Although there were a lot of questions I would've liked to have asked A.P. Carter, I hesitated about getting too personal, afraid he might run me off! But I really treasure that time with him. He was always so thoughtful, and thinking the whole time he was talking. I never recall him having a jovial moment, not that he was downhearted or depressed, but just sort of solemn. I believe he was always thinking about the music though."

9 'Foggy Mountain Top'...
Midst the Bluegrass

"You caused me to weep, you caused me to moan,
You caused me to leave my home...
Oh, the lonesome pine, and the good old times
I'm on my way back home..."

"My father-in-law – Mr. Forbus – was in the produce business. He'd truck produce in from Florida, places like that," explains Wiseman, who in the fall of '47, departed Bristol to work in Waynesboro again. "We'd sell a case of celery and five cases of oranges to local merchants. I could handle that easily for him and he was free to truck in the produce. I stayed there until March 1948. He'd done me a favor, letting us stay there earlier, and it was payback time."

Of course, that move also meant disbanding his Country Boys. He had no idea that departing Blue Grass Boys' Lester Flatt and Earl Scruggs would soon come into Mac's life.

"At that time, I listened to the *Grand Ole Opry* and knew that Flatt and Scruggs were with Bill Monroe, who was having some big hits on Columbia Records, like 'Lovin' Another Man' and stuff like that. Those were good songs, solid. Being honest with you, I didn't know which one played the banjo at that time. That's how smart I was.

"Unbeknownst to me," says Wiseman, "Monroe liked what I was doing, especially my early morning show. Anytime they were going East, he would always get in the car and go to sleep. So he'd tell the guys when he left there (Nashville), 'Now, when we get up near Bristol, wake me up. I like to hear the boy on the Bristol station'... Then, out of the blue, I got a call from Earl who said, 'Listen, me and Lester both left Bill. Would you like to join us?' I thought, what the hell do they need with me? But I joined them anyway down in Hickory, North Carolina, to do a radio show."

So it was in 1948 that Flatt & Scruggs had formed their original Foggy Mountain Boys. As Mac explains, Lester and Earl came up with their band's name, by borrowing it from an old A. P. Carter tune, "Foggy Mountain Top."

In those pre-band-bus days, the boys found themselves literally crowded into their available transportation: "Back then, Lester had a 1939 Ford Station Wagon, one of those old Woodies, with a canvas top and I had a black 1939 Studebaker Commander, so Lester and I would alternate driving to the shows."

Besides Wiseman, there were Howard Watts, another ex-Bill Monroe bandsman, who played standup bass and did comedy as Cedric Rainwater, and Jim Shumate playing fiddle.

"The reason they went to Hickory is because Shumate lived there. He had a wife and three little girls and worked at a furniture store. He had recommended and brought Scruggs to Monroe. But he fit into that kind of music just great and they wanted him in the original band. Being an old pro, he wasn't going to quit his job

54

at the furniture store and get in on a split deal where he couldn't support his family, until he was sure that bird was gonna fly. He also had that show on a little old five hundred-watt radio station, WHKY.

"But, honest-to-God, we were playing to twenty dollar houses. And that was the gross! Anyone could see this bird wasn't going to fly. I don't think that little radio station got off the roof-top. Well, I told them I knew the Bristol territory, and we should hit that *Farm & Fun Time* audience.

"I called the WCYB program director with whom by this time my integrity was high enough that he believed me when I told him how good our band was. He said. 'Come on over,' and we did a couple of tunes and that was it, we were in. I did all the bookings. But just to show you how fair Lester was performing, without any talk or argument, he and I would swap out. One time he would do a solo and the next time I did a solo; and I sang tenor to him when we did duets and I also sang tenor in a quartet."

Shumate recalled , "Lester, Earl, and Cedric Rainwater came over to the house and said they'd pulled out from Bill and were organizing their own show and were going to call it the Foggy Mountain Boys... and they needed me to play the fiddle. I debated around a while because I really didn't want to, but I thought well, since they went to all this trouble, I may as well. So we decided to just split down the board.

"Lester said they were going to need one more man, so they were going to hire Mac Wiseman. I'd never met Mac. So we got set up and did our first program over WHKY in Hickory. I think we worked a week there. We went from there to WCYB in Bristol and there we set the woods on fire. Everywhere we went, we turned them away. We played everywhere - at schoolhouses, ball parks, auditoriums, and airports.

"Wiseman kind of acted as our agent. He could type and was a pretty good bookkeeper. The letters would come in from people wanting us to come to so and so, and Mac would answer back and give them the terms and open dates, and there'd come back a contract, and we would sign it. That's all there was to it in those days."

Flatt & Scruggs and their Foggy Mountain Boys' popularity was growing like wildfire. Little did they know how iconic Flatt & Scruggs & their Boys would become. In fall 1948, they landed their first record pact with Mercury Records, then a relatively new label. Mac points out they recorded at WROL-Knoxville: "The reason for that is we 'bootlegged' that session due to a union strike then taking place, so at the time there was a recording ban going on nationwide."

Shumate said some of the tracks they cut were "Cabin in Caroline," "We'll Meet Again Sweetheart," "God Loves His Children" and "I'm Going to Make Heaven My Home." On "God Loves His Children," he remembers Earl, not known as a vocalist, sang baritone. Shumate added, "I did the fiddle kickoff to 'Cabin in Caroline.' When I was playing that song when we were on stage, I'd pull the bow on the kickoff. But on the record, I pushed the bow because I couldn't take a chance of squeaking the bow. You are subject to screech on the fiddle when you're going both ways. If you go the same way all the time, you ain't going to screech. It'll come out smooth."

The most memorable track featuring Wiseman was "We'll Meet Again, Sweetheart," on which he sang tenor with Lester and it's still regarded by aficionados to be among the best bluegrass performances. Instrumentally, Mac recalls playing rhythm guitar, and also did a lot of second guitar fills and runs.

"I played guitar all the time on shows with Flatt & Scruggs. Lester was the main guitarist, but I stood over there beside Earl and learned more banjo stuff off my guitar playing than anybody in the business, because I learned his runs and his stops. But with Lester carrying the rhythm and the string-bassist's strong, solid underpinning, I was just over there really goofing around if I wanted to, so far as playing, and it wasn't really up to me to keep the tempo. I didn't play out of time, but I wasn't responsible for it... So it was a big training ground for me without anybody really knowing it, you see."

At that milestone Mercury Records session in November '48, Flatt & Scruggs and the band were produced by Murray Nash. It was Lester and Earl's first recording as a duo. It was also the last that featured Mac, though two decades later he and Lester would pair up for the RCA label, and there was an odd session or so pickin' with Scruggs. After departing Wiseman's Country Boys, Curley Seckler went on to play with Flatt & Scruggs for nearly a dozen years, his distinctive tenor harmonies are featured on classic cuts like "Salty Dog Blues," "Rollin' in My Sweet Baby's Arms" and "I'll Go Steppin', Too."

Flatt & Scruggs joined the WSM *Grand Ole Opry* in 1955, with their own sponsor Martha White Flour, which still advertises on the station. Monroe reportedly did not desire the duo on the Opry, but Martha White gave WSM an ultimatum to take them or lose their ad money. Despite disbanding in 1969, Flatt & Scruggs were elected as a duo to the Country Music Hall of Fame in 1985; and similarly enshrined in the Bluegrass Hall of Honor in 1991, along with former boss-man Bill Monroe.

Mac shared some anecdotes from his days with Flatt & Scruggs: "One of the things that happened while with Lester and Earl, we played a small school back up in the mountains and upon driving back to Bristol on a dirt mountain road, the generator went out on Flatt's 1939 Ford Station Wagon. By this time, it was 11 o'clock or later at night, and while we could see the odd light in the windows on the side of the mountain, none of us was brave enough to go up and knock on the door. While going to the schoolhouse, we stopped at the printer in Abington and picked up two hundred window cards, which we used to send out to advertise our upcoming show dates.

"While sitting there in the darkness wondering if we were going to have to wait until daylight to leave the mountains, I came up with the idea of sitting on the right front fender of the station wagon, and burning those window-cards as a torch. After burning quite a few of the posters, we made it down to Abington and to a service station where we got the generator fixed."

Similarly, another event a few months later involved the posters: "We were going to another show and just outside of Richlands, the local sheriff pulled the station wagon over. He got out with his gun drawn, came up to the car and demanded we all get out and put our hands on top of the vehicle. His reason for such actions was that five men had escaped from a road gang, and he thought we might be the escapees. Where the posters came in handy, we had our band picture on there and showed it to him," adds Mac. "So he accepted that and we were on our way."

At this time the Foggy Mountain Boys were having great success with shows in the Bristol area: "One weekend particularly, we would play the Starlight Ballroom in Hurley, Virginia, near Grundy, on a Saturday. We would play the courthouse in Hindman, Kentucky, Sunday, and on Monday the courthouse in West Jefferson, North Carolina. All of these dates were on percentage, and for that three-day weekend we split twenty-five hundred dollars profit, netting each band-member five hundred dollars. I would book that same weekend of dates every two months and we'd do just as well each time."

Mac recalls a performance in Pikesville, Kentucky, where a local bootlegger came to see their show: "He wanted Earl and me to ride around with him awhile in his Cadillac. At 3 or 4 o'clock in the morning, he'd stop at these little shacks on the road he traveled, which he owned and rented out, to pick up some booze. He'd go in and lift up the mattress and there would be a whole layer of half-pint bottles of booze between the mattresses…"

Shumate told of a fiddling competition which featured Wiseman as support instrumentalist. Although Jim only worked with the Stanleys a week, Leslie Keith had been their regular fiddler. Shumate was with Flatt & Scruggs when he first met Keith.

"That Keith was some fiddler. But the worst I ever saw Keith hurt was when I beat him in a fiddler's convention. He'd take that 'Black Mountain Blues' and win every convention in the country. He could do that thing. When a man writes a song, it's his, you know, and he could handle it like nobody else. So we did a show at the National Fiddlers Convention at Richlands in 1949. We had Buck Ryan on the program, who was playing fiddle for Jimmy Dean at that time; Leslie Keith, who was doing a show out of Bristol; Chubby Wise, who was working with Hank Snow in Nashville; and myself. I was fiddling with Lester and Earl. There was a huge crowd, about nine thousand best I can remember."

True enough, Keith played his "Black Mountain Blues," Wise did his "Orange Blossom Special," Buck Ryan played "Listen To the Mockingbird," and Shumate lit into "The Lee Highway Blues," which did the trick for Jim.

"I remember that Mac Wiseman backed up all of us on guitar. That way, they'd be no feudin'. Nobody could say 'If I just had so and so behind me, I could have won.' The only disadvantage I could see to those guys was that Mac was working with us at that time, and he knew that 'Lee Highway' up one side and down the other. Every time I'd turn, he'd be right there. So that was a lick in my favor, too."

Eventually, Mac drifted away from the Foggy Mountain band due to finances: "Well, there was a misunderstanding. Earl came to me in the late fall. Now, we were on equal shares and making good money. He said, 'Lester wants to put everybody on salary.' I thought he meant the fiddle player and the bassist, as I was such an integral part of it, handling the booking and all. I told him I thought it was the wrong time to put them on salary. It's such a lean time of the year: 'Don't you want to wait until spring? Then they won't mind so much.'

"Then I noticed that he was kinda nervous, and he said, 'Well, that means you, too.' You see Earl was sort of spokesman for Lester at the time. In the meanwhile, we had made an audio tape I sent over to WWVA-Wheeling, a hot station at the time. But we hadn't got an answer out of them. Anyway, I gave them my notice, though we worked on with no quarrel or hard feelings, and then I said I was going to another place."

Actually, a friend from his days at WNOX-Knoxville, Bill Carlisle - fresh from his split with brother Cliff - contacted Mac about a possible stint at WSB-Atlanta, where he was working. Bill had created his "Hot-Shot Elmer" comedy character, which proved popular with fans.

"Just before I was to leave for Atlanta at Christmas time, Earl came to me and said, 'We got an answer from WWVA, but the only way they will take us is if you come along.' Of course, I had been the pitchman for the deal. They had nothing against the rest of the band - they were good - but Lester and his singing didn't cut it. Talk about your sweet revenge. I said - and I might have shot myself in the foot - 'No, the first time, screw you, and the second time, screw me, if I let it happen again.' I want you to know they didn't get it (the *Wheeling Jamboree* contract)!"

In the meantime, Bill Monroe came through, working a local theater and as was the custom, appeared on the Foggy Mountain Boys' radio show to plug his gig: "On that noon show, he said to me right on the air, 'If you ever want a job over at the Opry, just call me.' It burned Lester up that he'd do that right on the air. I said, 'Well, thank you, I'm flattered.' And I was."

As it happened, Mac had already committed to WSB-Atlanta, owned by the *Atlanta Journal-Constitution* daily newspaper, and he could thank good buddy Bill Carlisle for the gig. *The Barn Dance* boasted headliners Martha and James Carson, Hank Penny & His Radio Cowboys, which would feature Boudleaux Bryant at one time. Former WLS-Chicago and *Renfro Valley Barn Dance* entrepreneur John Lair had helped set-up the *Barn Dance* programming in coordination with J. Leonard Rensch, WSB's station manager.

From its official kick-off on Saturday, November 16, 1940, Harrison (Chick) Kimball managed the *Barn Dance* portion, which usually consisted of from twelve to fifteen musical acts. Among those through the years were Aunt Hattie & The Hoot Owl Holler Girls (including Martha Carson and sisters), Pete Cassell, Chick Stripling, Cotton Carrier, Harpo Kidwell, Dwight Bratcher, The Sunshine Boys, Glenn & Jean Hughes, and the Swanee River Boys.

Mac notes, "I had asked Bill what the possibilities for me were down there. He called back to say, 'They'll give you a daily show of your own and my band can back you, and we can do the Saturday night *Atlanta Barn Dance* together. We can play shows out together like a little package deal.' I went down there in January 1949, and Martha and James - the *Barn Dance Sweethearts* - worked a lot of those shows with us."

Mac and Bill Carlisle, long-time friends.

It was ideal for Mac because it also meant he didn't have any band payroll, and the troupe attracted SRO crowds; Carlisle rode his King record cover hits "Rainbow At Midnight" (number five, 1946) and "Tramp On the Street" (number fourteen, 1948). James & Martha Carson were major gospel favorites, thanks to touching ballads such as "Budded On Earth." Wiseman himself always had a soft spot in his heart for inspirational music, and indeed would himself record gospel albums, notably his Dot LP "Beside the Still Waters" (1959): "It was something that my mother was proud of."

By spring 1949, however, rumors circulated that the troubled *Atlanta Barn Dance* would soon be closing down [and officially went off the air February 18, 1950]: "I called Monroe the first part of the week to ask if his offer still stood? He said to meet him in Huntsville, Alabama, on Good Friday (April 15), where he was doing a show. I did. You know, I got a lot of mileage out of our association. It got me on the *Grand Ole Opry* and this wasn't part of the arrangement, but Bill gave me a solo every Saturday night we were in town. The Solemn Ol' Judge George D. Hay introduced me, and he got his background history right, so you'd think I was a 'star' on the show."

"The deal was, if you were in town and not doing gigs, you had to play their early morning shows. I stayed down the street at the old Tulane Hotel, which is now a parking lot at the corner of Eighth and Church. It was just a walk up the hill to that National Life Building for the 6 a.m. broadcast."

"Sometimes one would show up, sometimes two and sometimes Bill didn't even show. Boy I liked that, because I was The Man. One time after he had finished, Jimmy Dickens asked, 'Do you want my band to back you?' I said, 'No, I'll just do it.' He was only trying to be helpful, but I liked going on alone, just my guitar and me. Announcer Grant Turner talked about that until he died. He said, 'Mac never was late for an early morning show.' They didn't know it, but I preferred being solo."

Wiseman's stints on WSM by a couple months preceded Hank Willliams, whose debut on June 11, 1949 drew six encores for the skinny newcomer from Alabama. Both he and Hank appeared on the Red Foley-hosted Prince Albert portion of the Opry, then being broadcast by the NBC network, reaching some ten million listeners nationally, according to backstage manager Vito Pellettieri.

In 1948, WSM introduced its *Friday Night Frolics* in Studio C, which gave the artists yet another showcase for their talents when in town. The story goes that WSM created the Frolics - September 24, 1948 - hoping to keep the nationally popular Eddy Arnold on the Opry, after he announced his intention of doing his own CBS network broadcast. That ploy didn't work, but the Frolics continued on the air nonetheless, eventually becoming known as the *Friday Night Opry*.

Hank Williams' milestone song attracting so much applause was "Lovesick Blues," while the first song Wiseman sang on the Opry was one learned from Buddy Starcher: "It was (the uptempo) 'Four Walls Around Me,' not the later Jim Reeves number one ballad 'Four Walls,' and I later recorded it."

Mac also recalls a time promoter Les Hutchins leased a Trailways bus to carry the acts on tour, all the way from Lake Charles, Louisiana, to Minneapolis, Minnesota, with about twenty show-dates sandwiched in, while he was with Bill Monroe's Blue Grass Boys.

"I opened Bill's segment as an opening act, and it was customary on package shows not to sing another artist's material. But I'd heard the song by Molly O'Day, so I did 'Six More Miles,' and Hank was waiting in the wings to follow me, and as I came off he slapped me on the shoulder and said, 'Well, I'll never sing that goddamn song again,' which to me was complimentary.

"On that same bus tour, late at night while the others were asleep, Monroe, Hank and I were awake, when he mentioned his new song called 'I'm So Lonesome I Could Cry,' and said, 'Now maybe you boys can help me with this one I've got started.' I know I contributed a line and Monroe came up with a couple, but old Hank never did acknowledge our bits... ['I'm So Lonesome I Could Cry' became the B side to Hank's fall 1949 release 'My Bucket's Got a Hole In It,' a near chart-topper.]

"One thing I remember is Hank didn't drink during that tour, even though some of the other fellows offered him a beer or some booze, but he refused. I guess he was the kind of guy who couldn't drink just one and leave it at that."

Mac adds, "Many years later, I related the songwriting incident to Jett Williams, who said she didn't know about that, and was pleased to hear more about her daddy. Her husband, attorney Keith Adkinson, called me to say he was a big fan of mine, so I sent him some CDs, and during our conversation somehow the subject of family reunions came up. Keith made a colorful remark, saying, 'Well, when Jett and me have a family reunion, we hold it in a telephone booth!' Obviously they don't have much family left. Anyway, I thought it was funny."

Jett was Hank's illegitimate daughter born to girlfriend Bobby Jett days after Hank's death, and was taken in to raise by Hank's mother Lilly. After Lilly's death the family placed the baby up for adoption, and she was raised by a couple who didn't disclose her origins. Later, with the legal assistance of Keith Adkinson, Jett discovered her true identity and then became an artist in her own right, not so ironically touring with Hank's surviving Drifting Cowboys band.

"Although I had been to Audrey and Hank's house when Hank, Jr., was a baby, I hadn't seen him after he'd started his career," says Mac. "Later, a group of us were taping a sing-along Christmas special at the Opry House, and I was standing by Junior. I introduced myself, and with a surprised look on his face, Hank said, 'Mi'God I know you, you're purer than water!'... his exact words."

Incidentally, Hank's debut on the Opry may have been a showstopper, but as time wore on, he didn't fare so well with management, mainly due to his well-publicized drinking. Actually he was let go in August 1952. Afterwards, Hank returned to play the *Louisiana Hayride* once more, prior to his untimely death four months later.

"There was this restaurant down by the river where like the twin cities St. Paul and Minneapolis did in Minnesota, Bossier City and Shreveport sat on separate sides of the Red River; well, this was a favorite restaurant, catering to the Hayride cast in the back room, giving us some privacy to eat and visit. You know, I never saw Hank take a drink there on Saturday nights like almost everybody else did... I remember when we heard he died. I'd just come down to Johnny's car lot for our remote broadcast in Baltimore from there for WBMD. It must've been a New Year's morning broadcast, because Hank had just died the night before in Oak Hill, West Virginia, while en-route to a package show in Canton, Ohio. I was stunned. I mean I knew he was having physical problems, but didn't realize how bad off he was. I believe that damned doctor [Toby Marshall, not a true M.D.] that he had was just over-prescribing pills and shots for him. What a shame, and what a waste of talent."

'Can't You Hear Me Callin'...
Loud And Clear

"Sweetheart of mine,
Can't you hear me calling?
A million times I love you best
I mistreated you, I'm sorry
Come back to me, is my request..."

"When I came down to Knoxville in the fall of 1946, you couldn't find an apartment to rent. They had signs out saying no dogs or kids," Mac recalls, regarding the postwar housing shortage. "I finally found us a cabin at a motor court to rent by the week. So there was Alberta with our six-months-old baby, living out in the Knoxville boondocks, and lacking insulation those cabins weren't that warm. I'd leave early to do the morning show. Though I'd come home every night, after doing our radio program - we often played a show in the evenings, so she'd be home alone much of the time.

"Alberta didn't drive at all at the time, so she was absolutely stuck out there. You didn't dare get friendly with anyone staying there, as most of the tenants were riff-raff. We stayed there until Christmas I guess. Remember I went to Chicago near Thanksgiving to record with Molly O'Day, and we stopped overnight in Renfro Valley, so I was gone awhile, leaving her and the baby there alone."

Working the road has played havoc on many a musician's marriage. It was only after a mutual decision to break up in 1948, that Mac learned Alberta was about to make him a dad again. Actually, Randy's new sister, Linda, was born January 16, 1949.

"Thinking back, I realize how difficult it was for them," muses Mac, referring to his former wives, "though neither ever criticized me."

Wiseman strived to keep his career and his private life separate, especially with media: "In show business, you have a tendency to put the whole blue-eyed world on to some extent, maybe we kid them, but I don't kid me! The decisions I make had better be right, if I'm going to live by them. That's the advice I have for people coming into this business. I like to see them follow their dreams, but don't take short cuts. Get you a job that will pay the bills, because you cannot be creative if you've got marital or money problems. I've seen that all these years, and if a man had those problems, I didn't want him to start, or if it developed after he hired in, he had to go. People cannot concentrate on being creative, if they have marital problems and money troubles. It's just that simple. It sounds elementary, but I believe that."

Bill Monroe's private life was no model for a perfect marriage. While married to the former Carolyn Minnie Brown, mother of their children Melissa and James, Bill became involved with a younger woman: Bessie Lee Mauldin, who played token bass for the Blue Grass Boys.

When marital discord occurred in his own life, Wiseman was quick to resolve the situation as best he could: "Even when I was in the lean years - my family was never mistreated, I mean they weren't hungry or barefoot, but there were some lean years, boy, I'll tell you that – well I tried to conduct my career like a business. I was realistic. If I hit a stumbling block, I didn't lay there and wallow in it, I got up and tried to figure out another game plan."

After Mac met the Monroe band in Huntsville, inadvertently he found himself making his *Grand Ole Opry* debut the next night on the 10:15 p.m. Wall-Rite-sponsored segment, during which Monroe generously gave him one of his song spots. It thrilled Mac to have that opportunity, and also gave him a taste of just how hectic the Blue Grass Boys' schedule would be, for the next day - Easter - meant yet another road show, this one in Indianapolis.

When Mac left WSB-Atlanta, it was the new love of his life, Emma Kilgore Cassell, who accompanied him thereafter. The couple had met by chance at one of his shows, but she seemed to be just the pick-me-up needed, considering an increasingly troubled home-life. What started as an innocent flirtation soon became a serious new commitment for Mac and Emma, coping with marital problems herself.

Meanwhile, Bill's bassist Bessie Lee became the fly in the ointment regarding Mac's working relationship with Monroe. The younger man wouldn't give her the time of day when she made a flirtatious pass, and apparently she resented that: "After he'd given me the solo spots during our Opry appearances, it proved to be quite popular." Mac said the rebuffed Bessie encouraged Bill to reschedule Mac's solos to the closing segment, "which meant I couldn't always get a whole song in."

Obviously she was causing Bill concerns otherwise, as Mac found him and fellow bandsmen hitting the road for weeks at a time minus their star attraction. Usually out on tour, the Blue Grass Boys could rely on being back in Nashville every weekend, as Bill was resolute about meeting his requirement of playing weekends on the Opry, later cut back to twenty-five weekends annually. If the Monroe troupe was in Florida on a Friday, they'd head back in time to play the Saturday night Opry, then maybe drive back to Florida for a scheduled Sunday show. Often, this meant catching Z's on the run.

Wiseman remembers well both of Bill's youngsters: "When James was three or four years old, he was real shy and would hide behind his momma's skirts. Now Melissa started singing with her dad when she was twelve... she sang like a mockingbird. At one time she had a Columbia contract and recorded several things." (Of course, James Monroe is a full-time performer these days, as is his guitarist-son Jim. Melissa died on March 12, 1990.)

Despite what others had asserted, Mac found Monroe wasn't always a temperamental sort: "Not for me anyway. I've seen him shoot down some other people and I was ashamed to be within hearing distance. He was terribly jealous and really had a mean streak, very vindictive. But we never had a cross word between us. He knew I was doing more than I was supposed to; I mean I sold tickets and made the payroll. He respected me. I guess I'm the only man in the world he doesn't owe something to, because I paid myself out of that box (containing the show's receipts)."

Mac felt fortunate that when he left Bill, his reaction was quite different than when Lester left as Monroe didn't speak to Flatt for twenty years: "It was a very amiable departure between us. And you know, the only criticism I ever heard about Lester from Bill, was when he said, 'Lester's voice wasn't strong enough for me.' That was it."

On the other hand, Mac's distinctive, clear tenor was heard to good effect in what was considered Nashville's first major bluegrass recording session, October 22, 1949, which also marked Monroe's last recordings for Columbia.

"I didn't think I was going to get to record with Bill, because he had a long-standing feud with Columbia after they signed the Stanley Brothers. I heard Uncle Art tell him, 'Bill, we signed them to protect you. They're getting pretty popular out there. If we don't sign them, somebody will. By us signing them, we can control their recordings and do what we want to with them on our label.' But Monroe wouldn't buy into that. Decca had already offered him a deal; however, he owed Columbia one more session and fulfilled it. That's the only way I got to record with him."

There was that fickle finger of fate again working on Mac's behalf. Out of that final fall session came two classic numbers pairing Bill and Mac - "Can't You Hear Me Callin'" and "Travelin' Down That Lonesome Road" - and according to Wiseman, grinning, "I was with him when he wrote them. We used to ride along in the car and sing 'Can't You Hear Me Callin',' that way and did it very high. You have to hold one foot up to touch that (hitting those high notes)!"

Bill was the youngest of the Monroe brothers. He cut his teeth performing with fiddler Birch, born in 1901; and guitarist Charlie, born in 1903. Bill, born September 13, 1911 in Rosine, Kentucky, became especially adept on mandolin, and developed his famed "high lonesome" tenor. Bill crafted a sure-fire presentation of experimental arrangements, performed by the best musicians he could muster, for his songs such as "Kentucky Waltz," "Scotland" and "Uncle Pen."

Over time, Bill's Blue Grass Boys boasted some legendary names like Clyde Moody, Jimmy Martin, Don Reno, Carter Stanley, Chubby Wise and Wiseman. Monroe, who joined the Opry in 1939, saw his hits - "Uncle Pen," "Kentucky Waltz" and "Blue Moon of Kentucky" - recorded later by the likes of Eddy Arnold, Elvis Presley and Ricky Skaggs.

Mac adds candidly, "This may sound crude because I liked Bill and enjoyed what he was doing, but so far as being part of the Blue Grass Boys, it held no attraction to me. Yet, I always wanted to be on the Opry by hook or by crook and for that, I was truly grateful to him."

The guitar slinger is also thankful for the opportunity it gave him to hit the road with some of the era's greatest name acts to grace the stages for WSM's *Grand Ole Opry* broadcasts. At times, as Wiseman recalls, their promoter would charter a Trailways' bus, before the customized, air-conditioned luxury buses today's entertainers use, with only seats to rest in, not bunks. Considering the costs incurred, these were mainly booked for the bigger package shows.

Among Opry notables they toured with while playing package shows were Hank Williams, Uncle Dave Macon, Cowboy Copas, Little Jimmy Dickens, George Morgan, Sam & Kirk McGee, Minnie Pearl and Lonzo & Oscar. Wiseman was keenly aware Monroe's set on the Opry's Prince Albert portion was picked up by NBC, giving him rare national exposure early in his career.

Uncle Dave was known for taking along a bottle while on the road, smiles Wiseman. One time before departing on a tour headlining with Bill and Sam & Kirk, Uncle Dave rode with Kirk, Mac and Don Reno in Kirk's older car. Mac recalls Macon saying, "Boys, it's gonna be a long way to Nashville. We need to get us a little toddy."

Thus they all chipped in and Kirk found a liquor store still open and got a fifth: "Uncle Dave immediately took possession. Well, he opened it and Uncle Dave and I would drink and pass it up front so Don and Kirk would take a drink, then pass it back to Uncle Dave. He and I would take a drink again and he put it away. We were double-timing them and that went on for an hour or so when we finally finished it off. Then everybody settled down to sleep as Don was driving. Then about 4 or 5 o'clock in the morning, Don turned around to where I was sitting behind him, reached back and pinched my leg, saying, 'You wanna drive a little? I'm getting sleepy.' So we changed places.

"Along about daylight, I was driving and they were sleeping until Kirk woke up, smacked his lips, rubbed his eyes and said, 'You wanna drink?' I told him we'd finished off the fifth, but he opened the glove compartment and took out a pint, which he'd bought at that liquor store. He opened it, took a sip, then passed it to me, saying, 'Don't let the old man see you or he'll take it away from us.' Well, indeed Uncle Dave popped up, asking, 'Hey, good buddy, whatcha got there?' So we handed it to him and never saw it again!"

When touring, Uncle Dave - known in billing as "The Dixie Dewdrop" - was known to favor Jack Daniel's Tennessee whiskey, and would usually hoard his package in the backseat, just taking sips from it himself. One of the McGee brothers riding with him decided to warn Macon that when they reached the California state line any unused booze had to be turned in, as you couldn't bring out-of-state bottles across the state line.

"Well, an uptight Uncle Dave decided rather than turn it over to the damned border patrol, this time he would share it with his fellow riders and empty it before they reached California. In passing the bottle around, Uncle Dave would first take his sip, then hand it up front, but sip again when it was passed to the backseat. When he discovered it was all a ruse, he just chuckled, acknowledging the laugh was on him. He was, after all, a practical joker himself."

A colorful character noted for his gates-ajar collar, plug hat, goatee, and gold teeth seen through "a million-dollar smile," he boasted the "loudest voice in radio," while carrying three beribboned banjos, each color signifying the key in which he kept it tuned.

Macon was also booked on Opry road shows with black harmonica player DeFord Bailey, which provided problems regarding overnights in Southern states. That meant Bailey spent many a night sleeping in their vehicles. Finally at one hotel, Uncle Dave barged in ahead of the troupe and bellowed a request to the desk-clerk: "Ya got two rooms, Cap, for me and my brother out there?" The clerk shot back, "We sure do," so Macon yelled, "Come on in DeFord!." Seeing Bailey, the innkeeper stammered, "Is uh... is that your brother?" Taking the stunned clerk aside, Uncle Dave stated, "Don't tell him, Mister, but he had a colored daddy... and it just might hurt his feelings!" As the man stared after them, the two Opry stars strode off to their respective rooms.

On another occasion as the boys were tuning up in their dressing room, Dickens came running up to Mac: "Why he slapped me right in the face, and then took off running. I yelled, 'Come back here you little S.O.B. and I'll whip your ass!' He got out of there in a hurry." Although he and Jimmy have re-

64

mained life-long friends, Mac never knew what prompted that action, whether it might've been a bet or a dare Dickens took.

Mac grins, too, in recalling the time Emma brought Carolyn Monroe to one of their road shows to surprise their husbands. Considering the on-stage presence of Bessie, the "Carolina Songbird," Mac muses, "I told Emma don't ever do that again!"

Another plus with Monroe was working with fiddler Chubby Wise: "Yeah, he was with Bill while I was there. We roomed together quite a bit on the road. Later (1982) we did a whole album - 'Give Me My Smokies & The Tennessee Waltz' (a double LP) - produced by Johnny Gimble, together at Gilley's in Texas."

Discussing Wise brought back an early memory: "In the fall of 1947, Earl Scruggs got in touch with me, saying that he and Chubby Wise were thinking about leaving Monroe. They were looking for a job - wanting to join my band!

"Can you imagine how I would've loved that, having Earl and Chubby in my band? But the radio station (WCYB-Bristol) wasn't paying much and our main source of income was from doing p.a.'s, so I had to level with them, and confided that I was heading back to Waynesboro myself for the winter."

Mac's pal Chubby a.k.a. Robert Russell Wise, hailed from Lake City, Florida. He went on to work with Clyde Moody, with whom he said he co-wrote the million-seller "Shenandoah Waltz," Hank Williams, Red Foley and Hank Snow. Chubby claimed co-writing "Orange Blossom Special" with fellow fiddler Ervin Rouse, though the latter insisted he created it solo. In old-time country bands, the fiddle carried the lead, while the guitar and bass fiddle provided the rhythm, and "Orange Blossom Special" became a fiddler's anthem.

While with Monroe's Blue Grassers, Chubby defined bluegrass fiddling during the 1940s. He combined the sounds of the droning double-stops of mountain music, with the bent notes of blues or an uptempo twang of train tunes like "Orange Blossom Special." After departing Monroe in '50, Wise did sessions and recorded solo. When asked why he chose to pursue music, Chubby replied, "The fiddle bow fit my hand a lot better than them plow handles did."

Another artist Mac admired who toured for a time with Monroe was Max Terhune: "While working with Monroe in 1949, Max worked as part of Bill's show as an added attraction. What a talent he was! We wound up in Vincennes, Indiana, at Thanksgiving. Max had a sister living there and we had Thanksgiving dinner with her and the family. He and I became good friends, and did you know that's where the comedian Red Skelton hailed from."

Terhune initially made his mark entertaining and doing magic tricks on WLS' *National Barn Dance*, and later became a film sidekick mostly known as "Lullaby," first for Gene Autry and more often The Three Mesquiteers - initially with Ray Corrigan and John Wayne, until Wayne hit in "Stagecoach." A ventriloquist, Max had his own movie "sidekick," a dummy he dubbed "Elmer."

"While with Bill Monroe, we were on the road touring about all the time, usually doing at least twenty days at a time. For instance, we played a number of weeks appearing along with the movie 'Roseanna McCoy' (released in October 1949, starring Farley Granger and Joan Evans). Bill and I watched that movie so many times, we had its dialogue memorized. This was up in Illinois and Ohio. We'd be riding along in a car and I'd recite one of the character's lines, and he or somebody else would come back with the other actor's line from the film."

Mac pauses, "I think Bill being from Kentucky was why they booked him as the live show to accompany this film [a romanticized version of the Kentuckian Hatfield-McCoy feud]."

Mostly they traveled to their gigs in cars, with Mac often a driver: "We stopped at service stations for gas, and would grab a quick lunch, eating something like sardines, cheese and crackers, Vienna sausage or balogna sandwiches, usually bought from a little old country store."

Another friend Mac met through Monroe was Boudleaux Bryant and his wife Felice: "I remember first meeting them when they lived right behind the theater we played in Moultrie, Georgia, with their little boys, Dane and Del. I recall that first time because they invited Bill and me to eat with them."

Later the couple became Hall of Fame songwriters known for standards like "We Could" and "Rocky Top." Their son Del Bryant became head of Broadcast Music, Inc., a trade organization that collects royalties for writers and publishers

Once Mac's divorce was final, he and Emma were married. She gave birth to their first daughter, Christine, in October. Then just before Christmas 1949, Mac called it quits with the Blue Grass Boys.

By early 1950, a somewhat disillusioned Mac was back in Virginia, where he'd reformed his Country Boys band, this time including Ralph Mayo and Ted Mullins, and again landing a berth at WCYB-Bristol. Mac also cut a self-promotion record at WCYB, recording "From the Manger To The Cross," "A Broken Heart To Mend" and "Grey Eagle."

"I thought I could get a label in Nashville, but when nothing turned up, I headed back to familiar territory," Mac explains. "Those times I went back to Virginia, I just did it to re-group, knowing I could make a living, while getting another game plan together."

Wiseman recalls a time when Syd Nathan invited him to record for his Cincinnati-based independent label King Records: "When I was playing Bristol's station, Syd approached me to record - and he'd had great success with Hawkshaw Hawkins doing covers on Ernest Tubb. That's about all 'Hawk' did then, covers, and it damned near killed his career. Well, Syd offered me a contract, if I could sing like Bill Monroe. I had nothing against Bill, but, hell, I didn't want to establish myself as somebody else. I wanted to be me, and the royalty rate was very minimal - a half-cent or something like that. I kept Flatt & Scruggs from going the same route, when we went there in 1948. I said, 'Boys, we can do better than that. You don't need to do that. Just wait a little longer.' And they did."

King, of course, thrived on cutting covers of other artists' hits, directing label singers like Cowboy Copas to re-record them, including "Filipino Baby" first charted by T. Texas Tyler; revising Nat Shilkret's number one "Dancing With Tears in My Eyes" as "Waltzing With Tears..."; covering George Morgan's "Candy Kisses"; and Mac's "Tis Sweet To Be Remembered." Esco Hankins, a Roy Acuff soundalike, cut "Low and Lonely," "Precious Jewel" and "Fireball Mail."

It wasn't that Mac didn't want an independent label, as indeed he had a collection of tunes he was straining at the bit to record, but hoped to showcase his talent, not somebody else's. It concerned him that he wasn't on a label, because without records, Mac felt his career would stagnate. He was confident that given the chance he could break out of the rut of being regarded as a regional artist.

"After playing demo discs for most of the major labels, I couldn't buy a hello - and I had been on fifty-thousand watt stations around the country, appearing on the *Mid-Day Merry-Go-Round, Atlanta Barn Dance, Grand Ole Opry* and finally *The Louisiana Hayride*."

Actually it was in the spring of 1951 that Wiseman went to KWKH-Shreveport. Mac and his Country Boys soon became a welcome act on their weekend *Louisiana Hayride*. KWKH's popular Saturday night program debuted April 3, 1948, with the likes of the Bailes Brothers, Johnnie & Jack with Kitty Wells, headlining. It soon became home to Hank Williams and a number of future stars such as Webb Pierce, Slim Whitman, Jim Reeves, Faron Young, Red Sovine, Goldie Hill and the Wilburn Brothers. Later notables included George Jones, Jimmy Newman, The Browns, Floyd Cramer, Johnny Horton, Sonny James and yes, Elvis Presley. For the first ten years, Horace Logan was program director and eventually - and rightly - hailed as a star-maker.

On Mac's home front come January 31, 1951, he and Emma welcomed daughter Sheila into their family. Certainly the domestic pressure was now on Mac to expand his career horizons, due to having more mouths to feed.

By then, Wiseman had added youthful Joe Medford to his Country Boys, then consisting of Mayo, Mullins and Shreveport bassist Don Davis, not Pee Wee King's Golden West Cowboy of that name who played steel. As "Smokey," Don also did comedy skits, adds Mac: "Joe Medford was the first banjo player I ever had. His dad brought him to me in Bristol, just before I was to go to Shreveport, and he played so much like Earl that I decided to hire him. He was on my first Dot session,

Mac's young daughters, Chris and Sheila, by his 1946 Chevy.

and all four sides were successful for me.

"We did a couple gospel songs and the ballads; as a result, the banjo became part of my sound. I always felt a banjo was too raucous for the ballads I liked to do, but I also knew you didn't get off a winning horse. When Joe left me, he went with Charlie Monroe, who was going to WNOX. Consequently, I kept the banjo on my recordings, though more and more I used a subdued sound on the banjo. For that reason, I was the first to hire a Dobro in a bluegrass band, as I wanted a subdued sound on my ballads. The first Dobro guy I hired was Burkett 'Buck' (a.k.a. Uncle Josh) Graves, who also played mandolin for me on the uptempo things."

KWKH, Shreveport's fifty-thousand watt clear channel station, proved a good stepping stone for Mac, but without discs to promote, it limited his earning power: "Me and my band got fan mail from the East Coast and from the West Coast. I also had a five o'clock morning program that generated a lot of letters, so we made a lot of personal appearances, as far away as Florida. If I had to be out of town, I'd record my radio show.

"I'd always done morning shows, because I felt that was the most potent time to be on the radio. Growing up, I'd go do my chores and get back inside for breakfast in time to hear Curly Fox fiddling songs like 'Fire On the Mountain.' But an artist needed records. You know years later, Curly and I had a mutual friend named Tom Morgan, who took Curly in and cared for him in his final years in Dayton, Tenn." [Off the record, Mac out of regard for Curly's talent would send Tom some "dirt money" on occasion, a hundred dollars here and there, to help with Curly's care.]

"We also played drive-in shows out in Oklahoma when I was doing the *Louisiana Hayride,* though not there quite a year. While in Shreveport, Jim Bulleit, who ran KWKH's Artists Services Bureau, booked us at a drive-in near Tulsa and we did two nights up there. You know, nearly forty years later, I did an annual festival in McAllister and on my way there, glanced over and that damn drive-in was still there!"

"Incidentally," he adds, "I played that McAllister festival for twenty-five years. I remember back then Bulleit booked T. Texas Tyler and me together a lot. [Known as 'The Man With a Million Friends,' Tyler had hits on sentimental songs such as 'Deck of Cards' and 'Dad Gave My Dog Away.'] T. Texas and his wife Claudia, who traveled with him all the time, used to keep a washtub full of beer iced down in the trunk of their car. But we drove separately, as I had the Country Boys back then. He'd do his part of the show solo, like he recorded it, but then used my band for backup."

Regarding KWKH, Mac reflects, "Union scale was all we got for playing the *Hayride* and I got paid zip for the morning shows. Red Sovine was the only one who had a sponsor on his show [inheriting Hank Williams' sponsor Johnny Fair Syrup] and was known as 'The Old Syrup Sopper.'

"The trouble with going from one station to the next, you had to be on there awhile to draw a crowd to your shows. If Shot Jackson, steel guitarist with Johnnie & Jack, hadn't been a damn good shade-tree mechanic, I couldn't have stayed. He'd do all the work on my car and all I could afford to pay for was the parts. That 1946 Chevy had over one hundred thousand miles on it."

It didn't take too long to augment their *Hayride* appearances. Bulleit who handled bookings, was a former Nashville record executive: "I knew Jim a little. He was an acquaintance and we got a good camaraderie going. Bulleit, founder of Bullet Records in Nashville [producing the multi-million-selling 1947 Francis Craig Orchestra pop recording, 'Near You'] was booking everybody on the *Hayride.* We worked through him on a percentage basis, but no guarantees. KWKH claimed like five per cent of our take, similar to WSM's artists bureau.

"Besides Florida and local shows, we had a lot of dates in East Texas, Mississippi and Arkansas. In Arkansas, there were mainly poor people who depended on the cotton crop, so you didn't draw as well there. Roads were in bad repair and there was open range, all particularly hazardous. I mean you'd go around a curve and there'd be a cow, in the middle of the night, lying down on that pavement to keep warm."

After depart-ing KWKH, Mac re-members Webb Pierce proved to be quite a businessman, though former banker (W.E.) "Lucky" Moeller was Webb's road manager and an agent for Jim Denny's Nashville booking agency. Webb insisted Lucky deduct any taxes or fees due, so whatever money Lucky gave him, was free and clear.

Ralph Mayo, Ted Mullins and Mac in Toronto, Canada.

"Lucky later set up exclusive booking arrangements at the Flame Club in Min-neapolis. Texas Bill Strength, a very popular DJ, did their bookings. I was the first to be booked there or it may have been Tex Ritter, anyway I was among the first. [As was Webb.] On that same radio station was an announcer, John Talley, who was later at WENO radio, Madison."

Webb, then a salesman in the men's department at Sears & Roebuck in sub-urban Monroe, started at KWKH doing announcing chores until Horace Logan finally let him sing and soon engaged him as an artist on the *Hayride*.

"Webb and I had an 8:15 morning program, for thirty minutes weekdays. He and I lived across the street from one another. I recall Slim Whitman being a mail-man. He'd come in the station, set his mailbag down and do fifteen minutes by himself, then pick up the pouch and go make his deliveries.

"Slim's morning show followed Webb and I. At that time, Johnnie & Jack, Kitty, Webb, Slim and I were all barely just making ends meet, but within twelve months each of us had a hit record. Webb told me one time he didn't know how he missed recording 'Tis Sweet To Be Remembered,' because of all the requests com-ing in for it and his 'Wondering.' He'd give me the mail to read, too."

Bulleit, who sold Bullet Records, replaced Hubert Long at KWKH. Accord-ing to Mac, Jim was also a close friend to Randy Wood, then just getting started on the recording scene.

"Randy had a mail-order thing going with WLAC-Nashville, and local radio's Big Jeff Bess & His Radio Cowboys were recording on his label. Randy told Jim he sought an artist who could sing high a la Bill Monroe, so Jim said he had just the singer for him. Randy then came to Shreveport to check me out. Well, we hit it off from the start.

"We recorded my first four sides for Dot on May 23, 1951, my twenty-sixth birthday, at the station, using my Country Boys. Randy asked, 'What you got to record?' I told him 'Tis Sweet To Be Remembered,' and I wanted it to be my first recording and also the first release. Due to its change in tempo, Randy said, 'No, we can't do that because we'll never get it on the jukeboxes.' By that time I'd have given my left nut to get on records, but I came up with a retort that if we couldn't have that song as the first, to just forget the deal. In one way, I didn't really know who was doing whom a favor on this deal, as I figured Randy's best distributor at the time was the backseat of his car. So he consented to cut and release 'Tis Sweet To Be Remembered.'

"It hadn't been out but a week when he called me to say I'd been right and from then on I could pick the songs. Oh, Randy would submit songs, but mostly I had the final word on everything. And you know we stayed together thirteen years."

Years later, Mac ran into Randy's buddy Jim Bulleit in an airport, and learned he was selling cemetery lots at that time.

One of the key sounds on Mac's first cut much to his chagrin was a banjo, but certainly not to banjoist Joe Medford, who was thrilled. Never a fan of the instrument, though it has long been a staple of bluegrass, Mac felt it not a particularly good fit for ballads.

"It seemed to me like banjo players were more vulnerable, too; that is, you could pull jokes on them being seemingly more naive," joshes Wiseman. "For instance, one time while working in Shreveport, I needed a banjo player, so I came back up to Bristol to get Herbert Hooven. As we crossed the Mississippi River into Vicksburg, Herbert was asleep and we had about two hundred miles to go to Shreveport. So he didn't know what I did to cross the Mississippi River. Soon after that, on our way to Florida to play some shows, I made idle talk while driving from Shreveport towards Vicksburg. I made a comment that if they didn't charge so much in tolls, we could make some good money on these shows.

"Herbert, wanting to be very accommodating, asked, 'How much do they charge?' I said five dollars a piece (when actually it was fifty-cents for the car and all its occupants), so Herbert spoke up and said, 'If you want to put the instruments up in the backseat of the car, I'll get in the trunk and you can save my five dollars,' adding, 'You'll have to let me out as soon as we get on the other side of the river.' I agreed, saying we always gas up on the Mississippi side. We did stop at the service station and an attendant came out to fill up our car, as all the rest of us got out to go into the station for drinks and snacks. On my way past the rear of the car, I knocked on the deck-lid and he replied with a similar knock, and the station attendant almost dropped the gas hose!

"Well, we all got back in the car heading east again, and every once in a while Herbert knocked on the deck-lid, calling out, 'Let me outta here! It's getting too hot!' He was about six-foot, two-inches. I'd carried him almost to Jackson, Mississippi, a hundred miles or so, and suddenly stopped, ran back and unlocked the trunk, apologizing for leaving him in there so long. By then, he was so angry he wanted to 'whup' me! When he got into the car with the rest of us, he kept on jawing about me leaving him in that trunk. To get him to shut up, I threatened, 'If you don't hush up, I'm gonna tell everybody backstage how dumb you were to get into that trunk in the first place.' That did it because he didn't want other musicians to know that he agreed to do it."

Yet another incident involving the Country Boys' banjoist sticks in Mac's mind: "When Herbert, who was from North Carolina, went out with us, the first day we worked, we stopped at a diner and I guess he hadn't been in a restaurant much, if at all. So when we ordered, he asked for corned-beef and cabbage. Our little waitress was shy and tried hard to please us. When she sat his dish down in front of him, he sat and stared at it. Then she asked, 'Sir, is there something wrong with the food?' He had this deep voice and blared, 'Where's my corn? I want my corn!' He thought he was gonna get corn, beef and cabbage. When I told Homer and Jethro about that, they laughed so hard, they decided to use it as a part of their act: Jethro would pull it on Homer."

Mac hung in at KWKH several months, feeling the pinch of sparse bookings, as Dot wouldn't release Mac's single until Labor Day. Wood wasn't keen on releasing a record in the summertime. Meantime, Clyde Moody, who had been a *Hayride* regular, recommended Mac get in touch with an agent-booker he knew over in Raleigh, North Carolina.

"Because my record hadn't been released, we were picking shit at Shreveport. So we took what money we had and went to Raleigh, the first and only time I did something like that without a commitment for my next job. This friend of Clyde's was handling our bookings and we depended on him. Well, I did a lot better when I had done our bookings. I pawned everything I could get my hands on to keep us going. Clyde lived there and he and this guy liked the World Series, so they watched the games and let us starve."

By then, Clyde was a regular and major attraction on WANO-Raleigh, when they engaged Mac and his Country Boys. "Yes, Clyde was doing fine," reasons Mac. "I remember though there was this little diner we'd go to after the morning program, and I'll never forget 'til the longest day I live how me and my boys were sitting there drinking coffee because that's all the money we had. Clyde and that old man who was supposed to be doing our bookings were sitting over on the other side having a nice big breakfast.

"Then the jukebox man came in and started taking records off the jukebox and changing them with new ones, and it hit me that I might get some breakfast here. Randy had sent me a box of my first single, so I went out to the car and got one. Well, I showed it to the guy at the jukebox, who said he'd had the odd call for that title, and he bought all I had.

"Now you talk about three fellows sitting and eating their full, we sure did! I didn't know what to charge him, but we decided the going rate at about forty or fifty-cents apiece. But I'll never forget that day in the diner. It sticks with me."

It remained nip and tuck for the Country Boys until after Labor Day weekend when Mac's first single "Tis Sweet To Be Remembered" was released: "Right away we did all right."

But by then their bills had piled up. He and bandsmen Mayo and Hooven were living in a room over a beer joint with a jukebox: "It played all night long and I remember a raunchy song that was so popular, it played over and over on that damned jukebox."

When Glen Thompson of WDVA-Danville, who ran a Saturday night barn dance, offered Mac and his boys a hundred dollars to perform, they were happy to oblige: "After our gig in Danville, we threw our luggage out the window in the middle of the night heading for Mt. Airy, North Carolina... Herbert was really a hard-luck guy. After we went to Danville to do the barn dance, on the way back Herbert was driving, and I was in the backseat asleep. It was late night as we came through Mt. Airy and the town policeman pulled Herbert over. He took Herbert's driver license, looked at it, and said, 'Herbert Hooven! That's like Herbert Hoover, the worst president we ever had! We had corn-meal for breakfast, miss-a-meal for lunch, and corn-meal for supper under him.' He threatened to take our Herbert in because of that name similarity!"

After dropping his bandsmen off in Mt. Airy: "We disbanded completely, and I gave each of them twenty-five dollars a-piece." Indicative of Wiseman's career dedication, "Sunday morning I went by WPAQ-Mt. Airy and asked for the station manager and they said he was out at his house getting ready for church. Reluctantly they gave me his address. I went out, knocked on the door, and he came out with lather on his face, ready to shave. I told him why I was there, and he said, 'I really don't need anybody.' I told him, 'Yes, you do, you need me!' He said if I felt that strongly about it to come by the station in the morning to see him. I did and he hired me, just me and my guitar playing on the radio. I stayed until spring 1952, and organized another band.

Mac at WPAQ - Mt. Airy.

"I next went to WDBJ-Roanoke, Virginia, where I had an hour at 6 o'clock in the morning and fifteen minutes at noon for the Dr. Pepper beverage company. Before I went there they, the folks at WPAQ, told me nobody listens to that station anymore. On impulse that first morning on WDBJ, I mentioned that anybody listening who would write to say they heard us, I'd send an autographed eight by ten picture free of charge…

"By Tuesday, we had several hundred pieces of mail, and the manager came in and literally chewed me out, saying don't make offers on the air without first clearing it with him. I apologized and by Thursday we had five thousand pieces of mail and the same manager came to me and said if I'd let him give the addresses of those writing to the sales department, they would pay to mail out the pictures. I've heard it said that each letter represents a hundred thousand people, so that was pretty good for a station that supposedly didn't have any listeners."

While at WDBJ, Mac's best source of income was coming from his tie-in with the NASCAR (National Association For Stock Car Auto Racing) people. This, for very little effort on his part: "They had started a weekly race at the fairgrounds every Wednesday night, so they came down to WDBJ to make a deal with me to come out each Wednesday to sing a song while lining up the cars… after four or five weeks, they had their routine down good enough, we didn't have to even take our instruments out of the car. We'd go watch the race and then go by the office to pick up our check.

"The race was run by Bill France, Sr., who formed NASCAR. Then there was Curtis Turner, who was one of the early top drivers, and we became great friends. He listened to my program and got so he came down every morning at 6, then after my show he'd take me out to his house for breakfast. Usually it consisted of a couple coffee-laces (whiskey and coffee), country ham and eggs. He was a daredevil kind of fellow and he'd come get me in a pickup truck and on the way back to his house there was a bridge right in the middle of a curve on the road, and Curtis would scare me each morning by approaching the bridge, doing his thing by going through that bridge nearly sideways, which scared the hell out of me. I told him, 'If you do that one more time, I ain't ever going to ride with you again.' Well, next morning, he really did it! . . . Five or six years later, when I was then living in California, whenever I'd come through the valley, I would stop and stay at his house.

"Curtis for some reason drove on the highway, like he did on the racetrack. As a result, he got so many tickets they revoked his driver's license. So he went out to the local airport to take flying lessons, and rented himself a plane. Some years later [October 4, 1970], Curtis crashed and died in Pennsylvania, along with a golfer, Clarence King. He had been a great timberman, too, who could fly over a wooded area and estimate what the timber was worth. Actually, Curtis made a fortune selling timberland, but developed a reputation as a party boy, that ate it up."

Mac continues: "Years later, I went to a number of car races and Elmo Langley, a full-time driver of the pace car, would let me and my friend ride the whole race in his pace car. While in Charlotte one time, going by the office trailer, Bill France, Jr., stepped out of the trailer, and my friend introduced me to him. Bill, Jr., said, 'Oh, I know Mac. I used to hang out at the Roanoke racetrack when I was eleven years old,' and that's where Curtis and Bill Senior promoted their racing on my radio show. I found that so flattering to think that boy remembered me from that far back. And yes, I'm still a big fan of NASCAR."

Mac and George Nesbitt with NASCAR's Elmo Langley.

'Tis Sweet To Be Remembered'... Time And Again

"As I travel o'er this world/Just to soothe my rovin' mind
Tender messages I get/From a dear one left behind
They were filled with sweetest words/That so touched me when I heard
Never ever can I forget/These are some things that she said...
'Tis sweet to be remembered/On a bright or gloomy day
'Tis sweet to be remembered/By a dear one far away
'Tis sweet to be remembered, remembered, remembered
'Tis sweet to be remembered/When you are far away..."

"My first release for Dot was "Tis Sweet To Be Remembered,' which had been released in September 1951 (backed with 'Are You Coming Back To Me'), and by the early part of 1952, the record was doing quite well, as was my early morning radio show," notes Wiseman, that early show being at WPAQ-Mt. Airy.

"'Tis Sweet To Be Remembered" had first been a country success for the WLS-Chicago *National Barn Dance* duo Mac & Bob, who met while both were studying music at the Kentucky School For the Blind. Lester "Mac" McFarland played piano, trombone, guitar and mandolin, and became a music teacher; while Bob Gardner was a piano tuner, who possessed an ear for perfect pitch and tone. They teamed up professionally in about 1922, and subsequently recorded over two hundred songs, resulting in sales of more than a million.

On a personal level in the early 1950s, Mac had some concerns about his brother who was serving in the Korean War: "Kennie was in Korea with the Army to be exact. He had an important job, a lineman or something like that. I was in Knoxville at the time."

Like big brother, Kennie had worked the family farm and as a farmhand for the bigger landowners. "You know, Kennie was like seven years younger than me, so I was pretty much up and gone before he did much work on our farm. He did later work for others and as I recall worked for farmer Shaver, as he was great buddies with the farmer's son."

Mac adds proudly that Kenneth made it home safely, and was discharged from the military: "Kennie went to work for DuPont and stayed with them until retirement time, and he's doing all right. Our dad, as a matter of fact, worked on that DuPont building, the construction of it, when he was a young man. Unfortunately, Kennie recently lost his son (in 2011). I talked to him about a week ago and, of course, he's still sad about it. His boy Bill didn't leave any will or anything and he had some property, some money and stuff like that. He wasn't married."

Incidentally, Kennie's daughter Debbie was residing in Nellie Gochenour's trailer court, across from the 340 Snack Bar in Crimora, at the start of this writing. Regarding Mac's older sister Virginia, she married a Navy man, stationed at Norfolk: "She'd met him somehow, though I don't know the particulars of that. His name was Allen Davis, but they divorced when their only child was of pre-school age. They lived out in El Paso, as he was from Texas, and I visited a few times when I was passing through. Seems as though he couldn't hold a job, so she left him to live back home in Virginia.

"Virginia was only two years younger than me, so we came through that Great Depression together as kids so-to-speak. Naomi was at least 10 years younger. I did help pay for her nursing school, and she worked in Waynesboro and primarily in Staunton, the county seat, as a nurse until she, too, retired and is now a widow."

In January 1952, Wiseman received notice Wood was ready to produce Mac's second session, this one at WHIN-Gallatin, Tennessee, after sunset when the radio signed off the air, as required under its license. Besides having to hang heavy quilts on the walls to retain the sound, Mac chose his own songs and helped Randy round up the studio musicians. These included some of Nashville's best, notably Ernie Newton on standup-bass; Tommy Jackson on fiddle; Rollin (Oscar) Sullivan on mandolin; David Akeman on banjo; and Mac's guitar accompanied his vocals. The songs, all of which Mac had "tested" on radio were "I'll Still Write Your Name in the Sand," "Four Walls Around Me," "Georgia Waltz" and "Dreaming Of a Little Cabin."

"I had a flow of material that I test-marketed in all those radio markets I'd worked, from five thousand to fifty-thousand watt stations. By that I mean I had played the songs and in so doing, could judge by the feedback what listeners wanted to hear. I'd go by their mail whether they liked a song or not, because they'd write in and request to hear them again. If they didn't, I would cut that song out. That testing method accounted for some of the great early successes that I enjoyed on the Dot label."

In February 1952, Dot released Mac's second single pairing "I'm a Stranger" and "Little White Church." Its singer continued to hold court at WPAQ until spring 1952. It was in March that he returned to Gallatin, this time taking along Jim Williams (mandolin) and Russell Vass (banjo) to link up again with Wood, Jackson and Newton in the studio.

As Mac recalls, Williams and Vass were hired as Country Boys at Mt. Airy: "We used Russell's wife Lorene as a vocalist on our gigs, but not as part of the radio show. She and I wrote songs together, including 'Let Me Borrow Your Heart Just For Tonight,' which I recorded."

Regarding earlier session players, Mac points out that Rollin Sullivan was half of the *Grand Ole Opry*'s zany duo Lonzo & Oscar, who scored the Top Five *Billboard* novelty number "I'm My Own Grandpa" (1948). They also traveled some together. Ernie Newton, a string bassist from Connecticut, had earned his spurs at WLS-Chicago, performing with Mac & Bob, and became part of the Les Paul Trio, also featuring Chet Atkins' half-brother Jimmy Atkins.

"Ernie had a unique drum-head contraption on his bass, where he 'noded' with his left hand, picked with his right hand and played the snare with the same hand at the same time. It made the same sound as playing the snare drum. As he picked, it made a little extra beat, using the brush instead of sticks... Ernie was one helluva bass picker and that's why we used him so much. He was also a very personable fellow."

Alabama native Tommy Jackson, like Mac the son of a barber, became Nashville's most commercial session fiddler, whose single-string style enhanced number one records like Hank Williams' "Lovesick Blues" and Ray Price's "Crazy Arms" and playing in bands for such luminaries as Red Foley and Price. Although it's little known, he was a tail gunner on B-29 flight missions in 1944 and '45, earning himself four bronze stars and an Air Medal. (He died in 1979.)

David Akeman's serious clawhammer style banjo pickin' learned from Opry icon Uncle Dave Macon, set him in good stead with Wiseman. Best known to the public for his comedy antics on the Opry and later TV's syndicated series *Hee Haw*, he wore an outlandish costume consisting of tousled hat, long striped shirt and short, low-belted long pants, helping justify his nickname Stringbean.

Sadly, Akeman endured an untimely end, as he and wife Estelle were murdered by burglars, after arriving home from an Opry gig, November 10, 1973. The killers were caught and sentenced to life terms. Dave was also Bill Monroe's first Blue Grass Boys' banjoist, and performed, too, with Bill's brother Charlie Monroe's Kentucky Pardners.

"I used to just drop in on String at his three-room cabin in Goodlettsville, and we'd just sit and talk like good old country boys on the porch. I remember my feet dangling onto the ground while sitting there. You know how he looked on TV, well he was always so well-dressed otherwise. Come to find out, String hunted squirrels and dug up a lot of ginseng in the mountains, which he gave George Morgan. Morgan ('Candy Kisses') in turn, would give him all his used clothes. String was a mountain man, that's all there is to it. Ginseng was quite expensive, and being a mountain boy, he could recognize it, though I wouldn't know it if I walked through it."

Mac remembers they held a public sale after the couple's death, with an auctioneer touting their personal effects and his career items: "The auctioneer came across a set of glasses, which he said were specially monogrammed with String's 'S' on them, noting, 'I know you good folks will want to own these, which will have to be bought in a set.' Truth is, String had stolen the glasses from the Sheraton Hotel chain."

Aside from the search for the killers, there was yet another controversy that arose in the wake of the murders, when surviving kin of Estelle and String, sought to determine which family got what: "The burning question then became who died first, her or him, because that would decide which family got the bigger inheritance!"

Another Stringbean memory brought a glint to Mac's eyes, recalling how Akeman would greet him: "He played on both my singles 'I'll Still Write Your Name in the Sand' and 'Four Walls Around Me,' and yes, if he caught me in a crowd of several people, he'd say, 'How ya doin' Chief?... Yeah, I made Mac a star, and then he never used me again!' He said recording those songs with me was his favorite little gig. You know, old String played a good two-finger roll on the banjo instead of the usual three..."

Yet another time at a ball field south of Nashville, Mac recalls, "At the time, String had a new record out, and at intermission there was a black family sitting up in the stands and they bought one of his records which he autographed. When he came back down to start our second show, he said, 'Chief, I'm hot in all fields!' He was a character."

It was during 1952, Mac tuned in station WEAM-Arlington, Virginia, and heard his record played, and the DJ calling him "The Voice With a Heart." The announcer - Don Owens - would become a good friend to Mac. Meantime, Mac's camp picked up on the tag, plugging Wiseman as "The Voice With a Heart" in promotional efforts.

Wiseman was at WBDJ-Roanoke through August 1952. In July, Randy Wood summoned Mac back for his final session at WHIN, with session players Jackson, Newton, Jim Williams (mandolin) and Ed Amos (banjo).

"Ed lived in Roanoke, where I hired him. He was a brother to singer Betty Amos, who played with the Bill Carlisle family on the Opry. I also hired Johnny Haskins, who was from Danville. After Ed Amos was drafted into the military during the Korean War, I didn't hear from him for a year or two.

"Then I was on the West Coast doing a concert with Bob Wills, Lefty Frizzell and the Maddox Brothers & Rose, and right in the middle of my singing 'Love Letters in the Sand,' the audience perked up, so I peeked behind me to see what the reaction was all about. It was Ed in uniform. He just came on and joined in, and I thought that was something. Then it seemed like only a couple months afterwards, I heard he was in a freak car wreck. I mean he didn't crash into a tree or anything, but when the car rolled over a small embankment, he was trapped in the door and killed. It may have been he was trying to open the door to jump out."

Mac was always ready to record because he had a huge repertoire of tunes that had passed his listeners' test: "These were songs that I had performed on the stations where I had been, and knew they could be hits, simply by judging the responses received.

"Some years later, I was playing a concert in Dayton, Ohio, where we did an afternoon and an evening show. Between the two shows, I walked across the street to a little shotgun diner to get a pack of cigarettes. While there, I checked the jukebox out of curiosity, and was amazed to find sixteen sides of my records. Now it wasn't one of those huge Wurlitzers, so I dare say I had a good fifteen or thirty per cent of the selections on that damn box."

He was welcomed back to Knoxville by WNOX's station manager Lowell Blanchard in September 1952. There he worked some shows with a married duo, singer Bessie Lou & Red Murphy, a comic, but it proved to be a temporary stop.

"We had a nice little package show we did together," Mac explains. "We remained friends through the years. After being squeezed out of the entertainment business, Red worked as a bellhop at a downtown Nashville hotel."

What finished Mac's WNOX affiliation was the proverbial offer he couldn't refuse from WBMD-Baltimore, complete with a sponsor. Mac's contact there was DJ Ray Davis, who regularly played Mac Wiseman records on his show. That airplay and its response from listeners sparked Mac's October move to Maryland.

"For my first winter in Baltimore, I had bought my first house-trailer in Knoxville, to pull up there myself. It was a twenty-seven-footer, which I hauled behind a 1951 Chevy. My wife Emma and our two little girls were with me, and on the way, while driving at night, I got sleepy. I left my wife and girls in the car with the heater running, then went back and climbed into bed in the trailer to stretch out. I damn near froze to death, because back then trailers weren't that well insulated. The trailer was also very confining, which we found out rather quickly... and we didn't yet have a TV.

"Baltimore was a big town and they couldn't change movies fast enough for us, as we'd go to two or three movies in a day… I was doing an early morning radio show for Johnny's Used Cars on Lafayette Street which was Route 40, and Ray was our announcer. The studio was at Johnny's car lot and we did our remote for WBMD, and old Johnny was a sharp cat.

"Actually Baltimore was really hot and happening at the time. The sponsor money was enough to keep my band and me going, and with my records being played, our shows did well. I believe myself and a pair from North Carolina did Baltimore's first weekly television country show for a half-hour every Thursday night, sponsored by a beer (Hudepohl Brewery) company."

That WBAL-TV teaming of Mac with Ola Belle Reed & Alex Campbell, a celebrated regional sister and brother duo, proved popular with viewers. Singer-banjoist Ola Belle, had written "High On a Mountain," and with Alex ran New River Ranch, a Maryland country music venue.

Mac points out that Alex later had the hour following the WWVA-*Wheeling Jamboree* broadcast, and came to own Campbell's Corner, a popular small store in central Pennsylvania during the 1960s: "They were all good country folks. I stayed with Ola Belle and her husband Bud Reed several times."

Regarding his own family, that topic was off-limits in interviews. Even wife Emma was somewhat in the dark: "I remember the time my mother told me she had seen Alberta over the weekend, and Emma asked why she kept talking about my ex-wife? I quickly explained that mom was not talking about my ex, but about my *Aunt* Alberta. She was married to my father's brother Marvin, and had been a secretary at the mill where the brothers worked."

By late 1952, Mac's Country Boys consisted of mandolinist Jim Williams, banjoist Wayne Brown, fourteen, and fiddler Chubby Collier, who doubled as a rube comic: "We would do 'cross-fire' comedy; that is, I'd be the straight-man and lead him into his routines. Initially I was very shy because of the limp when I first got started. I couldn't say shit with a mouth full. After I entered a lot of contests, did guest shots and had done announcing on the radio - it all gave me more confidence."

"I got so usually I would feature a comedian. We'd do an hour-and-a-half just the band. I'd hire regular comedians, too. I remember engaging Tom Ashley, who did blackface as *Rastus.* When the folk craze came along, I kept seeing the name 'Clarence Ashley' as being popular on the folk circuit. Tom was living in Shouns, Tennessee, when he came to me at the station in Bristol.

Country Boys (from left) Chubby Collier, Mac, Jim Williams and Wayne Brown, 14.

When I went to play the Newport Folk Festival in the late 1950s, I found Clarence Ashley was booked, then I saw him and knew he was Tom, who had worked for me."

As a youngster, Tom had learned a novelty number "Coo Coo Bird," which became a popular record for him and Doc Watson. He's also credited with being the first to cut "House of the Rising Sun," as "Rising Sun Blues" in 1933, credited to writer Alan Price, and which Mac later recorded.

Multi-talented Ashley was down-on-his-luck, doing odd jobs in Shouns to support wife Hettie and two kids, when he approached Mac in Bristol, seeking work. His career flourished after the college set discovered his old records as Clarence Ashley. Tom, seventy-one, died June 2, 1967, in a Winston-Salem hospital, and requested burial on a hill near his house, which he wrote about in his song "Little Hillside."

During February 1952, Dot decided to release a third Wiseman single: "I'll Still Write Your Name in the Sand" with "Four Walls Around Me" on the flip-side. Both sides proved winners for Mac and Dot. The A side, of course, was a tip of the hat to Buddy Starcher, who wrote and hit with his own earlier recording.

While at WBMD doing Johnny's Used Car program, Mac was pleasantly surprised to receive a check from Dot, his first royalty payment: "Yeah, I had a couple records out by then and remember picking up my mail there at Johnny's, and opened that envelope containing a check for more than twelve hundred dollars. That was probably for the first release - representing a cent-and-a-half per record - which gives you some idea of what my sales were. Back then that was a substantial sum, though today it would be chump change."

Dot could sell one hundred thousand records alone to the jukebox operators: "Randy was a big caterer to the jukebox trade, because he believed in the power of the jukebox. They were everywhere back then, bars, pool-halls, restaurants, dance halls and truck-stops

"I would regularly attend the Music Operators of America conventions in Chicago where people like Mitch Miller were attendees. That's where I met the great gospel singer Mahalia Jackson and sat next to her at dinner. I found her to be a very fine lady, and we shared a most interesting conversation. I was quite familiar with her work and was just blown away to find I was seated next to her.

"While I was at MOA, I also ate my first Chinese food, dining with publisher Wesley Rose, who was originally from the Chicago area. Jimmy Work (of 'Makin' Believe' fame) was with us, but he wouldn't eat, saying it all looked so unappetizing to him. But I enjoyed it."

Another concept Wood believed in was releasing records on a more accelerated basis: "Back then the pattern of the record companies was to withhold a follow-up release until it was apparent the current record had run its course. Randy and I put our heads together and figured we'd put a single out every six weeks. We didn't care what was happening with the previous record. As a result, we would have two or three playing on stations at the same time, and that's the reason we built such a large catalog so quickly."

Mac soon learned Randolph C. Wood originally hailed from McMinnville, Tennessee; graduated in 1937 from Middle Tennessee State University; and served in the Army during World War II.

"After the war, Randy ran a repair shop for radios and used electrical appliances, a hangover from his military days," acknowledges Wiseman. "Then he began putting used jukebox records in a bin to sell for a quarter, as a service to customers (in 1947). He got them for next to nothing, but they were just gobbling them up. Randy said he thought then, 'Man, if I can sell other people's records like that, I could sell my own.' So he put one thousand dollars in the bank and never touched it, to start his own label initially calling it Randy Records."

When Mac made his 1951 pact with Randy, however, the label was called Dot Records. That made Mac the first to be officially signed as a Dot artist, where the others had cut a few recordings on a handshake deal only.

Upon military discharge, Wood moved to Gallatin, opening an electric appliance store he called Randy's. Among his reduced-rate records, Randy noted the more popular sellers were the Race Records, then *Billboard's* chart title, covering black artists like Cecil Gant, Roosevelt Sykes and Joe Liggins.

Wood picked up on the fact their songs were in great demand on WLAC-Nashville, and being played by DJs such as "Hoss" Allen. This nugget of knowledge prompted Wood to launch a mail-order business (1948), advertising heavily on WLAC, and the amount of incoming orders amazed him. WLAC programmed a late night radio show titled *Randy's Record Shop*. Incidentally, on June 25, 1949, *Billboard* revised its Race Records chart to the then more politically-correct Rhythm & Blues chart.

By 1950, Randy's mail-order business had become a top priority, prompting his store's new name, like the radio show: Randy's Record Shop. In tandem with Gene Nobles, he created Randy Records, producing early works like Richard Armstrong's "Gene Nobles' Boogie," as well as Cecil Gant, who earlier enjoyed a number one single "I Wonder," then under Wood's guidance recorded titles like "Cryin' To Myself" and "With All My Heart." Another act produced was George Toon & The Tennessee Drifters, a teen band from Nashville's East High School, with a regional hit, 1950's "Boogie Beat Rag," and then there was Cuzzin Clem & His Country Cuzzins' "Love or Indigestion."

Talk about diversity, Mac grins, "Actually, Randy gave Gene about ten per cent of Dot Records. I think that was in exchange for all the radio station plugs on WLAC. Gene was very crippled, but he hung in there until Randy sold Dot to Paramount in 1957 for three million dollars. Of course, Paramount kept Randy Wood to serve as president (a position he filled for some ten years)."

During the early 1950s, Randy also became half-owner of radio station WHIN-Gallatin. He began producing local artists under the Dot banner. Attesting to the influx of orders, the over-burdened branch post office had to expand, as *Randy's Record Shop* doubled the amount of its incoming mail. According to Mac, Frank Hamilton ran his mail section, while Frank's wife Christine became Randy's right arm, so to speak.

Among the acts Dot recorded were pianist Johnny Maddox, who spent some twenty years with Dot, on songs such as "Hula Blues." Such successes lured other R&B artists to Dot, including Ivory Joe Hunter, Joe Liggins, The Four Dots, Big Three Trio, Brownie McGhee, Shorty Long & The Counts, who hit Top Ten with "Darling Dear" in 1954. Wood also recorded country names, like Mac, Lonzo & Oscar and JamUp & Honey, with more to come, though Mac was the first signee.

Wood was convinced that jukeboxes could create hits. Initially it was Randy's reasoning that "'Tis Sweet To Be Remembered," a 1902 tune copyright by William Marshall Smith, was not jukebox fodder. Mac says when Randy first heard the song, he "felt the tempo change in it, like where you go into three-quarter time, then uptempo, and then waltz time," hurt its appeal for jukebox play.

Mac reminds us, "He'd said, 'No, we can't record that!' When I asked why, Randy said, 'Because we have to get it on jukeboxes and the tempo changes will affect their dancing.' Now I had used it as a theme song ever since my Molly O'Day days, a good five years. I just sweated blood for fear somebody was going to record it. I knew it was going to be a hit. I'd go into these different markets I told you about. Then a week or so later, after being on the air, I'd get into a cab and the driver would be whistling or singing it, everywhere I went. I just knew somebody was going to beat me to it.

"It's also quite coincidence that there's a banjo on my first recording that typifies me as bluegrass," reiterates Mac. "Mostly, I felt the banjo was too raucous for my ballads, so on the ballads that banjo would lay in the background. Many of the banjo pickers didn't even play fills. They'd play the same melody you were singing. That's what makes it raucous."

As Mac predicted, King Records quickly covered his first record with Cowboy Copas, whose version hit the Top Ten in 1952; as did Mac's former band-mates Flatt & Scruggs' rendition on Columbia, which charted one week only. Having originally heard it by Mac, their record became their very first Top Ten *Billboard* charting (and the duo inadvertently credited Wiseman as the composer).

"Jimmy Skinner, I think, did it on Capitol [as flipside to his 'Penny Postcard']. I remember hearing on the Opry, before Copas sang his version of 'Tis Sweet To Be Remembered,' he told the audience, 'I wasn't the first guy to record this. Mac Wiseman recorded this on Dot Records.' I thought how wonderful for a guy to plug me when he had a new release on it, you know."

Dot got its first pop hit thanks to The Hilltoppers, a collegiate group featuring Billy Vaughn, Don McGuire, Seymour Spiegelman and lead singer Jimmy Sacca, with their recording "Trying" (Top Ten, 1952). Follow-ups included their million-selling "P.S. I Love You," "I'd Rather Die Young," "From the Vine Came the Grape" and "Till Then."

Billy Vaughn and Nashville's Beasley Smith co-wrote "I'd Rather Die Young" for The Hilltoppers, whose version was rushed out prior to the performance Wood had Wiseman cut, though the song seemed like a fine fit for Mac. Vaughn, something of a musical genius, went on to be Dot's pop A&R music director, and also fronted his own orchestra with hits such as "Melody of Love," "Shifting, Whispering Sands," "Sail Along Silvery Moon" and "Raunchy."

Vaughn's orchestral backing enhanced many Dot artists' fare, notably Pat Boone ("Ain't That a Shame," number one, 1955), Gale Storm ("I Hear You Knocking," number two, 1955) and Tab Hunter ("Young Love," number one, 1957). Incidentally, Dot's success with movie idol Tab Hunter's "Young Love" and "99 Ways" (1957), spurred his home movie studio - Warner Brothers - to form its own disc label to issue Hunter's 1959 Top 40 "Apple Blossom Time." Tab's recording career soon slid down hill when gossip magazines like *Confidential* outed the teen-agers' heartthrob as gay-oriented.

All My Memories Fit For Print

No one-hit wonder, clean-cut Boone boasted some sixteen million-selling singles for Dot, and his longest charting number one was 1957's "Love Letters In the Sand," inspired by Wiseman's cut. It was in 1953 that Mac recorded his "Love Letters In The Sand," which Ted Black's Orchestra had a pop hit on in 1931, and it's loosely based on 1881's "The Spanish Cavalier."

Noting its audience appeal, Randy passed it on to Pat, a quintessential college crooner, who signed with Dot, and recorded it. It was his seventh million-seller, and its smashing reception convinced Randy to re-release Mac's recording of the song.

Listeners may have wondered if Mac was hung-up on singing sweet nothings on the beach when he recorded "Love Letters In the Sand," having already cut "I Still Write Your Name In the Sand." Wiseman's Dot version of the latter title was recorded in January 1952, at radio station WHIN, and he cut "Love Letters..." at Castle Studios in downtown Nashville's Tulane Hotel in July 1953.

"Love Letters In the Sand" was co-written by J. Fred Coots and brothers Charles and Nick Kenny, notes Mac. Nick was a columnist and radio editor for the *New York Daily News.* Their creation was initially a hit for Black's Orchestra featuring vocals by Tom Brown. Regarding the Kenny siblings, Mac says, "Right on the damn radio in N.Y. when they appeared, the announcer credited Pat Boone with reviving it, and they stated, 'No, it was originally Mac Wiseman who recorded it first for Dot.' The way the song came about, Nick had actually found this lovelorn fellow down at the beach who had it bad for a gal, and was actually writing her name in the sand. I believe he was a major singing star, but didn't record the song he had inspired."

Mac confides that he never heard Black's "Love Letters" and knew it only from hearing Fiddlin' Arthur Smith sing a snippet on the radio. He recalls an Amish fellow approaching him after a show at Sunset Park in Pennsylvania, wondering why Mac didn't record the song? Mac replied because there weren't enough lyrics for a full record, whereupon the guy told Mac it indeed had some great verses and later sent him sheet music on the song: "And I still have it."

The year 1953 saw Mac doing three studio sessions, at Castle Studios, first in February, when Mac utilized twin fiddles on his session, a first in country though routinely used on Western Swing records, thanks to the talents of Tommy Jackson and Dale Potter. Heading up the session players was guitarist Grady Martin, whose Slew Foot Five band was fresh off two Top 10 collaborations, first with Burl Ives for "The Wild Side of Life" and Bing Crosby on "Till The End Of the World," both pop hits, as well. That always meant more money in royalties, something dear to Grady's heart.

Mac says he wrote "When I Get the Money Made" with then-gospel duo Ira and Charlie Louvin, the same boys who didn't show up in Bristol, after making that terrific band test tape. "They never did bring that subject up." The fourth song "Rainbow In the Valley" was a country cover on a pop song Wood heard another artist do. Guitarist-vocalist Jim Eanes, who was on the session, had played briefly with Flatt & Scruggs' Foggy Mountain Boys, three or four weeks at the most, just prior to Wiseman joining. Virginia native Eanes declined to depart Danville, where he was making enough to support his family, and wasn't anxious to take a chance on a small radio station in Hickory with an unknown group. Ultimately, they were

indeed floundering in Hickory, until
Mac's urging helped Flatt & Scruggs
and the Foggy Mountain Boys turn their
fortunes around at WCYB.

Come April 1953, Mac's session included his and Lorene Vass's "Let Me
Borrow Your Heart Just For Tonight,"
while among pickers booked was newcomer Jackie Phelps on banjo. Phelps,
incidentally, played the first electric
Spanish guitar, and was also comedy foil
Cousin Ish on the Lonzo & Oscar show.

Mac chuckles remembering in May
1953, when session ace Hank Garland
wanted to treat him: "So Hank got these
tickets and took me down to see a Jersey

Mac and Smilin' Jim Eanes.

Joe Walcott championship fight at the old Paramount Theatre across from the Tulane Hotel on Church Street. By the time we got inside and sat down, the fight was
over, as Joe was kayoed by Rocky Marciano in the very first round."

During that spring, Mac was invited to talk to the powers-that-be at WRVA-
Richmond, home to the *Old Dominion Barn Dance* weekend program, regarding a
move to the station, a CBS affiliate. The fifty thousand watt WRVA, owned by the
Edgeworth Broadcast Service, had its own theater at Ninth & Broad streets downtown and for years showcased the talents of Sunshine Sue Workman.

"My records were selling well in Richmond. A guy named George (Pop) Pop-
kins was playing them on WXGI radio there," adds Wiseman. "I felt that his efforts
helped create the excitement that made them come to me, and though I didn't know
it at the time, WRVA's *Barn Dance* was on its last legs. Not being boastful, but when
we played there they stood around the block to get in to see our show. I think what
hurt the *Barn Dance* was Sunshine Sue, who was so demanding and anybody who
wanted to work the station had to have her say-so.

"I remember that first
meeting I attended when
we were discussing price
and she was there. Well,
the Program Director told
me, 'You'll be working for
Sunshine Sue,' and I spoke
right up and said, 'I'll
gladly work with her, but
there's no way I'll work for
her!' I was determined that
I wouldn't be under her,
because I heard that broad
was malicious."

Country Boys at WRVA (from left) Lee Cole, Buck Graves,
Mac, Donnie Bryant and Curtis Lee.

All My Memories Fit For Print

Mac's original assessment proved right. For example, in 1953, WRVA's CBS network portion was part of a rotation policy between Richmond and a few other stations, and every third week or so WRVA had the network broadcast.

"Sue would usually schedule me towards the last half-hour, the final portion of the broadcast, and a couple times we got cut off as they ran out of time. Finally one night, I told my boys, 'Let's go back down to the dressing room,' and I heard her announce me, but we didn't go up. So Sue stood there with egg on her face. Believe me, that is the last time she put us on last. But she had that sort of control."

For the uninformed, Sunshine Sue, who became known as radio's Queen of the Hillbillies, was born Mary Arlene Higdon. After her marriage to musician John Workman, they performed with his brother Sam. The Workmans hailed from Iowa. From January 1940, Sue worked at WRVA-Richmond, then in 1946 became one of the original stars on the station's newly-minted *Old Dominion Barn Dance*. As one of the first female emcees, she literally determined the *Barn Dance's* talent roster over time, including Wilma Lee & Stoney Cooper, Grandpa Jones, Mother Maybelle & The Carter Sisters with Chester Atkins, Rose Lee & Joe Maphis, and Don Reno & Red Smiley.

That is all except Mac, whose band-members at WRVA over time were Allen Shelton, Donnie Bryant, Eddie Adcock, banjos; Chubby Collier, Scotty Stoneman, Curtis Lee, fiddles; Lee Cole, bass; Jim Williams, Don Hoaglin, mandolins; and Buck Graves, dobro/mandolin.

While still based in Baltimore, Mac began booking his boys at newly-popular outdoor drive-in movie sites in eastern cities to augment his schedule of show-dates: "Drive-ins. They were really coming into their own at the time and receptive to live entertainment between screenings. To us, those drive-in theaters were a big item along about that time. Remember them?

"I was doing my own bookings and while at WRVA, would go into Washington, D.C. or Norfolk, those places where they would book 'B' movies, and I'd schedule shows two or three months at a time. All I had to do was bring in my calendar, sit down with the guy and fill in the dates. I didn't have to pay anyone else to do it. Don't misunderstand me that that was a millionaire's dream, but we had some big crowds. We played on the top of the concession stands, wherever. They would honk when they liked your show. It was different."

Yet another bright spot for Mac was Sunset Park in Chester County, Pennsylvania: "The old gentleman who owned Sunset Park, Uncle Roy Waltman, called me at the radio program and asked me to come see him at the park. When I got there, he made me an offer that he would use me every Sunday that summer that I wasn't booked somewhere else. So that summer of 1953, we worked twenty-six consecutive Sundays, at parks in Pennsylvania, Maryland and West Virginia. When we were there in Richmond, we were doing as high as three hundred 'one-nighters' a year. Absolutely! Only time we were home was to change underwear or get some clean clothes."

Mac points out there were such parks all over Pennsylvania, Virginia and Maryland they played in summer, while their other venues consisted of theaters, town halls, school auditoriums and gymnasiums. Later, banjoist Wade Macey would present Mac with an Afghan quilt depicting Sunset Park. Wade, who had a Ph.D, by then was head of a college in North Carolina.

Jogging his memory further, Mac remembers back to 1947: "While in Bristol, I stole an idea from Bill Monroe. I'd put me a basketball team together and book that team into the schools. Our team played against their team. We did our show - and then they got the game!

"Some schools wouldn't allow us to use their auditoriums because they were afraid our crowd would mess up their floors. That was especially true in southern Virginia after receiving funds to refurbish their auditorium or gymnasium. They'd use folding chairs and in a lot of schools the gym doubled as their auditorium. I got the idea to do shows early in the day during school time - usually 9 a.m. to 3 p.m. - in the auditorium or gymnasium because the kids would bum mom and dad for a quarter to go; otherwise, they'd have to stay in class. We did as many as three shows a day that way."

During a guest stint on Washington, D.C.-based Connie B. Gay's *Town & Country Time* telecast in neighboring Arlington, Mac performed "I Saw Your Face in the Moon" and "You Can't Judge a Book By Its Cover." According to Mac, "Connie booked me on a lot of dates while I was in Richmond."

Mac especially liked when Connie booked him gigs on the Potomoc River: "We would ride on a boat that sailed from D.C. to Mount Vernon, where you could get off, take a pee, then get back aboard and sail for home. I was performing on it one time with Jimmie Davis (of 'You Are My Sunshine' fame) and did well. My records were hot up D.C. way because Connie saw to that."

One amusing incident Mac recalls concerned Gay's booking of Hank Williams, with Moon Mullican as his opening act. Moon, of course, was on the Opry and had the 1950 chart-topper "I'll Sail My Ship Alone," but this was a couple years later.

"Connie's assistant Jane Trimmer was usually very efficient. But one time while acting as paymaster for him, by mistake she handed Moon Mullican the paycheck sum meant for Hank Williams. She didn't realize what she'd done until it came time to pay Hank. Connie put out a search party for Moon, who they found over in Maryland sitting on a stool, munching a 'burger, but he had cashed the paycheck. Meanwhile, Connie had made up the difference in Hank's check and had Moon work out the over-payment from additional bookings."

Yet another Moon memory surfaces: "During Governor Jimmie Davis' second run for the state office in Louisiana, Mullican traveled as part of the Davis campaign. He put on a concert wherever they stopped to promote Jimmie's candidacy. Knowing Jimmie as I did, apparently he didn't compensate Moon for his shows. When he won the governorship again, however, he made Moon 'Commissioner of Highways' in payment for his efforts. Jimmie went all the way by putting Moon's name on a door in the highway department, but old Moon never darkened that door."

As Mac points out, Connie Barriott Gay was manager and concert promoter to the stars, boosting the careers of Billy Grammer, Jimmy Dean, Patsy Cline, Roy Clark and George Hamilton IV. He bought into a number of radio and TV stations, having originally initiated WARL-Arlington's *Town & Country* program. He was founding president of the Country Music Association, and inducted into the Country Music Hall of Fame in 1980. He died December 3, 1989, at age seventy-five in Fairfax, Virginia.

Gay was proud of the artists he helped along their way, none any more so than Patsy Cline, a lady whose records still sell, some five decades after her death. Back when Cline was very popular in the Washington, D.C. area, she hadn't yet cut her first breakthrough record "Walkin' After Midnight" charting number two, 1957. It was then Mac met her, on the Connie B. Gay broadcasts, which was either late 1953 or early 1954, he believes, remembering she was already a seasoned singer.

Mac recalls a later package show at Hartford, Connecticutt, in which she was a headliner and made a provocative comment that stuck with him through the years: "It was a big show with Bill Anderson, Little Jimmy Dickens, Leroy Van Dyke and Patsy. We came out, a bunch of entertainers from backstage, between shows after the matinee, to get in cars they furnished to go to dinner. Patsy had on an evening dress. When she started to step into the limousine, she caught her heel in the hem of that damn dress she had on, then looked up at me smiling and said, 'Ah, no harm, Mac. It's just like some other things, it'll stretch a mile before it tears an inch.'"

Mac was also proud of his Country Boys band-mates. He continues to boast of their talents: "I mean they're all good, but some stood out, like Eddie Adcock, Scott Stoneman, Wayne Brown, Donnie Bryant, J. D. Crowe, Buck Graves and Herbert Hooven. Eddie Adcock was sixteen when his mom brought him to me, and she said, 'I've been listening to you on the radio and I think you'd treat my boy right.' They lived in Lynchburg, Virginia, and heard me on WRVA's *Old Dominion Barn Dance*. Both Eddie and Donnie Bryant played banjo. J. D. Crowe also played banjo for me, and his daddy sent him from Cincinnati to work one summer with me. He was sixteen. I even had a fourteen-year-old banjoist once named Wayne Brown, who had to get a special work permit in order for me to use him, because he was so young. He later played lead guitar for Brenda Lee.

"I can remember when J. D. Crowe's school term was starting up, I encouraged him to go back to Cincinnati to continue his schooling. That was something I always did with the younger musicians. I literally had to fire them to get them back to school."

By then, Mac was trimming his band down, using a banjo, mandolin and fiddler: "I didn't need a bass because I could cover that using my guitar."

Jim Williams and Buck Graves were multi-talented instrumentalists, which helped in Wiseman's cut back on band-members: "You know, according to Buck Graves, I was also the first to use Dobro in a bluegrass band, primarily because of my ballads. Incidentally, that's when Flatt & Scruggs heard him and hired him to play as a Foggy Mountain Boy. They hired him and ruined him, because they had Buck playing the Dobro like a banjo. But I used him later on a lot of sessions, because he played so beautifully.

"When he came to me, Scotty Stoneman of the Stoneman family was probably a teen-ager, too, and I liked that because they learned easily, and secondly, I could sort of mold them to play as I instructed. Despite what you hear about him, Scott never gave me a minute's trouble. For one thing, when I hired my musicians, one of my steadfast rules was no drinking; I told them if they were drinking, they didn't need to show up as that would save me sending their asses home. I remember Wayne and Scotty on long trips would stretch out long-ways across the station wagon's back seat to sleep, and sometimes just to wake myself up, I'd hit the brakes and throw them both onto the floor, and quickly say, 'That damn dog darn near wrecked us,' to cover my action."

'Ballad of Davy Crockett'...
Hat's Off

"Born on a mountain top in Tennessee
Greenest state in the land of the free
Raised in the woods, so's he knew ev'ry tree
Kilt him a b'ar when he was only three
Davy, Davy Crockett, king of the wild frontier!"

"Mac has been my godfather so-to-speak," says banjoist extraordinaire Eddie Adcock. "From Mac Wiseman, I learned the business inside and out. I didn't learn anything from Bill Monroe, but by the time I worked for Bill's band, I already knew much more than they knew. I didn't act like it or I didn't show off. Mac was so intelligent when it came to everything, but was extremely so about how to make a living in this business.

"You know Mac was on a bigger station and he had a little more record airplay, so we traveled a lot when I was with him, and we would also stop and play Wheeling quite often," continues Adcock. "As a matter of fact, Mac was extremely hot in Canada. Every time the car left Richmond, if you were trying to go west, it would pull to the right because it wanted to drive to Canada."

Eddie was barely sixteen when Mac agreed to take him on as a member of his Country Boys. It marked his first stint with a nationally recognized artist, though he would achieve greater renown as a member of the original Country Gentlemen with John Duffey, Tom Gray and Charlie Waller. A favorite on the folk and college circuit, the Country Gentlemen were inducted into the Bluegrass Music Hall of Fame (1996).

Regarding Mac, Eddie recalls he was headlining the WRVA-Richmond *Old Dominion Barn Dance* when he joined his band in 1954: "We played parks and theaters whatever, working everything in that line. Mac was driving a Mercury wagon back then, probably a 1954 or 1955. He always had a Mercury in those days, almost always new. I remember we did good when radio was the thing. Television took away some of that little niche we had, supplying entertainment live to the people."

Mac at the time recalls he could have afforded a Cadillac, but purposely didn't because he felt pulling up to the venues in a "Caddie" might be considered flaunting his success to the people who had brought him there.

Working for Mac taught young Eddie a lot of tricks of the trade: "Mac was never ever not thinking about his business. He said he's got one commodity to sell and 'that's me.' He was talking about himself.

"We would stop at the jukebox people's places, sometimes for an hour or two in a town," continues Adcock. "He'd talk to them about trying to get records on the jukebox, and at the same time he'd urge them to buy the records - and not give them for free. So it became a double whammy! And it worked. At the time, a lot of artists weren't on the jukebox, but Mac really worked the jukebox scene and at the same time he'd regularly stop at radio stations. Mac was smart because he remembered names. I guess he must've had a note-pad with the DJ's name and that of their wives and kids, because you couldn't possibly remember all that stuff. He was a smooth, smart operator, really one of the most intelligent persons I ever worked with and that's not to knock the others really.

"I learned a lot from him. He's one of my favorite all-time entertainers to work with, and you know, Mac is also a really good cook. Later on in life when we'd meet out on the road - now I remember when I was then with the Second Generation group playing somewhere up in Maine, he said, 'Let's see if we can't find us some lobster,' and he got a pot and we went to the store and got some fixings so we could cook in the room. He had plenty of money and we weren't broke either, but he liked to cook and we appreciated his cooking skills. Mac's quite the chef."

Eddie later earned bigger salaries, like when he and wife Martha were a duo with David Allan Coe, receiving a thousand dollars weekly: "But it wasn't any more than the ninety dollars clear I made with Mac all those years ago. Naturally money went further back then, you see. You could go to a movie and get a bag of popcorn and a Coke for a quarter. Try that now."

According to Adcock after Mac disbanded his group, he worked mainly as a solo, though some promoters would insist he have a backup band. In those cases, Wiseman had it written into his contract that the booker would absorb the band cost, if he or she felt it was necessary. He saw how T. Texas Tyler did that.

"A number of musicians had bad-mouthed Mac, telling wrong stories that he didn't pay the musicians backing him," recalls Eddie. "Well that's not so. Whenever Mac worked by himself, if a promoter insisted on him performing with a band, Mac had it covered by putting in his contract that the promoter was responsible for paying them.

Mac sings at Rebel Records show, while Del McCoury's band takes a break.

"Unfairly, word got around where a musician would say, 'Let me give you something better than money. I'll give you a famous Mac Wiseman handshake.' In other words they were implying Mac wouldn't pay, but merely give you a 'thank you' handshake and that would be it. That was so far from the truth. Mac heard about it after an occasion where one of the McCoury boys, Del's son, played for him. When the promoter didn't pay, the guy called Mac who called the promoter and said, 'If you ever want me to work for you again, you'll pay these kids the money you owe them!' Anyway that was a time when Mac heard about it, but some of the earlier bandsmen didn't bring it to anyone's attention. So Mac got a bad rap and didn't deserve any of that crap."

In retrospect, Wiseman recalls being surprised that one of the musicians took umbrage at Mac's comment after appreciatively introducing each player to the audience for a round of applause, "Whoa! That's enough. Next thing you know, they'll expect to be paid," not knowing they weren't being paid. The instrumentalist said, 'You say that again and I'll leave' ...I did and he did."

At a Graves Mountain Festival, the booker got Del McCoury's boys to back him, notes Mac, who had contractual agreement with the promoter "to furnish one at no cost to me," but didn't.

"He never did pay them a nickel," adds Wiseman. "I didn't know that until one time Del let it slip out. I remember we did a bang-up job, as they knew my music. So then I heard they did their show, then came out and worked another complete set (probably forty-five minutes) playing for no pay! That still embarrasses me to think about it. Norm Adams would get acts such as the Osbornes or Jim & Jesse to back me, but I didn't know what he paid them, though they seemed well-satisfied."

Mac's audiences were content, hearing him sing solo and only playing guitar.

Adcock insists Mac's never tight with the people he works with whatsoever: "He'd give you whatever you needed to help you out. I know for a fact. I'll tell you what he won't give you is a free record. He'd come right around and give you a hundred dollar bill or even a thousand dollars cash if he knew you needed it. But he won't give away anything having to do with business.

"I can give you one example of how free and open-hearted he is, if you're interested... I was out in Smithville, Tennessee, when Martha and I were between jobs and had dropped our band. We were financially embarrassed if you will. I had a car sitting in the driveway without a drop of gas in it. A lot of musicians go right down to the wire and not have anything left at all, and will go hungry before they'll ask for help. Usually I'm that way.

"But this one time I called Mac, who lived seventy-two miles away from where I was. I said, 'Mac, I need a little help. I'm in some trouble.' He said, 'What do you need, boy, tell me?' I told him I needed to borrow some money, saying, 'I hate to ask you, but I really need it. I wouldn't ask you if I didn't.' Mac said, 'I know you wouldn't. How much do you need?' It wasn't a small sum, but I needed enough to tide us over until our next booking. He said, 'No problem. C'mon and get it.' I added, 'That's the catch, Mac. I don't have any way to get there. There's no gas in the car. We're sitting here hungry and I don't have nothing going for me except the rent's paid on the house. But I haven't any way to come get it.' So Mac brought the money out to me. That's the kind of guy he is. I love Mac. He's a big, kind and gentle person."

While Adcock was with Wiseman, his boss had a Top Ten, "The Ballad of Davy Crockett," which enjoyed a sixteen-week run. Mac cut the song in February 1955, with players Grady Martin, Hank Garland, Donnie Bryant, Tommy Jackson, Dale Potter and Ernie Newton. They also cut a second song: "Danger, Heartbreak Ahead." That single was released February 21.

According to Mac, it was his label's idea he sing about the fabled nineteenth century frontiersman: "Randy sent me that. A pop jock out of Cincinnati sent it to him after the Walt Disney TV show *Davy Crockett* starring Fess Parker started getting so big, saying, 'Here's a song for Mac. It's gonna be a smash.' Nobody was more surprised than me."

Walt Disney Studios originally produced a trio of TV segments on former Tennessee Congressman and frontier legend Crockett, first telecast December 15, 1954, via ABC. It created a national phenomenon that resulted in the subsequent

Columbia Records' disc by title player Parker, and a big screen movie, "Davy Crockett, King of the Wild Frontier," which premiered in June 1955, co-starring Parker and side-kick Buddy Ebsen.

"The Ballad of Davy Crockett," co-written by George Bruns and Thomas Blackburn, proved a major pop hit, especially among the younger set, most notably as recorded individually by pop crooner Bill Hayes on Cadence Records (charting number one, 1955), Fess Parker (number five) and Tennessee Ernie Ford on Capitol (number five). Nonetheless, Wiseman's popular Dot country cover peaked at Top Ten on May 28, 1955, five days after his thirtieth birthday, a nice belated present for the burly balladeer. Its B side: "Danger! Heartbreak Ahead," was co-written by Edith Lindeman and Carl Stutz. Mac points out, "Both Edith and Carl were (media people) from Richmond. They just had the number one 'Little Things Mean a Lot' for pop singer Kitty Kallen [and in 1978, a number three country hit for Mac's friend Margo Smith]."

"You know Tennessee Ernie had a five-day-a-week TV show, so I had to work to try to beat him. Randy gave me a thousand dollars to promote our record, and told me just to keep on flying, visiting radio stations and such, until I ran out of money. That didn't take too long... The procedure I used was to call on the major radio personalities in an area. I remember in Louisville, one of the good old boys met me at the airport, and that same guy hooked me up to other DJs there, so within a couple hours I was done in Louisville.

"In Cincinnati, I'd made the mistake of telling the top DJ about Randy giving me the money to promote our record. He suggested if I gave him a slice of the promotion money he would assure me a number one record. I quickly told him I'd used up most of the money by then, but having said that, he had little choice but to promote our song. That guy was well-known for kick-backs."

Mac actually ran out of the limited advance promotion money in Dallas. Although the ballad had many verses, Mac's version was, of course, scaled back to the standard three-minutes for airplay, with the familiar intro: *"Born on a mountain top in Tennessee, greenest state in the land of the free/Raised in the woods so's he knew ev'ry tree, kilt him a b'ar when he was only three/Davy, Davy Crockett, king of the wild frontier!"*

The song literally became part of the national culture, thanks to the film and its sequel, and TV's *Walt Disney Presents*, plus Crockett merchandise that sold in excess of three hundred million dollars by the end of 1955. Mac's boy Randy was peacock proud of Dad's recording, but he wasn't alone: "It got so some high school kids would drive by my house singing 'Davy Crockett,' and you know several high schools even had fan clubs for me. That was a hot damn time for me, I'll tell you!"

Linda and Randy, a miniature 'Davy Crockett,' target Dad's new hit.

90

Actually, prior to Mac recording "Davy Crockett," Eddy Arnold and Hank Snow's former manager "Colonel" Tom Parker approached him with a management deal: "It was in 1955, just before Easter when I recorded 'Ballad of Davy Crockett' [actually February '55] and the record ended up being the reason why I left him. He wanted me to wear a coonskin cap, leather jacket and all that, and that just wasn't me. I didn't even wear a hat back then, as I had a healthy head of hair. But he did get me a lot of good show-dates in the Midwest, anywhere the record sold well (his package shows featured Minnie Pearl and the Willis Brothers)."

With eyes smiling, Mac recalls how the Colonel got him a pay raise with Dot. Parker and Wood were friendly rivals, and when the Colonel heard Wiseman couldn't get a pay hike, he told Mac, "Tell Randy you want a five per cent raise because that's what I'll get you to sign with RCA." So that's how the Colonel got Wiseman a raise.

Of course, Parker went on to guide a younger star on the rise, namely Elvis Presley, and indeed got him a record upfront fee from RCA for a newcomer in November 1955, consisting of a reported forty thousand dollars, plus a five thousand bonus for the singer. Little did they know how his successes would impact the pop, rock and country markets in the decade ahead.

Mac was also on good terms with Hank Snow, who initially signed Elvis to Hank Snow Attractions and suggested his label RCA sign him, only to be snookered out of the deal by Parker, who dropped Hank to manage Presley full-time.

Wiseman didn't really know Elvis personally: "Yeah, Elvis worked in Richmond at The Mosque, then a leading venue there, like the downtown Bridgestone Arena is here. One of the WRVA announcers, Herb Clark, who went from Richmond to WCAU-Philadelphia and stayed there the rest of his career, used to ride herd on my business when I was out of town working so much. Well, just a few years ago out of the blue, I got a letter from him. Herb and his wife had been down near Marion, Virginia, for a visit and on the drive back heard one of my records, which prompted him to write me. He said, 'I'll never forget the time that you introduced me to Elvis Presley backstage at The Mosque.'

"Funny, I didn't remember that at all, but then how can you recall everything. I remember a time though I played Cleveland, Ohio, when Elvis was just getting started, and working a theater there. Well, the show's promoter came up to me and said, 'You know Elvis put on one helluva show at the matinee, but he shacked up with this little gal between shows and wasn't worth a damn for the evening show.' I knew he could pack them in because he was opening shows for big-name country stars and soon was closing their show (usually the star slot), because nobody wanted to follow him. He was so dynamic."

Regarding "Davy Crockett," Wiseman recalls another incident that occurred years later while performing with gospel's Lewis Family at their annual music festival in Georgia: "Little Roy Lewis, who played five-string banjo, was a noisy little S.O.B. and like all banjo pickers played melody all the time. He and his sister Polly, who sang some duets with me, would stay on stage after their performance to help with my show. Little Roy slipped up behind me and said, 'Sing some songs you did on the Carnegie Hall Concert.' Then adding, 'Do a little of 'Davy Crockett,' your hit.' Well, I hadn't done it in years, and said, 'Little Roy, I'll tell you, I'm not going to sing 'Davy Crockett' now.' He said, 'Oh yeah, don't you wanna be on the next Lewis Family Festival?' So right then I started singin' *'Oh Davy, Davy Crockett, king of the wild frontier,'* and everybody burst out laughing."

According to country music's longest-running newspaper columnist Don (Ramblin') Rhodes of Georgia's *Augusta Chronicle*, Mac's 2001 pairing with Polly Lewis on "I'd Rather Live By the Side of the Road" is a special favorite of his. It was recorded for a Lewis Family album at Opryland, as was another Wiseman guest spot earmarked for a Porter Wagoner album.

Mac adds, "I think that was the one that also included the Osborne Brothers, which was recorded at the Opryland's Theater By The Lake, also featuring Hal Rugg and Leon Rhodes backing us. It was released in 1982, by RCA Records."

It was back in 1955, that Dot also released Wiseman's first album of songs - his only EP, usually consisting of four to six songs - titled "Songs From The Hills." Randy Wood was quick to realize the sales potential for LPs (long-play albums usually had at least ten songs) and didn't scrimp on the number he put out on such artists as Mac, who matched or exceeded the LP output on fellow artists like Carl Smith, Sonny James, Faron Young or even Flatt & Scruggs.

Mac on a Willie Nelson set with (from left) Maxine, Martha & Eddie Adcock, and Harold Morrison (that's a cardboard cut-out of Willie).

"I never did play on Mac's sessions when he was at Dot, but since then I've probably played on more Mac Wiseman recordings than any other banjo player, and I've cut TV shows with him," says Adcock. "When he did guest TV spots, he would call me to back him and that was good exposure. When I had Second Generation, he put them on TV and after I married Martha, he put us on. I mean these were shows like Carl Smith's, syndicated across Canada and the northern U.S., plus other big ones booked by Jim Halsey.

"My first ocean cruise was on the *SS Rotterdam* with Mac, and he got me paid separately from him. Every good thing he got, he would help me get work on. He's my best friend and in the music business these days, there's not a better friend than Mac Wiseman."

Another 1955 song of interest was Irving Gordon's title tune "The Kentuckian," which Mac recorded in April 1955. It was from the United Artists' film, directed by Burt Lancaster, who also starred. Others recording "The Kentuckian Song" included The Hilltoppers and Eddy Arnold.

"I must say Al Bennett promoted the hell out of my records, along with Billy Vaughn's and Pat Boone's. He later bought Liberty Records, and was a party man if ever there was one," notes Mac. "I think he died young because of it."

In October 1955, Mac was back in Castle Studios - with leader Beasley Smith, the veteran musician-bandleader who wrote such hits as "That Lucky Old Sun." By now Mac was using more mainstream country instrumentation on his records, though he maintained his bluegrass booking connections.

Beasley was one to offer challenges for artists. The session included Dave Bartholomew's vocally challenging "I Hear You Knockin'," also recorded pop by Dot's Gale Storm. "The phrasing on this one proved a problem, just trying to get it the way we wanted," Mac explains. The Bartholomew band's 1955 cut "I Hear You Knockin'," with vocals by Smiley Lewis, was a near-number one on the R&B list for Imperial Records.

In December 1955, Dot booked Castle Studio time for Wiseman to record four more songs, among them Mac's collaborative co-writing with Paul Keys, "I'm Eatin' High On the Hog." Virginians Keys and Wiseman were also fellow hunters.

Mac wrote such as "The Bluebirds Are Singing For Me," but insists, "I didn't have much success writing, because I was too critical. I always felt what other people wrote was better."

At that Christmas season session, Mac had Chet Atkins playing electric lead guitar, Newton on bass, Jackson and Potter on fiddles, and Donnie Bryant on banjo. Regarding "These Hands," an Eddie Noack cut: "Eddie pitched us his song 'These Hands,' saying Hill & Range were offering us exclusive rights to record the song. Apparently they had said the same thing to Hank Snow and Johnny Cash... Randy wouldn't accept their music after that."

Mac humorously recalls saying to Chet Atkins, "I hope you'll play this song ('I'm Eatin' High On the Hog') like you do on your RCA hits. I was only kidding Chet, as we were good friends. We also used banjo on it, but it was very subdued on that track."

Incidentally, that novelty number ended up in a United Kingdom release on the indie Cactus label, titled "Hillbilly Compilations: Rockin' Hillbilly, Volume 6," one of thirty-two songs with other acts, though only Mac's face appeared on the cover.

Donnie Bryant's first session with Mac occurred in the fall of 1954: "I started with the Country Boys in August and in September we did a session. I didn't know the tunes to some of the songs until we practically got into the studio. I mean a couple we cut - 'Wabash Cannonball' and 'Fireball Mail' - I was somewhat familiar with, having heard Roy Acuff singing them. We had very little rehearsal, so I literally had to learn them on the spot. I just kept it simple.

"At a later session, I was stunned to see Chet Atkins walk in the door carrying his guitars. We were at the Castle Studio. I was in awe. Chet's sitting there on a stool playing one song after another at my request. Finally, I looked over and thought Mac was getting agitated because we were on studio time. So we had to knock it off and get down to business."

In time, Bryant would play with both Lester Flatt and Bill Monroe. Donnie especially values his friendship with Mac and looks back upon his days as a Country Boy fondly.

93

"While I was there we had guys like mandolinist Don Hoaglin, a lead singer, Curtis Lee on fiddle - Curtis and I still stay in touch - and there was Buck Graves. I got to know Buck very well. That was the reason I was selected to sit in for Earl Scruggs, when he was injured in a bad automobile accident. It wasn't as though I was the most logical choice from a musical standpoint. It was one of those *it's who you know* things, because Buck and I worked together about a year in Mac's band. At the time of Earl's mishap, Buck was well-seeded in Lester's band, and he knew I had my head on straight and probably could do as well as about anybody else. Nobody could fill Earl's shoes, but I did the best I could and I was flattered to get the opportunity.

"Understand I never was a Blue Grass Boy, so the only time I did anything with Bill was after I stopped playing full-time, and that was thanks to Mac... Now the reason for stopping was I got drafted into the Army for two years, and it gave me a good opportunity to assess things.

"I decided I was not going to devote my life to five-strings, as I really didn't care for the traveling aspect of it too much. So I applied for the police department in D.C. and that proved a good move, for I had a fine career and retired as a police captain. Anyway, during that time in the 1960s, Mac was living in Nashville by then and he'd contact me on

Jammin' with Donnie Bryant.

weekends; for example, if he were going to be at some place like Gettysburg for an outdoor gig within a couple hours of D.C., frequently he would come through and pick me up to do the dates with him, as he knew I could do the job. One time in the 1970s, I even went to Europe with Mac, but I didn't record anymore with him because we were not allowed to be in a union you know."

Bryant was born and raised in the Washington area, "At the time it was a major hot-bed for bluegrass music. My parents were big bluegrass fans, especially of Bill Monroe, so I was exposed to bluegrass growing up.

"But you know I never really was into bluegrass that much myself," continues Bryant. "As a teen-ager, I loved playing guitar. Oh, I wasn't a fancy player but I understood the chord progressions easily. In the early '50s, I was hearing Mac on his first recordings and he did a lot of neat guitar runs. So when I heard he was playing locally in a place called Mount Airy in Maryland, I went over in the spring of 1952, to hear him, not knowing anything about his band really. Well, he had Jim Williams playing mandolin, who was very, very good, and had done a lot of recordings with the Stanley Brothers, and he also had Ed Amos, who I believe was a Roanoke-area guy, and another fellow named Johnny Haskins. When I went there that night to their show, talk about a life-changing experience! I was totally zapped by the whole sound. I loved Mac's voice and within no time I'm sure I forgot all about his guitar playing, because Ed Amos knocked me out with his banjo, and Jim Williams with his playing and singing duets… I had never heard anything like it in my life.

"I think it was within a couple days after that show, I borrowed a banjo from somebody. I'd been playing guitar with a flat pick, nothing exceptional, but now I had to start playing the thing with my fingers. I don't remember what I had as a frame of reference, but I knew I used two fingers and a thumb. So I started fiddling around with that banjo. There was an old man living near me, who didn't play anything like Scruggs' style, but he did play, so I started playing simple tunes like 'Oh Susannah,' and to my surprise found it came easily to me. I had the dexterity in my hands and it seemed like overnight I could play tunes on that thing.

"Then as time went on, I found there were some great players around the area like Roy Clark, Smitty Irvin and later Don Stover, who had been with the Lilly Brothers playing banjo. He came down from Boston, I think, in the summer of 1953, and by then I'd been playing banjo almost a year. Well, we got together and he helped me a lot. Smitty was another fine player I knew.

"The ironic thing about all this after seeing Mac's Mount Airy show and getting zapped by Ed Amos, within two years I was a member of Mac's Country Boys! It was in the summer of 1954 that he appeared in Warrenton, Virginia, and I was introduced to Mac by an area DJ, Don Owens, a mutual friend to me and Mac. Don told Mac I was a banjo picker. Somehow or other it happened that I auditioned for Mac out in a field where he'd been doing an outdoor concert. I think it was August 1954, as the player Mac had then wasn't a great banjoist.

"Well, I played for Mac and when it was done, he said 'OK. Can you be in Richmond Tuesday, day after tomorrow?' The DJ - Owens - was standing there and I said 'Yes, sir!' I remember when Mac hired me, he said, and I'll never forget this - 'I'm hiring you to make me sound good. I don't like a lot of fancy stuff. I don't like to be upstaged. I want you to play solid, simple stuff.' I certainly always tried to do that. I didn't try to do any Scruggs' licks and played to make all the notes fit what Mac was singing.

"What I began to realize was the more you to try to do that the better you sound, because the people paid to hear the singer. They're not there to hear you. So if you make him sound good, you're gonna sound good. If you try to do a little lick in there once in a while that's on the flashy side, then it wasn't too good, at least with Mac's band. He was so good vocally, that he didn't need that. To this day - I play every day as a hobby - I wish I knew then what I know now. It served me well.

"To me, Mac was/is the ultimate singer and he wasn't the easiest to play behind because he has a little bit of - I don't know if this is technically the right word - *syncopation* that is his own style, which is to his credit, but in backing him you had to be very careful of the way he phrased his words. If you weren't cautious, you would sound like you were out of time. I mean he might be a bit early or a bit late, depending on how he chose to phrase the lyric, and he certainly was within the beat, but if you didn't pay attention you could clash with him. Keeping it simple made it a lot easier for me. I did play a lot of standard fills and that's what he wanted. It pleased me because I was never all that fancy a player anyway."

Mac also offered his Boys mini-solos while singing his songs, giving them a shot in the spotlight. According to Don, "I got a lot of that. Most of his tunes were designed to take a break on… but you had to know when to do it. That was a regular part of the playing, though some of the slower songs we didn't do a break on. It got so the one I was most featured on was the 1956 number 'The Ballad of Davy Crockett,' a big hit for Mac.

"We worked on one microphone in those days," continues Bryant. "That was kind of neat though. Today, if you look at a bluegrass band that's got five or six members, they're gonna have five or six microphones, and they just stand there and play. I mean it sounds good, but there's something to be said about the choreography that took place in a band where a member would step up to the mic, take his break, then step back out. To illustrate what I mean, you've got the main man - Mac - standing behind the sole mic singing, then picture this, he's got a banjo player on his left, a little bit behind him, then a fiddle player on his right, and maybe a Dobroist there somewhere.

"All those guys had to be able to work their way up to the mic, so when it's time to take your break, you step in at the right time, moving into the mic. The beauty of it all was it let the audience know you're moving in, and they think, 'he's coming in to play,' that's a bit of anticipation and lends itself to a little excitement. Of course, the singer can see in his peripheral vision that you're moving up for the break, and you have to be right on the mark."

Bryant saw Mac as a no-nonsense sort of bandleader: "Mac was both boss and mentor to me. When I went with him he was still in the early stages of his career and there was no nonsense. That meant he wanted no fooling around because it was his career on the line. Still, he was good to work for, and he would let you know when you're doing a good job; however, if there was something you were doing he didn't like, he would let you know in a heartbeat. Sure he was stern but that was the attitude he had and you'd better adhere to it. I would've been the same way."

Musically speaking, Mac was at the top of his game, adds Bryant, "Mac was in his prime, and he sang in that beautiful tenor voice with such feeling. He was my personal favorite and at times when working with him, a couple times I'd be listening so closely to his singing, I forgot what key I was in. I'd have to get hold of myself and say 'now come on, Donnie.'

"Another thing about why I liked working with Mac is he didn't play beer-joints. We also did a lot of big package shows with Opry stars like Little Jimmy Dickens, Marty Robbins and other guys like Slim Whitman, so we had bigger venues to perform in and a lot of times we'd open up for them and we stole the show."

Mac points out the time he shared the bill with Kitty Wells, Queen of Country Music, and Johnnie & Jack ("Poison Love") at an outdoor concert: "Johnnie knew if they didn't do the first show by 6 o'clock, they wouldn't get paid by the promoter. Back then, if you were an Opry member you had to play every Saturday night, and it didn't matter where you were, it was compulsory to play the WSM Opry on Saturday night. Usually it was a rough damn ride after playing the Opry to try to make it to another gig, ironically enough, booked by the WSM Artists Bureau, for a Sunday show in Pennsylvania or wherever.

"I mean you were driving those two-lane roads before the Interstates, and it got to where they might get in there late. Most of the folks attending those park shows were farmers and country folk, and they had to leave around 5 or 6 o'clock to go home and do the milking and the feeding and stuff like that. So the parks got to where they put in the contracts if the acts didn't get there by 6 o'clock to do their concert, then they would only get half their money. That's what brought this thing about with John. They were traveling in two cars, him and Kitty in the front car, and Jack and the band in the second car. Well, there was a storm and a tree blew down after Johnnie had passed, but it fell on the road blocking Jack's car, which slowed him down. There was nothing they could do, so the first car took off, trying to keep the show-date in Pennsylvania, while the others tried to get some help moving the tree so they could continue on.

"They pulled in - and those were the days when he was imbibing a bit - then Johnnie came up to me and said, 'Why don't you go on with me and I'll tell them you're Jack.' That way he could be assured of being paid; however, I told him, 'Hell John, I've already been on about three times holding the crowd for you to get here.' But it wasn't long before Jack and the boys arrived, and they went on and did their show. It just amused me that he wanted me to go on with him in Jack's place. Johnnie, Jack and I became good friends while I was down there in Shreveport at KWKH, and Johnnie and I kept up our friendship ever since."

Donnie Bryant earlier played with bands of Buzz Busby and Bill Harrell, mostly playing bars and honkytonks: "Now don't misunderstand me, Mac wasn't as big a star at the time as an Eddy Arnold, but the people were coming to know him and they liked what they heard. He had them in the palm of his hand. I recall being backstage with Mac, getting ready to go on - and he wasn't big on rehearsing - he'd say, 'Alright boys, let's give them both barrels,' to fire us up. He was a joy to work with."

Another plus for Mac was his natural ability as a salesman, attests Bryant, "He had a great reputation for being a good pitchman. Mac also liked practical jokes. He would kid with me and we had a lot of laughs together. Once, going to Florida, as we drove along I saw this grove and said to him, 'There's some good-looking oranges out there. I'd sure like to have one, wouldn't you?' Well he said 'Yeah,' so I told him pull off to the side of the road and I'd get us one. He stopped, I got out and when I went to get the oranges, he drove off! I stopped and stood there watching him and knew better than to pick oranges and stand there with stolen fruit in my hand. He rode down the road about a quarter mile, before driving back to pick me up. I was a bit pissed, but he was laughing heartily. That was his odd sense of humor."

Bryant treasures the times traveled with Wiseman: "We'd be driving along like at three in the morning, and there were two guys sleeping in the backseat, and I'd get him to sing some of those old ballads like 'Mary Of the Wild Moor' or 'Put My Little Shoes Away,' and he'd sing in his natural voice without any strain. I'd think, 'God, if people could only hear him singing like this. It was beautiful.' I've heard Mac sing Bob Wills' stuff and I know he could sing with anybody. He had a natural tenor with all the range needed."

While with the Country Boys, Don played a 1927 raised-head Gibson banjo: "Mac really liked that banjo. It was loud but didn't come out loud on recordings, though engineers can do whatever's needed in the studio. When we were out on tour, I didn't have to get up too close to the mic because that thing would take the paint off the walls. I used a Gibson circle top. A few years later, I sort of got into the old Gibson flat-heads. I've had a Martin guitar since my teens. I have three today."

Bryant retired from his police job and spent ten years with the Defense Department before totally retiring in 1990, to live in Colorado Springs, Colorado, content with his memories.

"Mac was a good rhythm player and did some fine flat pickin'. Back when I was sitting in for Earl with Lester, I let Mac know when I was through, and he invited me to do a tour with him in Florida. I jumped at the chance, and we worked just the two of us that time. Then frequently there would be reunions, like at the Newport Festival and Mac would invite me along. I remember a time when the promoter got Mac and Bill Monroe together to sing 'Can't You Hear Me Callin',' and I played behind them. That was memorable. It became more like a friendship between Mac and me, and we've kept in touch through the years."

Regarding his bandsmen, Mac recalls he always had a waiting list of players to choose among musically: "Usually, I'd audition them at the time and then keep them in mind when I needed them. I didn't always carry banjo. I did carry mandolin, I wanted a Merle Travis-style guitar, and I wanted the fiddlers to have background to my songs you see, fills and such. I carried the rhythm because I had no bass. I did play a lot of runs and fills. You know, Grady Martin and Merle Travis made the remark - 'You know you're the best flat-top picker in the business' - and coming from them that was quite complimentary."

Early Country Boys' line-up (from left) Johnny Hall, Donnie Bryant, Don Owens, Buzz Busby and Pete Pike.

Another set of Country Boys (from left) Chubby Collier, Jim Williams, Mac and Allen Shelton.

98

13 'Waitin' For Ships That Never Come In'... On Stormy Seas

"I'm waiting for ships that never come in
Watching and waiting in vain
It seems that life's stormy sea
Holds nothing for me
But broken dreams and shattered schemes
With each day of sorrow, I love to pretend
One more tomorrow and waiting will end..."

"It was their first session for Capitol - James & Martha Carson - and we had to wait on them as they were a little late," recalls Mac Wiseman, waiting with fellow musicians Bill Carlisle, Sandy Sandusky and Georgie Tanner, as the husband-wife gospel duo recorded in Atlanta. "I know the recording session was all they talked about enroute to the show - and I listened, as I was interested in how Capitol conducted theirs."

Mac, of course, had recorded a few years earlier with Molly O'Day in Chicago. Martha was a much more volatile vocalist, who might've made a major rock and roller if not so dedicated to inspirational songs.

For his last session at Castle Studios, April 4, 1956, Mac recorded Martha Carson's "Be Good, Baby" and "The Meanest Blues in the World." Although little known today, the late fiery singer was then called queen of country gospel. She was a prolific songwriter, whose pen produced "Satisfied," "I'm Gonna Walk and Talk With My Lord" and "I Can't Wait (For the Sun To Go Down)." It was also the first session noted Nashville studio guitarist Bob Moore, who in 1961 recorded an in-strumental Top Ten, "Mexico," sat in with Mac, and later the likes of Elvis Presley, Pat Boone and Brenda Lee.

Think Martha and you remember her second husband, booker Xavier Cosse, who worked for a time with another forceful agent, A. V. Bamford: "X. Cosse booked Martha, Ferlin (Husky) and I on a ton of show-dates, and I remember the time he had us scheduled five days in Florida, and we wound up in Tampa on a Friday night, drove into Richmond and did the WRVA *Old Dominion Barn Dance* on Saturday night. We had Sunday off, then drove seventeen hundred miles ending in Bismarck, North Dakota, for a Monday night show, with George Morgan, Martha and me headlining. I drove the biggest part of it, and I had my band - all three of us were self-contained units, using our own bands.

"We then played throughout the Dakotas on tour and wound up Friday night at a college in Columbia, Missouri, and were booked the next night again at the *Old Dominion Barn Dance.* In order to make Richmond, I drove every mile of the way. When we gassed up, the boys would grab snacks or drinks whatever, as we didn't have time to stop at a restaurant. I drove a thousand miles in twenty hours on two-lane roads, and that included old Route 60 through the West Virginia mountains.

99

Cosse would buy tours, like for ten-day periods and sometimes as high as twenty days per tour. Most of the time, I did my own bookings, often coordinating through different booking agencies, though I always handled the paperwork. Usually Cosse was the paymaster, the one who collected the box office take on his tours.

"When I played theaters," continues Mac. "I played on a percentage basis; that is, I would get the starting number of tickets and the final closing number, which was supposed to give me an accurate number in attendance. But, I learned that the tricky theater owners would sell from the middle of their roll of tickets, meaning the crowd was different than what they indicated ticket-wise. I learned to get little counters and check out the number of people actually coming into the theater, then approach the guy with my count and let him know we knew he was selling from the center of the roll."

Recollecting his travels with Morgan, Mac adds, "You know Morgan liked to pull pranks. Having driven from Richmond to Bismarck, I was one tired pup, and went to bed to get some rest. When I came down to the coffee shop, I didn't notice any of the other entertainers there. After ordering, I sat trying to clear my head and heard the hotel page *Mac Wiseman*. I went out to the desk, and they said they didn't page me. Went back in very puzzled and sat down. Again, I heard the same page… so a second time I went in and they hadn't paged me. On my way back, I saw George sitting in the back, and smiling. He was the one paging Mac Wiseman. I have some funny-ass stories about that S.O.B.

"One in particular took a week or ten days to bring off. Only one guy in his band was aware of the prank George was pulling: Don Davis to be exact (earlier he played steel guitar for Pee Wee King). So George began moping around, and seemed gradually withdrawing into himself all the time. Of course, he was doing it purposely. Pretty soon the band members were inquiring as to whether anything was wrong. There was one guy, Don (Suds) Slayman, who could make coffee nervous. All George's band came down for breakfast one morning, and George didn't. The bandsmen said they were really worried about him. So Davis sent Slayman up to George's room to make sure George was OK. He hurried back to the coffee shop, white as a sheet, saying George had committed suicide! When he got up to George's room, he was sitting nude in the tub, and all he saw was red (mercurochrome), thinking it was blood, and jumped to the conclusion that George had killed himself. When they all got up there, George jumped up scaring Don half to death.

"There was no end to his pranks. Don Davis and Morgan both had convertibles. One decided as a prank to buy some eggs and throw them off at the other convertible in passing. So the other decided he'd get him a dozen eggs and toss them over at the other vehicle. Finally, both traded in their vehicles, as they didn't smell too good with dried rotten eggs in there."

During a memorable extended twenty-eight-day tour in September 1956, Mac drove ten thousand miles and did sixty-six shows arranged by A. V. Bamford, a Cuban-born booker based in Texas. The reason for the high number of shows was that Mac and Slim Whitman did a week at a Toronto theater doing five shows a day.

"Slim and I came back into the States, adding the Marty Robbins show, thanks to Bamford, and for the remainder of that month, we played Western states, like Idaho and Montana and came back up into Canada, including Calgary, Edmonton and Winnipeg, among others. We each had our own band.

"I played San Diego for him one time - with Lefty Frizzell, Ernest Tubb and the Maddox Brothers & Rose - and he oversold the arena in San Diego and the law stepped in and told him to stop selling tickets. Actually, the firemen came in first and asked him to stop, but he didn't, so the law was notified.

"It was an arena where they had ice underneath the floorboards and heat from the bodies was melting the ice, sending up vapors. [Obviously a hockey arena.] That same night we went to Long Beach and the law was looking for him, but A.V. didn't show up, as he knew they would be looking for him. After the show in San Diego, we went down into Mexico, as A.V. could speak Spanish. Mexican singer-actor Tito Guizar [who'd appeared in Hollywood films with Bob Hope and Roy Rogers] was featured vocalist at a club we went to in Tijuana. We went down out of curiosity mostly, and had a nice time.

"Bob Wills joined us for the Northern California tour, just for three or four dates. I met him and told him how much I admired him and his music. I did ride a lot with his manager in his car to the shows. The first time I met Lefty Frizzell was on this same tour, when we opened in San Antonio on a Sunday. I was working as a single at the time, so I flew into San Antonio. Bamford made arrangements for me to ride with Lefty, who had a driver, a big guy named Al Flores. That was a Sunday night when we did our first show. Monday morning we got up and left for Phoenix to do a Tuesday show, and I'm in the backseat and Lefty was up front in the passenger seat. He wouldn't eat anything, but ate cheese and drank beer all the time.

"As we got acquainted, he said, 'You S.O.B. I wanted in the backseat so I could lay down.' Guess he didn't feel he knew me well enough to tell me to ride in the front seat at the time. Lefty had a drinking problem and they wouldn't let him have a bottle backstage, so they'd frisk him looking for whiskey, as he came in for the show. He had a big thermos he carried, however, and they thought he had coffee in it, but Lefty had it filled with whiskey. He did his shows all right, but he had his pick-me-up, thanks to that thermos.

"You know I found my records were selling quite well out there in California. So much so that Bamford would book me on separate shows elsewhere in clubs in other towns with their house-band backing me, while the rest of the package went on together... Another time, Slim Whitman and I played a week together in Montreal, five shows a day. That was murder doing five shows a day. Those were pretty prestigious venues, as he was right at his height of fame, thanks to such hits as 'Indian Love Call,' 'Secret Love' and 'Rose-Marie.'"

Later that summer of 1956, Mac included yet another of Martha Carson's songs, "Hey, Mr. Bluesman," as he recorded for the first time on the West Coast, specifically August 17, at Radio Recorders Studio in Hollywood. Musicians assembled included jazz guitarists Barney Kessel and Jack Marshall; Larry Breen on bass; plus most notably Shorty Rogers on piano and Alvin Staller on drums, another first for a Wiseman session. Drums and piano worked well on the pop-oriented tunes picked - "I'm Waiting For Ships That Never Come In," "One-Mint Julep" and "... Bluesman" which went unissued until decades later when Bear Family included it on their 2003 Wiseman box-set - for the production helmed by Billy Vaughn.

"One-Mint Julep" relates how a man tries forgetting in a bottle: *"One early morning as I was walking/I met a woman, we started talking... ,"* Mac sings, closing with the tell-tale lyrics, *"I don't want to bore you with my trouble/But from now on I'll be thinking double."*

Musician Smokey Rogers' haunting ballad "Gone," which on April 6, 1957, struck number one for Ferlin Husky, was recorded January 31, 1957 by Wiseman at Radio Recorders, along with "Step It Up and Go" and "Sundown."

Earlier in 1957, Capitol's Sonny James' single "Young Love" had been topping the pop chart one week, until Dot's cover by screen star Tab Hunter edged out James' record on the trade charts February 16, staying on top six weeks. Ken Nelson was fit to be tied, sparking a short-lived feud between him and Randy Wood, which may have influenced Dot's decision to shelve Mac's version of "Gone."

At age ninety-three, Ken Nelson related his side of the story: "I had so much faith in the record ('Young Love'), I put it on rush release. We recorded it in October, disc jockeys received it in November and in December it was number one on the country chart [actually it wasn't number one country until February 2, 1957, but indeed first charted *Billboard*, December 22, 1956].

"In those days, it was quite common for record companies to cover a hit record; that is, to rush out their own version in hopes of cashing in on it. Randy Wood, owner of Dot Records, immediately covered the song, recording it with Tab Hunter, a movie actor. He copied our arrangement to a T. In 1957, both records became number one on the country charts at the same time [not so, Mr. Hunter charted only pop and R&B]. Sonny's version also became number one on the pop chart and Hunter's version number six on the pop chart [as noted above, Hunter's version succeeded James as a pop number one]. Both records combined sold about five million copies."

Apparently Nelson got back at Wood in 1957, when Dot's near-chart-topper "A Fallen Star" was racing up the country chart starting May 20, until Capitol's Ferlin Husky cut entered the chart July 1, 1957, spending thirteen weeks on the *Billboard* list, peaking at number eight. Newman's disc spent twenty-one weeks peaking number two, but also crossed over to Top Twenty pop. Incidentally, Husky's crossover smash "Gone," number one on 1957 country charts ten weeks, is regarded by many music historians as the first Nashville Sound country style cut bordering on pop, replete with background chorus and pop-oriented instrumentation. It was this uptown country mix that helped reignite country sales.

Backing Mac's recording of "Gone," Barney Kessel and Jack Marshall were on guitars, Dick Shanahan supplied drums and the Jack Halloran Singers added harmonies, under the production wand of Billy Vaughn. Rounding out his trio of tracks was "Sundown," co-written by Paul Keys and Mac, with the uptempo "Step It Up and Go" derived from rootsy blues guitarist Blind Boy Fuller.

As 1956 rolled along, Wiseman was growing weary of the early morning shows and touring grind, and decided to disband, ending his WRVA-Richmond association in October. About that time, Mac recalls a life-changing call: "Now Randy used to phone me every Sunday night wherever I was, just to keep up-to-date. One night he called, after I had just quit the station. I was just burned out, as we had worked so many shows all those years. Right then he said, 'How would you like to come out to California and build me a Country & Western department?' I damned near dropped the phone!

"By the mid-'50s, rock and roll and rockabilly were taking over with Presley, Cash and new guys like that. We were used to going out with four or five-pieces to play schools and theaters and drew tremendous crowds. But with TV so strong, the little single act day was gone. It got to where folks weren't going to miss *I Love Lucy* on the tube, to come out and see our little show. Back in the heyday of country, we could draw as many people as any other act, and I say that with as much modesty as I can muster. But it seemed like it wasn't going to exist anymore," continues Wiseman, who remembers Randy's prophecy, "There will be no more country music as we know it."

Rock & Roll was raking in all the dough at the box office, a fact Randy was faced with, but he was determined Dot should go with the flow. In the studio Mac encountered material reflecting the times, as he recorded the titles "Teen-Age Hangout," "Because We're Young" and "Shame, Shame, Shame," April 12, 1957 at Radio Recorders. These were far from the artist's usual acoustic-oriented ballads, and not unexpectedly some fans criticized this change of pace. "Shame, Shame, Shame" was unissued until Bear Family leased the masters for its "Tis Sweet To Be Remembered" 2003 box set.

Later, Wiseman learned that DJs, notably in the South, tossed "Teen-Age Hangout" and "I Hear You Knockin'," into the waste-basket: "They did, but I'd developed a Northern market that was playing that kind of music, which off-set that other market loss and even helped broaden my scope."

Enough so that Mac found himself playing a sock hop in Minneapolis for a benefit sharing the marquee with pop acts Andy Williams ("Butterfly") and Elaine Rodgers ("Miracle of Love").

Mac's decision to tackle the A&R chief position was further influenced when Randy said he could play concerts, as long as it didn't interfere with his day job: "The way it worked, I was to go out there to stay about a year or two, to learn the inner workings of the label, while returning to Nashville to record, then finally come back to Nashville to open their branch office."

Wood assured Wiseman that he was the man in charge of his department: "He said, 'If I've got to tell you what to do, I don't need you.' That's the kind of trust he put in me. That first day I was at Dot in L.A., come lunchtime, Billy Vaughn and I went into a place popular at the time, Hamburger Dan's, next door.

Dot's publicity shot of Mac.

It's where everybody hung out. As we were coming in, Rex Allen was coming out and we stopped to chat. He was guest hosting Spade Cooley's show that day and asked me to come over to Riverside Rancho, where they were doing the show; it's a freeway now. So the first night I was there, I was guesting on television."

For Dot, Mac produced his first album on bluegrass duo Reno & Smiley, April 15, 1957, titled "Sweethearts in Heaven." He recalled, "I had heard that one as a Buck Owens' cut (1956). It was our lead off single. I sang with them, the third part on several tracks. One in particular was 'Where Did Our Young Years Go?' Bobby Osborne called me one time to ask who was that singing the high part, and when I told him, he said, I knew it was you. Reno had been with Monroe when I was with the Blue Grass Boys. I wasn't all that acquainted with Smiley, but he and I became good friends. After Don and Red split, I booked Red and his new band on shows."

Mac reiterates mainstream country radio wasn't programming a lot of blue-grass music then: "Probably one of the reasons country radio didn't program more bluegrass-style music wasn't because they were discriminating, but they associated it primarily with Bill Monroe and Carter Stanley. Both were quite popular at that time and both sang nasally, so often their words were indistinguishable, and most of the time played so damn fast you couldn't catch them for years."

Dot, in fact, didn't sign a lot of bluegrass acts - Reno & Smiley being the ex-ception - though the label prided itself on its diversity. They were Mac's pals.

"I also produced a lot of Tommy Jackson's instrumental albums at Dot, and he had played on a good number of my records. One thing I did that pleased him very much was after we had recorded all the old fiddle tunes Tommy knew, I had a good friend, who was president of BMI-Toronto named Harold Moon, who gave me some good fiddlin' tunes for Tommy to cut that were popular, but not well-known in the states. Among these were 'Whiskey Before Breakfast,' 'White Water Jig' and 'Grandma's Chickens.' The fiddle was very popular in Canada, and those tunes Tommy cut, I got the U.S. publishing on them."

Another production angle Mac approached while A&R for Dot, was welcom-ing prominent DJs into the studio, who felt they had talent: "We produced records on T. Tommy Cutrer (KWKH-Shreveport) and Bob Jennings (WLAC-Nashville), who were among the top DJs in their respective areas at the time. That also may have made them more receptive to playing Dot records when they received them."

Mac also got a taste of TV while at Dot on the West Coast. On *The Town Hall Party* out of Compton, Merle Travis and Johnny Bond were pals Mac shared the stage with: "We were a three-hour live TV show and because of union rules had to take a ten-minute break on the hour and during that break Johnny Bond would do that bit trying to beat the clock, like on the game show (*Name That Tune*). Local merchants would donate silverware and such for gifts, and if we couldn't do sixteen bars of the songs requested among the three of us, they would win the prizes. But you know, they didn't win a helluva lot. It was just some kind of fun, and Merle and I had a thing going for years about that when he seen me, he would say 'I got one you don't know.' We did that every Saturday night as a side-set to *The Town Hall Party*. Johnny Bond was quite a humorist, in a very subtle way, he was disarming and the most laid-back fellow you ever saw. He had been very popular working with Gene Autry (*Melody Ranch*), and was quite a songwriter ('I Wonder Where You Are Tonight') as well."

Merle himself had recalled in December 1979, "Remember Mac, when you, Johnny Bond and I called ourselves the 'Panel of Experts' on the old TV show *Town Hall Party*? (Host) Jay Stewart would announce that one of the three of us would know any old-timey song that the viewers would send in. The following week we'd line up and Jay would call out songs. Johnny knew an awful lot of them. I knew one once in a while. But you, you rascal, proved that you knew more old songs than anybody I've ever met!"

Mac emphasizes *Town Hall Party* was a good show with a big cast: "It was the hottest thing in L.A. at the time. Tex Ritter was on it, Skeets McDonald, Eddie Dean, Lefty Frizzell, Rose Lee & Joe Maphis, great musicians, and a couple of kids, Lorrie & Larry Collins (whose hits included teen titles like 'Beetle Bug Bop')... Johnny Cash had a crush on Lorrie.

"I remember that Ricky Nelson also had eyes on the little girl and used to come hang out at our show, to be around her." [As a result, teen-aged Lorrie landed a recurring role as Ricky's girlfriend on the popular family TV series *The Adventures of Ozzie & Harriet.* Larry Collins went on to become a successful songwriter with hits such as "Delta Dawn" and "You're the Reason God Made Oklahoma."]

"Regarding Joe and Rose Lee, their family and mine got together and would have barbecues and things like that while we were in California. Nice people. Of course, Joe's now gone (1986), and it was sad their son Dale died so young."

Although a great opportunity with Dot, Wiseman was frustrated at the growing lack of airplay for country. Among other country acts he worked with on Dot were Leroy Van Dyke, Leon McAuliffe, The Sunshine Boys, Jimmy Work and Jimmy C. Newman. The latter artist enjoyed a string of Top Ten tunes for Dot, notably "Cry, Cry Darlin'" and "A Fallen Star," also a pop success. Mac co-produced Bonnie Guitar, whose biggest seller was the crossover hit "Dark Moon," and she also would produce him for Dot, making her a pioneer among female producers.

"I recall recording Bobby Bare, working all night at a studio in Bakersfield owned by Lewis Talley and Fuzzy Owen (credited as co-writers on the number one song 'Dear John' with Billy Barton)... never did get a keeper so-to-speak," muses Mac. "The next morning we went quail hunting. It was so damn foggy, you could see the quail running on the ground, but was so thick they wouldn't fly. We just followed them around and waited for their take off. About mid-morning when the fog lifted, we got some hunting in."

Mac remembers advising Bare not to sign with a particular label that made an offer, and as a result he was ready when RCA pitched him an offer, leading to his "Detroit City" smash. Yet another promising newcomer, Buck Owens of Bakersfield, wanted Mac to sign him to Dot. He had just placed one of the songs he'd co-written, with Decca, "Mommy For a Day," giving Kitty Wells a 1959 Top Five, and himself scored a minor success on the indie Pep Records with "Sweethearts in Heaven."

Wiseman adds: "Yeah, Buck came to my office at Hollywood & Vine, wanting me to record him. I told him if I did, he'd just be coming back in six months or so, mad at us because nothing was happening. He told me he'd been to see Ken Nelson who was on the fence at the time about signing him, so I told Buck, 'You go talk to him and tell him if he don't sign you, I will. That'll make him get off the fence, but if he don't, I'll be glad to sign you.' As we know, he signed with Capitol Records, the start of an ultra-successful recording career. Buck reminded me a number of times in the dressing rooms where we were about that, and it made me feel good."

The former A&R leader also recalls having tried to interest Randy in signing hot newcomer Johnny Cash, fresh from his Sun Records introductory rockabilly hits, but the fly-in-the-ointment there was Cash wanted ten thousand dollars up front: "He was well worth that, but it turned out Randy had just turned down a similar sum for Frankie Laine [who had numerous pop million-sellers including 'Jezebel,' but his career was on the downslide], and he didn't think it would be right. That was a big disappointment for me. In retrospect, I've read (bassist) Marshall Grant's book and I couldn't have put up with his drug problem back then. I believe Marshall's book, because he was right on about so many things with which I was familiar. So maybe Randy's decision was a blessing in disguise. Signing him might have ended the friendship I enjoyed with Johnny all those years."

While on the West Coast, Mac appeared regularly on *The Town Hall Party* and Tex's syndicated *Ranch Party*. It provided him a good opportunity to plug Dot's 1957 release of Mac's first full-length LP (album), "'Tis Sweet To Be Remembered," a compilation of previous singles.

Mac with good buddy Tex Ritter.

"In 1957, while working with Dot, I was glued to the radio listening to the World Series games between the Milwaukee Braves and New York Yankees, and in that particular series, Lew Burdette was pitching for the Braves, and won three complete World Series games [pitching two shut-outs, earning the year's Most Valuable Player award]. The Braves beat New York to win their only series pennant.

"As I sat in Hollywood listening to that third game, I thought, if he won this game, I'm going to record him. Now I'd never heard him sing, but I figured him being from West Virginia [actually Nitro, West Virginia], he could sing a little. To give you an example of how efficient his manager was, I tried to reach Lew in New York shortly after the game, but with all the celebration going on was unable to get him, but left a message.

"Much to my surprise, at midnight the same night, his manager called to see what I had wanted - me being from Dot Records. The following season, every time the Milwaukee Braves came to L.A. to play the Dodgers, Lew and Warren Spahn both came to my office to spend some time. By then, I had recorded Lew. We did a song that Cowboy Copas had, titled 'Three Strikes and You're Out' and on the flip-side we put 'Mary Lou,' as Lew's wife was named Mary. After Lew retired and went to Florida, he coached Little League teams and whenever I came into the area, he'd call and come to see me."

Mac smiles recalling Dot had a publicist, who on the slightest news peg had Mac featured in the *Hollywood Reporter, Daily Variety* or the *Los Angeles Times* newspapers: "That gal knew how to get us in the columns."

There was also a Hollywood agent adamant about trying to talk Wiseman into working as a supporting actor in movies: "He called me an Edgar Buchanan-type. I think Jonesy, our p.r. lady, gave him the idea, as she hoped to get some press on it in the trades."

From the deep recesses of his memory bank, Mac emphasizes there were also things he did that he'd certainly not want the public or Randy Wood aware of, especially back then: "I remember one time at the Plaza Hotel in Hollywood. Tex Ritter and I would always have a little drink to take the chill off. Now believe me, Tex would scare you to death driving sober, but one time I was into my cups and he said, 'I'll drive you home.' Well he pulled up to this place and a Spanish lady came to the window, and Tex said, 'How are you Mamacita ('Little Mother')? Have you got a bottle for me?' Well, he pulled up to the Plaza to let me out on Sunset Strip. He jumped out of the car to let me out, and I said, 'Damn Tex, I think I'm gonna be sick!' Well I run over to this spot, and all I remember was there were lots of pine trees, and I let go! Well, Tex got me up to my room at the Plaza and put me to bed.

"I saw Tex six months or so later, and asked, 'Where did you take me that I got sick?' He said we went to Nicodels, a popular watering hole. He lived in the San Fernando Valley, and this guy lived on the corner by Tex's house, 'That night after I got you to your hotel, I 'transplanted' a tree in my neighbor's yard!' Dorothy, Tex's wife, was upset, and wanted to know who he'd been out with drinking. 'Now Texas Bill Strength (Minnesota DJ) can't come to my house because of you. I told her it was him.' I also knew Texas Bill Strength from the Flame Club in Minneapolis. Bill was the one who initiated booking big names in there. I think Tex was the first and I was the second one he booked. They asked him 'What kind of cowboy is Wiseman?' Bill said, 'He's a Jewish cowboy, *Weismann*!'"

As A&R honcho in L.A., Mac aided Randy in getting back at the Auerbach brothers, Jean and Julian, the publishers who broke a promise earlier to Dot: "The Hill & Range brothers whom Randy fell out with because of the screwing they gave us with 'These Hands' supposedly giving us an exclusive, then gave three other guys the same exclusive. When I went out to L.A., they came up to me trying to get back in with Dot, and so I let them make their pitch, and they later sent me a contract from New York. Well, I never signed it or sent it back. It was a pretty good deal, best I can remember. I mean they were offering me pretty good money to get the songs on top. But it remained in my drawer."

It was in 1957 that Wood had actually sold Dot to Paramount for three million dollars, but he was retained as label president for another decade. That gave him the opportunity to engage the label talent he had full confidence in, and obviously Wiseman was at the top of his list, having just released his first LP.

"At Dot, mostly I had the authority, the ability, the privilege of signing anybody, recording them and releasing it, but that's where it stopped," continues Wiseman. "You'd ship it to radio and, hell, you couldn't get it played. We couldn't tell if the people liked the records or not, because you couldn't get any concentrated action in markets like Pittsburgh or Dallas, places like that."

Then at one point, Mac had an opportunity of leasing Four-Star Records music: "That would've given us a helluva catalog, but Randy wouldn't have anything to do with the label's Bill McCall, who had a reputation of exploiting his artists and their songs in a negative way that enriched McCall."

During that turbulent time for indie labels, however, Mac says Dot began buying masters to regional hits, such as the Dell-Vikings' "Come Go With Me," Mickey Gilley's "Call Me Shorty" and Ned Miller's self-penned "From A Jack To A King" obtained from Fabor Robison's Fabor label: "These were songs that might break out regionally, and we felt had the potential to hit nationally."

Another such song was Jimmy Newman's "Cry, Cry Darling," a hit in the Southwest. Jimmy became the biggest hit-maker for Dot's country division, thanks to additional singles "Blue Darlin'," "Seasons Of My Heart" and "A Fallen Star." He first came to Dot in 1954, after Wood bought the "Cry, Cry Darling" master from Khoury Records in Louisiana.

According to Newman, "When I came to Nashville, I started with Fred Rose and he produced my first session, I believe, at his home studio. How it all came about was due to my signature song 'Cry, Cry Darling.' Released first by Khoury, it was an unbelievable hit for me down in Louisiana, and Dot bought it up. I wrote the song, but J. D. Miller added a chorus and there went half the song. During the early 1950s, J.D. and I were with Feature, an independent label, which didn't have much success.

"Then George Khoury out of Lake Charles offered me a deal to write a couple of songs and record them. I did them at J. D. Miller's studio in Crowley. J.D. had the Nashville connection with Murray Nash, one of those guys who traveled around for a publishing company, and Murray got us hooked up to Acuff-Rose. That's how all that came about.

Jimmy C. Newman and Mac.

"Fred Rose got me my contract with Dot. I thought I was going with Hickory Records [Acuff-Rose's own label], which first had a success with 'Good Deal, Lucille' (by Al Terry, 1954). But I guess Fred liked Dot's distribution better. Big labels like RCA, Columbia and Capitol had the major distribution deals, as they were firmly entrenched.

"Every time I'd start to think about going with a major label, Randy would talk me out of it. He'd say, 'Let's do another album.' We had some good hits like 'Daydreaming,' 'Blue Darlin',' 'Seasons Of My Heart' and yeah I had a Top Ten with 'God Was So Good,' which has J.D.'s wife's name - Georgia - as its writer, but it wasn't a big seller for us. Now 'A Fallen Star' written by James Joiner was big in both country and pop (Number two, 1957). It had a good song on the flip-side, 'I Can't Go On This Way,' which had been a hit years before for Bob Wills (number four, 1946), written by Fred Rose. I was a big Bob Wills' fan."

Being a Louisiana native, Jimmy was well versed in the musical sounds that emanate from the Bayou country along with Creole-based, Cajun-influenced Zydeco. As a result of his unique talents, upon joining the Opry, Jimmy added a "C" to his name, indicative of his performing Cajun country music. "A Fallen Star" was not in this vein.

"My record of 'A Fallen Star' would have been an even bigger seller if Capitol hadn't covered us with Ferlin Husky's recording. Well, Ferlin and I were good friends, and he just had a smash recording 'Gone,' which was equally big on the pop charts. I also knew Buddy Killen well, who had just started working with Jack Stapp who ran Tree Music. I said, 'Buddy, do you have one of those songs like 'Gone'? I think I could sing one of those type tunes.'

"That was on Saturday night at the Opry and he said, 'Come over Monday. I think I may have one to play for you, and that's how 'A Fallen Star' came my way. Now let me explain, after 'Gone' was such a big hit for Capitol, they had no other 'Gone' type song for Ferlin to follow up on... Now the way I heard it is the labels were feuding. Randy had covered Capitol's Sonny James' hit 'Young Love,' by having film star Tab Hunter record it on Dot. Remember? That cut into Sonny's sales, and Ken Nelson was rarin' to get back at Randy. Capitol had great distribution and they could sell a lot of records. When my record came out on 'A Fallen Star,' Capitol rushed out a cover by Ferlin and they sold a bunch, but I still beat them. Back then there were a lot of cover records released, so it was pretty common. You don't see that as much today. Throughout all that, Ferlin and I remained good friends."

It was during his final year with Dot that Randy had Mac produce Jimmy, who regarded Mac as bluegrass: "Back then bluegrass was Bill Monroe period, and he was on the Opry. Mac and I became friends, but we didn't work a lot together. He was A&R for our session, which was in 1957 or 1958, and we did four songs. It was pretty much the end of my career at Dot Records, though Randy tried another record on me, Jim Reeves' 'Need Me,' but that didn't work either."

Newman chuckled when asked if Wiseman was stern in the studio: "I don't know that Mac would be a hard man to deal with anywhere." Jimmy went on to enjoy further hit singles for both MGM and Decca Records, including "You're Makin' a Fool Out Of Me," "A Lovely Work of Art," "DJ For a Day," "Artificial Rose" and "Back Pocket Money." The half-Cajun Louisiana native specialized in novelty numbers like "Alligator Man," "Bayou Talk" and "Louisiana Saturday Night."

Hank Locklin, of "Please Help Me, I'm Falling" fame, might take issue with Newman on Wiseman being so easy-going. As Mac recalls, "We were playing in the states and also had some scattered bookings in Canada. Well, I decided to drive up there to the next gigs because we had cleared the customs, and cleared all the product, and wasn't looking forward to going back through customs again. Well, Hank was on this tour with us and elected to ride with me. After driving many hard miles over less-than-first-rate roads, I was thinking maybe I should've gone back into the U.S. which had better roads. But, what I didn't need was Hank's continuous bitching about my decision. Finally,

Hank Locklin and Mac.

when he said once more how we should have used U.S. roads, I said, 'Look, you S.O.B., this is my car and you asked to ride with me! If you don't shut the hell up,

I'll stop this car and leave you on the side of the road to fend for yourself!' Well, that shut him up the rest of the way."

For his one 1958 session at Castle Studios, with Mac at the helm, Jimmy C. recorded the following numbers: "With Tears In My Eyes," "Step Aside Shallow Water (Let the Deep Sea Roll)," "Carry On" and "Bop-A-Hula."

As producer and artist, Mac himself commuted between L.A. and Nashville on a regular basis. It was August 20, 1957, that Mac re-recorded "'Tis Sweet To Be Remembered" and "I'll Still Write Your Name in the Sand," capturing those gems with a pop flavoring, at Radio Recorders Studio.

While out on the West Coast, the Wisemans rented a bungalow with three bedrooms: "We were about ten miles south of L.A. in a new township called Santa Fe Springs, next to Whittier. I think my daughter Sheila had just started school, and she and her sister Chris seemed to like it fine. What was good is that my wife Emma's old girlfriend, with whom she went to school, also lived out there. That gave her a good friend to help occupy her free time.

Emma and daughters Chris and Sheila.

"*The Town Hall Party*, which I worked, was about ten to fifteen miles from where we lived," Mac continued. "Man, I even went to a gym nearby and lost fifty pounds. The fellow, who instructed there, was a boxer and he helped strengthen my polio leg. It enabled me to go hunting with my buddies for quail and deer, and I was able to keep up with walking up and down the terrain."

During his September 1957 session, Mac recorded two new numbers, "A Promise of Things To Come" and "Thinkin' About You," that were special. Mac says, "That's the first song Fred Carter, dad to Deana Carter (of 'Strawberry Wine' fame) had written - 'Thinkin' About You' - and I cut it; and 'A Promise of Things To Come' was by a New York songwriter, Aaron Schroeder. It was interesting to me that they knew enough about me to let me record their songs. Schroeder said he was surprised that I used a double rhythm on his song, which I worked out with Billy. Another thing I learned with Billy was how he mixed the harmony above the lead. Again, it's a feel and not an obvious thing. I used that on our Tommy Jackson sessions after that."

Regarding Vaughn, Mac smilingly admits, "I wasn't sure what Billy meant when he said, 'You have amazing intonation.' Later, I learned that was a nice compliment."

Wiseman's final recording stint for 1957, in October, assembled for a single track, the vintage W. Lee (Pappy) O'Daniel song "Put Me in Your Pocket," a song dealing with a soldier's girl giving him her picture to carry in battle. That recording may have been for a split session in which Mac produced another artist, as he did on February 21, 1958, when he cut the public domain ballad "When the Work's All Done This Fall." Carl T. Sprague adapted that song for his August 1925 recording from an old cowboy ballad "After the Roundup" by Western writer D. J. O'Malley in 1893, concerning cattle drovers. Backing Mac in the Gold Star Recording Studios were Joe Maphis, guitar; Pee Wee Adams, bass; Jimmy Pruitt, piano; and Skeets McDonald, guitar.

Reflecting the changing musical tide, artists like Webb Pierce and Hank Snow weren't topping the charts in 1958, quite so regularly. Meantime, Elvis Presley's bombastic "Jailhouse Rock" did, and was followed by additional number ones, "Don't" and "Hard-Headed Woman." Elvis took his cuts into the country, pop and R&B charts. Another newcomer, Johnny Cash, set country's woods a-fire with "Ballad Of a Teen-Age Queen" and "Guess Things Happen That Way," both written by Jack Clement.

Mac has recalled having missed out on some classic country songs over the years, including "Wedding Bells" and "You Pass Me By," both recorded by a pair of Hanks, before Mac landed a label: "Claude Boone offered 'Wedding Bells' and taught it to me when I was with Molly O'Day, before Hank Williams cut it (number two, 1949); and 'You Pass Me By' was pitched to me by Eddie Nesbitt, who said he was a fan of my singing. Hank Snow recorded it (as B side to his number one 'Rhumba Boogie,' 1951). Claude bought 'Wedding Bells' from Arthur Q. (Pritchett) Smith in Knoxville. He's the fella that sold songs cheap."

Two of the biggest country cuts of 1959 had crossover appeal, indicative of the times: "The Battle of New Orleans," recorded by Johnny Horton; and "The Three Bells," a former French hit originally cut by Edith Piaf and *Les Compagnons de la Chanson* and a.k.a. "The Jimmy Brown Song." Both of those country hits also became number one pop.

Although Mac wasn't a pal to Horton, he did know The Browns pretty well: "I remember one time when Ferlin and I were on tour with Martha Carson, each with our own bands. We had done a show in Missouri and drove all night to Lake Charles, Louisiana, getting there just at daylight. Everyone was beat and went to their rooms to rest. Not Ferlin and I. We rented a boat and went fishing all day. That night after the concert, we left, headed back towards Nashville. When we got to Pine Bluff, Arkansas, about two a.m., we found this all-night diner open. When we got settled in there with the musicians, somebody remarked that this was The Browns (Maxine, Jim Ed and Bonnie) hometown. Their father used to grow watermelons there as I recall. Well, Ferlin said we ought to call them up. We did and would you believe all three of them came out to visit with us."

Wiseman volunteers yet another Husky story: "This one happened in Canada. Ferlin had worked the Edison Hotel in Toronto, and I was across town at the Horseshoe Club. Both booked acts a week at a time. Ferlin's gig ended an hour before my set was finished. So he came over to the Horseshoe and when I was done we'd go party a little. One night, Ferlin was a bit in his cups, so he wanted to go to Chinatown and eat at Lichee's Gardens, a leading restaurant with wonderful food. After we were seated, Ferlin ordered a chaser and pulled out a bottle he had; however, they were slow bringing it, so he reached over and chased his drink with Soy Sauce! I almost lost my lunch, when I saw that! Ferlin was really a funny guy."

Another "road story" came to mind, regarding a ten-day tour in the Canadian Maritime Provinces. Next up, Mac had a club booked in New Jersey, before proceeding on to a weekend spot at WRVA-Richmond: "We drove all night to get to that gig in New Jersey, only to find when we got there the club had burned down! That had never happened to me before, but it happened again for a later show scheduled in Omaha, Nebraska. We checked into the hotel and before show time, the club had caught on fire! But that time Mack Sanders (Omaha station KOOO) rebooked us into another venue."

Mac recalls that after a week's booking in Ontario, they were returning for the WRVA *Barn Dance*, traveling in his new Mercury towards Buffalo, New York.

"That was a beautiful car, a sea-green color, with white and red upholstery. Well, just before we came to the Canadian-American border, we hit a bump and my car quit, as though somebody had shot the engine dead. My bandsmen and I pushed the Mercury across the border into Buffalo. First thing we saw open at the end of the bridge was a service station. It was in the wee hours of the morning, but fortunately there was a mechanic on duty.

"After he examined the engine, it was determined when we hit that bump it cracked the rotary button. There was no place open to buy a part. After pondering our situation awhile, we took a fiddle string and wrapped it around that cracked rotary, and that damned thing held all the way to Richmond, and we were in time to play the *Barn Dance!*"

But that wasn't Mac's only problem with his new Mercury on that trip: "About forty or fifty miles outside Richmond, we pulled into a service station to gas up, and since we were going right back to Canada, I hadn't changed my currency. So in paying the attendant, I mistakenly had Canadian dollars in with my American money, giving him the Canadian bucks. Well, he grumbled, 'What kinda damn phony money is this?' Of course, we collected enough American dollars to take care of the charges."

As though bad times come in threes, the next morning - Sunday - Mac received a call from sister Virginia saying their mom was in the hospital: "Oh, it wasn't death-threatening, but I thought I'd best drive over to see her and find out how she was doing. Approximately thirty miles out of Richmond, riding on a two-lane highway, I rear-ended another car and tore up the front end of my Mercury.

"I thought to call the Mercury dealership and had the car towed back to Richmond. My salesman came down with several mechanics that Sunday afternoon to repair the vehicle. They got it all patched up with a new hood, radio, and everything, except they didn't have time to paint the hood. So there I was driving my Mercury back to Canada with a new brown hood on it. That was an eventful weekend, believe me."

Still ahead for Mac after he relocated back to Nashville was another hit single: "I came back and had our offices out in Gallatin and worked the town here, making the rounds of the publishers, seeking material, not only for my artists, but for his pop artists as well. Pat Boone was probably the biggest, but he wasn't that big to start with. Randy had to nurture him and bring him along. He never did get Pat to stop hissing his S's or popping his P's. But man, he sold records. When he released his 'Love Letters in the Sand,' it sold so well, we re-released mine and got another success out of that."

112

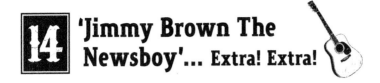

14 'Jimmy Brown The Newsboy'... Extra! Extra!

"My mother always tells me, sir/I've nothing in the world to lose
I'll get a place in Heaven, sir/Selling the 'Gospel News'...
I sell the morning paper, sir/My name is Jimmy Brown
Everybody knows that I'm the newsboy of the town..."

"When we started the Country Music Association (CMA) in 1958, there were only about one hundred and fifty stations in the entire U.S. playing any country, and I don't mean full-time stations. Some were programming it early mornings or on Saturday, whatever," explains Mac Wiseman, who cites then-prominent rock and rockabilly. That small number of stations was down reportedly from an earlier peak of some one thousand, five hundred country-oriented stations.

Country had been termed "hillbilly" music, but troupers like Ernest Tubb began feeling that was derogatory and didn't take into consideration the strides made by the genre. Substituted names were folk, then country, and later broadening it to cover Western-themed songs, it became Country & Western (C&W). Rhythm & Blues crossover star Ray Charles latched onto Don Gibson's "I Can't Stop Loving You" in 1961, recorded it, making it number one in both Pop and R&B, while some reviewers even labeled it Jazz.

According to a column in publisher Charlie Lamb's *Music Reporter* magazine, in the wake of Ray Charles' smash, the writer mused, "Guess what, man? It's hillbilly music. Originally the music came from the hills, but it belongs to anyone who wants to sing it or listen to it. Hillbilly music is just a handle... true, it is outdated. If it hurts, call it country music, or call it folk music, or just alphabet soup. Just never forget, the music's 'hillbilly' heritage."

As if lack of airplay weren't enough of a problem for promoting country music in 1958, rock 'n' roll DJ Alan Freed opened the floodgates when in Boston he railed against the law coming down on broadcasters, spearheading a "payola" scandal. That term, concocted by combining pay and Victrola (a vintage term for record players), referred to record labels enriching "jocks" who played specific singles, generating higher trade chart numbers and subsequently better record sales. Reports indicate certain country promoters weren't above such wheeling and dealing, and in some instances offered an influential DJ a portion of a song's future royalties to ensure success.

"Randy would fire a man in a minute, if he thought one of his people were involved in that sort of stuff," stresses Wiseman. "His handling of the Four-Star leasing proposal with Bill McCall, and not wanting to pay the ten thousand dollars advance to Johnny Cash, after turning down Frankie Laine, are good examples of his integrity."

Artist manager-musician Tillman Franks, whom Mac knew while both worked at KWKH-Shreveport, unabashedly admitted he was a "pioneer" in currying favor among radio announcers. At the outset of Webb Pierce's astounding career, Franks worked feverishly to promote Webb's first charting "Wondering" in 1951, noting: "Webb and I would go down to Del Rio, Texas, to see Paul Kallinger, who had a show on that powerful Mexico (border) station XERF. You could hear that station all over the world. Wayne Walker and I had written a song called 'Bow Thy Head' and I gave Paul half writer's credit to help me promote 'Wondering.' I told Paul he could get rich from the song, which was gospel, but he would have to play Webb's record at least twice each night and really brag on Webb as 'Mister Hit Maker.' Paul did it...

"Nelson King at WCKY-Cincinnati was one of the nation's top DJs at the time. I told him if he would make 'Wondering' by Webb number one within three weeks, I would give him fifty per cent of 'Three Ways Of Knowing.' I had just written it and put the publishing with Jimmie Davis, who took half the song (listing himself as a co-writer). I wrote the song and ended up with nothing from it (as Johnnie & Jack's RCA cut 'Three Ways of Knowing' became a 1952 Top Ten). Then Webb said, 'Go to Chicago and see Randy Blake (at the time, top DJ in the U.S.).' So the next day I flew to Chicago. I had written a tune that Webb later recorded, called 'I Haven't Got the Heart.' I gave Randy, whose real name was Harry Winston, half the writer's royalties of the song (which hit Top Five), to make 'Wondering' number one on his program. Within two weeks, I had the nation's number one and two DJs making 'Wondering' the number one song on their programs. (On March 1, 1952, the Decca release hit number one nationwide.)"

Tillman Franks had long been in Mac's corner, noting back in 2000, "There is no finer, crystal clear voice in country and bluegrass music than Mac Wiseman's. I have been a friend with Mac ever since he first came to the *Hayride* in the 1950s."

Wiseman, in turn, was wise to treat DJs on a more personal level, mainly inspired by a great respect for them, but obviously aware, too, that radio airplay was a necessity in making hit records. Having been an announcer himself, Mac recognized their role in the cycle, calling, writing or visiting stations whenever in the area. Like Webb and Mac, Sonny James was yet another artist who made a point of familiarizing himself with DJs and their families, and no doubt that helped Sonny become the first artist to score sixteen successive number one records, including "Running Bear," which Mac later recorded.

Dot made every effort to service the smaller stations, along with larger-watt broadcasters. Mac explained it to WSM's Eddie Stubbs: "If there were three disc jockeys (at a station), we'd send each one of them a record, and I called each one and wrote each one. It was very important. For example, a little jockey in Minnesota - I forget what town it was; it wasn't a leading city up there, a little 250-watt station - (where) I was playing some dates through there, and I heard about him, so I called him and sent him the record. Well, about five years or so later, he's the program director on the biggest station in Atlanta.

"He hadn't been getting any record serviced on that little 250-watt station up there - their feeling was he wasn't big enough for the record companies to fool with - but the fact that we were kind to him and sent him some programming material mattered. They'd sit there without a lot of records to play on those small stations, unless they went out and bought them themselves and they didn't have a budget for that. That's the reason I got my foot in the door with some of those Northern markets, and a lot of people didn't, because I catered to them you see, but it's always been a business to me. I had a mailing list that wouldn't quit... when it got too heavy, I'd farm it out on a temporary basis or whatever (to accomplish the mailings)."

Along about 1953, Nashville industry folk launched the first Country DJ Festival in Music City, as a means of thanking radio for its role in helping to popularize artists and songs. Co-founders included Chuck Chellman, Tom Perryman, Bill Lowery, Smokey Smith, Charlie Walker, Tom-Cat Reeder, Len Ellis, Cousin Ray Wolfenden, Ramblin' Lou Schriver and Charlie Lamb. This was unusual for a music genre to attempt, but proved to be a popular precedent.

Joe Allison was another who helped promote the Country Music DJ Association, which proved something of a role model and influence for the Country Music Association, founded in 1958. Allison, who wrote number one hits for Tex Ritter and Jim Reeves, was a DJ in Nashville when in 1952 he succeeded Tennessee Ernie Ford doing a daily radio program on KXLA-Los Angeles. He would also come to host ABC-TV's *Country America.*

Mac smiles in recalling a three-day party in Long Beach, put on by an all-country station, and co-hosted by Allison, Charlie Williams and Squeakin' Deacon (Carl Moore), DJs all. "Barbara Fairchild and I had been to this three-day affair and were flying back to Nashville. We were both beat, and she excused herself to go to the restroom. Well, she was gone so long, I was worried and I asked the stewardess to check on her. Barbara was sitting on the toilet where she had fallen asleep!"

Jim Reeves and Mac made a five-day tour including stops in Calgary, Stettler and Red Deer, and according to Mac, "He was a joy to work with. We were both carrying a band at the time. Neither of us had a bus at the time, and anyway back then the highways wouldn't rightly accommodate them. Years later, Jim and I were on the same package show in Hammond, Indiana, promoted by a local DJ, Uncle Len Ellis. Between the matinee and evening shows, Uncle Len, Jim and I went to dinner. I was sitting in the backseat and Jim in the front passenger seat, and most flatteringly he turned around and said to me, 'I don't do this to many people, but I just want you to know you're welcome at my house anytime you want to visit.' I was flattered because Jim's reputation was he didn't have parties or such social things going on."

When the Reeves plane crashed, Wiseman was at the Tennessee State Fairgrounds watching a NASCAR race, and it was announced over the loudspeaker they had located Jim's wrecked plane out in the Brentwood area. They had searched several days all over the surrounding area and hadn't yet spotted the wreckage: "Marty Robbins came to the officials and told them they were searching in the wrong area. He had been out in his yard after washing his hair and wanted rainwater to rinse it, and heard what he thought was a plane in trouble, sputtering, and indicated what part of Brentwood he thought might be the site.

"They subsequently looked where Marty indicated and found Jim's plane at the foot of a big tree where it apparently nose-dived in. There was a house just a few yards away and they didn't even hear the crash, due to the thunderstorm. I drove out there and was very saddened, of course, and especially so when I saw them put

115

what was left of the plane in the back of a pickup truck."

Wiseman always strived to attend the DJ conventions when available, nurturing relationships with those on the airwaves. It was easier after July 1958, when Mac reopened Dot's office in suburban Gallatin, keeping in mind that his daughters had to start a new school year in September. Plus it was a lot of fun and gave artists not only a chance to visit with the jocks on their own turf, but also to renew friendships with fellow performers in town for the event.

Many feel that DJ festival led to the eventual organizing of the CMA. Wiseman was also among its founding members, serving as first secretary-treasurer and also as an executive board member. Others giving an assist were behind-the-scenes honchos Jim Denny, Wesley Rose, Jack Stapp and Walter "Dee" Kilpatrick, each of whom kicked in one hundred dollars to help fund it. At their first meeting of the CMA Board of Directors in 1958, with Mac were Oscar Davis, Ernest Tubb, Ken Nelson, Wesley Rose, "Cracker Jim" Brooker, Vic McAlpin, Hubert Long, Harold Moon, Connie B. Gay, CMA's first president, and Charlie Lamb of *The Music Reporter*. At thirty-three, Mac was then the board's youngest member and ironically is now its sole surviving founding father.

Mac felt flattered to be invited to be part of the new project, as CMA's first Secretary-Treasurer, recognizing that it was due to his position with Dot: "It was touch and go for a time. I thought I could help by getting my buddies such as Marty Robbins, people like that, to join. But they felt they were doing well enough that they didn't want to fool with an association, wanting no part of it. I can't tell you how many board meetings we had where we passed the hat to take up a collection to pay the postage for our correspondence."

The lady who became the CMA's first permanent staffer, administrative secretary Jo Walker (now Walker-Meador), became a life-long friend to Wiseman. She later became its long-suffering Executive Director, and partially in payback an honored member of the Country Music Hall of Fame in 1995. When Mac's time elapsed as a board member representing a label, rules were finagled to allow Wiseman to continue serving, this time as an artist member - attesting to how high fellow officers regarded him and his input to this fledgling organization.

"Jo had been secretary to a lawyer who was a Tennessee Secretary of State (G. Edward Friar), and she confided that she knew nothing about country music when she was hired as the CMA's first full-time employee. She's since mentioned that I gave her a crash course in country music history, but she did more than anyone in expanding the CMA's growth, for under her leadership, we organized the Country Music Hall of Fame, Fan Fair, the annual awards program and promoted country music overseas."

According to Jo, "I had never even been to the *Grand Ole Opry*. I'd heard of Minnie Pearl, Roy Acuff, Ernest Tubb and Hank Williams, but I didn't delineate the different styles because I didn't think about country music, and that was fine with those who offered me the job. They had already formed a board of directors, and didn't care to hire someone who wanted to be a singer or songwriter, but someone as an administrator, someone who could set up an office and do all the behind-the-scenes work. The first executive director was Harry Stone, formerly manager of the Opry and vice president of WSM radio, but he was only at CMA a short while mainly because they didn't have enough money to pay both salaries. Since my salary was much less, I was the one who got to remain."

It wasn't until 1961 that the CMA inaugurated the Country Music Hall of Fame, posthumously inducting its first members, ironically songwriters all: Singers Jimmie Rodgers, Hank Williams and music publisher Fred Rose. King of Country Music Roy Acuff became the first living artist inducted in 1962, and oddly enough no new inductee was named in 1963, with the CMA claiming not enough votes.

Meanwhile, waiting in the wings to be inducted were such 1920s' pioneer names as Vernon Dalhart, Ernest Stoneman, Uncle Art Satherley and The Carter Family, all voted in much later, though they were pioneers whose achievements more than qualified them for induction. Then, of course, there were additional veterans Monroe, Pee Wee King, Jimmie Davis, Gene Autry, Patsy Montana, Red Foley, John Lair and Lulu Belle & Scotty, but they had to wait, and sad to say Lair and his WLS-Chicago discoveries Lulu Belle & Scotty are still waiting. They are now deceased.

The Country Music Association, more than three decades after the first country recording success, hasn't escaped some finger pointing. Reportedly, Country Music Hall of Fame members were initially anointed by a secret panel of a hundred industry stalwarts, but now numbers some three hundred, most of whom seem not cognizant of number one artists of yesteryear, including Al Dexter, Elton Britt, Jimmy Wakely, Hank Locklin, Skeeter Davis, Johnnie & Jack and Dottie West, all yet to be inducted.

Mac Wiseman resigned from that secret committee when he discovered co-members unaware of the accomplishments of 1960s' pop-country phenomenon Brenda Lee, pondering, "What the hell are they doing serving on that panel?"

Still younger fans like TwinPaula7, who via *U-Tube* posted this comment upon listening to Mac sing "Shackles and Chains" (with the Osborne Brothers) on an Internet website: "Wow! Was there ever any artist who could sing a song like Mac does this one? I cry each time I listen to this song, but the legendary artist is one whom I could listen to every day. Mac's wonderful distinctive voice is such a treat. The Osbornes are great accompanying him."

As Mac points out, the CMA sponsored the first Country Music Hall of Fame inductions in 1961, with the first three being deceased artists: singer-songwriter Jimmie Rodgers, who died in 1933; Fred Rose, a singer-songwriter-producer-publisher who died in 1954; and his artist-writer protégé Hank Williams, who died in 1953. No one could quibble with their selection, nor the sole honoree in '62, Roy Acuff.

Additionally in 1967, the CMA started its annual awards program that eventually would become a televised ratings winner, and its very first Entertainer of the Year was Eddy Arnold, thanks to his country-pop crossover hits "Lonely Again" and "Turn The World Around." This came a year after his induction into the Country Music Hall of Fame, an honor usually bestowed on artists past their prime. Oddly enough, Ernest (Pop) Stoneman, a 1920s breakthrough artist, earned the first CMA vocal group award with his family group, The Stonemans, marking a comeback for Pop. Stoneman died the following year at seventy-five. Despite having been a star at the Bristol Recording Sessions in 1927, which

117

marked the first field recordings for newcomers Jimmie Rodgers and The Carter Family, Stoneman wasn't inducted into the Country Music Hall of Fame until 2008, forty years after his death.

A Carter Family's success brought Mac back into the winner's circle, A.P.'s tearjerker "Jimmie Brown the Newsboy." Dot changed its spelling from Jimmie to Jimmy for whatever reason. Recorded March 23, 1959, Mac went into the studio primarily to do covers for Dot, none of which were expected to even chart. Yet that particular single hit Top Five on *Billboard's* country chart for Mac on October 26, 1959, charting a grand total of twenty weeks, as the public responded in a big way, prompting DJs to spin the requested disc.

Reportedly, Carter adapted his version from a nineteenth century public domain ballad by Will S. Hays, who also composed "The Little Old Cabin in the Lane" recorded in 1923 by Fiddlin' John Carson, meaning "Jimmie Brown" dates back to 1875.

"LITTLE JIMMY BROWN, THE NEWSBOY"

MACWISEMAN

Mac's fluid vocalizing wrapped itself around such mournful lyrics as, *"I sell the morning paper, sir, my name is Jimmy Brown/Everybody knows that I'm the newsboy of the town/You can hear me yelling 'Morning Star,' as I run along the street/I've got no hat upon my head,* no shoes upon my feet/I sell the morning paper, sir, my name is Jimmy Brown/Everybody knows that I'm the newsboy of the town..."

As Mac's single climbed to number nine on the Top Ten charts of *The Music Reporter*, Faron Young's "Country Girl" topped the list October 26, 1959. Another Dot chart entry was Wink Martindale's "Deck of Cards," number four. Meanwhile, Mac's single on *Billboard* that same week hit number five, while Wink's record stalled at number eleven on that chart. A former DJ, Martindale generated much fanfare hosting the TV game show *Tic-Tac-Dough*.

"You know, Chet played some fabulous guitar on that session," boasts Mac. Chet, of course, in that same time frame, produced The Browns' mega-hit "The Three Bells," charting *Billboard* a week before "Jimmy Brown The Newsboy." Mac's hit song charted twenty weeks, a week longer than The Browns' disc.

"I learned that their song was actually subtitled *The Ballad of Jimmy Brown* and that caused confusion," muses Mac. "People would come lookin' for my record 'Jimmy Brown The Newsboy' and stores would say, 'We're out of it,' substituting 'The Three Bells' instead. I told Jim Ed about that, jokingly saying, 'I shouldn't even talk to you!' Actually, RCA had much bigger distribution anyway than Dot did, so we were at the mercy of independent distributors. They owned their own distribution outlets.

"I did the arrangement on 'Jimmy Brown The Newsboy' for a folk album, and really wasn't trying for a single, but I think the arrangement is what made it take off. It was getting action even before the album got out, though Randy hesitated putting it out as a single. You know 'The Battle of New Orleans' was out by Jimmie Driftwood, and I wanted Randy to let me cover it on Dot, but he didn't and that was before Johnny Horton's version came out [and would hit number one country and pop]. That was the beginning of the end for me with Dot. I felt if I couldn't get their support, to hell with it."

Still, his "Jimmy Brown The Newsboy" was a big seller, and equally hot north of the border, notes Wiseman: "A company in Toronto was putting it out up there, and every night it seemed we'd have to go over there to pick up more singles to sell. That's how fast they were selling. Grandpa Jones was with me on that tour, and I remember him whining, 'Do we have to go to *Torontie* tonight?' Actually, Ray Price, Wilma Lee & Stoney Cooper, Grandpa and I did twenty days up there, starting on Labor Day 1959, I guess, at about the time my song became a hit. We opened the tour in Kingston, Ontario."

Just prior to that prosperous session producing "Jimmy Brown... " Mac got to fulfill a long-time desire to do a gospel album for Dot. In three sessions at Bradley's Quonset Hut, Wiseman handling guitar and vocals, accompanied only by bassist Joe Zinkan - January 22, 23 and 26, 1959 - cut twelve songs. One, "Beside Still Waters," became his album's title.

Once settled back in Nashville's suburbs, Mac became a familiar figure on the music scene. He was in the studio a lot, though mainly putting other artists through their paces. Mac, meanwhile, made four more treks to the Nashville studios for himself in 1960, even re-cutting his premiere chart hit "The Ballad of Davy Crockett." Mac covered two hits by The Browns, their number one "The Three Bells" and their Top Five "The Old Lamplighter."

One cover he did stood out in Mac's mind, "El Paso," written and recorded famously by good buddy Marty Robbins: "Gordon Stoker and I recorded this like a duet, just the two of us and he sang a wonderful tenor... now that's a long song and we got it done from top to bottom in a single take. It gave us a different sound from Marty's record. For that session, I had them play harpsichord; I think the pianist, Pig Robbins, brought it in."

As Mac remembers it, Hank Garland, who had a friendly rivalry with session leader Grady Martin, was pleased to have the chance to pick on "El Paso" for Mac, as Grady had played on Marty's hit version.

"Hank used to say he liked my fills. I remember for one song, I had it all in my mind how I wanted Hank to play, and after I explained it to him, he said, 'Why don't you play it?'... I did and when I heard the playback it sounded just the way I wanted it."

For Mac's February 1961 recording date at the Quonset Hut on Music Row, his producer Beasley Smith invited the backing of Papa John Gordy's Dixielanders Band, an interesting change for *The Voice With a Heart*. Despite having fairly recently hit with "... The Newsboy," Mac thought it time to bow out as Dot artist and A&R executive: "It just wasn't happening. There wasn't any action. I didn't feel I was doing Dot any good, and they were going more and more with pop acts. Randy was signing Hollywood stars like Gale Storm, Tab Hunter and even (opera diva) Helen Traubel. It became one of those things where I was feeling like I was stealing every time he sent me my check.

119

"So we just agreed to part ways. Actually I tried to leave several times, but bless his heart, he would say, 'No, let's do another album.' I had two or three albums out already, while most of the big acts didn't have any. Remember Randy had the forethought that the LP would be the coming thing."

Mac's decision to depart Dot was followed by a personal conflict that marked the beginning of the end in his second marriage. Not surprisingly, Wiseman found himself in financial straits. It all weighed heavily on his mind when he paid a call on former touring pal Marty Robbins: "I went to see Marty out on Eighteenth Avenue, and during our chat I said, 'Hey Marty, think you could loan an old country boy a few dollars?'

"He smiled and replied, 'How much would an old country boy need?,' and when I said a couple thousand, he said, 'An old country boy wants a whole lot.' At the time, Marty's steel player was Jimmy Farmer, who also worked in his office. It was about quitting time and as Jimmy started down the steps, Marty called out, 'Jimmy, write Mac a check for two thousand!' When he gave me the check, I asked Marty did he want me to sign a note or something? He said, 'Hell no! If I had to have you sign a note, I wouldn't let you have it.'

"Anyway, I paid him back in increments of five hundred dollars. Just to give you an idea of his wry sense of humor, when I was ready to pay him the final installment, I thanked Marty backstage at the Opry for having helped me out. I was especially appreciative, because he hadn't even charged me interest. Then he suggested we play a little joke on some of the old boys backstage, with him coming up to me and saying, 'Mac loan me five hundred dollars,' and I was to just whip out the money and hand it to him. Marty said, 'It'll drive them crazy.' But I simply couldn't do that.

"I also remember the time Marty heard about this down-on-his-luck fellow who lived under a bridge had died a vagrant. So he says to some of his cronies, 'Let's give that old boy a royal send-off!' He knew they would just bury him in Potter's Field. There were only about four or five people at the service, but he lay there in that casket in all his splendor, and Marty picked up the tab."

15 'Your Best Friend And Me'...
Hank's Heartache

*"Today I met the friend you talked about
She's everything you said, beyond a doubt
You told me that I'd like her and how right can you be
But I'm afraid we'll hurt you, Your best friend and me..."*

As Mac picked himself up and got through his marital turmoil, he was in negotiation with RCA Records, a major recording label, and he had some good friends in the business to socialize with during those discordant days.

Hawkshaw Hawkins and Jean Shepard and Mac had become good friends from the late-1950s into the early 1960s: "It got so Jean, Hawk and I used to get together for dinner a lot, and Hawk and I used to train bird-dogs. Then, as we got busier in our careers, however, we didn't see each other for a while. Finally, Jean decided to put an end to the procrastination. She issued a union-type contract to dine at a specific time and date. Now whoever didn't show had to pay for all the dinners anyway. You know when I called to congratulate her on her (2011) induction into the Country Music Hall of Fame, we got to talking and that little incident came up and we both had a good laugh."

When in 1961, Ken Nelson got wind of Mac's possible signing with RCA, he didn't hesitate to offer a counter-proposal: "You know Ken Nelson was on that CMA board with me, and Chet Atkins had just proposed a deal for me to come onto RCA, and during conversation with Ken, I mentioned I was going to record for RCA. He said, 'Oh damn, if I knew you were available, I'd love to have you on Capitol and promote you like The Kingston Trio,' who were big at the time from the folk standpoint.

"I said, 'Are you serious?' and he said, 'I'm dead serious.' Now Chet and I had a few meetings and already picked some material, including 'Freight Train' and 'Bluegrass Fiesta' for a first session, but we hadn't signed any papers. We had been friends and didn't see any big hurry in signing an agreement. I was a good-enough friend with Chet that I sat down with him and told him about Ken's offer, and how he wanted to promote me like a folk artist.

"Chet said, 'I think that would be great for you, Mac, and the only thing that I was concerned with about recording you is that I might not be able to produce you myself. I've got so many artists on my roster, that I might have to sub-let you to another producer.' That didn't appeal to me a damn bit. He added, 'I don't know but that might be the best deal for you,' and as I got up to go, Chet opened his desk drawer and pulled those songs out of his desk, saying, 'You might as well take these, too, as I'm not going to do them with anybody else.' We did record them later."

Mac flew out to California for a press conference about his scheduled signing with Capitol Records, but during the flight contracted a virus and was hospitalized. He was placed in isolation once doctors diagnosed a sinus-connected affliction as contagious:

"I mean when I was first hospitalized they asked if I wanted a TV? I said no, I was in too much pain to watch TV. Well later, when I asked about having a TV, they said no, because they would have to destroy it if I used it. They got rid of the utensils I ate with because I was very contagious. The trouble was with my right sinus."

Additionally during hospitalization, Mac also suffered a staph infection. Aside from that life-threatening situation, Mac was worried about mounting healthcare costs. He contacted Capitol, which declined advancing him one thousand dollars, apparently not sure how he would sell (or perhaps whether he would live). During his week's stay, however, despite the quarantine, Saul Holiff, Johnny Cash's manager, and singer-actor-friend Sheb Wooley ("Purple People Eater") came to see Mac. At the time, Holiff was handling both Cash and George Jones.

"They visited awhile and as Holiff departed, he pressed a check in my hand for one thousand dollars from Cash to help cover my hospital costs. Saul was an agent, booker and manager from London, Ontario. When I called Johnny to thank him, he told me that he was going to play a date at Carnegie Hall. I said that was an artist's dream playing Carnegie Hall, and he asked if I'd like to do the show with him. Would I? Now I guess Saul had to take somebody off that bill - I don't know who it might have been - but that was quite an honor to me."

Meanwhile, Mac was all too anxious for release from the hospital. His doctor was the same physician that treated movie star Jeff Chandler, who died June 17, 1961 at Culver City Memorial Hospital. Chandler, known for such movies as "Broken Arrow," had been under the primary care of Dr. Marvin Corbin. Reportedly, he went in for simple outpatient treatment for a spinal disc herniation on May 13, but suffered a staph infection that necessitated subsequent surgeries. The six-footer was forty-two when he died at the hospital, prompting family members to file a one-point-eight million dollars' malpractice lawsuit [finally settling out-of-court for two-hundred and thirty-three thousand, three-hundred and fifty-eight dollars and forty-two cents, which went to his two daughters].

A frustrated Wiseman couldn't get the go-ahead to get out of the hospital: "My doctor wouldn't release me after my surgery because he said if I'd fly back, it would close up again. He had been in the military and lost a couple pilots who were treated for sinus infection and went back up in the air too soon, and died. I asked, 'Would you release me if I promise to ride a train?' He looked at me very seriously and said, 'Only if you promise me that for sure... I will.' So I got on a train from L.A. to Toronto and that was the longest, most boring trip I ever took in my life. I had to go back there because that was where my car was parked. I remember we rode into Chicago and then went on up to Toronto, and the Canadian trains were ten times better than ours."

While many artists would've been discouraged by Capitol's refusal to advance him money for his hospital bill, Mac reasons, "I was working in Toronto when this press party idea came up with Capitol to introduce me as a folk artist in the tradition of The Kingston Trio. They had a press conference set up at The Ash Grove in south L.A., one of the leading folk venues there at the time. I had to miss that. My second-guessing was that Ken Nelson might've been ticked off because I didn't attend the press party. I probably could have gotten it from Dot, but I wasn't on their label, though Randy and I were still good friends and he would have done it, because they would have recouped one thousand dollars in my next recording check, you know."

Obviously Mac's pact with Capitol wasn't off to a smooth start: "Well, we didn't have any problem really, and I recorded with them and cut a couple things that got some pretty good airplay, notably 'Bluegrass Fiesta,' which got played on Top 40 and country stations, as well. There were others that got fine airplay, but didn't enjoy huge sales."

It was December 20, 1961, when Ken Nelson first scheduled Mac's initial Capitol recording session in the Quonset Hut. Musicians on the time card were musicians he was familiar with, as were the songs. Pianist Marvin Hughes, however, was producing the second session, January 17, 1962, utilizing the same studio musicians and songs scheduled suited Mac's style.

Often Nelson, Capitol's A&R chief based in L.A., engaged Hughes to handle production chores for the label's Nashville sessions. Nelson wasn't one to ride roughshod over his artists in the studio: "No, Ken just left it up to me, much like Randy. But we had Marvin Hughes to contend with. He used to take a little nip before coming into the studio, and the first session I was on, he and I sort of locked horns. I knew my part and had worked out the arrangements with the guys in the studio. Well, I'd get about two or three lines into it, and he'd stop the session saying, 'We didn't get that, could we go back to *blah, blah, blah...*' Then about the third time, I got to looking around at the musicians and the dubious signs were 'I wonder how many times Mac's gonna put up with that shit.' Well, the next time I got about half-way through the song, he did it again, and this time I called a stop to the whole session, and went in, got right in his damn face and said, 'Listen you S.O.B., don't stop these things until I get a take, and then if you don't like it, we'll do it again. Don't stop me in the middle of it, until I make a damn mistake.' I didn't have any trouble with him after that. He just kept in his damn place.

"The way I was able to do a lot of good things in the studio was by surrounding myself with good engineers like Mort Thomasson and Shelby Coffeen. To my knowledge Shelby engineered the first stereo session done in this town and it was just the two of us musicians, Joe Zinkan and me; but he recorded us on separate tracks when we did that Dot gospel thing (January 22, 1959) in the basement of the Quonset Hut. It was for 'Beneath Still Waters,' and the talk at the time was that it was the first stereo recording here, back when they were experimenting with it, which seems sort of odd, as we only had two instruments on that (three-day) session for sixteen sides."

Wiseman's February 9, 1962 session with Hughes went well. With the exception of Chubby Wise being replaced by Tommy Vaden, the players were the same. One of the tracks was "Bluegrass Fiesta," a number well suited to Vaden, a longtime Hank Snow fiddler.

"That number 'Bluegrass Fiesta' boasted a kind of rhumba beat and it got lots of Top Forty radio airplay," explains Wiseman. "Later, I recall traveling to San Francisco and was pleased to hear one of their top pop stations playing it. It was a big request number."

It was on May 10, 1962, that Mac accompanied the Johnny Cash troupe for a Carnegie Hall concert in New York City: "Cash was wanting to play Carnegie Hall on his own to prove to the industry that he could draw in big metropolitan cities. It was quite a package, George Jones, Mother Maybelle & The Carter Sisters, Merle Kilgore and myself.

"John came to my room early the next morning after our concert carrying the newspapers, saying 'I just wanted you to know that you got the top reviews on our show.' He had stayed up, waiting on the newspapers to come out. Hell, Johnny was suffering from a hoarse throat and would have stolen the show with no hesitation had he been in good shape. He had been to a hypnotist or guru trying to get his voice in shape - it was the same guy Harry Belafonte used."

A *New York Times* reviewer declined to say any more about the star than noting Cash "was suffering from a throat ailment, which made it difficult to judge his performance." Further, Columbia Records' A&R chief Don Law, who had journeyed north to record Cash for a 'live' album at Carnegie Hall, refused to tape the performance and signaled his engineers to quit recording. Cash bandsman Marshall Grant recalled, "Johnny could hardly talk. He was high, and he was so hoarse. He'd been up for three days, maybe longer."

The day before their Carnegie Hall concert, the acts all went to The Bitter End, a coffee house in Greenwich Village, notes George Riddle, rhythm guitarist and harmony singer: "I remember when I was backing George (Jones) during his Carnegie Hall show, it was a sell-out. We stayed at the Barbizon Plaza Hotel a whole week, but you could hardly get Jones out of the room. He didn't care much for the 'Big Apple.' Well, we all performed in Greenwich Village at the Bitter End, which was a rehearsal type thing and old Mac got up there and stole the show, singing songs like 'Wabash Cannon Ball' and 'Wonder How the Old Folks Are At Home.' He blew them away! Them long-haired hippies seemed to love those old songs."

Mac remembers, too, Cash went to the Taft Hotel where Jimmie Rodgers had stayed on his last recording stint in New York (1933): "This hotel let Johnny go into their basement where they stored old artifacts and they found an old coal-oil lantern that Jimmie had used working for the railroad (as a brakeman), which he'd brought with him. They let Cash display it in Carnegie Hall during our concert... Cash came on stage swinging the lantern, garbed in a railroad cap and jacket to complete the image."

Actually the folk craze - spearheaded by such acts as The Weavers ("Wimoweh"), Kingston Trio ("Hang Down Your Head, Tom Dooley"), Harry Belafonte ('The Banana Boat Song'), and Peter, Paul & Mary ("If I Had a Hammer") - reignited Mac's career, sparking accelerated personal appearances nationwide.

"It really did. I started doing the Newport Festival and played Carnegie Hall again with a folk festival, the Philadelphia Folk Festival, the Mariposa Festival in Toronto, and a lot of others. All the folk festival bookers picked me up on their own, I guess because I drew well at those things, just working as a single. I was in some damn good company, as far as getting attention, working with the likes of Doc Watson, (Canada's) Ian & Sylvia, Taj Mahal and a lot of the black singers, and was well-accepted."

Mac also guested on Tyson's TV show in Canada, and Dick Clark's in the U.S., among many others. Suddenly Wiseman found himself nearly going Ivy League. At the time, Mac especially hailed bluegrass festivals as "the last type of music which lets the entire family attend... arena concerts cost too much, because the tickets must be scaled so high. We're picking up on these kids now."

Actually, being from the heart of the Appalachian mountain region - from which a body of songs originated that told the story of Americans struggling to carve out an existence in the new country - recalled Mac's very own roots. Ballads derived from experiences expressing people's suffering and sorrows, and spurts of satisfaction and happiness, ruled.

"I like to think I paint a picture with my story songs, trying to put as much sincerity into the singing as I can," explained Wiseman, who was heavily influenced by a pioneer in delivering story songs, Bradley Kincaid. We wondered if Mac ever shared the stage with the Kentucky balladeer, advertised on radio as "The Original Authentic Folksong Singer" on stations such as WLS-Chicago and WLW-Cincinnati.

"Back when I was running the Renfro Valley Festival, I would schedule an old-timers' program, Bradley was one of the artists I called up in Ohio, and he said no, feeling that he'd been retired too long and didn't feel he should do a show anymore. Well, the day we started doing this thing he showed up and was standing on the sidelines and I went over to chat, but didn't ask him again as I thought he had given me his final answer. Finally he said, 'Y'know, I'd be glad to sing a couple songs if you really want me to...' Of course, I did and when he got up on stage, you couldn't get him off. Why someone would call out a request and he was in his element. That made a wonderful memory for me, having Bradley Kincaid on the show. I don't believe I realized initially how much of an influence he had on me as a youth, listening to him on radio and the way he was in talking to an audience."

One of the finest pioneer performers was Huddie (Leadbelly) Ledbetter, who hailed from Louisiana and created such classics as "Goodnight Irene," "Have a Drink On Me" and "Cotton Fields," which Mac recorded.

"Really, I feel I was instrumental in setting myself up with colleges," Mac muses, marveling now that those students are mostly in their 60s and long since grandparents. "Back in the early 1960s, I sat down at my house in Nashville and wrote every college station in the country, told them what I did and the music I had, and if they felt my recordings would fit their programming, I'd send them records, and received a tremendous response. I sent two albums each to the stations replying, and they played them.

"Then the first thing I knew they invited me to play little listening rooms, coffee houses and concerts. I played Vanderbilt University here several times, just individual things, upstairs, where kids would come in, sit on the floor and I just played little acoustic sets. That's the reason I became so entrenched on the college circuit."

Playing solo suited Mac's style: "Any time I was in a pinch, I would just resort to that. It worked in the bad times of the year, and saved me having to pay for a band. With a band, the hell of it was in the winter you had to work when weather and circumstances weren't favorable, because you had musicians on payroll."

Thanks to his rave reviews at Carnegie Hall and the folk festivals, Mac garnered greater gigs: "Johnny Cash did his first major tour with me aboard. I opened for him about a year, playing prestigious places like the Hollywood Bowl, Rice University in Houston, and though that just fell in my lap, it was great for me. When

I left Toronto, I had to go to New York and decided to drive there rather than fly, because I still wasn't quite up to snuff. But I just couldn't pass up that opportunity. One thing I remember while we were in New York, there was this top folk venue there where it was decided we would do like a dry run with a captive audience. Well, the guy running that was Ed McCurdy, a DJ from Frederick, Maryland, when I went there with my first little band. So when Ed introduced me on the stage, he built me up like crazy, and I ended up stopping the show. George Riddle mentions that every time I see him, saying, 'Mac was working that show with Johnny Cash and George Jones, and he gets up there and blows them away.' George and I served together on the Reunion Of Professional Entertainers' executive board."

Being solo and singing solo are two different things. During his visits and performances in Canada, Mac became a fast favorite. It wasn't like Mac Wiseman could do no wrong in Canada, though indeed he could fill the show's seats. During a booking on Prince Edward Island, "Running late, I was speeding but got pulled over by the Royal Canadian Mounted Police. They issued me a ticket to pay the next day in Halifax (Nova Scotia). Well, I caught the ferry over to P.E.I. for my gig. Then when the show was over, I caught the ferry back to Halifax for the night, thinking I'd get out of the speeding fine. The Mounties, however, were smarter than me. They were checking license plates before we drove onto the ferry. Well, I had to pay my fine right then and there."

On another memorable occasion, Mac, in mid-winter, was on the ferry crossing over between Halifax and Prince Edward Island when the boat became ice-bound: "So we had to spend the night. Ice was breaking up the next day as we sat and watched the seals floating by on the pieces of ice."

In September 1962, Capitol scheduled a session for Mac during which he re-recorded his first Dot success, "'Tis Sweet To Be Remembered," along with "Goin' Like Wildfire," written by his former band mate Speedy Krise (from the O'Day days), and well-received by Wiseman fans. Closing out the session was "I Like Bluegrass Music," co-written by Johnny Ringo and Fred Madden, an ironic title considering the artist's adversity to being typecast in a single genre. That September 24 studio time, under the production hand of Hughes, clocked in Cecil Brower on fiddle.

Memorable, too, at Mac's September 24 recording stint were added harmony vocals by Mother Maybelle and the soaring soprano of Millie Kirkham, augmenting choral backing by The Jordanaires. Again, Hughes booked the Quonset Hut, which became the Columbia Recording Studio on Music Row. (Mil-

lie, a favorite vocalist of Elvis Presley's, performed in her 90's doing Presley tribute-type shows with The Jordanaires and Ronnie McDowell.)

"Millie had such wonderful control. And yes, it was my idea to get Mother Maybelle on there singing harmony for "Tis Sweet To Be Remembered.' She didn't play the autoharp for us, but I knew she would give that song more of an original sound. On that particular rendition, I had Cecil play like a violinist and he was classically trained. It didn't take him a minute to switch from fiddle to violin."

Incidentally, Brower signed with Jimmy Dean in 1963, appearing on Dean's ABC-TV variety series. Oddly enough on November 21, 1965, after playing Carnegie Hall, the Texan went to a party at the Waldorf-Astoria Hotel, and died there suddenly, a week shy of his fifty-first birthday. "A great loss," says Mac.

Regarding recording with Mother Maybelle, Mac notes further, "She blew me away, and only later I found she really liked me. I remember one time during a party down at The Cannery in Nashville, Marty Stuart sidled up to confide he'd asked Johnny Cash (his then father-in-law) if Mother Maybelle ever had any flings, and Johnny laughed and jokingly said, 'Well, if she did, it would've been with Mac Wiseman because she really liked him.' (Mac smiled in telling that.)"

Earlier, while on the West Coast on tour, Mac found himself walking on the beach with Maybelle, along with Jan and Harlan Howard: "When we came up off the beach there was this little club facing the street, with no steps, and as we looked up, saw that the black comic Moms Mabley was the entertainer. The front was open and so we just wandered in and sat down, while she was doing her stuff. There was no stage, so she was working on ground level. We really got into her comedy, which was risque, but hilarious. When she caught on that we were fellow players, she really laid it on us ...You know, Jan still remembers that night. Sometimes when she sees me she'll say, 'Mac, you want to go walk on the beach?' We enjoyed that."

Grinning wider, Mac assures us that Moms Mabley had no copyright on using suggestive material in her act, recalling one of his laugh-getters, a conversation between a woman and her grandson: "An elderly lady called her grandson to tell him his granddaddy passed away. The boy said, 'I'm sorry to hear that,' then asked what did he die from? Grandma said he had a heart attack. The boy asked her, 'What were y'all doing when he had the heart attack?' The woman reluctantly said, 'We were a doing it!'

The grandson said, 'You knew he had a heart problem and y'all were doing it?' She said, 'Yes we were making love to the church bells chiming ding, dong, ding... and were doing alright until the damn Good Humor truck drove by!'"

Amusing, too, but maybe true, Mac relates the experience of two good old boys working in Jimmy Dean's early band in the D.C. area. After picking up a couple girls, they couldn't find a spot out of plain sight for a little necking. One knew a fellow who had a service station, however, and arranged for him to put their car up on a grease-rack so they could enjoy their "groupies" in private. When finished, one who had a bottle of booze said, 'Go get us a Coke and we'll have a little drink.' Not thinking, the other musician promptly stepped out into mid-air, dropping downward on a cement floor. Although bruised, fortunately the picker survived his fall, grins Mac.

It was in February 1962, that Capitol issued Mac's first single for the label: "Footprints In the Snow" with "Just Outside" as its flipside. That was followed by the "Bluegrass Fiesta" June release, coupled with a prophetic backup "What's Gonna Happen To Me?" Rounding out the year came "Pistol Packin' Preacher" backed by "Sing Little Birdie" in October. None made *Billboard*'s charts.

Capitol also issued Wiseman's debut LP, "Bluegrass Favorites By Master Folk Singer Mac Wiseman" (Capitol ST-1800), which today commands anywhere up to two hundred dollars in mint condition among collectors. According to top collector-historian Jerry Osborne, only Mac's Dot release "Keep On the Sunny Side" (DLP-3336), ranks higher as a collectible.

Meanwhile, thanks to his folk fan following, Mac was enjoying a boom in bookings: "When the 'Hootenanny' craze came along, I was fortunate enough that college crowds took a liking to me. I went through another generation and did colleges and the Hollywood Bowl!"

Wiseman didn't really make any significant change in performing for the folk audience: "I always just did my thing acoustically, usually going through my 1950s' repertory of songs."

For many years, Mac would close out his shows with a rendition of "Will the Circle Be Unbroken," often turning it into a sing-along with his audience: "It's a good friendly way to close out. The crowd loves it."

It didn't matter whether he was starring in a country show or booked alongside headliners like Andy Williams, Judy Collins, Joan Baez, Ian & Sylvia Tyson or Gordon Lightfoot - whom Mac later honored via a tribute album of his songs - Mac simply stuck with his winning formula.

Bob Dylan, who started hitting his stride in New York City's Greenwich Village folk clubs, became main man on the booming folk scene. It was at Newport that Mac met the future folk superstar: "Oh yes, at the time he was following Joan Baez about. Another fellow I met at the same time was Ramblin' Jack Elliott ('Talkin' Blues,' 'Fifteen Cents'). He sang a lot of the same songs I enjoyed singing through the years. At the Newport Folk Festival, probably the first time I saw Dylan, I was watching Joan Baez introducing him around, and he hung to her coattails like a little kid."

Mac remembers, too, the first time he met Mississippi John Hurt: "I was surprised to see him because the word was out that he was dead, but somebody found him down in Mississippi singing on street corners. People would

pitch coins into his hat. I watched him at the Newport Festival and saw kids surrounding him as he sat under a tree with just his guitar, just pickin' and singin'. They were transfixed by him and his talent."

Despite the upsurge in gigs, there was one difference Mac was determined to make in his private life: "When I was home, I would spend more quality time with the family."

Maxine and baby brother Scott.

128

All the same, he remained fully focused on his career, committed to making his deal with Capitol succeed as best he could. Regarding Mac's April 12, 1963 session, he recorded four songs a month after the loss of Patsy Cline, Hawkshaw Hawkins, Cowboy Copas (whom Mac had produced) and his pilot son-in-law Randy Hughes in a plane crash. Tragically, Jack Anglin was en-route to their memorial service when an auto accident claimed his life, ending the Johnnie & Jack team. Later that month, Curly Fox's wife Ruby died in a trailer fire, all had been Opry performers.

Thus the town was in a funk over this heavy loss for country music. Mac, friend to all of the deceased, was still in a state of mourning, but perked up when he heard a new song pitched by writer Hank Cochran, "Your Best Friend and Me." Marvin scheduled it on the April 12 session, which also included the dramatically-titled "Scene Of the Crime," the vintage "When the Moon Comes Over the Mountain," popularized by Kate Smith, and the novelty number "What a Waste of Good Corn Likker."

"You know 'Good Corn Likker' proved a big request number," notes Mac, though "Your Best Friend and Me" became the session's bona fide hit: "When I first heard that song, it just knocked me out, and Cochran was there for the session. (Hank's co-writer was Gail Talley.)"

Mac especially liked the lyrics to this provocative ballad: *"For awhile we talked about me and you/But we also talked about me and her, too/I don't know what happened, but it happened you see/So won't you please forgive us/Your best friend and me?"*

It became another near-Top 10 for Mac, garnering generous airplay throughout North America. According to *Billboard* it charted September 21, 1963, and peaked number twelve the week of October 26, his only single charting for Capitol. The label's promoters seemed too busy hawking the singles of its longtime artists like Sonny James, "The Minute You're Gone"; and another newcomer Roy Clark's "Tips Of My Fingers." That year, too, red-hot Buck Owens was burning up the charts, with his number one Capitol titles "Act Naturally" and "Love's Gonna Live Here."

Meantime, Hank Cochran was riding high with a couple other compositions from his Pamper Music catalog: "Make the World Go Away," Ray Price, number two; and "You Comb Her Hair," George Jones, number five. "Your Best Friend and Me" was merely more frosting on Hank's cake.

Mac and Hank became close buddies. A wild one, Cochran was rather unpredictable. Around the Fourth of July, he and Mac were walking on Lower Broad, Nashville's honky-tonk district. Hank, by the way, had a pocketful of firecrackers.

"You remember when they started selling suits with two pair of pants, back when they had cuffs?" asks Mac. "Well, I had just bought me a new suit which had two trousers. Hank and I were walking along and every once in awhile he'd light up a 'cracker and toss it out to scare some passersby. Suddenly, I smelled smoke and looked down and saw my pants a'fire. One of his firecrackers had ended up in the cuff of my pants!"

16 'Bringing Mary Home'... Next Stop: Vegas

"I was driving down a lonely road, on a dark and stormy night
A little girl by the roadside stepped up in my headlights
I stopped and she got in back, and in a shaky tone
She said my name is Mary, please won't you take me home..."

Mac himself was hotter than a firecracker as an artist, when in the fall of 1963, he made his performing debut in the entertainment mecca of Las Vegas, with a three-week engagement at The Mint. According to Mac that booking began via an unexpected turn in Caseda Springs, California, when he was there to play the Hollywood Bowl with Johnny Cash's troupe the next night.

"Songwriter Joe Allison ('He'll Have To Go'), June Carter, Mother Maybelle and I rode out to the Cash house from Hollywood. They were doing a round-robin picking party. That's when John was still married to Vivian. We were all sitting around in their living room, passing the guitar. Usually each person would do two songs and pass the guitar to the next one. I took the guitar, did a couple songs and then Cliffie Stone, who hosted the *Hometown Jamboree*, asked me to sing another.

"I ended up doing five or six songs, which embarrassed me because I didn't want them to think I was hogging the scene," continues Mac. "But they all gave me a big hand. I was unaware that a Las Vegas booker was there. When I got back to Nashville, I got this telegram from the guy who did the booking for The Mint in Vegas. He explained he heard me at Johnny Cash's house and said The Mint was doing a series of folk-style shows, featuring headliners like Red Foley and Roy Acuff. He wanted to know if I would do a three-week stint. Hell yes! I was knocked out because I knew they also paid good money. I hadn't made any effort trying to line-up a booking there at all; in fact, I'd never been to Las Vegas before agreeing to that gig."

It was another instance of being in the right place at the right time. Of course, Mac needed a backup band, obviously one that could handle his style of music: "Initially I thought about bringing out the cream of the crop in studio players like Grady Martin, Ray Edenton and Pig Robbins, but the more I thought on it, I realized Vegas already had its share of great musicians. Since it was a folk-oriented theme, I felt The Stonemans would be a good fit.

"I knew them from their days back in the Washington, D.C. area (and of course Scotty had been one of Mac's Country Boys). There was also an excellent entertainer I knew from Mississippi, bassist Smitty Smith, who had been at WSB-Atlanta with the likes of Cotton Carrier and Paul Rice. I invited him to ride out with me, Marge and our months-old baby girl Maxine, born in August 1963."

Even before that, Mac made a preliminary trip to Vegas to check out the terrain: "I stopped to case The Mint after playing dates in California. Leon McAuliffe was booked at the Golden Nugget there, and he had been one of my artists at Dot in the 1950s. So I went by to visit with Leon and mentioned to him that I was going to fly back to Nashville the next morning. He said, 'I've got my private plane here and I fly each night after the show to L.A. Stick around and I'll give you a lift there.' Leon was a steel guitarist with both Pappy O'Daniel's Light Crust Dough Boys and Bob Wills' Texas Playboys."

In Nashville, Pop Stoneman headed up his family band of grown youngsters, who had just recorded for Starday. The Stonemans' music neatly complemented Mac's style. The family wanted to follow Mac out West in an old tour bus they picked up. Roni recalled that Van, not exactly an experienced bus driver, almost smashed into Wiseman, who'd made an unexpected traffic stop ahead. When Scott took the wheel, he nearly collided on a bridge with a semi-truck.

Wiseman: "I was aggravated as hell with them. It took sixty-six hours to go from Nashville to Las Vegas [more than twice the time needed for the eighteen hundred and ten-mile trip]. It was their first old bus, however, so if they heard the slightest noise they had to stop and get underneath to make sure something wasn't going to give. I could understand they were scared of being stranded somewhere, but it was nerve-wracking, stopping so much. I finally told them I was taking off and if they wanted to follow me to Vegas, they had to keep up, and they stayed right on my tail the rest of the way. To be on the safe side, I'd even arranged for a possible replacement."

Mac never had a bus, back in the early days. "Didn't matter, because there weren't any roads fit to travel on back then," though he recalls Highway 60, stretched across West Virginia onward. "I drove that road so much, I could've probably managed it with my eyes shut. You had to cross those mountains to go into Ohio."

Once in Las Vegas, the Stonemans opened for four one-hour shows, then remained on stage to back Mac for his star segment. Reportedly, the long sessions on stage sometimes got to Pop, occasionally dozing off while strumming his guitar, but never stopped playing, just sort of slowed down, until someone nudged him and then he perked up, playing even faster.

Mac was pleased how the sophisticated Vegas patrons took to the Stonemans, as it confirmed his choice: "Pop and his kids simply knocked them out. Man, the fans and the media were very impressed by their performances. Scotty was wild as a buck though and got into gambling all his money away. He messed with slot machines, even in a bathroom, and had to make a draw on his pay to get by. Roni was naturally funny, but Pop kept putting her down, discouraging her efforts to step out comically. He said it was unladylike for a woman to tell funny stories. I told Pop to turn her loose and the audience would love her, and that she wouldn't say anything risque.

"I remember the reaction to her first joke. She was talking about the new Maidenform Bra advertisements: 'I bought one of those Maidenform Bras today, but I don't know what to feed it!' Of course, she was straight as a stick, and the audience went wild."

A big fan of Marjorie Main of "Ma Kettle" movie fame, banjoist Roni adopted Ma's raspy vocal delivery and finally found comedy fame as Ida Lee, the nagging wife in hair curlers, on the long-running syndicated *Hee Haw* TV series.

Roni herself credits Mac with helping to launch her comedic talent there at The Mint: "I just love Mac. My father warned me, 'Act like a lady while you're out there on stage.' Well, I was bored to death on stage and just wanted to let loose and have a good time. Mac saw what was happening and he said, 'Pop, let her alone. She won't do anything to embarrass you.' And it worked. They had known each other a long time, back in D.C."

Mac adds, "You know, on his death bed, Pop told me that my inviting them to play The Mint not only got them out of the Washington, D.C., area, where they were in a rut, but also led to getting their syndicated TV series which gave him a comeback."

Pop died June 14, 1968, at age seventy-five, several months after his new troupe won the first CMA best vocal group trophy.

"I recall a time when I'd recorded a sweet ballad 'When the Snowflakes Fall Again' and I saw Pop backstage and gave him the first score, telling him, 'I just recorded this. What do you think?' He smiled and said, 'I think that's pretty good. I wrote that one.' I didn't know Pop Stoneman wrote it, and that was embarrassing for me (not knowing)."

Not many remember Stoneman once competed on the national CBS-TV quiz show *The $64,000 Question* (1956) and won ten thousand dollars for his efforts, says Mac: "He looked like he wasn't smart enough to come in out of the rain, but he blew them away, buddy! He also worked for the post office at one time."

Mac became good friends with Roni's older sister Patsy Stoneman Murphy, who worked hard on behalf of ROPE in her later years, and was a champion of her father's belated induction into the Country Music Hall of Fame.

"I liked her husband, too. Whenever I attended a ROPE event, 'Murph' blocked off a space for my car, so I wouldn't have far to walk. He even watched for my arrival and came out so that I could lean on him to walk inside. That was so thoughtful." [Jack Murphy was Patsy's late husband.]

Wiseman cracked up hearing on a road trip that Patsy asked Murph to pull off the highway and drive to an area cemetery containing her second husband's grave. He had been very abusive to her, and the lady squatted down on his grave to relieve herself, sighing, "I always wanted to do that!"

On a melancholy note, the November 22, 1963 assassination of President John F. Kennedy cast a pall over the entire nation, and by then Mac's single "Your Best Friend and Me" had also run its course. It would

Mac with Janette Carter and Patsy Stoneman, daughters from country's first families.

be his last *Billboard* charting for five years. Meanwhile, the country seemed to be coming along fine under the new leadership of Lyndon B. Johnson, the President who initiated the Great Society, seeking the elimination of poverty and racial injustice.

Well, LBJ came to the Shenandoah Apple Blossom Parade in Winchester, Virginia, to crown daughter Lucy Baines Johnson queen of the festival. Mac laughs at the recollection: "It was in 1964, in the center of apple country, and I was there to ride in the parade. Lucille Ball was its grand marshal. Well, Arthur Godfrey was also there and he and Lucy were enjoying themselves backstage, and when it came time to ride in the parade, you could tell they were more than feeling good."

"You know another song I did along about that time I was flattered with was 'An Old Pair of Shoes' by Cindy Walker. It was just a good song with fine chord progressions in it," Mac says. "I remember that Cindy's mother (Oree) traveled with her all the time, coming in from Texas, and she was a pretty good pianist. Cindy asked me to listen to her song. Instead of cutting demos, that's how Cindy would 'shop' her songs. She'd have artists and publishers come to her when she was in Nashville. The first time she showed that song to me was in the ballroom down at the Andrew Jackson Hotel. I was very impressed by the song and recorded it (February 13, 1964), and we got some mileage out of it though it never became a hit."

Cindy was on the CMA board during the early 1960s, so she and Mac developed a lasting friendship: "Whenever I sent a Christmas card, I suggested she give me a call - and she did. We chatted a long while, the two of us. Through the years, she pitched me several songs."

On Valentine's Day '64, an additional dozen songs were scheduled for Mac to record. Apart from the usual suspects, musicians assembled included Lew Houston, Dobro; and Donnie Bryant, banjo.

That same afternoon, Hughes added Junior Huskey on bass, as Zinkan had a conflicting studio date, while Charlie McCoy played harmonica, and Josh Graves added his Dobro to the mix. During the session, Mac recorded "Katie Waits For Me," with Marion Worth (of "Shake Me I Rattle" fame). Marion had recently cut a Top 20 duet with George Morgan, a revival of Floyd Tillman's "Slipping Around," coupled with Floyd's "I Love You So Much It Hurts."

Mac recalls hearing Marion singing "Katie Waits For Me," written by Curley Putman, while traveling on Marty Robbins' bus to a package show in Phoenix: "It had a great sound, so I got her to teach it to me and we started singing it together. So I invited Marion to sing it with me at my next session, which marked my first duet with a female."

Being on a major label like Capitol added to Mac's prestige for bookings and guest shots, but they didn't always please the artist, including not releasing the Wiseman and Worth duet as a single.

Through the years, Mac developed an easy-going onstage style that reflected a riveting rapport with his audiences, who looked forward to his between-songs patter and the occasional tickling of their funny bone.

A particular audience favorite Mac sometimes told, concerned "this jack-legged handyman who was hired by the town-folk to paint a church steeple when nobody else volunteered to do it for free. Now he was one of those fellows who worked awhile then once he got a few dollars in his jeans, laid off working until he was broke again. So he took on the task and was nearly done painting when he'd worked his way up to the top of the steeple and saw his paint bucket was almost empty. Rather than climb down two feet to replenish his paint, he remembered he had a little libation in his coat pocket to keep the chill off. Thinking he could use it as a paint-thinner to finish up, he poured the liquor into the paint, giving him enough to complete the job. Looking at the finished work, he stood quite proud of himself, admiring his effort, when all of a sudden a flash of lightning and a crash of thunder came from out of the blue, and a loud voice admonished him, calling out, 'Thou Shalt Repaint! And Thin No More!'"

Mac was bemused during a panel session he and DJ Eddie Stubbs were conducting during the International Bluegrass Music Association week-long trade conference in Nashville, shortly after the turn of the twenty-first century, when an attendee requested Mac retell that decades old play on the religious refrain: "Thou Shalt Repent! And Sin No More!"

"It was a fellow from Florida, I can't recall his name just now, but I was some surprised that he still remembered that old story," says Wiseman. Joking aside, however, Mac has always kept the faith instilled from his childhood: "I've slipped and fell a number of times. I worked hard and I partied pretty good too, but He always scooped me up and pointed me back in the right direction to try again."

A test of his faith in his fellow man occurred in 1964, when Mac discovered he and some other Capitol contractees were put on the back-burner so-to-speak, spelling the beginning of the end recording at that label, which turned its full attention on the recent British rock invasion.

"Several of us asked for our release from Capitol, because of the impact that The Beatles were having. [The British foursome scored back-to-back number ones, 'I Want To Hold Your Hand,' 'She Loves You,' 'Can't Buy Me Love,' 'A Hard Day's Night' and 'I Feel Fine.'] The demand was so great, the label couldn't keep up with the pressings, so we were left sucking hind-tit as they concentrated fully on The Beatles. Faron, myself and Ritter, one of their first signees in the 1940s, and a great rep for them, well – we left. Tex had been the first to recommend me when he came through Bristol." [Neither Faron nor Mac went back, but Ken Nelson urged Tex to return to Capitol five years later.]

Mac's good friend Ritter was free to head up the CMA and actually made a move to Nashville, serving two terms as president. In turn, the board and voters pulled off a surprise announcement naming Tex the next member of the Country Music Hall of Fame. Some pundits wondered why Ritter went in ahead of Gene Autry, a much bigger star in movies and in record sales, who would instead be inducted five years later.

Tex was a good choice, notes Mac, echoing then current Chairman of the Board Frances Preston's assessment: "He is powerful, yet gentle. He is commanding, yet attentive. He is forceful, yet compassionate. When you talk, he listens. When he talks, everybody listens. If personal problems are being discussed, they are never his. If there is an inconvenience, it is never his. But when you need him, he is always there."

According to Mac, Tex came in from California unaware why they wanted him in so desperately, thinking he might be there to make a presentation: "It was supposed to be secret, but Jo Walker had told me he was being inducted that night. Tex was staying down at the Capitol Inn and I offered to pick him up at the airport. So when he got settled at the hotel, I took him over to the show."

134

Mac points out why Tex was unaccompanied on this trip: "His wife Dorothy was still in California to host a party he had planned for ball players - the Dodgers - as Tex was an avid baseball fan. So after the awards, I brought Tex back to the hotel and we sat and reminisced awhile."

At yet another awards show, Mac was scheduled to participate and sent his tuxedo to the cleaners. The night of the event, he pulled it out of its wrapper: "But the trousers wouldn't fit me, so in my haste, I tossed them aside and substituted a pair of black pants to go with the jacket. When I got there, Bill Williams [then WSM vice president and *Billboard* editor] came over to me and said, 'Damned cleaners got our suits mixed up. The trousers were too big for me.'"

Another friend to Wiseman was Jim Reeves. When both were in town, Mac would stop out at Jim's Madison home and office for a visit. Both had been at KWKH-Shreveport, though at different times, but they became fast friends in playing package shows and such.

Mac was stunned to learn that on July 31, 1964, Jim's single-engine Beechcraft plane had been caught up in a rainstorm and crashed near Brentwood. Reeves was the doomed plane's pilot, accompanied only by his pianist Dean Manuel, flying from Batesville, Arkansas. It took two days for their remains to be identified. Jim was just forty years old and three years later was inducted into the Country Music Hall of Fame.

Mac had yet to tour overseas, but had built up a huge following north of the border, beginning in his Country Boys band era, playing the Maritime Provinces. Thanks to all those bookings north of the border over the past decade. Mac was also a good friend to an influential music man there by the name of George Taylor.

"I was having big success with shows and record sales in Canada at the time, and George had one of the biggest labels up there then - Rodeo - and was a big friend of mine. We partied when I appeared in Halifax, Nova Scotia, as he had a place there."

There was another chap in Halifax, who owned a bar across from a military base and was a good pal: "He also had a grocery store adjacent to the tavern with an apartment for him and his family. He would throw lobster feasts for us and was a good fellow, but a boisterous kind of good old boy who had one eye that drooped the more he drank. You knew when that eye completely closed, he was done for the night. We sat up there and ate lobster for hours and he had *puh-lenty* of whiskey. I remember he said, 'Eat slow, you can eat more like that.' What a guy!"

Thinking back on his early Canadian recordings, Mac's memory is amazing in its detail: "We recorded in Montreal (July 1965) because that was where a lot of musicians we wanted to use were, including Papa Brown from The Family Brown up there and Ward Allen; Ward was one of the highlights for me, as he was one of the most popular fiddlers in Canada. He was right on his last legs, and in fact was so ill, we had to stop the session from time-to-time to let him rest. I believe that was the last thing he did before his demise, and I was particularly pleased to have him on there."

Indeed, Ward Allen died two weeks after Mac's session, on August 3, 1965, while doing a gig in Hull, Quebec at age forty-one. A champion fiddler, Ward played two years with Wilf Carter - Mac's boyhood idol - and recorded for Sparton Records in Canada. Allen wrote many of his instrumental numbers, including his most famous "Maple Sugar," a lively two-stepper Mac recorded, featuring added lyrics by Hank LaRiviere.

According to Mac, not all the LP's numbers were recorded in Montreal: "When I started my label, Wise Records, I recorded 'Bringing Mary Home' and 'Maple Sugar Sweetheart' here in Nashville. I was between labels and I'd heard The Country Gentlemen sing 'Bringing Mary Home' and they just recorded it, and it flipped me out. You see we were in Toronto playing separate clubs and we'd get together after the places closed. I didn't have a label at the time, so when I came back here, I just went down to the bank and raised me enough money to start a damn label myself."

The haunting ballad, co-written by Country Gentlemen John Duffey, Chaw Mank and Joe Kingston, proved to be a much-requested song at Mac's concerts. It's also one of his finest recorded performances. It's eerie message of a missing daughter, struck just the right chord for Mac's listeners: *"But thirteen years ago today, in a wreck just down the road/Our darling Mary lost her life, and we all miss her so/ Thank you for your trouble and the kindness you have shown/You're the thirteenth one that's been here, bringing Mary home..."*

Subsequently, Mac's Canadian recordings were issued there and also in the states on Wise Records as "Mac Wiseman At the Toronto Horseshoe" in 1966. Although admittedly the songs were not recorded at the club, its owner had helped subsidize Taylor's recording sessions at the RCA Studio in Montreal. Payback was sweet.

Ever the businessman, Mac also started his own publishing company, Wise-O-Man Music and for booking purposes, created the Wise-O-Man Talent Agency. Since its inception, Wise Records remains a busy promotional entity. Some additional selections among Mac's Canadian cuts: "Legend of the Irish Rebel," "The Ghost of Bras d'Or," "Prince Edward Island is Heaven To Me," written by guitarist Hal "Lone Pine" Breau [hubby of Betty Cody, who had the Top 10 answer song "I Found Out More Than You Ever Knew About Him"], "My Nova Scotia Home," co-written by Hank Snow, and "My Molly Bawn," a 19th century ballad popularized by Irish tenor John McCormack.

Just before his recording stint in Montreal, another milestone in Mac's life occurred. The entertainer was playing a date in Bemidji, Minnesota, the home of Paul Bunyan and Babe the Blue Ox, as depicted in a giant statue downtown. It's also birthplace of bosomy 1940s' screen siren Jane Russell and NFL Hall of Famer Dave Casper, and proclaimed as the first city on the great Mississippi River: "I saw a sign that said you can step across the Mississippi at this point, which I did. It's really kinda like a big stream up there where the river begins."

Meantime, Mac was anxious to get back to Nashville after wrapping that Fourth of July show there with Lefty Frizzell. As Mac recalls: "I got into Chicago on that holiday weekend, but couldn't catch a flight out in time, so I missed my son Scott's birth in Nashville by a few hours."

Ironically, where Mac chose to skip over his middle name, both of his children of the 1960s, chose to go by their middle names in lieu of their parental first names, discarding Marjorie and Malcolm in favor of Maxine and Scott. "You know, I've played every state but Hawaii, and all the Canadian provinces but British Columbia," boasts Mac, who from 1966 on helped to turn around the sagging fortunes of WWVA's *Wheeling Jamboree* in West Virginia.

"I was there four years. When it changed hands, the old gent who bought it - Emil Mogul (Basic Communications, Inc.) - a Jewish gentleman out of New York, was fair. He'd come and keep his finger on what was going on, but he never bothered me or criticized. It was my ballgame so-to-speak. Well, it was about to fold when I went there in May 1966. I believe in the year 1965, it had grossed something like thirty thousand dollars. By the end of 1966, we split eighty grand. That's how much it came up. I burned the midnight oil trying to figure a way to turn things around. I instituted an Artist of the Month plan. WWVA was twenty-four hours country on a fifty thousand watt station. Demographics at the time showed we covered at least thirty per cent of the population in the U.S., the entire East Coast."

Due to the increased attendance, the Saturday night show had to be shifted from the Rex Theater to the larger Wheeling Island Exhibition Hall, situated across the Ohio River. Mac's Artist of the Month plan, that helped put WWVA in the black, appealed to the powers-that-be in Nashville: "In Nashville, I ran a plan by some agents, guys like Hubert Long and Lucky Moeller. This is the offer I made them, a 'Godfather' deal they couldn't refuse; that is, I guaranteed their artists a play once an hour for thirty days, if they came in the last Saturday night of the month and played the show free. That was fabulous for them. My first artist under that program was Bill Anderson. He had a new record out and we were a fifty-thousand watt station guaranteeing airplay."

A regional hit could escalate on a national level. Mac had everybody who was anybody at the time participating, including George Jones, Merle Haggard, Buck Owens and that *All-American Country* package Buck had with Freddie Hart, Tommy Collins and Dick Curless, among others. Regular members Mac presented were Kenny Roberts and Darnell Miller.

Regarding the arena, Mac explains, "It was a skating rink normally with bleachers on each side. In the space in the middle, we put folding chairs, as we packed them in. I had fifty per cent of everything baby, including the popcorn."

He sold out three shows in that big building: "Our headliner was George Jones and that S.O.B. didn't show for the Saturday night booking. By Saturday afternoon I knew he wouldn't make it, so I called Nashville bookers I knew trying to get Hank Snow or Johnny Cash, but was too late, as those sort of stars were already en-route to gigs. We had tour buses in from Canada, among others, so I got on stage and announced Jones a no-show. He already had a reputation for missing gigs, so the audiences weren't too angry. I offered rain-checks or a cash refund. I recall not many asked for their money back. I don't think we had but a dozen ticket holders request a refund, and those who did were mainly Canadians who knew they couldn't get back there."

Wiseman added every talent available to the nightly show line-up to entertain the crowds. Mac also scheduled his own spots on WWVA, "I had their *Saturday Night Record Shop,* which was on an hour after the Jamboree, just like Tubb was doing at the Opry with his WSM *Midnight Jamboree.* You know, I kept that Record Shop a year after I came back to Nashville, which featured Lee Sutton as host. I'd just send scripts on what I wanted on it and the orders would come to a post office box here."

Lee Sutton was WWVA program director when Mac came aboard, and Gene Johnson was in charge of talent. His old friend from WSVA-Harrisonburg - Lee Moore - hosted the station's *All Night Show.* WWVA was first licensed October 6, 1926, as the first radio station in West Virginia. Incidentally, both Lee Moore (2000) and Don Owens (1989), who were connected with Wiseman's early days, were inducted into the Country Radio Broadcasters' DJ Hall of Fame. Don, of course, known in the Washington, D.C. area as "Mr. Country Music," not only wore the wax off Wiseman recordings, and dubbed him "The Voice With a Heart."

On January 7, 1933, the *Wheeling Jamboree* debuted, boasting such early star acts as Grandpa Jones & his Rhythm Rangers, Doc Williams & his Border Riders, and Joe Barker & The Chuck Wagon Gang. Other notables who spent some time on the station included Hank Snow, George Morgan, Ken Curtis, Hawkshaw Hawkins, The Stanley Brothers and an early female favorite Chickie Williams, Doc's wife. Wilma

Music festival attractions (from left): James O'Gwynn, Mac, DJ Don Owens and Curtis Gordon, circa 1960. It was Mac's first Jimmie Rodgers Festival in Meridian.

Lee & Stoney Cooper and their Clinch Mountain Clan were also regulars before joining the *Grand Ole Opry.*

After being bought by Clear Channel, the *World's Original Jamboree* continued on a locally owned station WKKX, and once again was back in the newly-named Capitol Music Hall. In 1977, the program sponsored the first *Jamboree In the Hills,* which featured the country's biggest acts and still showcased newcomers, such as twelve-year-old Brad Paisley, who made his debut there in 1984. Now he's a superstar member of the historic Opry.

Lee Sutton, incidentally, produced Mac in April 1966, for Uncle Jim O'Neal's Rural Rhythm Records, recording a staggering twenty-five tracks, which were issued on "Mac Wiseman Sings Old-Time Country Favorites," a double-LP: "It wasn't that difficult because I had my songs set when I went into the studio. I only had to familiarize the musicians and that didn't take long."

Rural Rhythm was founded in Arcadia, California, in 1955 by O'Neal, whom Wiseman said shared a love of old ballads with him: "He was originally from Arkansas, and used to invite me out to his home in California. In fact, he would send me tickets to fly out and the most of what we did during my stay was to talk about old songs. He liked that I would know most of the titles he came up with. It was odd but his wife didn't share our love of the vintage songs. She may have hated them, but it paid for those nice clothes she wore."

As Mac recalls, the session was conducted in Canton, Ohio, though some insist it was in Akron. Musicians were mainly local players, notable for the inclusion of a female Dobroist, Peggy Peterson.

"I'd just recorded three albums for Dot in Nashville, then went up to Canton and recorded twenty-five sides in one day for Rural Rhythm. So that was fifty-six sides recorded in that month, and by September, all four of those LPs were out. For

138

Dot, one of those was bluegrass, which Bobby Osborne was on. We did one of folk songs, and then one with strings and stuff like that. I remember at the time I had enough foresight that I had the Dot albums all set up on separate contracts, because I knew the bluegrass would pay for itself quickly and the one with strings probably never would," chuckles Mac.

Wiseman was given an opportunity again to play the prestigious Carnegie Hall, sharing the stage four years later, once more with Johnny Cash and a truly star-studded line-up landing in the Big Apple for the New York Folk Festival.

"Truth is things got so rowdy at the Newport Folk Festival that they were asked to take it elsewhere," muses Wiseman. "It was always a big event and I was pleased they called me to be a part of it."

The 1966 folk gig included Mac, Cash, June Carter, Bill Monroe & His Blue Grass Boys, Doc & Merle Watson, The Blue Sky Boys, Ramona & Grandpa Jones, Dock Boggs, The Statler Brothers, Jimmy Driftwood, Sarah Ogan Gunning, The Greenbrier Boys and Billy Edd Wheeler.

Their segment "Grassroots to Blue-grass to Nashville," conducted on Friday night and Saturday afternoon, proved a high-light of the multi-days' schedule. In other segments appeared the likes of the New Lost City Ramblers, Mississippi John Hurt, Skip James, Almeda Riddle, Dave Van Ronk and Son House, though clearly the fans went

With Grandpa Jones at Appalachian Festival.

wild over the country and bluegrass artists. Although advertised as "the first annual New York Folk Festival," it did not manifest into a yearly event.

During his 1966 portion of the festival, Wiseman was only accompanied by a fiddle and banjo - "I'm sorry, but I just can't recall who backed me on that show" - performing several favorites from his catalog, certainly "Jimmy Brown The Newsboy." Mac's cover on Acuff's standard "Wabash Cannonball," with the fiddler recreating the sound of a train roaring along the tracks, also proved a crowd-pleaser.

Wiseman and company were excited that the sophisticated audiences were won over by their downhome country format. Apparently enough were still aware of the day of outdoor plumbing, as they gave a favorable whoop and holler to one-hit vocal wonder Billy Edd Wheeler, whose claim to fame was a tongue-in-cheek ditty "Ode To The Little Brown Shack Out Back" (number three, 1964).

Actually, Wheeler was a rare exception in country music, as he had a 1955 college degree in English from Berea College, Kentucky, and continued his studies at Yale University. The West Virginia native also wrote the Johnny Cash & June

Carter hit "Jackson," and Kenny Rogers' "Coward of the County."

In an interview, Wheeler recalled, "I was invited to be one of the minor acts at the New York Folk Festival and Johnny Cash was headlining. He told me, 'If I ever think I'm losing the audience, I whistle for June and she comes out and we do 'Jackson' and it brings them right back up.' Normally a star will record your song and then go out and promote it, but he was trying it out on the road before he got around to recording it in 1967."

Wiseman and Cash again worked the Newport Folk Festival together, though this time it was 1969, back in Rhode Island. It was a diverse line-up of talent that included Van Morrison, Joni Mitchell, Big Mama (Willie Mae) Thornton, Ramblin' Jack Elliott, John Hartford, James Taylor, Arlo Guthrie, Muddy Waters, The Everly Brothers and, of course, June Carter Cash.

"Johnny was hotter than a firecracker, because he had his popular TV show at the time (and chart-topping records 'Daddy Sang Bass' and 'A Boy Named Sue')," adds Mac. " I remember that one was conducted in July (16-20)."

Ruth and Howard with their four children (from left) Kennie, Virginia, Naomi and Mac
(on one of his infrequent hometown visits).

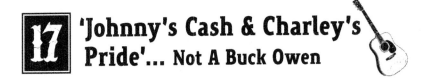

17 'Johnny's Cash & Charley's Pride'... Not A Buck Owen

"If I had Johnny's Cash and Charley's Pride
I wouldn't have a Buck Owen on my car
I'd get Dolly a Parton a good life
And buy me a Bonnie Guitar
I'd Sue Thompson for driving Conway Twitty...
I'd have Johnnie Wright there
Digging oil Wells, Kitty..."

"Everyone has a pet peeve or a frustration; mine is trying to explain that I do much more than bluegrass, without offending the bluegrass people, because God knows, bluegrass has been good to me," opines Mac Wiseman, reflecting on a long, bluegrass affiliation, but not keen on being "boxed" into a specific musical slot.

So between labels in the mid-1960s, Mac was especially receptive to ex-boss Randy Wood's invitation to record material enough for three albums, to be compiled in a trio of LPs: bluegrass, gospel, and standards. Soft-spoken Bonnie Guitar would co-produce.

Randy and Lois Wood at home.

"Yeah, 'Master At Work' was done with Bonnie Guitar. She was only part time, not full time, but she did projects for Randy. Incidentally, about a year-and-a-half ago, she got in touch with me and we had quite a conversation. She said she's still getting out, playing a few supper clubs, things like that, and lives up there in Soap Lake, Washington."

The May 1, 1966 session kick-off Mac produced, as it was a bluegrass set. Again the session was held at Columbia's studio, featuring Bobby Osborne assisting on vocals and playing mandolin; brother Sonny Osborne on five-string banjo; Joe Zinkan, bass; Tommy Jackson on fiddle; and Willie Ackerman, drums. The numbers were mainly well-worn ballads like "We Live In Two Different Worlds," "Tragic Romance," and "I'll Be All Smiles Tonight," though lesser known numbers made the line-up: "A Million, Million Girls," "How Lonely Can You Get," "New Black Suit," Mac's "The Bluebirds Are Singin' For Me" and "Since the Day You Went Away," plus two penned by WWVA rube comic Cousin Elmer under his name Smilie Sutter - "This Is Where I Came In" and "You're the

Best Of All the Leading Brands." Mac's take on the Sutter songs enjoyed ample airplay among country DJs and became fan favorites.

"A Master At Work's" titles were mostly covers, among them "White Silver Sands," "When It's Springtime In the Rockies," "The Isle of Capri" and "Forever and Ever." One of the original tracks was skillfully written by Opry star Stu Phillips, a Canadian, called "The Lonely City Park."

It concerns a young fellow flouncing out of the house after arguing with his sweetheart, headed for a private pity party: *Along a city park I strolled/A lonely man was I/The memory of those angry words/That made my sweetheart cry... As I strolled around the park/I paused along the way/I chatted with an aging man/Who had these words to say... Sit down my son and rest awhile/But soon you must be gone/For it's just a park for broken hearts/Who lingered here too long... So go my boy and dry her tears/Mend her aching heart/For if you don't, you'll spend your days in some lonely city park..."*

Mac brought to it all the passion and emotion called for, capturing the essence of its aching refrain, thanks in part to an equally compelling melody. Sadly the song didn't make it as a single, despite superb musical backing, including Pete Drake, of talking steel guitar fame.

The Sunday, May 1, 1966 session concluded with songs that later comprised Dot's "Songs Of the Dear Old Days" LP, such as "The Letter That Never Came," "Put My Little Shoes Away," "The Letter Edged in Black," and "May I Sleep In Your Barn Tonight, Mister?"

Randy revived his old budget label - Hamilton Records - to release Mac's albums. It was one of Wood's final decisions at Dot, for he departed the label he had founded in 1967, after also helping friend Lawrence Welk buy back all his masters recorded for Dot.

Mac recalls becoming good friends with Welk's manager Gabby Lutz, who on occasion invited Wiseman to join him and other VIPs for deep-sea fishing cruises between L.A. and Catalina Island.

"The songwriters Don Robertson ('I Don't Hurt Anymore'), and Fred Stryker (Fairway Music) went out with us. Gabby's wife made the best tuna fish sandwiches, and he shared them with me. You know, I caught the biggest tuna. Don's married to one of the Dinning Sisters, Lou, who had a lovely voice, and years later in Nashville at a benefit for ROPE, we did a show around Christmas time. I remember Zeke Clement was there, and I sang on 'When It's Springtime In the Rockies' with the Dinning Sisters. I thought it came off beautifully. That was a hoot!"

"When it's springtime in the Rockies, I'll be coming back to you/Little sweetheart of the mountains, with your bonnie eyes of blue/Once again I'll say I love you, while the birds sing all the day/When it's Springtime in the Rockies, in the Rockies far away..."

Co-written by Mary Hale Woolsey, Robert Sauer and Milt Taggart, this sentimental waltz tune had been a number one big band hit for Ben Selvin in 1930, and later the title tune for Gene Autry's popular 1937 Western flick.

In 1967, Mac was invited to co-produce old bluegrass friend Don Reno's next album for Rural Rhythm Records. Reno had split with his former partner Red Smiley in 1964. Bill Harrell was Red's successor for this February '67 Ohio session, with Mac and Lee Sutton at the helm. At their split, Don had retained the band

142

name Tennessee Cut-Ups. As late as March 14, 2006, Rural Rhythm re-released this set as "Best of Mountain Bluegrass."

Lee and Mac worked well together, one complementing the other throughout the session, as the latter recalls: "I enjoyed all the songs, though I worked in some different chord changes and such to give it a fresher feel."

That year Canada celebrated its centennial in a huge way, by hosting the International Exposition (Expo '67) or World's Fair at Montreal, Quebec. At the time it was hailed as the most popular World's Fair (conducted from April 27 - October 29, 1967). Some fifty million visits were recorded, with a one-day attendance record of more than a half million on the third day.

Mac was among those visitors, though he was in town for a booking: "I took Ma and Dad... and my kids (for a week). While I was at WWVA-Wheeling, I was doing exclusive bookings for a club in Montreal, where I was booked that week, as well as the Tommy Hunter TV show. Well, this promoter in Montreal arranged for us to have a three-bedroom apartment while I was there, which was especially nice considering all the hotels were booked up due to the World's Fair. We all just had a wonderful visit together. The kids other grandmother and my folks would just take turns watching them, so everyone had a chance to see the exhibitions (there were sixty-two nations represented) and such. The children (Maxine and Scott) were just small at the time."

In 1968, the industry was abuzz with news that Gulf-Western bought Dot from Paramount and expanded its country music output to include the likes of Roy Clark, Tommy Overstreet, Billy (Crash) Craddock, Joe Stampley, Barbara Mandrell, Freddy Fender and Donna Fargo. Attesting to Mac's claim that Dot was a pioneer in promoting the album format, when Gulf-Western sold Dot, which had merged with ABC, it was reported that since 1955, Wood's label had produced more than 1,000 LP discs. As Mac points out, "I told you, Randy was way ahead of the pack, when it came to producing albums."

Maxine and pet cat.

When Mac was working with WWVA, daughter Maxine remembers they lived across the river in St. Clairsville, Ohio: "I attended the first and second grades there."

It was after Mac renewed his acquaintance with Cowboy Jack Clement, producer and sidekick to Johnny Cash, that he began getting the itch to move back to Nashville. In fact, Wiseman's recording sessions from 1968 to 1970, occurred under the "guidance" of Clement, who said of Mac, "I knew him around Washington, D.C., and I believe he was also on some radio station in Baltimore."

As Mac points out, "Initially Jack and I talked about wanting to work together. He said, 'RCA's interested in you, but I can't get them to make a final commitment, because they really don't know whether you'll sell in this period of what's happening in country music.' Jack said he knew the people at MGM and felt they would at least 'go along for one record with me.'"

On May 3, 1968, Mac joined Jack at Clement's home studio situated on Belmont Boulevard, where their first selection was "Got Leavin' On Her Mind" which Jack had placed a couple years earlier with RCA's Bobby Bare, who included it on his 1966 hit album "Talk Me Some Sense." The second offered was Vince Matthews' "She Simply Left," which sounded like it might've been an answer to the A side. Nonetheless, MGM decided to release it in 1968, and it charted seven weeks starting November 9, stalling at number fifty-four.

"As a result of 'Got Leavin' On Her Mind,' and its success, Chet signed me to RCA with Jack producing me, and he had negotiated the deal. He was also having great success with Charley Pride at RCA."

The following summer - June 9, 1969 - Mac and Jack were back on Belmont Boulevard, recording Clement's "The Things You Have Turned To." Three months would pass before the team reunited, this time to try a new Cy Coben novelty number "Johnny's Cash and Charley's Pride," this one would be Mac's first charting for RCA, peaking number thirty-eight, January 17, 1970. It was paired with the vintage weeper "Put My Little Shoes Away."

Cy Coben, a well-respected country songwriter, had four number ones by Eddy Arnold: "I Wanna Play House With You," "There's Been a Change in Me," "Easy On the Eyes" and "Eddy's Song." Spurred on by the increased airplay on Mac's single "Johnny's Cash and Charley's Pride," RCA suggested Jack produce Mac singing Cash and Pride hits. With that as its theme, Mac recorded covers of the Johnny and Charley songs, which Jack had a hand in producing and sometimes originally writing the familiar refrains. Some dated back to 1958, while others were of more recent vintage.

"Johnny's Cash and Charley's Pride" was a tongue-twister to perform, featuring names of many of the artists in town, including Stonewall Jackson, Dottie West, Warner Mack, Minnie Pearl, Jeannie C. Riley, Sheb Wooley, Tex Ritter, Hank Snow, Ferlin Husky, Carl Belew and Jim Ed Brown. The song proved equally popular in Canada and the UK.

According to Mac, "Cy Coben was pleased with the way it came off. It was one of the more cleverly written songs I'd heard. He did something similar for Eddy Arnold called 'Eddy's Song,' but personally I didn't think it was as good as this one... I was over at WWVA-Wheeling when I got the 'Johnny's Cash and Charley's Pride' demo and liked it. Along with the other songs, I worked on it, though I wasn't satisfied with the way I heard it...

"Then I got over to Nashville, and told Cy I wasn't satisfied, so he took time to teach it to me as written. I was well prepared when I went into the studio to cut the song, thanks to Cy. I always had my songs ready when I went into the studio, as well as tentative arrangements, always subject to change. I'd tell the band, 'Don't be afraid to make suggestions, but I do reserve the right to reject the changes, once we run through it.' That way there were no ruffled feathers if we did it differently."
It would be Mac's last solo Top 40 *Billboard* chart single.

"I first got to know Jack when I was in Richmond and he was instructing at an Arthur Murray Dance School in Washington, D.C., and he told me he was teaching the waltz to my recording of 'The Waltz You Saved For Me.' Then we both knew Johnny, of course. About the time when we were doing the album 'Johnny's Cash and Charley's Pride,' we were in the Sheraton Hotel dining room and Johnny said to Jack, 'Remember when we used to listen to old Mac's records down in Memphis?' Anyway, I think he got a kick out of our recording."

On Monday, February 2, 1970, Jack assembled top session players and with RCA picking up the tab, celebrated his modernized facility, known as The Cowboy Arms Hotel & Recording Spa, by recording Mac. Originally the brainchild of Clement and his chief engineer, Charlie Tallent, the studio was completed December 10, 1969.

According to Tallent in a summer 1972 interview, "Everybody was cutting at that time; the music business was really hot. Then, next year, the music business was down, nearly crushed. But we still had a ten per cent increase over the previous year, and we've continued to beat every record we ever set."

In addition to recording Wiseman, Clement was also working with talents like Rex Allen, Dickey Lee, Doc Watson and newcomer Townes Van Zandt. Production assistants aligned with Clement included executive-songwriter-guitarist Allen Reynolds, who would also record with Mac down the road.

To complement Mac's hit record "Johnny's Cash and Charley's Pride," RCA called for the concept album of that title, with four days set aside for Mac's take on hits created by Cash and Pride. Incidentally, Charley Pride's songs were all recorded under the RCA banner, but Cash's hits were for Columbia Records. The colorful Cowboy Jack, who had produced many artists' hits, has since said, "My favorites were Mac Wiseman records."

In seeking a new direction, it's easy though to see why Wiseman would place himself in the hands of such a successful producer-tunesmith as Clement, who came up with two potential winners: "Got Leavin' On Her Mind" and "Johnny's Cash and Charley's Pride."

One incident in the studio stays fresh in Mac's mind: "Unbelievably, Jack had this stack of steel guitars on my session. I mean he had Lloyd Green, Joe Talbot and every other top steel man playing, just stacking them and then he even added his own steel playing. It could've been a unique sound, but he mixed out everybody's but his steel playing. I also remember I got sick of singing the same damn song over and over... Then when we was recording one day, Chet (Atkins) came in and said, 'Is this the million dollar recording I heard about? - and I don't mean in sales, but the session!' Jack wasn't worried about budgets."

By 1970, Mac was ready to call it quits with WWVA-Wheeling, and he had accomplished his mission: building up attendance for the historic show. Wheeling was fine for settled artists like Doc Williams, who harbored no further ambitions as an artist nationally, but not Wiseman.

"It was time to go and I had my deal with RCA," admits Mac. "I remember I pulled out when school let out in June 1970, as the kids were able to finish up their school year."

Meanwhile, Wiseman was frustrated by his lack of major success with Clement, who told his artist, "I just don't know what to do with you." Wiseman wasn't sure what that meant, though his other artists like Cash and Pride were some years younger than he.

"Jack's genius part is there's more in his head than he can say or do," Wiseman articulates. "But Jack's the guy who got me on RCA… and also the one who got me off. You know, after the 'Cash and Pride' record, it was another year before he got me another record. He'd leave a session just to go out and smoke pot in the parking lot. It bugged the hell out of me, but I sort of hung in there waiting to see if we could do something. Jerry Bradley (then RCA's A&R country chief) later said, 'Every week we held our meetings, we wondered how long before Mac would get tired of putting up with Jack's shit.' There was Bob Ferguson, and then I got Allen Reynolds producing. He's the guy who became wealthy after working with Garth Brooks."

Roni Stoneman confided The Stonemans had similar problems when produced by Clement, so much so that Billy Grammer really handled his studio chores when Jack was absent so much: "It was horrendous working with Jack, the most horrible experience I've had in music. He would hold up production, belittle us, calling us the 'Stonehypers' and *hillbillies*. He'd be smoking that stuff, and we didn't even know about marijuana at the time. I remember that he also absolutely hated girl singers, and mostly wanted us to record his songs. Daddy went along with it because he wanted to see his children do well."

In his defense, Jack said years ago, "We're in a fun business: entertainment. So I've always said if we're not having fun, we're not doing our job." Mac was open to having fun, but during work hours, he was there to be serious and hopefully succeed.

Finally, not too keen on his solo prospects at RCA, Mac seriously considered an offer in 1970, from former Pamper Music publisher Hal Smith, to become involved with the Renfro Valley, Kentucky, enterprise, which Hal had bought into a couple years earlier.

The original *Renfro Valley Barn Dance* had been founded by John Lair, who first made a name for himself working the WLS-Chicago *National Barn Dance* show, which originated April 19, 1924 as the *Chicago Barn Dance*. Ironically it had been organized by George D. Hay, the Solemn Old Judge, who a year later founded WSM's historic country program. WLS, call letters that stood for *World's Largest Store*, meaning Sears & Roebuck, which originally owned the station. WLS became home to such talents as Gene Autry, Smiley Burnette, Rex Allen, Jenny Lou Carson, Karl & Harty, Red Foley, Lulu Belle & Scotty, Patsy Montana & The Prairie Ramblers, Bradley Kincaid and George Gobel.

Lair also nurtured the talents of the Three Little Maids (Jenny Lou Carson and sisters), Lily May Ledford's Coon Creek Girls, Martha Carson and her sis-

With John Lair, owner, Renfro Valley Show.

ters as the Hoot Owl Holler Girls. In 1937, Lair left WLS to launch his own country program at WHAS-Louisville, later moving it to WLW-Cincinnati, before settling in Dayton. Relocated to Mt. Vernon, Kentucky, the show evolved as the famous *Renfro Valley Barn Dance* on November 5, 1939.

"Mr. Lair and I became very good friends. He came through Richmond, while I was on *The Old Dominion Barn Dance* and invited me to go with a Norfolk package show he was presenting there - the *Renfro Valley Barn Dance* program - but I had too good a thing going in Richmond, so I respectfully declined. I considered doing that show a couple times in the early 1960s with him, but being honest with myself, I realized it would mean moving to Renfro Valley to be a full-time member. That would mean losing my national image, which we had built up through my Dot recordings and also I just had that hit on 'Jimmy Brown the Newsboy.' So I put the idea out of my thoughts. At one time, Molly O'Day was a headliner at Renfro Valley."

In 1969, Hal Smith, who had played fiddle in bands for such stars as Ernest Tubb and Carl Smith, along with guitarist-wife Velma Williams, before running the ultra-successful publishing firm Pamper Music, was beginning to divest himself of his Music Row business interests. These had included management, publishing and booking agencies, as well as a partnership with Haze Jones in Hal Smith's Artists Productions, which promoted the likes of Tubb, Willie Nelson, Ray Price, Hank Cochran, Lois Johnson, Benny Martin and Don Reno. Hal also syndicated the popular *Ernest Tubb Show* for television.

It was in 1968 that Hal bought the Renfro Valley show from Lair and ran it for about ten years. He later confided, "I found out two things: absenteeism is a bad thing; and if you're gonna be successful in something involving tourism, you've got to have something else going on besides the pickin' and singin' out in the boondocks. We had a certain following, but there was nothing else to go to.

"There's nothing as lonely as being in the business world and looking around and seeing you have no friends," continued Smith. "There's no one to ask for advice. Mom or Dad or Uncle Tom can't help you, so you play everything from the seat of your pants."

*With bluegrass festival founder
Carlton Haney.*

Running that operation required steady commutes between Nashville and Renfro Valley, no easy task for a man. In an effort to turn things around, Hal called on old friend Wiseman. Apparently the challenge to work with Hal appealed to Wiseman; however, he didn't want to work the actual *Renfro Valley Barn Dance* near Mt. Vernon, as Hal requested.

"I came up with the concept of a *Renfro Valley Bluegrass Festival*, which made it the third biggest festival in the business, right behind Carlton Haney's Berryville in Virginia, and Bill Monroe's Bean Blossom in Indiana [where

Mac's a charter inductee in the Bean Blossom Bluegrass Hall of Fame]. It would be an annual event. I ran the first full weekend - Friday, Saturday and Sunday - in July. I ran it for thirteen years that way. Knowing it was always the first full weekend in July, people could remember it that way."

Mac remembered years earlier, Carlton Haney calling him with an idea to comprise a weekend bluegrass and country concert outdoors: "He would ask me for my input and whether I thought it would work," and subsequently Haney launched his 1965 Festival at Cantrell's Farm in Finecastle, Virginia. Mac, of course, played it and Haney's effort sparked many more bluegrass festivals.

Amazingly, Mac's *Renfro Valley Bluegrass Festival* earned a profit its very first year: "I booked my acts just as heavily as the other festivals, and even though rule of thumb is that it usually took three years to realize success, we made a good profit that first year."

First up booking-wise were Lester Flatt & Nashville Grass, Bonnie Lou & Buster (who had the first theater in Pigeon Forge), the Shenandoah Cut-Ups, Chubby Wise, Red Rector and quite a few of the top bluegrass and folk acts of the day. In order to be competitive with the big festivals, Mac advertised and promoted the Renfro Festival very heavily, using a lot of major newspapers in places like Cincinnati, Louisville and Nashville, as well as in country periodicals.

"Hal was very easy to work with. He let it be my ballgame, the festival, while he ran the *Barn Dance*. Before I took on the festival, I would ride up with Hal, who went every Tuesday to check his *Barn Dance* operation, because he had a lot of concession stuff and such. We'd leave like 4 a.m. and because the turnpike wasn't built then, drove up through Lexington, then drove straight South about forty miles to get to Renfro. I knew Hal since he was a fiddle player, and he and Ernest Tubb started one of the first booking agencies in this town. Hal had a lot of history to tell."

One festival coup Mac made, came about with Coca Cola, when he went to Berea to their main distribution plant and made a deal "where they would put a collar on each six-pack of Coke, listing not only the dates of our festival but our talent line-up, as well. It didn't cost us a penny, but, of course, we stocked only their product, which included Coke and orange soda. Similarly, Mac approached a meat supplier to furnish a refrigerated van in exchange for using only their hot dogs and hamburgers.

"Another feature was selling corn-on-the-cob, and it was about two weeks ahead of the crop coming in up there, so I made a deal with a farmer in South Carolina to obtain his sweet corn, shipping it in to coincide with our festival. We would take a refrigerated truck over there, and bring back the corn. As I recall one year, we sold three hundred dozen ears of corn!"

According to Mac, he and Hal split fifty-fifty on the entire operation; that first year - 1971 - Mac's talent bill was forty thousand dollars (reflecting what bluegrass boys were receiving, while an artist like Johnny Cash could command that much alone). Not all was smooth sailing. Mac recalls a time when the self-proclaimed "king of bluegrass" Jimmy Martin was booked on Renfro's star-studded show.

"I put Jimmy Martin on early after telling me he wanted to hit the road in a hurry, due to a Pennsylvania gig the next day. Hell, he got on stage and you couldn't get him off. I told the emcee to get that SOB off there, so the other acts could go on.

Well, Jimmy had some fellow drunks there in the front rows cheering and egging him on, so he kept right on joking and playing.

"Waiting in the wings to go on were hallowed duo Lulu Belle & Scotty, then up in age after having enjoyed their heyday in the 1930s and 1940s. When Scotty came up to me in the wings, and said that he and Lulu Belle needed to get on and do their bit, because he was getting tired and wouldn't be worth a damn, I'd had enough. I went out there and chased Jimmy off the stage, so the other acts could continue. You know after telling me he had to hit the road early, he stayed on until the festival ended. Then while pulling out, his bus hit the radio tower. That was the last time I ever booked Jimmy Martin!"

There was no shortage of talent waiting to play Mac's Renfro festival. He recalls when inviting Lulu Belle & Scotty, "At first Scotty was hesitant to do it, as they had been retired so long. Then he called back to say after talking it over, they would play the festival after all. A big factor in their decision was the opportunity to see Mr. Lair again.

"You know besides their beautiful home in North Carolina, they built a couple cabins on their property for guests who came to visit. He and Lulu Belle graciously called me and invited me to lunch one time and I went. She had prepared a nice lunch and we had a wonderful visit. Scotty took me out to see one of the cabins and gave me a standing invitation to visit any time.

"The first time I ever met them was at Sunset Park, where we were all booked. Back then, Lulu Belle and Scotty had ridden the train from Chicago to Philadelphia, and the park owner made arrangements to pick them up. I guess I told you that from early spring of 1952, before I went to WRVA, the park booked me every Sunday I wasn't scheduled somewhere else... There's a housing development there now."

Another festival Mac was booked at annually was near McAllister, Oklahoma: "There was an old man who ran the festival there who at first wouldn't give permission for them to do it there in his fields. There were rows of trees, and some very rocky terrain. But he cleared it out and indeed it made good festival grounds. I played it for fifteen years or so and during that time bragged if it lasted for twenty years, I'd do it that year for free. You know that he didn't forget what I said. So I played it and he made me keep my word, but he told me, 'Hell, I've got to give you eight hundred dollars just to cover your damn expenses!' That was near the Oklahoma State Prison... Years later, I learned that Joe Diffie's parents had taken him to see those festivals, so he was familiar with my music when we got together."

18 'We'll Meet Again, Sweetheart'... Reunited

"So goodbye now, don't be blue
Try to be happy and be true,
And remember what I say
Sweetheart, we'll meet again someday..."

"At a festival in Myrtle Beach, South Carolina, I was on ahead of Lester Flatt and as I came off, he was standing in the wings ready to go on. Lester said, 'Why don't you come back on and we'll sing 'We'll Meet Again, Sweetheart,' the one we recorded for Mercury. After he got into his show, Lester called me out and when we sang that song, boy, the audience went into a frenzy. I couldn't believe it. Lester looked at me and said, 'Damn! Maybe we ought to do more of that.'

"So we came back to Nashville and he had his deal with RCA when I was also on the label. That's when we did 'Lester 'N' Mac' (1971)... It went over quite well, so we did 'On The Southbound' (1972) as our follow-up album, and 'Over The Hill To The Poorhouse' (1973). All three sold well. I think 'Lester 'N' Mac' was one of the first bluegrass albums in the Top Hundred *Billboard* pop charts to my knowledge." [It did indeed make the Top Hundred, as did another of Lester's, 1964's "Flatt & Scruggs At Carnegie Hall."]

Mac and Lester Flatt at 1971 show.

Indeed Mac and Lester's collaboration gave Wiseman his first Top Forty LP charting on *Billboard* (number forty-two, 1971). Bob Ferguson had produced the first session, then Clement added his input as co-producer with Ferguson for the remaining sessions teaming the bluegrass pioneers. At one point, Lester even suggested perhaps he and Mac should team up, but that wasn't something Wiseman wanted, though willing to do show-dates with his old friend, thanks to their albums scoring well with fans.

Their collaboration on "Someday, We'll Meet Again, Sweetheart" was garnering ample airplay across the country: *"Oh sweetheart, I'm leaving now/Yes, I'll soon be on my way/Each night upon my knees I pray/Sweetheart we'll meet again someday..."*

Mac recalls Flatt had a house on Old Hickory Lake, originally built by Roy Acuff to live in, right across the street from then-Governor Frank Clement: "I went out there a number of times and we'd rehearse and plan our next album, coming up with the material that we'd use."

Back then, Don Light was doing most of their bookings: "We worked a lot of colleges together, as well as bluegrass festivals. He would do his show and I would do my set, then Lester would come out and we'd do another twenty minutes together, performing songs from the albums. We got along fine, performing together three or four years, with never a cross word between us."

One incident Mac remembers occurred en-route to a gig when he ran out of smokes. He bummed one from Lester, who was driving. By the time he'd asked Lester for a second, he was feeling a bit like a moocher, and told Flatt: "When we get to a stop up ahead, let me buy you some cigarettes." Lester drolled, good-naturedly, "I don't need cigarettes. Better buy yourself some!"

Two of Mac's personal favorites among their numerous collaborations were "The Bluebirds Singing" and "Sweetheart, You Done Me Wrong." The final Flatt-Wiseman studio effort occurred in October 1971, when the pair cut another dozen songs at the RCA studios, co-produced by Clement and Ferguson. One of the tracks on that final session was "You Can't Trust a Friend Anymore."

"While doing that tune on stage, Lester laughingly looked over at me after singing *'You can't trust a friend anymore...'* ad-libbing on mic, *'And I ain't too sure about you,'* and I pretended I was shocked, staring back at him."

While running the operation in Kentucky for Hal, there were still solo sessions being scheduled for Mac, as well. Wiseman had his work cut out for him, including the outside personal appearances. Yet another milestone music event occurred in April 1972, as the first Fan Fair was launched at the downtown Nashville Municipal Center, attracting some five thousand enthusiasts, compared to the one hundred and fifty thousand or so some forty years later. Mac would become a regular at this event, and promoted participation by the Reunion Of Professional Entertainers, during his years as ROPE president.

For the time being, the *Renfro Valley Festival* was his first priority, and acts tripped over themselves vying for bookings at the outdoor venue. As a result, John Lair had misgivings about having sold the historic show he had launched.

In his (1999) book of reminiscences, "It All Happened In Renfro Valley," comic Pete Stamper recalled how things were after Smith took over: "There were Appaloosa horse shows, rodeos, antique car shows and the bluegrass festival... During their first five years there was quite a bit, but it all seemed to come from the outside and only a little of it stuck.

"Mac Wiseman produced our first bluegrass festival in July 1971, and I'm proud to say it's still going strong. It's now called the *Old Joe Clark Bluegrass Festival*, but it's the one and same that began twenty-eight years ago."

Stamper indicated that Lair was determined "to buy the Valley back and left no stone unturned in pursuit of that goal..." and obviously that's why he held onto *The Bugle* newspaper and continued with the *Renfro Valley Sunday Mornin' Gatherin'* broadcasts. Both outlets reported on Renfro Valley events.

"I was doing a concert in Ohio, when Mr. Lair came and approached me after the show," says Wiseman. "He asked if I would consider 'buying' the *Renfro Valley Barn Dance* and he would be my silent partner, explaining he thought Hal wouldn't sell it to him. He had one hundred thousand dollars set aside to purchase the *Barn Dance* back. I told Mr. Lair that I really didn't want to do that, but thanked him for the offer. I felt that I would've disappeared from the music scene nationally, had I done that."

Actually, by then Hal was fed up with the operation and wanted out, so eventually did sell the *Renfro Valley Barn Dance* back to John Lair, but also wanted to enlist Mac to make the sale.

"It was odd the way they transacted the deal. It was akin to the Hatfield and McCoy thing, because Hal and Mr. Lair weren't all that friendly, but they used the same attorney to close their sale. They did this at a motel, with Hal in one room and Mr. Lair in the next room. So the lawyer had to go back and forth to make their offers and acceptances, until the deal was finalized."

"In the second year I ran the festival, there was a television crew in Louisville that had just purchased a modern mobile unit and were anxious to do a trial run to get the bugs out and to get acquainted with it. They asked to come down and did all three days of our performances at the festival. That footage became half mine and half Hal's. Years later when Hal decided to get out of the music business entirely, he called me and said, 'I can't think of anybody I'd rather have my half of these videos than you,' so he let me buy his half. I was very pleased by that. As recently as 2006, I sold the whole shooting match to Ronnie Reno. In addition, to getting a good price, Ronnie produced a new album and DVD on me, and then gives me coverage on the new RFD cable network, where he shows and sells the product." (That's the album that hit number twelve, 2010.)

The relatively new RFD network focuses on the nation's farmers, but beams music shows by Ronnie Reno, Marty Stuart, Larry Black, Ralph Emery, *Midwest Country,* as well as reruns of old country shows such as Porter Wagoner's, The Wilburns and *Hee Haw.*

Harking back to the topic of Renfro, Mac notes: "Mr. Lair had never presented his very popular *Sunday Mornin' Gatherin'* show any other place than his Renfro Valley Barn, but at my suggestion, he came down and did the show on my Festival, which was part of the three days shot by the Louisville TV crew. So that's part of what I sold to Ronnie Reno and he now has a DVD out on that and it's been shown on his RFD show, as well."

Mac's known Ronnie Reno all his life.

Mac was less than thrilled at the turn of events that occurred during a July 1975 show which son Scotty, ten, attended while dad was on stage entertaining. A drunk attempted to gain entry to the festival without a ticket; however, one of the show's security guards interceded, ordering the intruder off the grounds, but he refused. During the scuffle, the guard's gun went off, wounding the belligerent gatecrasher: "Scott was close enough to the security guy that he could've reached out and touched him. I decided to keep right on pickin' and singin' in order to avoid any panic in the crowd, as the security detail worked to calm the commotion in their corner."

152

Wiseman recalls how he came to engage that particular security crew: "I had played a festival in North Carolina and saw these guys doing such a good job of security that I hired them for my festival. It wasn't completely fenced in, and usually I hired state troopers or the local Sheriff, if available, to handle security. Well, one of those old boys from North Carolina was standing by a fence when he saw this guy and warned him not to come over, which he did and it ended up that the guard shot him. We had a tent out there used for the festival's security detail, and Scott saw inside and said they had an arsenal in there! They had all of that cleared out before the law arrived.

"Now I had to leave the area to go to upstate New York for a Sunday folk festival. Maxine was with me, but that crowd was so unruly I wasn't brave enough to take her out in the field to sell my product. Anyway, after I got back to Nashville, they called me to testify, as the guy who got shot sued me, being the festival manager.

"When I went up, I found the security guy had been in jail all winter awaiting trial. They'd gone to North Carolina to get him, and you know he never mentioned me all during that time. I thought that was right neighborly of him, so I bailed him out of jail that day. He could've involved me a lot to save his butt, because it was in my name.

"But before I went to court, I did my homework. We got information that the guy (the shooting victim) had been drinking and boasting he was going to break up the music festival. So I got witnesses who brought this out in testimony, showing the guy was a troublemaker... Miraculously, the bullet had entered into his eyelid, traveling alongside the socket, but exited and didn't lodge in his head. It must've been a smaller weapon, like a .22. I didn't know but what he was dead when from the stage, I saw them taking him out of there on a stretcher."

"In their later years, I'd take my mom and my dad to the shows and festivals I did. My wife and I took them to Renfro Valley or down in Georgia. I even took Mom to Texas with me one time. She just ate it up!," exclaims Mac. "Mom made so many pen pals, so that by the time she became incapacitated, she corresponded with people she met on those trips."

Nor does he forget Ruth's earlier interest: "My mother was a big wrestling fan when TV first came out and it was so big (remember the flamboyant Gorgeous George?). So I took her over to Roanoke to see the wrestlers... she did everything but throw chairs at the ones who made what she felt were bad calls."

Indeed, Mac made time for his family, despite a busy and demanding schedule.

On October 27, 1971, Jack Clement produced a three-song session for Mac, who sang, played rhythm guitar and picked up leader's pay for performing "I'll Still Write Your Name In the Sand," "I'd Rather Live By the Side Of the Road" and "Sing Little Birdie." They recorded again in RCA's Studio B. Others on their time card included Joe Allen, bass; James Isbell, drums; Chuck Cochran, piano and harpsichord; and on harmonica Danny Flowers, the chap who wrote "Tulsa Time."

Although "Sing Little Birdie" appears as a Mac Wiseman composition on RCA's time sheet, Mac clears up the confusion regarding the song: "Mine's just an arrangement. It's really just an old song from public domain."

Regarding Clement musicians scheduled, Mac notes, "I didn't know Joe Allen, but he was a good bass player. Now James Isbell I can't recall. Jack must've got him. Chuck Cochran did a lot of good things with me. Actually, he had just finished an album with me at MCA, when he got killed (in a 2007 car crash). That was a tragic accident indeed."

Cochran kicked off his professional career by playing piano for Bobby Vinton, and went on to tour and record with Don Williams and Neil Young. Stars like Don Williams, Emmylou Harris, John Hartford and Dr. Hook recorded Chuck's compositions. On May 18, 1972, Clement protégés, Allen Reynolds and Bob McDill, co-produced Mac's session in RCA's Studio B, as McDill and Reynolds each played guitar, with the latter collecting the leader's double scale. Former Pozo-Secos Singers' vocalist Don Williams provided harmony, along with co-producer Reynolds and Susan Taylor.

"Of course, Don would go on to be a major singer of country songs (like 'I Wouldn't Want to Live If You Didn't Love Me' and 'Tulsa Time'). We knew he was an exceptional vocalist. Susan? She was in the music business, more as a writer than anything, but a very sweet lady."

Mac found himself in youthful hands with McDill, then twenty-eight, and Reynolds, thirty-three: "I got to know them both well, and they were very competent, so I had confidence in them. There was no friction to any extent. If there were disagreements, we just spoke up about it and got them resolved."

Kickin' off their session was Scottish folk favorite Donovan's composition "Colours," which he'd charted in May 1965 in the United Kingdom, and saw it released a few months later Stateside.

"I didn't know Donovan then, but somebody ran his song by me - I heard it, I liked it, I cut it," says Wiseman, who continued by singing a portion of the lyrics: *"Yellow is the color of my true love's hair/Blue is the color of the sky in the morning when we rise... Mellow is the feeling that I get/When I see her, mm hmm/When I see her, uh, huh/That's the time, that's the time/I love the best..."*

Three originals from McDill and Reynolds were cut - "Song of the Wildwood," "At the Crossroads" and "Let Time Be Your Friend" (which Allen co-wrote with Susan Taylor) - says Mac: "That song 'Let Time Be Your Friend' is one of my favorites. 'Song Of the Wildwood' (by McDill) is another of my very favorites (again breaking out into song, singing the chorus). Guess you don't want to hear that, but it brought back a memory to my mind... Bob became one of my 'goodest' friends. He told me whenever he and his wife wanted to relax, that they light up a candle, get a bottle of wine, sit down and listen to my albums. That's the nicest of compliments."

Mac's session fiddler Buddy Spicher, cognizant of the easy way Wiseman segued from country to bluegrass, to folk to gospel or romantic ballads, feeling he could do it all, called Mac "the Frank Sinatra of country music."

MAC'S SCRAPBOOK

Ruthie with her parents Thomas and Susan Humphreys.

The Wisemans (from left): Howard, Marvin, dad Kenneth, mom Naomi, and brothers Luther and Ira.

Mac's granddad Thomas Humphreys.

Howard (from left) with Thomas and Susan Humphreys and their daughter Ruth.

Mac's grandfather Kenneth (seated) with his brothers.

Ruth's elder half-brother Lewis Humphreys, a pastor, with their Aunt Jane Sampson.

Uncle Jim and Aunt Esther Marshall at her parents' house.

The Wisemans moved here on Rockfish Road, when Mac was 2. He loved the sound of rain falling on its metal roof, lulling him to sleep.

Susan (holding baby Mac) and Thomas Humphreys with (from left) Jim Marshall and wife Esther and her sister Ruth, Mac's mom.

Aunt Mariah, Uncle Sal and their daughters.

Mac's Aunt Carrie lived to be 100.

Malcolm 'Mac' Wiseman, age 15 months.

Howard, son Mac and daughter Virginia, on the family Ford.

Howard with children (from left) Virginia, Mac and Kennie.

157

Little Mac, Mom, Kennie and Virginia
in early 1930s.

Pre-schooler Mac marks a birthday.

Virginia Louise, 1, and brother Mac, 3.

Wiseman kids – Mac, Kennie and
Virginia – get their own kittens.

Shenandoah College at Dayton, Virginia.

158

NEW HOPE HIGH SCHOOL SENIORS

First row—Left to right: Glenna Garber, Elizabeth Smith, Joan Cline, Mirna Belle Flory, Nancy Crisman, Mabel Suddarth, Verbanell Rankin, Mary Aldhizer, Charlene Yonce, and Miss Frances Cline, class sponsor.
Second row—Left to right: James Aldhizer, Dorothy Wiseman, Ellen Baber, Marguerite Foley, Jean Rankin, Mildred Weade, Reba Crickenberger, Thelma McAllister, Margaret Bulle, and Mary Herron.
Third row—Left to right: James Willberger, William Whistleman, William Robbins, Principal E. W. Chittum, Thomas Patterson, Samuel Diehl, Malcolm Wiseman, and Herman Small.
Not in picture—William Wampler, James Patterson, Bowman Parr, Everette Garber Jr., Charles Wine, and Lucius Beard.

The local paper carried this senior class picture, depicting Mac in third row, second from right; and that's his cousin Dorothy in the second row, second from left.

In sport jacket and gloves, student Mac looks pretty dapper (note his built-up right shoe) at the pump.

Here's New Hope High School as it appears today, a bit run-down.

That's young Mac out in the dooryard.

159

Mac Wiseman

FOLIO OF

Favorite Folk Songs

This is no doubt Malcolm's first publicity shot, at WSVA-Harrisonburg.

Mac's songbook that sparked a rift in his run with Lynn Davis's troupe.

Mac and his first-born, Randy, in the 'wilds' of Virginia.

Mac worked with Bill Carlisle at WSB-Atlanta, before joining Bill Monroe at WSM.

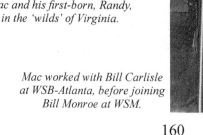

160

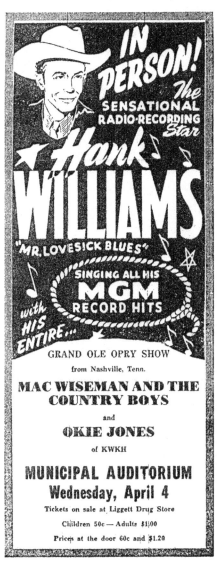

While playing KWKH-Shreveport's Louisiana Hayride, Mac gigged with Hank Williams in 1951.

Mac seems a happy roving troubadour during his Louisiana Hayride tenure.

This ad appeared in the *Winchester Star* for the August 14, 1960 show.

The Watermelon Park promoter must've thought Mac a fore-runner of Kinky Friedman, 'The Jewish Cowboy,' in plugging 'Max Weisman,' The Osbornes and Scotty Stoneman over the likes of Bill Monroe and Reno & Smiley, for this 1960 festival, in Virginia's Winchester Star newspaper.

161

Mac hawked this handsome, glossy 8x10 for $1 each for fans at his early concerts.

Little Linda checks out Granddaddy Howard's old truck.

Mac and Christine, his first baby with Emma.

Mac stops by the old South River once more.

Sheila and Chris sit up high as Aunt Esther, Dad and Grandma Ruth strike a pose at Knott's Berry Farm, Calif., 1957.

Mac posed for the photographer, maybe seeking an official Dot Records shot.

CMA board members in 1958 (front row, from left): Hubert Long, Harold Moon, Connie B. Gay, first president; and Mac; (rear) Oscar Davis, Ernest Tubb, Ken Nelson, Wesley Rose, Cracker Jim Brooker, Vic McAlpin, Walter D. Kilpatrick and Charlie Lamb. Mac was the youngest of the CMA founding fathers.

CMA executives (1962): Roy Horton (left to right), Jo Walker, Bill Denny, Steve Sholes, movie cowboy Gene Autry, president; Wesley Rose, Frances Preston, Hap Peebles; (second row) Hal Cook, Bill Anderson, Jim McConnell, Chuck Bernard, Jack Loetz, Ken Nelson, Harold Moon, Bud Brown, Boudleaux Bryant, Mac, Bob Pampe and Walter D. Kilpatrick.

*Mac never missed the annual Disc Jockey
Conventions in Nashville, mixing it up with
both label execs and media types.*

*Mac and Billy Walker visit
backstage at the Opry.*

Mac chats it up with DJ Jody Rainwater.

Mac makes the rounds of NC's Cherokee Festival grounds with booker Norm Adams.

This snappy Pontiac pacer caught Mac's eye at a NC track.

Race champ Richard Petty sports a cool hat, as Mac wears his Texas Ranger cap.

Mac made it home to help Dad celebrate Mom's birthday.

Ruth remembers Howard on his birthday, as well.

*Mac had the pleasure of entertaining aboard the SS Dolphin
seen here in Nassau.*

*Mac enjoys singing with The Lewis Family (that's Polly at left,
and Little Roy, right).*

*Ex-Congressman-TV actor Ben Jones (Dukes Of Hazzard's 'Cooter')
sidles up to Mac at festival.*

167

Chubby Wise and Mac were both Blue Grass Boys and recording buddies, seen here in the '80s.

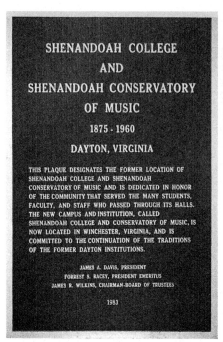

Mac has this reminder, a plaque commemorating his studies at the Conservatory.

Dad and Virginia catch up to the family's vagabond.

The home of Doc Bowman, who presided at Mac's birth and treated him often in his youth.

168

At Mac's Wildwood Valley Farm in Lebanon, he raised thoroughbreds.

Mac and Connie Smith share the Opry microphone.

Naomi, Dad, Virginia and Kennie, Christmas 1983.

Mac delights in a 'dueling banjos' bit between Donnie Bryant and Eddie Adcock.

169

Mac shares a moment with legendary harmonica player Lonnie Glosson.

At a bluegrass festival, Sheila and Chris hold up Wade Macey's carpet depicting his years with Dad's Country Boys.

Mac entertains his 101-year-old Aunt Alberta.

Sharing the stage are (from left)
Kenny Baker, Josh Graves and Mac.

Ramona Jones (Grandpa's wife) and
Euleta Kirby (Brother Oswald's)
with Mac at a house party.

That's great-grandson Ricky Taylor
checking out Mac's beard.

Patti and Randy guide son Mike
on a pony ride.

Mac snaps friends Frank Oakley, Shot Jackson
and Bill Carlisle at a get-together.

171

Ruth and Howard enjoy having grandson Mike Davis visit them.

Patti, Randy, Howard, Mac and Michael represent four generations.

Canadian balladeer Stu Phillips greets Mac at ROPE show.

After Acuff passed, Brother Oswald (chair) and Charlie Collins (center, guitar) teamed as Os & Charlie, seen here with their band and Mac.

Raymond Fairchild shares a new song with old pal Mac at Appalachian Museum in Norris, Tennessee.

Mac rekindles friendship with Claude Boone (credited with writing 'Wedding Bells').

Mac relishes a visit by granddaughter Kim (right) and husband Nathan, with children Olivia, Sarah and Logan.

Gov. Jimmie Davis takes time for a photo op with Mac, after Davis' show.

Mac, Virginia, Randy, Patti and Maxine aren't camera shy.

In 1994, Mac guested on WSM, 45 years after making his Opry debut with Bill Monroe.

Mac strikes a pose for a new publicity picture.

Chris Hillman, Mac and Marty Stuart laugh it up at an awards gala.

Texan Willie Nelson, and 'Dancin' Fiddler'
Mack Magaha perform with Mac.

Roger Sovine and Mac crack up over
a Porter Wagoner joke at ROPE.

Mel Tillis offers Mac
musical encouragement.

Singer Margo Smith lets 'Santa' have
the last word at holiday party.

175

Bluegrass legend Curly Seckler gets both Mac's hand and ear here.

Mac and George Hamilton IV attend Johnnie Wright's 90th birthday bash.

A pensive Wiseman ponders a new project.

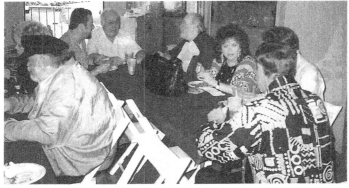

*Folks take a lunch break while filming Larry Black's Country Family Reunion
Show in the late 1990s. Mac talks to restaurateur John Hobbs, while next
to him, Jeannie C. Riley chats with Billy Walker (back to camera), and across
the way we see Johnny Russell. Mac also hosted a Bluegrass segment.*

*Earl Scruggs and wife Louise were noted for hosting jam sessions, replete
with refreshments. Here we see Mac (from left), Eddie Stubbs (obscured by Mac),
Kent Blanton, Glen Duncan, unknown mandolinist, Randy & Earl Scruggs,
Ricky Skaggs and Jerry Douglas (back to camera). What a line-up of talent!*

*While ROPE president, Mac
created a special caregiver plaque
– The Mac Wiseman Nightingale
Award – to honor those dedicating
themselves to caring for ailing loved
ones. Barbara Morgan, wife of DJ
Bill Morgan, was honored in 2004
(above). Among others awarded
have been Sue & Bobby Wright,
Euneta Kirby, Gloria Boyd and
Leona Williams.*

177

In '02, Randy visits Dad in Nashville (here at Cracker Barrel), along with son Michael and his daughter Samantha, making yet another four generations photo op.

Mac performed what he announced was his 'swan song' at the Nashville Symphony Center with John Prine, following the release of their 2007 album 'Standard Songs For Average People,' but he has made several appearances since, probably 'by popular demand.'

This photo opportunity occurred just after Mac's 85th birthday reception. That's Mac and Randy in front; daughters Sheila, Chris and Maxine behind them; and bringing up the rear are co-hosts Eddie Stubbs and David McCormick, with Mac's younger son Scott Wiseman. (– Photo by Patricia Presley)

In 2010 IBMA honcho Dan Hays honored Mac's longevity and legend on his 85th birthday.

Mac the good humor man.

Mac in the early 1980s.

179

OVER THE FLORIDA GEORGIA LINE

Utah-based booking agency - Country Explosion LLC - is suing **Florida Georgia Line (Brian Kelley** and **Tyler Hubbard)** over pay for their July 20 engagement at a Country Explosion Music Festival. Reportedly, the organisers of the program agreed to ante up $450,000 for their appearance, with half up front and the remainder the night of the show by cheque. The bookers allege the act's representatives **Darren Brady** and Stark Entertainment, also named in the lawsuit, caused the duo to breach a verbal agreement not to process the check until July 23, by attempting to cash it July 21, before the funds were deposited. Florida Georgia Line has since filed their own suit contending non-payment for their agreed-upon single show, though the artists admittedly received the advance payment. The Utah bookers further contend that their breach caused a bounced check, which makes Country Explosion "absolutely toxic among artists and booking agencies in Nashville."

Looking at the group's earning in the Forbe's listing of 'Country Cash Kings' (see page 5) it looks like pocket change for the Cruise hitmakers.

FGL have also announced the follow-up to their hugely successful 2012 debut *Here's To The Good Times*, with *Anything Goes* due to be released on Oct. 14. Speaking to The Associated Press, Kelley said of the pressure they are under to equal the double platinum success of their debut, "A little bit of that pressure creates some pretty good creativity... We just pushed really hard... little melody changes, adding little things here, an 808 drop there, a breakdown here, a different guitar lick there, whatever it may be, we really spent a lot of time on the little details."

The '808 drop' to which Kelley refers is a hip hop term - but that's how they roll! "There's a couple sad songs, there's a couple that make you think, but at the same time it's a party album. It's a feel-good album. Right when you get to the last song you're going to want to start it all over again. It's right exactly 100 percent where we are in our lives" he said.

California legal

On July 18, Marine Sgt. **Raymond Sharkey** of Camp Pendleton, Calif., was sentenced to a year in county jail plus three years' probation for beating **Zachary Zander** during a **Jason Aldean** concert in September 2012. Allegedly, Zander came to the defence of women being harassed by Sharkey, but then Sharkey was joined by several other Marines, who were not charged in the drunken melee. Zander identified Sharkey, who not only broke Zachary's leg, but caused extensive facial damages, requiring long hours of reconstructive surgery. Come September, the court will determine a monetary sum Sharkey must pay in restitution to the victim, and he cannot consume any alcohol during his probation period. Reportedly, the Marine is also being separated from the service, and his command is cooperating fully with the court.

Riding Away

The final night of **George Strait's** Cowboy Rides Away tour on June 7, 2014, was to a crowd of nearly 105,000 in Dallas and this month sees a 20 track live album of the event released.

The collection also features guest appearances from **Jason Aldean, Ray Benson, Kenny Chesney, Eric Church, Sheryl Crow, Vince Gill, Faith Hill, Alan Jackson, Miranda Lambert** and **Martina McBride,** as well as George "Bubba" **Strait, Jr.** who has written material for recent albums by his dad.

The 'event' has also been broadcast in a two-hour special on CMT. No word yet, but a special CD/DVD for the UK market we wonder?

Clay Aiken, a 2003 runner-up in an American Idol competition, was voted winner of a Democratic primary seeking a North Carolina congressional seat in the U.S. Congress. He faces Republican candidate **Renee Elmers,** 50, next November in the national run-off. Aiken, 35, had a Top 10 scoring via **Bryan White's** *Someone Else's Star,* and has a son Parker **Foster,** 5, with female record producer Jaymes **Foster,** though Clay is now openly gay.

Wising up

New Country Music Hall of Famer **Mac Wiseman** just completed a new folk-style album for Wrinkled Records, titled *Songs From My Mother's Hand,* co-produced by **Thomm Jutz** & **Peter Cooper.** Its official release date is Sept. 23. Mac, 89, must be setting some sort of record in recording another studio album, having made his first recordings with **Molly O'Day** in 1946, produced by Columbia's **Uncle Art Satherley,** in Chicago. The latest project couples him with mandolin virtuoso **Sierra Hull,** age 23, as well as the likes of veteran **Jimmy Capps, Mark Fain, Jelly Roll Johnson, Justin Moses** and **Alisa Jones Wall.** The selections recorded are derived from vintage notebooks Mom **Ruthie Wiseman** wrote down for her son while listening to the radio in the 1930s and early '40s, hence the album title. Meanwhile, Wrinkled Records' CEO **Sandy Knox** hosted an invitation-only listening party in RCA's Studio A, Aug. 22. Other artists on her label include **B. J. Thomas, Etta Britt** and **Jimbeau Hinson.**

UK fans learned of Mac's new solo CD last fall in the monthly
Country Music People magazine.

19 'On Susan's Floor'... Serenading

"Now that my song is sweeter,
Lord I'd like to greet her;
To thank her for the favor that she gave,
A stranger I came, my head bowed in the rain, to her door.
I sat and sang my songs on Susan's floor..."

"I did get to meet Shel Silverstein with Bobby Bare, but can't say I knew him well. Bobby and him were so close that Jeannie (Mrs. Bare) told me he was so torn up when Shel died (May 1999) that he couldn't go to his funeral."

Shel was a multi-talented artist, who co-wrote the touching ballad "On Susan's Floor" with Vince Matthews, the last track recorded by Mac at the aforementioned 1972 RCA session.

It was an ode to Sue Brewer, who opened her home to struggling songwriters lacking rent money or the price of a bowl of soup. Sue kept the burner hot under her stew pot, and if beds were filled, told the overflow to bunk on her floor until they saw the morning sun. Her Eighteenth Avenue home near Music Row became a hangout for down-on-their luck artists, who called it the Boar's Nest.

Mac wasn't one of those, but he liked "On Susan's Floor." Legend had it those better-heeled recipients of Sue's friendship - Faron Young, George Jones, Webb Pierce, Waylon Jennings - would occasionally slip her $100 or so to help pay for the soup and utilities in warming the stomachs of those in need. As Mac sang: *"Didn't feel so cold and tired/Stretched out before her fire/Rollin' smokes and drinkin' up her wine/And I remember candlelight and singin' songs/Till we could sing no more/Then fallin' fast asleep on Susan's floor..."*

When Brewer became ill, a bunch of "my boys" banded together to do a 1985 benefit produced by Jim Owens, to help out financially with medical costs. Thanks to the talent line-up, CBS-TV picked it up for beaming in October 1985.

Silverstein was a writer-artist who gained attention when his cartoons were printed in *Stars & Stripes*, the daily military newspaper, and later Hugh Hefner's *Playboy* magazine. His dark humor soon spiced up songs like Johnny Cash's "A Boy Named Sue," Loretta Lynn's "One's On the Way," The Irish Rovers' "The Unicorn" and Bobby Bare's "Marie Laveau." Shel also won acclaim for his children's books, including "The Giving Tree" and "Falling Up."

Since it was the fifth song on a session usually calling for four, one might have thought "On Susan's Floor" was something Mac recorded due to extra time. Not so, notes Mac, "Oh no, we really wanted to cut that song, and in fact it later got me on that Jim Owens CBS network TV show that Waylon hosted called *The Door Is Always Open*, and the only thing that qualified my being on was that I had the first recording on the song. A lot of the players were the patrons of her bailiwick so-to-speak. I never really was over there because I was out-of-town most of the time, though I knew Sue when she worked with Faron Young's paper *Music City News*. I liked her and the song."

Mac's September 27, 1972 Studio B session was again co-produced by the McDill-Reynolds combo. Mac's former Country Boys' Josh Graves and Eddie Adcock sat in playing banjo and Dobro, respectively, while tracks included "Eight More Miles To Louisville," written by Grandpa Jones, famed for his wry humor, but as a vocalist his only *Billboard* chartings are covers of others' hits: "All American Boy," a Top Twenty version of Bobby Bare's number two pop debut charting; and "T For Texas," Jones' Top Five revival of Jimmie Rodgers' number two "Blue Yodel" pop charting.

Most of his friends have a favorite Grandpa Jones story, and Mac is no exception: "There are so many to choose among, it would be pretty hard to pick just one. I remember the time he and I, along with Ray Price, Wilma Lee & Stoney Cooper, went out on a twenty-day tour in Canada. We started out on Labor Day, though I can't remember the exact year; anyhow it was the time Grandpa's nephew or somebody like that was building him a house out in Ridgetop (Tennessee), while he was gone. He rode with me because his wife Ramona needed to get their kids back and forth from school. At the time, they only had one car.

"Grandpa asked to ride with me, agreeing to share the driving and gas expense. We had a wonderful time together, but on a Friday night the last day of the tour, when we usually would spend the night before heading back home, Grandpa was so anxious to get home, he said, 'I'll help you drive if you don't mind, so we can go on back tonight.' We were in northern Ontario, so we drove right back, but didn't get there until 7 or 8 o'clock the next night. That's how far away we were.

"But when Grandpa walked into his new home, it smelled like three hundred rotten eggs! He said, 'Good God, Romany, what's that smell?' They had drilled a well out there before they built the house, which was smart, but they didn't test the water, which wasn't smart and it turned out to be that old black sulfur water. Ramona had just taken a shower and the house smelled like rotten eggs!"

Mac recalls Ramona telling him during that same time frame, Grandpa was on WSM's noon time program when in off the road. "In just routine conversation, fellow entertainers got to asking, 'How's that well coming along Grandpa, have you struck water yet?' He'd reply 'Nah, we ain't struck no water yet, but we're still drilling,' until finally he got so tired of being asked, he told the next guy asking, 'No, we ain't hit water, but we're smelling rice down there.' (Indicating they hit China.)"

Then there was the time Grandpa thought one of his cows was missing.

"He mentioned that on the Saturday night Opry, and Vic Willis and some other friends got together on Sunday to scout the hills up by his place searching, but couldn't find any trace of the cow... The following Saturday night, someone asked Grandpa did he ever find that cow? Before Grandpa could answer, his son Mark Jones spoke up to say, 'Yeah we found her. She was in the freezer!' He'd had it butchered but forgot about it."

Another time, "Grandpa decided to fence in some flatland to pasture his cows, so they wouldn't get out and roam around the hillside. He had his tractor there and everything, and spent quite awhile there, but trouble was Grandpa fenced himself in and hadn't built a gate to get out!"

182

The Opry cast knew sometimes Grandpa forgot names when hosting, especially guest artists on his portion. Billy Grammer was truly startled the time Grandpa forgot his own wife's name: "He had a mind like no one else. When he got his mind locked into a routine, then he'd forget everything else. When it came time to introduce me, he hemmed and he hawed then said, 'Here's this big-footed guitar picker...' Well, Ernie Ferguson, the mandolin player, he got right, but when it came time to introduce Ramona, he said, 'Here's a little girl who plays mandolin... she plays guitar... she plays fiddle... she plays zither,' while stalling, trying to recall her name; then in an aside, he whispers, 'What's her name?' By then the audience knew something was wrong, but he quickly called out, 'Yes, it's Romany!'" That's the nickname he called her off-stage."

Mac remembers a time Ramona was having eye trouble and the doctor advised her to keep off her feet until the problem was corrected: "She told me, 'You know Grandpa's not the easiest man to get along with, but all the time I was tortured by this eye trouble, he was so good to me. He would cook, clean the house and look after everything. Well, fortunately, before too long my eye got better. Now he's back to normal.'"

According to Mac, Grandpa didn't want drums on his recordings. One day he went into the studio to record, looked over and saw a drummer and his kit. After giving him a puzzled look, the drummer asked, 'Grandpa, don't you use drums on your session?' Trying to be diplomatic, Grandpa replied, 'Very little, if any.' He was a true character."

Bob McDill and Allen Reynolds scheduled Mac's November 8, 1972 session in Studio B. A pair of Carter Family classics were among the songs scheduled: "Keep On the Sunny Side," which gave the Carter Family a Top Ten in 1928; and "Will the Circle Be Unbroken," though A.P.'s version was titled "Can The Circle Be Unbroken (Bye and Bye)" (number seventeen, 1935).

"On 'Will the Circle Be Unbroken' we were supposed to do a fade on the end, and I finished up and repeated the last line, for the fade. Hell, I had the ear-phones on and the engineer wasn't fading, so I didn't want to have to make another take, so I just said very plainly into the mic, 'Well that's all I've got,' and when they mastered it they left that tag in there. It was cool. I was merely getting their attention that I didn't have any more to sing."

Canadian singer-songwriter Ray Griff pitched Mac his melodic weeper "It Rains Just the Same in Missouri (As It Does in Old Idaho)," a ballad that appealed to him, and should've been promoted with more vigor by RCA, having all the earmarks of a hit.

"That's been one of my most-requested songs," adds Mac. "Ray Griff wrote that and was living in Alberta at the time. He sent it to me on a little acetate."

Steve Goodman's "City Of New Orleans" was another powerful piece that seemed likely to reignite Mac's chart action: "Bob Millsap brought that one to me. Well, we were so pleased with what we done with it that we called the publisher to see if they wanted to hear our track, thinking they would be tickled to death we recorded the song. They had sent a tape with several other songs being pitched, but the publisher said, 'Oh my God, we didn't know that song was on there. That's a mistake and we can't let you release it.' You know the publisher can withhold a song that hasn't yet been recorded, so we couldn't put it out without his say-so. He really blew us away because we felt it would've made a hit for us."

Apparently the publisher had promised it - even though unbeknownst to RCA, Steve had already recorded it himself - to Arlo Guthrie, Woody's son, who scored a Top 20 pop hit with it in fall 1972. Mac thinks it was held for Waylon Jennings, though he never charted with the song, as duet pal Willie Nelson would (number one, 1984).

Incidentally, Reynolds and McDill had co-written a sure-fire success, "Catfish John," however, they had pitched it earlier to RCA's Johnny Russell. Mac recorded the song November 8, and Russell's version charted November 11, 1972, giving Johnny a breakthrough hit, a near-Top Ten. According to Mac, Russell, had been disgusted by his slow progress and was about to ask for his release. "Johnny had a lot of success getting songs recorded, but wasn't getting anywhere with his own recordings. One time we were both making phone calls to DJs at radio stations to plug our songs, when he said to me, 'I think I'm just going to give up recording and stick to writing.' I said, 'Oh no, John, don't do that just yet. You never know when the next one might be a hit. Just hang with it awhile longer,' and by damn the next one he put out was a hit - 'Catfish John' [followed by his 1973 Top Five 'Rednecks, White Socks and Blue Ribbon Beer,' written by McDill, Wayland Holyfield and Chuck Neese]. I was glad I talked him into that, and you know he repeated that story on stage one night at the Nashville Palace, the club John Hobbs had run. He told it when Don Light and I were dining there."

Johnny Russell and Mac stand tall.

Despite his disdain for Clement's erratic behavior, it was Jack back in the producer's chair for Mac's June 20, 1973 Studio B session, which called for a single cut: "You Can't Go In the Red Playin' Bluegrass." Co-written by Jack Speirs and Norman (Buddy) Baker, the novelty number expressed the situation for Wiseman clearly enough. Mac wasn't familiar with the team, but turns out Speirs and Baker were Hollywood writers working for the Walt Disney Studios, though Speirs, a West Virginia native, was the one more attuned to bluegrass.

"I know Bobby Thompson played a fabulous banjo on it. I mean he flat out beat the hell out of it! I did another 'Bluegrass' title earlier that Justin Tubb wrote, 'Bluegrass Music's Really Gone To Town,' which I brought into the studio myself."

Clement enlisted Bob Ferguson, who wrote "On the Wings Of a Dove," again to co-produce the next and last Flatt and Wiseman session for RCA on July 5, 1973, also in Studio B. Bringing his talent to the mix was young Marty Stuart on

184

mandolin. The Mississippi native was then fourteen, and his mom had given Flatt permission to use him in his Nashville Grass band, only if he studied and did assigned schoolwork.

Yet another session player that day was Johnny Johnson. "I knew Johnny Johnson as far back as Shreveport when he and his wife Jerry had a band down there," says Mac. "Now she was originally Jerry Leary, sister to Wilma Lee Cooper. The Leary Family had no boys only the three girls (the third sister was Peggy). Jerry worked awhile with Roy Acuff's Smoky Mountain Boys. After she and Johnny broke up, however, Jerry stayed on here around town (and for a time became her widowed sister's road companion). I don't know why they split, but Johnny was wild as a buck. I guess that may have been the reason."

Mac remembers that Wilma Lee "could play the hell-fire out of a guitar." In 1957, Wilma Lee & Stoney Cooper joined WSM's *Grand Ole Opry*. Stoney died March 22, 1977, but she continued solo with the backing of their band, the Clinch Mountain Clan. Their only child, Carol Lee Cooper, headed up the Opry vocal group The Carol Lee Singers for years. An ex-daughter-in-law to Hank Snow, she sung backup vocals on some of Mac's recordings. Sad to say, following a stroke, Wilma Lee resided in a nursing home, until her September 13, 2011 death.

On that July 5, 1973 session, Lester's listed as leader.

"Oh, Lester took the leader's pay?," repeats Wiseman, cocking his right eye. "No, I didn't give a crap, though it was of course a little extra money, but I'd simply steal it somewhere else."

Some of the session's songs stirred up memories for Mac: "Well, 'The Girl I Love Don't Pay Me No Mind' was a song I learned from Fiddlin' Arthur Smith of The Dixie Liners (featuring Sam & Kirk McGee). He co-wrote 'There's More Pretty Girls Than One,' at a time when he was with the Delmore Brothers (mid-1930s). Interesting thing about Smith is he went out to California in the 1940s to work with Jimmy Wakely, and got involved with American Publishing out there and copyrighted in his name a lot of old songs that the McGees had done, they said."

"Now 'Stranger in This World' was my song and also recorded in the first session I did for Dot, and was my second release. It says 'Over the Hill To The Poorhouse' was co-written by Lester Flatt. I think again that was an arrangement, because I came across its sheet music from the 1800s the other day... I don't think Lester was around back then, but he should've been."

Their chorus goes: *"I'm old, I'm helpless and feeble/And the days of my youth have gone by/And it's over the hill to the poor house/I must wander alone there to die."*

For some twenty years, Lester Flatt and Bill Monroe didn't speak to one another; however, Mac was there to witness their reconciliation: "It was at Bean Blossom and we were backstage, then a little porch-like thing there on the back of the stage instead of a dressing room. Well, they were standing there tuning up, looking at each other and I can't recall which one made the first move, but Bill and Lester shook hands, and I was standing there watching them do that."

It was also in 1973, that Mac broadened himself by accepting an offer to perform at the International Festival of Country Music in London from British promoter Mervyn Conn: "To talk about my overseas travel, I need to explain that I was on the CMA Board of Directors at the time, and we developed quite a pattern we created in order to get full-time country music stations going in places like Houston, New York or various cities like that. To coincide with that we wanted to expose our music abroad, especially with the Wembley Country Music Festival being launched in England by Conn. So we were taking the board over to meet and attend the show.

"In order to have a quorum, they came to me and wanted me to go, but I wasn't booked on the festival, which was around Easter. I didn't care to go at all and especially at that time of year wasn't the most responsible thing for me to do. But I did go. You also had to pay your own expenses for the damn thing, so I booked a few dates after I got there to help out. It gave me a chance to get my feet wet on short notice.

Mac meets with Dutch promoter Cor Sanne and German record executive Krugen Kramer.

"To qualify for the cheaper air fare, you had to stay at least ten days. Anyway, I went over and we had the board meeting and all, finishing in just a few days. Then everybody else scattered to travel all over to places like Paris, Cannes, Monte Carlo and Spain. I couldn't handle that you know, so I booked myself into little working-man clubs all around the London suburbs for next to nothing to help out."

Backed by staff bands, Mac drew good crowds, without much advertising. That let them know over there that indeed he had a following, and it didn't escape Conn's attention, adding Wiseman was the first bluegrasser to play Wembley.

"Bill Anderson and other artists initially went over there to work it at cost, simply for the promotion of country music internationally. I wasn't financially able to do that. When I went, I didn't get big money, but I was paid more than they got. Conn was the one who booked me on the European mainland, and one time with Bill Anderson for ten days as his opening act. I would open with his band and he would do the second half.

"Then I had this little college trio on tour and they were good to work with," continues Wiseman. "I even rode along with them in their van, and they took me to the battlegrounds and other historic sites. I mean we'd get off the main roads and stop in at pubs. Can't think what their names were, but traveling with them was fun and very educational."

Mervyn Conn subsequently got a reputation regarding his financial dealings with some acts (and in later years was accused of sexual harassment of young women).

"The promoter never shorted me a nickel. But Hubert Long and those guys in Nashville spoiled him, working their acts for nothing, mainly because they wanted to establish a rapport with English fans, which wasn't altogether wrong. But, I waited until he got ready to pay. He'd been promoting country acts two or three years before approaching me. Now, I didn't get big money or my regular price. I think I got seven or eight hundred dollars a day off him, which was more than the other guys were getting. Some went over with a band for five hundred dollars. I recall sometimes Conn booked me in Ireland and Scotland as well, just myself with a little backup band. We did pretty good for the most part.

"I took Donnie Bryant along with me another time, and him being a policeman in D.C., he enjoyed talking with the British police, you know the Bobbies," Mac points out, adding that he did eventually get booked on the Wembley Festival. "I was on the same package with Barbara Mandrell, who was at her peak. She and I were never buddies, but I knew her and her dad Irby in California. They were on that *Town Hall Party*. Well, she came on that Wembley stage and thought she was going to burn them a new one. But she was way too slick. She did her Vegas act, playing the saxophone and the steel, just bang! bang! bang! They came in within a hair of booing her off stage. That was not what they had paid their coins for.

"I came in right behind her and got the standing ovation she figured she'd get! Actually, I was sad for her. That was hard to take. Now, anywhere but there, she would've wowed them. That was a huge crowd and they came dressed in their cowboy outfits and stuff, their idea of how to come to a country show."

Barbara perhaps believes the British audiences were indeed hard to please, and some say they're more negative to younger artists and their material. Is that an accurate reflection?

"No. They weren't any different over there and they weren't behind the times, though their taste is more traditional," insists Wiseman. "They haven't switched over as much as American fans. I think that's excellent. That's also why I'm in love with Canada, for the same reason. They're more entrenched in what they believe in."

Wiseman remembered that Acuff-Rose music publishers were ecstatic when Ray Charles revived Don Gibson's "I Can't Stop Loving You," which sold Platinum-plus as a pop-country-R&B crossover single, and prompted another best-selling album.

"Acuff-Rose had publishing offices in London. So I went with Don on a big package show over there. We even went into France. Don's deal with his publisher was they'd furnish him a limousine for him and his wife, plus a driver. I'd known Don in his Knoxville days, so he invited me to ride with them, anywhere we didn't fly. That was a big line-up including Cash, Brenda Lee, Jerry Lee Lewis - it was a helluva package. I had a great picture of a bunch of us taken in front of the Eiffel Tower in Paris in which young Marty Stuart was standing. Not too long ago, he featured that picture in his photo book (now sold via his RFD-TV show)."

Don Gibson and Mac.

On another of Mac's overseas tours, he remembers: "I had the weekend off when Bill Clifton was living about a hundred miles out of London at the time, and invited me down to his place for the weekend.

I accepted and rode the train to his town, to stay at his house for the weekend. The bedroom he put me in had the most unusual rafters I'd ever seen, because they were about twelve by twelve... When I asked about their size, Bill explained the house had been built by a sea captain, who when he stopped sailing, had dismantled his boat and built the house from the timbers. The papers on this particular weekend were just loaded with Burl Ives getting remarried [to Dorothy Paul in April 1971], and that he was in England spending his honeymoon.

"Saturday night after dinner, Bill said he was going to take me up to a typical English house party and dance. When we got there, the place was just a big living room with the furniture moved out, and was already filled with people. When we walked in, me with my beard and plump size, a hush fell over the room and I could hear them whispering, 'My God, it's Burl Ives!' After introducing me around as Mac Wiseman, everything settled back to normal."

Clifton, like Mac, is a member of the Bluegrass Music Hall of Fame (2008), in recognition of having organized the first major bluegrass festival at Oak Leaf Park in Luray, Virginia, in 1961, and for his musical contributions in groups such as the First Generation band. Another WWVA-*Wheeling Jamboree* alumnus, Clifton lived and performed in the UK until 1978, when he moved back to Virginia.

It was in 1973, that Mac scheduled surgery he felt would be in his best interest, gastric bypass surgery, to slim himself down. He had to be placed on a waiting list; however, that same year, Hollywood icon Dean Martin wanted Mac to share the stage on his highly rated network TV variety series.

After being called on to guest on NBC-*TV's The Dean Martin Show*, for which he was notified in August 1973, Mac did a spot in downtown Nashville singing Steve Goodman's "The City of New Orleans," which had been recorded several months earlier by singer Sammi Smith.

"I sang that down on Lower Broad Street, looking out over the Cumberland River while seated in a boxcar. I remember it was a hot Sunday morning and I had a hangover."

The Dean Martin Show ran nine years (1965-1974), two hundred and sixty-four episodes, after which Dean did another series, hosting *Celebrity Roasts* that proved quite popular.

Mac's guest segment tied in with Martin's new attention-getting concept of going "a little bit country" for a portion of his program, designed to keep things fresh. When this came off so well, Martin's producer Greg Garrison wanted Mac to do yet another segment. The singer had to decline because of his October surgery date for which he'd waited so long. In order to accommodate his upcoming hospitalization - much to Mac's surprise - Garrison rescheduled their shooting date.

"They moved it up a week. This time we did it out at WENO-Ranch in Madison," muses Mac. "I did the first song early in the day, then hung around all day to do the second song 'The Baggage Coach Ahead' at twilight. That was a long-ass day. Donna Fargo was also there to sing her hit 'Happiest Girl In the Whole USA' (which sold a million records for Dot, and earned two Grammys)."

Mac's not sure what medley of songs they did, but he was also included in a finale with Dean and Petula Clark, walking and singing on Stage Four in Burbank. Martin also featured a spot where he was seated among comedian regulars such as Foster Brooks, Dom DeLuise and Nipsey Russell, who apparently was familiar with Mac's onstage storytelling, because off-camera Nipsey told the singer he ought to tell one on the show which, of course, was pre-scripted.

Mac had become concerned about his growing girth, thinking he'd have more energy with less weight to tote around. He was even making jokes about his three hundred pound form a part of his stage banter.

On one occasion, Mac confided to the crowd, "Friends they told me not to get too close to this microphone, as they are having some problems with feedback..." pausing to look down at the Martin guitar resting on his big belly, he joshed, "Ladies and gentlemen, I CAN'T get very close to this microphone!"

The artist had heard about a surgical process to enable overweight people to lose weight. Actually, the first reported bypass surgery in 1954 was conducted by Dr. A. J. Kremen, who did what he termed an "intestinal bypass" designed to aid endangered obese persons lose weight.

"What I had done was definitely a new procedure," continues Wiseman. "My doctors were the only ones doing that. What brought it to my attention was that New Orleans' trumpet player Al Hirt and his daughter both had it done right there at Richmond in the same hospital. I gave a lot of thought about having it done."

It would seem that Mac might seek out Al to find out about intestinal bypass before undertaking the procedure, but he says, "No, I didn't and if I had, he probably would've wised me up. I lost one hundred and sixty pounds in ten months (from a peak three hundred and twenty-five pounds). I see some of those pictures of me now from back then and it's scary. I heard that the word got out in the industry that 'If you want to see Mac Wiseman, you'd better do it soon because he's a goner!'"

Mac's bypass surgery occurred in late October 1973, at the University of Virginia Medical Center in Richmond. "I came home in time for Christmas with the family... Right after stomach surgery, I was like an inmate for thirteen years. My electrolytes got way down. You know your heart ain't nothing but a muscle and it weakens when your energy's down. My doctor warned me at the time while playing lots of shows, including wild places in New Mexico and West Texas, that if I kept it up, I wouldn't be around long - 'They're gonna pull the sheet up over you, if you keep this up!' - he warned."

Shortly after undergoing the surgery, Mac remembers getting a call from a struggling young singer and admirer, who had previously worked with Buddy Starcher and Ralph Stanley: "Keith Whitley called to ask if I'd manage him. But I wasn't feeling well enough to take on that extra responsibility. Before I was able to get him with someone I trusted to manage him, Keith had a bad car accident. That laid him up awhile. Afterwards, I was able to get him with Don Light, who not only managed and booked him, but got Jack McFadden for Keith, as well. The rest is history, as they say."

Indeed from 1973 thru 1986, Mac stuck with his gastric bypass: "That was a terrible time, man... and not to sound crude, but (his body) literally became a dumping station. I don't think that they're doing the bypass surgery now as much as they're doing the banding. For me, it was the worst thing I ever did. I'm still embarrassed by it with my family. My kids were small and I wasn't the most congenial fellow, and my wife waited on me hand and foot."

The singer made periodic returns to Richmond for exams and treatment: "Then my doctor retired or something, and he turned me over to a doctor at Vanderbilt Medical Center here."

Mac reflects on the aftermath, "Physically, I got so exhausted, and my nerves were right on edge, but during a ten-day tour in Canada, I only missed one date. Every other night though, I went into a hospital to check my blood pressure, and they pumped blood into me. We would be in a different town, and I'm in the hospital again. Finally, in an airport to fly back home, I was going to call Marge to let her know what time to pick me up, but as I reached up to drop coins into the pay-phone, suddenly I couldn't let loose of a quarter... My system froze - my arms convulsed

Mac at 1983 festival in Connecticut.

and two guys tried to straighten it out and couldn't. When I got back, I said, 'Take me to Vanderbilt Hospital,' this some thirteen years after my original surgery."

The first time his new physician worked with Mac, he was slated for a reverse surgery: "But I was in such a weakened condition and my electrolytes were so depleted, it took them nearly a week to get me in shape for the surgery (to reverse the procedure). Well, when they finished, it wasn't working and I kept bloating up. I mean they gave me laxatives and nothing would go through me. The gas built up in my stomach so bad that they came in and punctured a hole in me - and it was terrible! This stuff came flying out, splattering all over the place!

"Then when the doctor, who supposedly pioneered the process, came in, I asked him, 'Dr. Scott (H. W. Scott, Jr.), don't these things always work?' He hesitated, but told me, 'I've done over a hundred and this is only the second one that didn't work.' After a few more days, he performed the 'hook-up' surgery and this time it worked. I was kept in the hospital like thirty days."

Prior to being hospitalized, Mac had recorded with Tompall for an MCA album: "The day I came out of the hospital, Tompall had arranged for me to do a photo shoot for the front cover. I was all dressed in black when I went out to do that, and the photographer was concerned because the backdrop was black and wasn't sure whether it would work. But you know it came out great - and you couldn't tell I'd just got out of the hospital after that very stressful ordeal."

20 'It Comes And Goes'...
Fool's Gold

*"Like the beauty of a summer rose, it's a song everybody knows
It comes and goes, like breathin' out and breathin' in
You just gotta breathe again, ain't it funny how it comes and goes..."*

"I got so fed up with Jack Clement so bad that I felt I should've asked for a different producer sooner," says Mac, who on March 13, 1974, was assigned Ray Pennington, Chet Atkins' chief assistant, to produce what would be Mac's last session under the RCA contract.

Only three songs were slated, "It Comes and Goes," "Dixie Hummer" and "I've Got to Catch That Train," which Dave Kirby wrote. According to Mac, Susan Taylor co-wrote "Dixie Hummer," while Bill Dees penned "It Comes and Goes." Dees' major hits include Orbison's "Oh, Pretty Woman" and "It's Over."

"It Comes and Goes" represents one of Mac's finest works. Randy Wood would've welcomed it on Dot, as its tune's quite danceable, almost Samba-like with its basic two-quarter tempo and Latin rhythms. Dees' declarative *lyrics "La da de da da, La da de da da... playing my music so well/You can hear it when it stops..."* and Mac literally stops momentarily on the disc, returning vocally with *"It comes and goes, like the rhythm of the tide that flows/Like the weather, turning hot and cold."*

Apparently RCA didn't get behind the song, catchy and rhythmic as it is, and, of course, Wiseman was making his exit; nonetheless, "It Comes and Goes" became a single in May 1974, backed with "I've Got to Catch That Train."

Although Mac's family didn't get the opportunity to travel abroad with him, they did share a fun trip aboard a luxury liner, commencing off the Atlantic coast during the mid-1970s. Mac was co-headlining a summer pleasure cruise on the *SS Rotterdam* with Bill Anderson, sailing down to The Bahamas: "Coming back, however, we left Anderson down there, taking on Jeannie C. Riley, who switched over from another Holland America Cruise... I guess Anderson took her place on the other ship.

"I took Martha and Eddie Adcock as my backup. My kids Scott and Maxine accompanied us, seemed like they were eight and ten at the time. Well, we did one show down and another coming back. That was pretty easy. Poor Jeannie C., she had to do a few each day of the cruise, repeating her smash 'Harper Valley PTA'; however, I had made our arrangements before I signed on as to how many shows we'd do. It really was a nice cruise for us. We got to eat at the Captain's table one time and that required evening clothes. The food's unreal on those cruises, and my children had a ball. Soon as you got a mile or two from shore, there was gambling. Scott was little, but I let him play the slots a bit. Of course, he was standing by me, and only got to drop a coin in and pull the handle, but that thrilled him anyway."

Mac found himself back in the studio in late 1974, this time for Moe Lytle's Gusto Records, and among twenty-eight songs, the balladeer had a wide range of material to record with, including Bill Monroe's holiday tune "Christmas Times A'Comin'," vintage fare like "Barbara Allen," and covers such as "Poison Love" and "Rocky Top."

Mac would later record "Rocky Top" again with its original hitmakers - the Osborne Brothers, Bobby and Sonny - in 1981, recorded at Opryland. The song was co-written by Felice & Boudleaux Bryant, good friends to Wiseman.

On stage (from left) Sonny Osborne, Mac and Bobby Osborne.

"I met Boudleaux and Felice in Moultrie, Georgia, in 1949... Approximately eight to ten years later, while living in California, I was in Nashville producing some sessions and Boudleaux and Felice invited me out to their place on a Sunday, just to sit around and visit. Their house was most unique. Boudleaux had bought an old way station (stagecoach-type stop), using the timbers to have their house built. The floor in the living room was unusual because they had put it down with wooden pegs instead of nails, like it was at the vintage way station.

"On the way out to the Bryants in Hendersonville, there was a drive-in market, so Felice suggested we stop and she could pick up some (pre-cooked) chicken for supper. By late afternoon, Felice volunteered to warm up the chicken for us, and came in a few minutes later with her face longer than a Georgia mule's. Now she had shopped many times at this particular market and never got anything that wasn't first-rate. The chicken she bought, however, was full of maggots when she went to reheat it!

"Thereafter, she'd tease me every time I saw her, saying, 'If you come visit us again, I won't feed you any chicken.' That afternoon, Boudleaux was planning on singing some of his latest songs for me. He had just written one I really liked, titled 'Every Now and Then.' I was taping the Jim Ed Brown TV show the next day and sang it, then very proudly called Boudleaux and said, 'Hey, I recorded your new song.' Much to my surprise, he said, 'Oh damn, I've got to hurry, because I don't have it 'copywritten' yet.'"

Regarding Moe Lytle, Mac has only good memories, though some artists expressed regrets after working with him: "He's just a clever marketing man. Of those cuts I did for him, he's kept the same configuration, and keeps it going. My tracks were recorded at the old Starday studio on Dickerson Road, produced by Tommy Hill. When Moe bought up the Starday catalog, Hill sort of went along with it, having worked with Don Pierce. Tommy was the in-between guy, and got me the money I asked for from Moe, who paid good in my book. You know Moe owned a club in St. Louis, where he'd get up and sing some of my songs for the patrons. In fact, he picked the songs for my session. I later asked where did he hear about those songs? He said, 'I'm a fan of yours' and told me about performing at the club in St. Louis."

Unlike Lytle, Martin Haerle later mixed Mac's recordings on different albums, finding new ways for CMH to utilize them. Wiseman doesn't seem to have objected to his methods; obviously if paid accordingly that satisfied the artist and businessman in Mac.

During those early 1970s, Wiseman enjoyed reuniting with Lester Flatt for shows in support of their trio of RCA albums: "We played primarily colleges and bluegrass festivals. It was a wonderful reunion. In fact, he must've enjoyed it, too, because he talked about us teaming, but that wasn't for me. I'd been a solo act too long, though those records we did came out at a good time in my career."

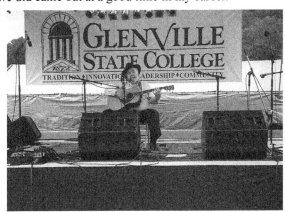

Meanwhile, on April 27, 1974, Mac's son Randy was admitted to the bar in Ohio. One of Mac's proudest moments was performing for his son's school, Glenville State College in West Virginia. Randy had also studied at East Tennessee State University, and the Capital University Law School in Columbus, Ohio, where he was a practicing attorney at the Bricker & Eckler law firm.

Mac plays at son Randy's college.

Incidentally, Randy was selected, by peers and independent research, for a listing among "Ohio Super Lawyers," from 2004-2008, a distinct honor.

In 1975, Mac journeyed to Cincinnati to record along with the Shenandoah Cut-Ups, under the production helm of Rusty York, known for his hit "Sugaree," at York's Jewel Studio. Cut-Up players included Tommy Boyd, Dobro; Billy Edwards, banjo; Buddy Griffin, fiddle/autoharp; Tater Tate, fiddle; and Jeff Terflinger, mandolin. They cut twenty-four tracks, ranging from familiar Wiseman cuts "What a Waste of Good Corn Likker," to P.D. standards such as "The Letter Edged in Black." The compilation was for Vetco, and re-released later by Rebel Records.

"The guy who had Vetco Records (founded in 1968 by Lou Ukelson) was a Jewish fellow and I worked for him quite a few times. He invited me to his home and served a Jewish meal. His mother and father were there and they explained the different dishes being served. That was so educational to me."

Mac's tracks appeared in Vetco's "New Traditions" album. After Rebel Records bought the label, subsequently his recordings were part of Rebel's 1989 "Classic Bluegrass" album; and "Mac Wiseman - Hits & Heart Songs" was released in 2009. Rebel was co-founded in 1959 by Dick Freeland, Bill Carroll and Sonny Compton, and initially placed in record stores on consignment. Rebel was sold in 1980 to Dick Freeman of County Records.

Well, it was back to merry old England for Mac in 1975, again to perform at Mervyn Conn's annual (this was his seventh) International Country Music Festival, March 29-30, at Wembley's Empire Pool. This time he was sharing the bill with co-

Mac checks out UK's Country Music People.

headliners Marty Robbins, Dolly Parton and George Jones, among others. Conn, always one to get his money's worth, also booked our boy at other venues abroad.

Following his return Stateside, Mac answered a call from friend John Hartford to join him for a Flying Fish session at Soundship Studios in Nashville, released in 1976, under the title "Nobody Knows What You Do." A Grammy Award winner for his composition "Gentle On My Mind," Hartford earned a small fortune from Glen Campbell's cover on his song.

"John was a user and abuser of products he wasn't supposed to use, you know. It was late, probably around 11 o'clock and I was about to go to bed. John called to say, 'Come on down here to the studio. I got something I want you to record with me.' I could tell he was flying pretty high already, but I regarded John as a good friend, so decided to go down, and we recorded his novelty number 'Granny, Won'tcha Smoke Some Marjie-wanna,' his way of saying marijuana."

The Hartford session called for a dozen cuts, produced by Mike Melford, including the far-out title "Granny, Won'tcha Smoke Some… " and less-controversial tracks: "You Don't Have To Do That," "John McLaughlin," "False-Hearted Tenor Waltz," "Joseph's Dream," "Down," "The Golden Globe Award," "Sly Feel" and "Somewhere My Love, We'll Meet Again, Sweetheart." Mac also supplied vocals on "Didn't Want To Be Forgotten" and "In Tall Buildings."

One of Mac's more satisfactory associations also got underway in 1975, with Martin Haerle. He shares some of Haerle's history on the music scene: "To the best of my knowledge, Martin Haerle did some great album covers for Starday Records. Don Pierce had brought him here from Germany in his early twenties, and Martin was responsible for all that fantastic art work. Apparently he had a drinking problem and his wife divorced him. But he attended AA meetings and straightened himself up. He had been in Nashville with Starday, then out in L.A. hooked up with Arthur 'Guitar Boogie' Smith to form CMH Records (1975)."

John Hartford, Marty Stuart and Mac.

194

Smith, however, had his own recording studios in Charlotte, North Carolina.

Wiseman adds, "Martin came to me when I was between labels, and I believe I was the first name artist to take a chance on him. He'd approached others like Don Reno and Lester Flatt, but they didn't trust him because of his drinking habit. Once they saw that I had come on his label, they all started recording with CMH... We became good friends. I stayed with him and his then-wife Glenda when I went out there."

Originally, Haerle had been influenced in his native Stuttgart by country music heard on the AFN military station, and became determined to make his way to the U.S. Following experience gained with Pierce, United Artists engaged Martin as general manager of its manufacturing division, and he also briefly worked at ABC Records. He found success by applying what he'd learned at Starday, and in signing name artists dropped by majors or between labels, including Mac, Flatt, Reno, Merle Travis, Joe Maphis, Grandpa Jones, Carl Story, Johnny Gimble, Carl & Pearl Butler and The Osborne Brothers.

Guitarist Smith's studio was frequented by such disparate personalities as James Brown, who cut his R&B smash "Papa's Got a Brand New Bag" and televangelist Billy Graham recorded his *Hour of Decision* shows there.

Smith's nickname came from writing the popular "Guitar Boogie," which he'd earlier titled "Banjo Boogie" (cut with Don Reno), both Top Ten 1948 *Billboard* records. Another instrumental he wrote in 1955, titled "Feudin' Banjos," is heard in the 1972 movie "Deliverance," but retitled "Dueling Banjos." It was played in the award-winning film by Eric Weissberg and Steve Mandel, but didn't credit Smith. Subsequent legal action righted the wrong, giving Smith composer credit and back pay in royalties for alleged copyright infringement.

"At Smith's studio, we recorded twenty tracks early in 1976, and had some fine musicians including Tater Tate on fiddle, Arthur, who produced, played that amazing guitar of his, as well as mandolin and Dobro, while his son Clay was on rhythm guitar," recalls Mac. "After we did several songs, I remember Arthur saying to me, 'Don't you ever make a damn mistake?' Hey, I just knew my part and kept going with it. He was used to doing several takes on other artists."

Tracks especially familiar to Mac like "Love Letters in the Sand" and "Dreaming Of a Little Cabin" made it onto CMH's album "The Mac Wiseman Story" released later that year. Mac returned to Charlotte to record nearly a dozen songs with the same crew, this time covers such as "I'll Sail My Ship Alone," "Don't Be Angry" and "Me and Bobby McGee," are heard on CMH's "Country Music Memories" (1976).

On December 12, 1976, a Country Road Records company claimed it produced Mac on thirteen tunes in Nova Scotia, citing as session players Vic Mullen, Eva Fogarty, Ralph Vidito, Dale Wood and Wendell Simm. Some of the songs featured were Arthur Smith's "Dueling Banjos," "Me and Bobby McGee," "Catfish John," "Keep On the Sunny Side" and "Will the Circle Be Unbroken."

Wiseman, regarding the alleged session, "That was strictly a 'bootleg' effort. I did a concert for this booker in Halifax, and without permission, he taped a live performance, during which I sang those songs. First thing I knew about it, this album came out 'Mac Wiseman - Live in Concert' on the Country Road label. I got screwed, lock, stock and barrel on this one."

Following that controversial gig in Halifax, Mac came home for a bit of relaxation and to enjoy the holidays with family. Ahead, however, were further studio sessions, one an album salute to distinctive Canadian singer-songwriter Gordon Lightfoot, more than a dozen years younger than Mac.

Seemingly out of character for Mac were ten tracks saluting Lightfoot, a contemporary artist who had his first hit recording in 1962, when he'd done nothing similar for his true music heroes like Buddy Starcher or Bradley Kincaid.

"That was Martin's idea... but I always had my stuff down pat. I like to wear them awhile before I record them," Mac replies, adding admiration for Lightfoot's music.

Wiseman sang Lightfoot hits like "Cotton Jenny," "Rainy Day People," "For Lovin' Me," "Steel Rail Blues," "Early Morning Rain" and "Sundown." Mac summoned Eddie Adcock to play banjo, as Arthur aligned himself with stock players Jim Buchanan, fiddle; Rob Thorne, drums; and son Clay on acoustic guitar. It was released November 15, 1977, as what else? "Mac Wiseman Sings Gordon Lightfoot."

"I never worked with Gordon, but I had been to his house in Toronto. After I recorded the Gordon Lightfoot project, I never heard from him, but remain a fan. The cover for that LP was taken across the street in a Charlotte cemetery. You can see I was a skinny fellow, whose legs were as big as my arms."

Mac learned one of his early solo recordings, Albert Brumley's song "Dreaming Of a Little Cabin" had been selected for inclusion in the historic one hundred-and-forty-three-track milestone recordings from 1922-1975, "The Smithsonian Collection of Classic Country Music," sponsored by the National Performing Arts Center. Mac had first recorded the tune in January 1952. The Smithsonian Collection, however, was released in 1981.

According to programmer and annotator Professor Bill C. Malone, then of Tulane University, "Mac Wiseman performances could easily fill up a couple of sides on any collection devoted to classic country music. 'Dreaming Of a Little Cabin,' the one chosen here pairs Wiseman's heartfelt tenor voice with the surging instrumental sound of the mandolin and fiddles (Wiseman introduced to bluegrass and country the concept of twin fiddling)... "

Mac emphasizes another reason he borrowed the concept of twin fiddling from Texas Swing's Bob Wills was that "it made the music more danceable," something that also made it more jukebox-friendly. Randy Wood no doubt approved.

Haerle wanted Wiseman to re-cut "Dreaming Of a Little Cabin" on CMH, and that was accomplished in Charlotte (1977), and is featured on the label's 1978 "Country Gospel Collection." Yet another CMH release on Mac (November 12, 1982 actually) was a compilation album, "Mac Wiseman Bluegrass - Greatest Bluegrass Hits," notable for classic cuts "Did She Mention My Name" and "The House Of the Rising Sun."

After Martin died, September 4, 1990 at age fifty-one, son David Haerle assumed leadership of the label. Wiseman remembers Haerle suffered a fatal heart attack during a mountain-hiking trip with David, with whom Mac shares an equally amiable relationship. David agreed to Mac leasing his former CMH albums not yet available in CD format, for a 2011 box-set titled "The Mac Wiseman Story," boasting a hundred and fifty-three tracks, issued under Wise Records' banner.

Yet another important contact for Mac was Robert Millsap, whom he met while a patient in Nashville's Baptist Hospital: "I knew of him, but hadn't met him. He and his wife were walking down the hall and my door was open. He looked, did a double take, and then they came in to chat. He said we should get together sometime, but I never thought he'd follow up on that comment."

When he did, Mac liked the sound of his suggestion. So it was with the good wishes of Martin Haerle that Mac joined producer Millsap in Nashville's Ironside Studio during December 1977. They recorded a pair of ballads, seemingly a good fit: Lindsey Buckingham's "Never Going Back Again," a Fleetwood Mac track from their "Rumours" album, and Coke Sam's "Goodbye Mexico Rose." On March 18, 1978, Churchill Records' release "Never Going Back Again" charted *Billboard* five weeks (number seventy-eight), with "Goodbye Mexico Rose" as its B side. Mac may have conjured up old memories, singing, *"She broke down and took me in/Made me see where I've been... Been down one time/Been down two times/I'm never going back again..."*

The Churchill label, an independent formed in 1975 by booking agent and artist manager Tommy Martin (Parrish) and Herb Gronauer, signed such artists as Woody Herman, Mamie Van Doren, Frank Sinatra, Jr., The Four Lads, and Mary Lou Turner, quite a variety of talents.

"As I recall, Churchill was out of Chicago in suburban Des Plaines," says Mac. "I stayed at Millsap's house several times in Branson, where Tommy Martin also ran Silver Dollar Records (for which Roy Clark and Pat Boone recorded, not Mac). I might've been on my way to Oklahoma and drove down from Springfield, or Bob would even come and pick me up. Bob also ran Ironside Studio there."

Mac's first charting for Churchill encouraged them to record a trio of tunes later that year on him: "Dancing Bear," "Scotch and Soda" and "Me and The Boys." The resulting single was Dave Guard's "Scotch and Soda," originally popularized by the Kingston Trio in 1958. Mac's version charted *Billboard* (number eighty-eight, 1979) three weeks.

It marked quite a change of pace vocally for Wiseman, "crooning," if you will, lounge lyrics like: *"Scotch and soda, mud in your eye/Baby, do I feel high/Oh me, oh my, do I feel high... People won't believe me/they'll think I'm just braggin'/That I feel the way I do/And still be on the wagon... "*

"During our sessions, I felt things were going smoothly, but Bob said to me, 'Mac, you know Chet quite well. Go see if we're on the right track.' Well, I took it to Chet, who played it from start to finish, but never changed his expression. Then he said, 'You son-of-a-bitch, you can sing anything!' I thought that was a nice back-handed compliment coming from Chet Atkins."

Working with Millsap led to one of Wiseman's most unusual musical pairings. In January 1979, Wiseman found himself at the Wax Works in Nashville, sharing the microphones with Woodrow Charles Herman, better known to 1940s' big band fans as clarinetist Woody Herman. It proved a most memorable session for Mac, who was even more surprised to learn how it all came about.

Woody featured his own upfront vocals, as well as such distaff singers as Lee Wiley and Frances Wayne, while calling his backup vocalists The Four Chips. Woody Herman & The Thundering Herd enjoyed jazz hits like "Caldonia," "At the Woodchopper's Ball," "Laura" and "Blue Flame" (the band's theme song). Herman's Herd also appeared in such movies as Sonja Henie's skate extravaganza "Wintertime" and "New Orleans" featuring Billie Holiday. In 1936, Woody married Charlotte Neste and they had one child, Ingrid.

Herman's last pop charting was "Early Autumn" (charting twenty-eight, 1952), though he and Mac made the *Billboard* country list via "My Blue Heaven" (number sixty-nine, 1979). Gene Austin's chart-topper "My Blue Heaven" December 17, 1927, remained at number one thirteen weeks, selling more than five million records for Victor.

On Valentine's Day 1942, Herman scored his own number one record, "Blues in the Night" for

Woody Herman, A&R chief Tommy Williams and Mac.

Decca Records. Woody continued as a bandleader into the 1980s, clearly enjoying what he did, noting, "The spirit of jazz is abandon. When you present it too grimly serious, you lose naturalness..."

It was Ingrid Herman Reese-Fowler who steered her father towards country, however, having already garnered her own kudos as a bluegrass fiddler with the Bushwhackers Band. She played guitar and fiddle, while Ginger Boatwright sang lead, Susie Monick played banjo and April Barrows was on bass, and the all-girl unit had an album on Laser Lady. Before breaking up in 1981, the band had made an impression touring Mac's old college circuit.

Ingrid, apparently a fan of Mac's standards, joined him on stage at Land-Between-The-Lakes, Kentucky, spontaneously playing fiddle backup for him, much to the appreciation of both audience and artist.

"I was running late and time I got there, they were already announcing me onstage. I didn't know she was Woody's daughter, but she sure could play hell fire out of that fiddle," recalls Mac. "Everything I sang, she stepped up and played on. So I walked up backstage to thank her."

For Mac, his collaboration with Woody on "My Blue Heaven," produced by Millsap, became a dream assignment. Not only had Woody's daughter endorsed Mac for dad's first Nashville session, but she was there when they recorded.

"Yes, Woody's daughter was at the session," smiles Mac. "She was just sitting there and I did a double-take, then walked up to her and we had a nice conversation."

There was no argument as to which song the unlikely co-stars should cut as the A side, for both agreed on the classic "My Blue Heaven."

"When whippoorwills call/And evening is nigh, I hurry to my Blue Heaven... A turn to the right/And a little white light/Will lead you to my Blue Heaven..."

As far as Wiseman was concerned, their rendition was indeed heavenly, a nice payback for his long days at WSVA announcing Big Band sounds.

"We did it in Nashville - seems like it was a basement studio in Donelson - and I liked Woody right off. He was so cordial and of course, such a pro. We purposely

198

sort of did it like the Crosby and Hope (Bing and Bob's 'Road' film fashion) inter-play, with Woody calling out my name, and I did the same. We kinda 'jammed' on that 1920s' Gene Austin classic 'My Blue Heaven' (co-written by Walter Donald-son and George A. Whiting)... Then Woody liked 'If I Could Be With You,' so we recorded it, though I thought it was next to nothing and had never heard of it. But I knew it wouldn't interfere with 'My Blue Heaven'..."

Actually, Woody had learned and played it with Tom Gerun's Orchestra, as it was his pop Top Five hit nearly fifty years earlier, when Mac was a five-year-old. Coupled with "If I Could Be With You" on the flipside as a medley, was an old Bing Crosby recording "It Must Be True" (number four, 1930) with the Gus Arn-heim Orchestra, co-written by Arnheim, Gordon Clifford and Harry Barris (one of Crosby's fellow Rhythm Boys from their earlier Paul Whiteman band days).

Little did Mac know Woody had backed Crosby on their 1941 Top 10 "G'bye Now," and Bing being his childhood idol, clearly he and Herman could've had a lot more to talk about between songs.

"I know what happened to the Woody Herman-Mac Wiseman record. It was up in the sixties in some charts and then they decided that's the bluegrass singer Mac Wiseman, and quit playing it, just like that! I know Churchill was promot-ing the heck out of it, and I was calling up stations myself. I want to believe it's just a lack of knowledge and that they thought bluegrass was Monroe and Ralph Stanley singing through their noses. So once they found out I was bluegrass, it became the kiss of death. That was the established image, and I'm not knocking those guys... Anyway, 'My Blue Heaven' was successful on one level (it charted). And that was such a high for me, to record with Woody, and at such an interesting period in my life."

That same month, Mac and Bob recorded two additional Churchill tracks: "Two Hundred Dollars" and "45's-8x10's." Both were ballads, and exceptional cuts; unfortunately, like the earlier "Me and the Boys in the Band," were never released. Thankfully, Bear Family's latter day box set "Mac Wiseman: On Susan's Floor," gives fans a chance to enjoy all three tracks.

Oklahoma-born Millsap had the goods as a broadcaster (KWTO-Springfield) and producer, but it was on the strength of his songwriting that brought him to Nashville in 1969. Signed to Tree Publishing, Millsap's songs included "Turnin' My Love On." Bob's "Me and the Boys In the Band" was cut by both Wiseman and Tommy Overstreet, whom he also produced (charting number seventy-two, 1980).

Bob and engineer Mike Poston designed and built Ironside Studios, while establishing a music publishing firm together. Among Millsap's top writers was Randy Goodrum, with hits like the number ones' "You Needed Me" by Anne Mur-ray, and "A Lesson in Leavin'," originally by Dottie West and successfully revived by Jo Dee Messina (number two, 1999).

Texas singer-songwriter Durwood Haddock ("There She Goes") tells about first meeting Millsap: "It was Sellers Studio in Dallas where we recorded. Jack Rhodes produced the session... there were two people on the session that I re-member, the rest I don't. Robin Hood Brians played piano and Bob Millsap played guitar... we later became friends in the music business in Nashville. Some of the best records I ever made were produced by Bob Millsap."

Wiseman also thought highly of Millsap, but didn't know Bob once headed a rocking vocal band, Bob Millsap & The Millmen. "One thing I've never lost sight of is that so many of the good things that have happened in my life occurred as though there were some kind of divine intervention."

Mac sees happenings as more than an accident of fate: "That is, my being in the right place at the right time; the failing of the physicals for the military, the rejection by Merck, the Johnny Cash thing, even Randy's refusal to take on the Four-Star catalog, and though we don't understand it at the time, if we're patient, He'll show us what it's all about. I believe that with all my heart. Then me being in the hospital at the same time as Bob Millsap, who just happened to be walking down the hall, exercising... how else can you explain it?"

At late 1950s Dot Records reception, label and WHIN-Gallatin ex-
ecutive Jerry Thomas addresses the crowd, while his label-mates
seem preoccupied. That's Hutch Carlock (from left), Thomas,
Randy Wood, D Kilpatrick and Mac (chatting with chap obscured
by table decoration).

eri.

21 'Shackles And Chains'... Non-binding

"And at night through the bars,
I will gaze at the stars
The plans that we've made were in vain
A piece of stone I will use for my pillow
While I'm sleepin' in shackles and chains..."

"I've enjoyed my friendship with Mac Wiseman as much as I have with anybody in the business. He's absolutely number one," says Bobby Osborne, a fellow member of the Bluegrass Hall of Honor (Class of 1994), adding, "Two guys that quickly come to mind that I've known, who were always the same from the day you met them, right up to the present, were Mac Wiseman and the late Don Reno."

Early in his career, shortly after returning from fighting the war in Korea, the former Marine teamed up with younger brother Sonny, performing as the highly influential Osborne Brothers.

Nowadays, Bobby is one of Mac Wiseman's oldest friends: "First time I ever met him, he was into bluegrass music, playing with Bill Monroe's band, and the first time I heard him singing that I'm aware of, he was with Flatt & Scruggs, singing tenor with Lester Flatt. You know Mac can be harmony singer or lead vocalist. He's got a different voice that went with bluegrass, country or big band music, just anything. I think he's tried a little bit of everything."

Pressed as to when he caught the Monroe show featuring Wiseman, Bobby explains: "I was in Middletown, Ohio, and they came to a tent show on a Sunday in 1949. I was on radio then with Larry Richardson on WPFB, and the show was out at Braden Acres, and you know it's still there."

It was Thursday, February 1, 1979, right after Mac wrapped up his January Churchill recordings with producer Millsap, cutting "Two Hundred Dollars" and "45s - 8x10s," that CMH scheduled Mac at Hilltop Studio owned by Jack "Hoss" Linneman in suburban Madison. There he linked up with buddies Bobby and Sonny to record "Mountain Fever," "'Tis Sweet To Be Remembered" and "I've Always Wanted to Sing in Renfro Valley" as their first tracks.

Considering the high gas prices that spiked during this time frame, Mac didn't have far to go travel-wise, merely driving out to Madison. On that session was a mix of Osborne and Wiseman players, all under the production hand of Sonny Osborne. The union contract lists Ray Edenton, guitar; Benny Birchfield, tenor guitar and vocals; Buck Graves, dobro; Jerry Douglas, dobro; Blaine Sprouse, fiddle; Buddy Spicher, fiddle; Jimmy Brock, bass fiddle; Wynn Osborne, banjo; and Robby Osborne, drums.

"Jimmy Brock had just came to work with us playing bass, and Blaine Sprouse is a great fiddler, who played twin fiddles on that session with Buddy Spicher," says Bobby, adding, "I think Bobby Moore played on a few of those cuts for us. Now Mac played real good guitar, and did so on all those CMH tracks we did with him.

"You know we played shows with him where he sang them old folk songs like 'Old Shep,' and just sat there on stage with only a guitar to entertain the people and they loved it. Mac was always prepared when he came into the studio. He's kind of like me that way. When I pull out of my driveway to go and play, I'm always prepared to get out there and do what I have to do to entertain the folks.

"Did you know we did an earlier album with him while he was still recording with Dot Records (in May 1966)? He produced it on himself, and was going to sing all solos on that album ('Mac Wiseman Bluegrass,' Dot, September 1966), but I think we sang some on that one, too. We had good players like Tommy Jackson, Joe Zinkan and Willie Ackerman. We never recorded as an act on Dot, only did those sessions with Mac."

Oddly enough, the CMH Wiseman and Osborne Hilltop sessions stretched out to include March, April and May 1979 studio time, covering a lot of material. Bobby was agreeable with younger brother Sonny being assigned as producer.

"Sonny handled production chores," he mused. "That never did bother me, as my job was to sing and play mandolin. Supposedly his was to sing and play banjo, but he always wanted to be a leader of some kind. I guess he felt that gave him a little bit of an edge over everybody, including me. It didn't bother me any that he wanted to do that. I might've wished I could've been invited to do some with him, but I never was. As it turned out, Sonny produced some pretty good stuff."

One such gem was the Mac and Bobby duet on the old Jimmie Davis song "Shackles and Chains" (Billboard number ninety-five, 1979), which they recorded during their April 25, 1979 session.

"Well, a lot of those songs Mac did solos on, and we just handled harmony. Then I began singing tenor with him, learning to phrase with him quite well, I think. My voice and his just fit together like fingers in a glove on that song. I liked what we did on that session."

Poignant lyrics: "Put your arms through these bars once my darlin'/Let me kiss those sweet lips I love best/In heartaches, you're my consolation/And in sorrow, my haven of rest..."

Two of the songs offered a tip of the hat to Mac's involvement with Hal Smith's Renfro Valley project: "I've Always Wanted To Sing in Renfro Valley" and "Take Me Back To Renfro Valley."

"Actually 'I've Always Wanted To Sing in Renfro Valley' came from some guys up there in Renfro Valley. I remember that one after someone got a demo on it, because it was so well written. I liked the part that mentioned Mother Maybelle Carter and her playing the guitar. Sonny actually had one of those guitars, so he played it like Mother Maybelle on that cut, and we put harmony with it. I think it was quite good. Now 'Take Me Back to Renfro Valley' - written by John Lair - was an old theme song for Renfro Valley Barn Dance's show up there... You know, Mac and me and Sonny had a trio of sorts going during those sessions."

At their final CMH session May 8, 1979, ironically, one of their tracks was titled "Mother Maybelle," co-written by Rose Lee and Joe Maphis. It was later recorded by such artists as Curley Seckler, Marty Stuart, Johnny Cash and, not surprisingly, Maybelle's daughter June Carter Cash. These Hilltop tracks have been incorporated into CMH albums "The Essential Bluegrass Album - The Osborne Brothers & Mac Wiseman" (released August 1, 1979) and "Fifty Years of Bluegrass Hits" (1985).

Mac had to travel a bit farther afield for his next CMH recording session, all the way to Dallas, Texas, co-producing with yet another musical legend Johnny Gimble, recording with a few former fellow Bob Wills' Texas Playboys. Wiseman tackled his first Western Swing-style set. Considering the

Mac, Bobby Osborne, Earl Scruggs and Pete Kirby after hours.

songs racking up sales, while topping the country charts that year, they boasted significant crossover appeal. Comparatively speaking, Mac's effort seemed little more than nostalgic.

"I'd always wanted to do a Western Swing album," grins Wiseman, who hailed Bob Wills as king of that genre, and could care less about adding to the crossover mix.

Among such 1979 number ones were: Eddie Rabbitt's "Every Which Way But Loose," Anne Murray's "I Just Fall in Love Again," The Bellamy Brothers' "If I Said You Have a Beautiful Body Would You Hold it Against Me," Barbara Mandrell's "I Don't Want To Be Right," Crystal Gayle's "Why Have You Left the One You Left Me For?" and Kenny Rogers' "You Decorated My Life."

Nonetheless, some regard this double album as one of Mac's finest efforts, spotlighting the balladeer singing superlative renditions of standards, blending a mix of Texas Playboys' tunes like "Bubbles in My Beer" and "(My) Home in San Antone," with such country classics as "Slippin' Around," "Yesterday's Girl," "Waltz Across Texas," "The Wild Side of Life," along with Mac hits "Love Letters in the Sand" and "I Wonder How the Old Folks Are At Home," done as never before.

In his extensive (December 1979) liner notes for Mac's "Songs That Made the Jukebox Play," Merle Travis states, "I don't think that you've sung better in your life! I'm not just getting carried away by the fantastic Western Swing band that backed you up either; you sound like you really enjoyed singing these songs... I can't think of another album quite as powerful as this one. These are truly 'Songs That Made the Jukebox Play.'"

There are twenty-two tracks, all produced at Sumet-Bernet Sound Studios, Dallas, on October 16-18, 1979. Mac remembers the musicians well: Jim Belken, fiddle; Will Briggs, Jr., clarinet and saxophone; Dick Gimble, bass; Curly Hollingsworth, piano; Bill Mounce, drums; Herb Remington, steel guitar; Eldon Shamblin, lead guitar; Bill Stone, trumpet; and Johnny Gimble, fiddle and mandolin. For Mac, it was sheer pleasure working with those fellows.

"When I got down to Dallas, I'll be damned if Bob Sullivan wasn't the engineer for the studio, and he had been the engineer when I did my first recordings for Dot at KWKH-Shreveport! Why, we had us a wonderful reunion."

Sumet-Bernet is a major studio there, with diverse clients like the Fabulous Thunderbirds, David Burns of Talking Heads, (actress-singer) Susan Anton and reportedly even the Rolling Stones cut tracks there. Mac was in good company.

"As I told you, we tried to locate as many of the former Texas Playboys' band members as possible," notes Wiseman. "You know I played rhythm guitar. My guitar backup was as much my trademark as my vocals."

Mac was no stranger to Dallas, having played the KRLD *Big D Jamboree*, when in the area, as did such other legends as Hank Williams, Kitty Wells, Ernest Tubb, Patsy Cline, Billy Walker, Webb Pierce, Hank Locklin, Johnny Cash, Carl Perkins, Charlie Walker, and Floyd Tillman. It was founded in 1947, as the *Lone Star Barn Dance*, before adopting its new name. The weekend program was conducted in the Dallas Sportatorium, also a home to professional wrestling.

"I would play the *Jamboree* when out on the West Coast and heading back to Nashville, usually backed by their house band. There was also a club there to play, which I can't think of its name just now," Mac notes. "Anyway, I didn't know what to expect that first time, but as luck would have it, Benny, the mandolin player, was from Parkersburg, West Virginia. He laughed when I came out and I knew things would be all right."

Mac's "Songs That Made the Jukebox Play" was released on February 1, 1980, and became a brisk seller for CMH.

Incidentally, a few years back when Mac was chatting with Texas singer-songwriter Darrell McCall ("A Stranger Was Here") and his songwriter-wife Mona, she told them about the time at a club in Montreal that she played drums, but being under-age, management made her play behind the curtain… and Mac was guest act at the time: "I don't personally recall it, but that's what she related to Darrell and me."

Mona, incidentally, later had a Nashville connection when she was hired to play drums in Audrey Williams' Cold, Cold Hearts band, before meeting Darrell who wrote Hank Jr.'s second number one song "Eleven Roses." Buck Owens also engaged Mona for his all-star *All American Shows* tours featuring fellow Capitol acts Merle Haggard, Tommy Collins, Rose Maddox, Dick Curless and Bonnie Owens. All of their associations with Capitol were a lot more fruitful than Mac's.

Still ahead for Mac was a reteaming with the Osborne Brothers, this time for a "live" session in the Theater-By-The-Lake at Opryland theme park, on October 11, 1981, for RCA Records, though neither act was signed to the label.

Bobby says, "I guess the reason they got us and Mac to do a show out there was they wanted a live album recorded at Opryland. We had some good musicians with us, guys like Buddy Spicher, Leon Rhodes and Hal Rugg, and they had Roy Acuff, King of Country Music, introducing us for the show. That's on the record. Then there's (WSM announcer) Hairl Hensley on the end of it, playing the part of the Solemn Ol' Judge George D. Hay. I seem to remember that they did one pressing that just had the Osborne Brothers on it, and the other with Mac and the Osbornes." This was released by RCA as "Bluegrass Spectacular" in the spring of 1982.

"When we left Decca, Martin was signing anybody he could get," recalls Bobby. "He got tied in with Arthur Smith over in Charlotte and they started CMH Records together. Martin stayed in California and ended up with CMH… We did about five LPs with him. Whatever you chose to do, Martin was fine with that. By contrast, I recorded three CDs with Rounder Records, but there was one guy I had to contend with there and he was never satisfied. This was some Jewish fellow from New York, who wanted to do this and that… Well, I did those projects with him and had nothing but problems. That did me in with Rounder."

According to Mac, Ken Irwin was A&R chief at that time: "You know Ken and I share the same birthday, May 23."

Osborne adds, "I talk with Mac every once in awhile. I call him on his birthday or he'll call me on mine. I was at his eighty-fifth birthday party out at the Ernest Tubb Record Shop where quite a lot of people turned out… that was really nice of David McCormick to do that for Mac at the shop's Texas Troubadour Theater, and it was good Mac was able to attend. Of course, Mac's played the *Midnight Jamboree* many times, even when Ernest Tubb was with us. Mac's been around a lot longer than me.

"I been trying to get him to do some more recordings with me, should he feel the urge to get out. The way things are now, I'm thinking very seriously about maybe just going to see him at his house, with a microphone and computer, to capture me and him singing together. I'd like to arrange things with Rural Rhythm Records to do it; I just went with them and they're great people. Rural Rhythm has been in California, but they're moving to Nashville."

For the past several years, since Sonny left the team, Bobby's headed up a new band he calls the Rocky Top X-Press. Sonny, who suffered a stroke in 2005, affecting his left side, has retired.

Another pleasant chore for Mac in 1982, was heading back down to Texas to do a double album with Chubby Wise for Gilley Records. They first met touring with Bill Monroe's 1949 troupe, even sharing a room on the road. Both had individually played the famed football field-sized country nightclub called Gilley's in Pasadena, Texas, near Houston and were crowd favorites.

Bill Monroe and ex-bandmates Mac and Chubby Wise.

At the time of their session, the Outlaw music genre was proving profitable that year, thanks to Waylon & Willie's "Just To Satisfy You," and Nelson's "Always On My Mind." It was a banner year for Mickey Gilley himself, with chart-toppers "Lonely Nights" and "Put Your Dreams Away." Fiddler Johnny Gimble, however, was assigned to produce Chubby and Mac's collection, titled "Give Me My Smokies & The Tennessee Waltz."

"Sherwood Cryer was the guy who instigated that project. I liked him. He became a good friend, and Sherwood's dad was a fan of mine. Chubby was living in Texas at the time and was very successful. He proved a big draw at Gilley's, and hotter than a pistol throughout the area."

Gilley's Club, founded by country superstar Mickey Gilley and his manager Sherwood Cryer in 1971, was the chief location for the milestone 1980 movie "Urban Cowboy" starring John Travolta. It made the Texas two-step more popular than ever, much as Travolta's "Saturday Night Fever" helped popularize disco dancing in 1977. "Urban Cowboy" earned nearly eighty million dollars at the box office and its subsequent soundtrack became a chart-topping country-pop crossover hit (number three pop), prompting a resurgence in country music.

After Gilley and Cryer broke up their partnership, Gilley's was closed in 1989, and destroyed by a mysterious fire shortly thereafter. Gilley, a cousin to both wild man Jerry Lee Lewis and controversial evangelist Jimmy Swaggart, continued recording, but his era of number ones, such as "Don't the Girls All Get Prettier At Closing Time?" and "A Headache Tomorrow," was behind him.

According to Mac, "Sherwood was into a lot of different deals down there. Just to give you an idea of how his mind worked, when he knew the filmmakers were coming in to do some exteriors for 'Urban Cowboy,' well, he had been anxious to replace the dinky 'Gilley's' sign. So he saw an opportunity and suggested to the filmmaker (director James Bridges) that they put up a bigger 'Gilley's' sign, as it would look much more impressive for their movie audiences."

Mac continues, "Now we actually did our recording 'live' in the club's main ballroom. It may have sounded a little funky, but that was natural because we were doing it at the club... Sherwood and I had a lot of interesting chats, and it was a time of successful acts adding a lot of contract 'riders' (a star's wish list, if you will, in addition to legitimate performance needs). He told me about some of the more ridiculous requests, recalling for instance that Waylon Jennings had a long list of exotic foods and beverages required... Sherwood said such riders were costing him a fortune, as well as a lot of inconvenience finding the oddball items. Well, the night Waylon was booked, he only did three songs, then went back out to his bus, drunk, and never did consume the food or drinks listed. Now that may not have been Waylon himself who added the riders and may have been his managers who did it. Personally, I think Waylon would've been happy with hamburgers."

One thing that irked Mac were entertainers who not only drank before doing their shows, but sometimes frequented competing venues where they mixed with the patrons: "Artists have a responsibility to the promoter not to mix with paying customers. I mean a lot of stars, like Webb Pierce and Charley Pride, would finish their show than head down the street to relax and let their hair down. But, often after a few drinks, they would get up on stage and sing. I always thought out of fairness to the booker who paid you to entertain at a specified venue, you shouldn't be going to another joint and give it away. Probably a lot of patrons figured why buy a ticket to their show down the street, when Webb would be down there after his own show to sing for free for a few drinks. I enjoyed partying as much as the next guy, but I wouldn't do that to the promoters who actually started writing it into an artist's contract not to do that anymore."

Since entertainers must, due to the demands of their profession, spend a lot of time touring and logging up the miles on vehicles, they are prone to accidents. Mac, who logged in some sixty years on the roads and interstates of North America, confides: "Back in 1952, when I had the Webster brothers and Ed Amos with me, we worked a North Carolina show-date on Friday night and then came in to work the *Tennessee Barn Dance* (WNOX-Knoxville), Saturday night.

"We then got in the car to drive on to Pennsylvania, that is eastern Pennsylvania, to do two or was it three shows? Then afterwards we got into the car to go back to Knoxville, and I was driving. Everybody else was asleep when we came into the city limits of Winchester, Virginia. I'd gotten pretty sleepy and I knew they were just as tired as I was, so I got out, walked around the car a little bit, just to try to wake up, then got back in and hadn't gone a mile until I cut down a mailbox post, a telephone pole and demolished the right side of the car. I didn't hurt anybody, didn't hurt me... but I felt so guilty... that's the worst wreck, actually the only major wreck I ever had that I remember. And to think of all those millions of miles traveled, isn't that odd?"

*Mac meets Mr. & Mrs. Wheatley (right) and their twelve children,
all of whom profess to be fans of the man from Crimora!*

22 'Clayton McMichen Story'... In The Pines

"Little girl, little girl what have I done
To make you treat me so
You have caused me to weep,
You have caused me to moan
You have caused me to leave my home
. . . In the pines, in the pines
Where the sun never shines
I shiver when the cold winds blow..."

"I always thought Clayton McMichen was ahead of his time really. He was so innovative musically," muses Mac, thinking back on McMichen, who played country, jazz and swing music. Clayton was also part of Gid Tanner's Skillet-Lickers, heard to such fine effect on the classic 1929 Columbia recording "Soldier's Joy."

That admiration made it especially memorable when Mac was asked to join friends Merle Travis and Joe Maphis to record a historic tribute to pioneer musician-songwriter McMichen (1900-1970) for CMH in 1981. This talented trio, along with Fiddlin' Red Herron, were themselves legends, well suited to the task.

In 1936, Merle was recruited into McMichen's Georgia Wildcats, and the fiddling bandleader soon nicknamed him "Ridgerunner." One account has it that nineteen-year-old Merle was love-struck over a mountain gal Mary Elizabeth Johnson, teen-aged daughter of a preacher, and both wanted to marry, but she was under age. Clayton, whom band-members called "Pappy," told the youth they'd cross the Ohio River from Cincinnati to get them wed in Covington, Kentucky, where laws were less-strict. Pappy and fellow fiddler Bert Layne agreed to be their daddies, so a justice of the peace would marry them. Unfortunately, they were later divorced, and Merle would wed a succession of wives: June Hayden, Bettie Morgan and Hank Thompson's ex, Dorothy.

"Clayton McMichen, Bradley Kincaid, Charlie Poole and Riley Puckett were among the pioneers that helped influence me," acknowledges Mac. "They were there at the beginning of the recording era. I've got Charlie Poole's box set yet. I was very much impressed by Bradley Kincaid and his story-songs... One time down in Atlanta, I was riding the elevator with Bill Carlisle who pointed out Fiddlin' John Carson - another hero of mine. He was the elevator operator!"

For the McMichen salute, Mac supplied both vocals and rhythm guitar stylings. Bassist Jackson D. Kane also joined the troupers. Their song list included twenty-seven tracks, a dozen of which were strictly instrumentals, such as "Fire On the Mountain," "Fifty Years Ago Waltz," "McMichen's Reel," "Lime House Blues" and "Waitin' For the Robert E. Lee." Other memorable songs: "Trouble in Mind," "Give the Fiddler a Dram," "The Convict and The Rose," "In the Blue Hills of Virginia," "They Cut Down the Old Pine Tree" and "Sweet Bunch of Daisies."

"We did that session in Albuquerque, New Mexico, and it was the last time Merle recorded before he died [October 20, 1983]. At the time, Merle had some sort of neurological problem and we could tell when he was missing, so we'd just take a break until he got right again."

Their effort was released late in 1982 as "The Clayton McMichen Story." A two-record set, the LP's artwork was unique and packaged like a movie poster, listing like a cast the musicians: Merle as himself "Ridgerunner" Travis and earlier guitarist Hugh "Slim" Bryant; Mac as singer-guitarist Jack Dunigan, McMichen's lead singer; Joe as Jerry Wallace and Blackie Case; Kane as Ray "Loppy" Bryant and Bucky Yates; and Herron as McMichen himself. (Incidentally Loppy's brother Slim later led the Wildcats and lived to be one hundred and one years old.)

Mac scored vocally on tracks like "The Convict and The Rose," "Trouble in Mind," "They Cut Down the Old Pine Tree," and "In the Pines" - a song on which he was quite versed - and later cut by the Grateful Dead, who credited as its writers McMichen and Slim Bryant.

Wiseman notes, "He had picked songs that Jack Dunigan sang nearly a half century earlier." The almost-spiritual "In the Pines" is regarded as traditional, and Mac's haunting version was right-on: *My daddy was a railroad man/Drove a mile and a half uptown/His head was found 'neath the driving wheel/His body has never been found... In the pines, in the pines/Where the sun never shines/I shiver when the cold winds blow... "*

McMichen retired from music, but ran a bar called Pappy McMichen's. Just prior to his seventieth birthday, he died January 4, 1970, in Battletown, Kentucky. So he never knew of CMH's recorded tribute.

"When we were done doing that album," continues Mac, "I recall as we left the studio, Merle was taking us all - five or six of us musicians - to dinner, and as Travis started to get into the limousine, he turned around and made the remark, 'There are two acts in this business, I can't get enough of, one's the Sons Of the Pioneers and the other's you.' I was simply speechless, because Merle was one of *my* music heroes."

"The Clayton McMichen Story" had yet to be released in CD form, when Mac made his pact with David Haerle. That deal resulted in Mac producing a 2011 CD box set that also contains the full McMichen album.

Sadly in 1980, Mac's mother died on March 4, after having suffered from heart trouble. Mac was out of the country at the time, booked for a week long gig in the Canadian province Alberta, but made it home for her funeral. Myra Ruth's grave-stone in Crimora carries the text, "Take no thought for the 'morrow, for sufficient unto the day is the evil thereof." [Matthew 6:34]

"You know my mother wasn't one to condone any mistakes or bad things I did, but she never chastised me about my failed marriages. I wouldn't have blamed her if she did, and she'd bend over backwards to get acquainted with my wives. Now when Alberta and I divorced, she was upset (having bonded with the grandchildren) and initially didn't want me to bring Emma to the house.

"As much as I hated to, I said, if 'Em' couldn't come, then I wouldn't come either. So we went down to Shreveport and the first ones to make an overture was my dad and brother Kennie, who drove down to Louisiana and stayed ten days with me. Then they went back and saw the Opry on the way home, and that broke the ice. By this time, we were having young'uns. That was the only time, and Mom didn't make a big deal about that, but she wasn't going to approve it by any damn means. My mother was a pal, so she never confronted me . . . I still miss her terribly in a good way, and think of the good things we had together, and what a great source of strength she was."

Dad's headstone in church cemetery.

The loss of his wife of nearly sixty years left Howard a lonely man. He died May 5, 1984, ten days prior to his eighty-third birthday. His headstone reads: "The Lord said, 'I Have Written Your Name On The Palms of My Hands'" - "Gone but not forgotten" crosses their individual markers.

"I still miss them both very much," Mac confides.

"In touring, one of the places that impressed and influenced me most was Switzerland. It gave me a realization of heritage, if you will. I saw such a similarity there with a lot of things like my father did. I mean such as the old machinery there like he'd used, things of that nature. While I don't know that anybody specifically drilled that into him, I think it was just handed down through generations of family tradition."

In retrospect, Mac's career encompassed both highs and lows like many other artists, but he's pleased that none of those whom he cared about, ever suggested he knock off being an entertainer and settle down into a regular job with a securer salary.

"My parents, my wives, children or even in-laws never said anything like that to me or even hinted at it," proclaims Wiseman, who is also grandfather of three and great-granddad to four. "And that is so flattering. I sit here now and reflect on a lot of things past, because I now have the time to do that, and one of the blessings is that they never criticized me for following the road I did, and were always supportive of what I did. Even when it seemed like it wasn't coming out right, they'd just stick with me. I feel so fortunate in that respect."

In 1983, Mac was honored during a special fifty-year anniversary commemoration for WWVA-Wheeling, as the city fathers joined the station to mark the occasion by installing a *Jamboree Walk of Fame* there with its first fifty stars, (a la the fabled Hollywood Walk of Fame). Wiseman was one of the half-a-hundred artists paid homage to on this historic October 15 reunion celebration, but unlike the others, he once managed it back into solvency again.

Another very special occurrence for Mac Wiseman was sharing the bill with comedy king Bob Hope: "I opened for Bob Hope at the University of New Mexico, and in the lobby of the concert hall was the most unusual Christmas tree I'd ever seen. New Mexico was known for its production of long red hot peppers. That Christmas tree had been sprayed entirely white and the only decorations were numerous pods of red peppers. It was so beautiful.

"The school would furnish us student musicians, but I told them we didn't have time to rehearse, and I played solo, just pulling up a stool to sit on. Being Bob's crowd, it was primarily made up of older people, so I just started singing all the old pop standards I could think of, and that audience was most receptive, to the extent Bob came out of his dressing room to see what all the excitement was about, as they responded to my music. I'd like to think he was probably wondering who was out there tearing them up?

"Along about dusk, I had been to dinner and was on my way back to the auditorium, as I saw maybe a quarter mile away, a line of people winding up a steep hill in a pilgrimage to a cross. What was so unusual about it is they had brown paper bags, and in the bottom of these bags were lit candles, and that gave off a great glow.

"Yes, I've had some wonderful times in this business. Songwriter Don Robertson was with us when we did that memorable fishing trip with Fred Stryker and Lawrence Welk's manager Gabby Lutz, going out to Catalina Island. Like the song says, I've lived a lot in my time. I found Lutz particularly interesting to know because I was such a big fan of Lawrence Welk's music."

Robertson, a bit of a rebel, wrote such number one songs as "Please Help Me, I'm Falling." Yet another Robertson, Mac met, was movie star Dale Robertson ("Call Me Mister," "Golden Girl") unrelated to Don: "He was at the same hotel, when I was playing an outdoor bluegrass park in Texas, and said he was there for a charity golf benefit. He was coming out of the hotel as I was going in, and he recognized me and we talked for awhile. I remembered him from the TV series *Tales of Wells Fargo*, and he'd also cut an album of Western songs on the side."

Mac had long admired Tom T. Hall, especially his writing talents. Hall's hits included such songs as "The Year That Clayton Delaney Died" and "(Old Dogs, Children And) Watermelon Wine" that he cut, as well as Johnny Wright's number one "Hello, Vietnam," and another he wrote that became a pop-country crossover number one for Jeannie C. Riley, "Harper Valley P.T.A."

"I went out to Tom T. Hall's studio to sing a song for an album with some girl singer once - I can't recall just now who she was - and it was summer and quite warm. Tom T. had been out on his tractor cutting the tall grass. He said, 'I was telling someone about how unique your voice was.' Well, he said, 'What's so unique about it?' I told him, 'To me, his uniqueness can best be compared to the flushing of a toilet. It don't matter who flushes it, you know how it's going to sound!' I believe that was meant as a compliment... He was a painter, too, and you know, I have a nice picture Tom T. did on me."

During a *Music City Tonight* (TNN) telecast, co-host Tom T. Hall called Mac "Country's Burl Ives." In that time frame, Mac guested with former boss-man Bill Monroe on TNN's *Bobby Bare & Friends*, which also featured banjoist-comic Mike Snider. Televised in 1984, the acclaimed program spotlighted laid-back Bare chatting with the pioneers about their early days in bluegrass. According to an ad for the show: "Monroe talks about his Kentucky roots and creating his own style of music in 1938."

Yet another popular TNN variety series, *The Statler Brothers Show*, had Mac in a special April Fool's segment. For this guest shot, Music Director Bill Walker scheduled Mac warbling his top hit "Jimmy Brown The Newsboy."

"That was an entertaining program, well done. It seems to me they had Rex Allen, Jr., and Janie Fricke as regulars," indeed so, and it was TNN's top-ranked show during its 1991-1998 run. Like *Music City Tonight*, co-hosted by Lorianne Crook & Charlie Chase, its producer was Jim Owens, Lorianne's husband.

Another good friend, one who toured a number of times with Wiseman, is the Opry's Bill Anderson. He attained success as both songwriter and singer, with his soft vocal style being responsible for his unique nickname, Whisperin' Bill.

Bill agreed to an interview regarding his friendship and association with Wiseman, shortly after the release of his CD, "Songwriter," which boasted several novelty-type tunes.

"I think so many fans, probably over the years - and people in your position (media) - because I've done so many serious kinds of things, I believe a lot of people think I'm just a real serious, sappy, syrupy sort of a guy. Listen to 'Still,' 'Mama Sang a Song,' 'Golden Guitar,' 'Five Little Fingers' and songs like that, and I guess that's what you would think.

"But I like to have a good time, I love to laugh, I like to think I've got a good sense of humor, and it dawned on me that I don't know if I've ever really showed that side of me on record before. That's kind of what I really had in mind when I went to

Bill Anderson

make 'Songwriter.' After making as many records as I've made, I thought it's time to show them something different, if there's anything different left to show them. That's what I was trying to do (via tracks like 'It Ain't My Job To Tote Your Monkey,' and 'That's When the Fight Broke Out'). Mac and I have had some laughs."

In addition to a Nashville Songwriters Hall of Fame induction, Bill's also a member of the Country Music Hall of Fame. Like Wiseman, Anderson's a true son of the south. Born in Columbia, South Carolina, he studied at the University of Georgia, earning a journalism degree, while working as a sports writer for the *Atlanta Constitution* newspaper and an announcer at a small radio station in Commerce, Georgia.

"I saw Mac the first time in concert at the old City Auditorium in Atlanta. Gosh, if I had to give a year, it was probably late 1951 or early 1952. I'd been aware of him, of course, due to his recordings and stuff. But that was the first time I ever saw Mac in person. It's really funny, and I'll tell you why - I don't know if I ever told Mac this or not - I was in the very back of the auditorium, I didn't have real good seats down front.

"Mac always kind of had a tendency I think when he does a lot of those ballads and great heartfelt songs, he closes his eyes when singing. From where I was sitting, I wondered if he was blind. I really did not know and was trying to get up closer somehow where I could really see. But I left the show that day still wondering if Mac was blind.

"The first time I ever remember speaking to Mac, he was A&R man in California working for Randy Wood and Dot Records. You remember those days? I had sent Mac a little recording of 'City Lights' I made down in Texas on TNT Records, because I was sending it to anybody I could find to send my record to.

"I sent it thinking wouldn't it be great if maybe Dot Records would pick this up and put it out. So Mac called me one day at the station and I couldn't believe I was on the telephone talking to Mac Wiseman from California! He was very interested in the song, but before he could do anything with it, my record had been pretty much covered by Ray Price at Columbia Records. Then by that time the horse was pretty much out of the barn. I do remember him calling me on the phone and I walked on air several days, saying, 'Hey man, I talked with Mac Wiseman on the telephone!' Yeah, that was pretty cool."

Bill and Mac are versatile in their musical talents. Anderson focuses on Wiseman's strengths: "There are several things about Mac that are just so remarkable to me. He knows more songs than anybody I have ever been around. One day, years ago, we were working a show together up in Ohio. It was Sunday and we did a matinee and had to do a night show. Between shows, one of the disc jockeys had us over to his house for a meal. We were sitting around, kind of killing time between the two performances and there was a guitar there. Mac picked it up and started singing.

"I said, 'Mac is there any song you don't know?' He said, 'I don't know. Try me.' So I sat there and I have a pretty good knowledge of old country songs, and I started throwing song titles to him, trying to stump him. I did not do it. I could not name a song that he couldn't at least perform a part of it. That stood out in my mind... I never will forget that day."

Anderson admires Wiseman's penchant for preserving America's roots music, primarily by recording it for posterity: "He has tried to preserve the old music and the heritage without trying to accommodate the latest commercial trend. He has stayed true to himself and what his roots are, what he knows and what he does so well. Mac has never sold out in the name of trying to be commercial. I think he's who he is and that says, 'Here I am and I hope you like it, and if you don't, sorry, this is still who I am!' There's nobody better to keep the old songs alive than him, because when Mac sings them, they have been sung."

In addition to playing numerous package shows together, they were both members of the Country Music Association executive board at the same time, and Bill later nominated Mac to be the AFM Nashville Musicians Association's next Secretary-Treasurer. Mac, who also received the endorsement of Chet Atkins, won that (Local 257) post and was most appreciative of their influential backing.

Bill says he's indebted to Mac for helping him while he was dealing with a former wife's recovery from a severe head injury, sustained when her car was struck by a truck, whose driver was drunk at the wheel, on October 13, 1984.

Anderson, who married Becky Stegall Davis, October 2, 1971, explains: "It was a very serious, very traumatic close head injury (and it was feared she suffered brain damage). She was in a coma for a month or two. Doctors gave her only a fifty-fifty chance of survival. When she seemed to come to, the doctor said to me, 'You need to surround her with things that she loves and things that are familiar to her.' In other words, don't bring up things not pleasing to her and he emphasized get things she really liked.

"Now Mac Wiseman had always been her favorite singer. She absolutely adored Mac and had a lot of his records, but it was far from a complete collection. Now I got in touch with Mac and told him the story. He sent me a package of albums and I have no idea how many there were, but there were many, many Mac Wiseman albums. What I did with them was transfer them over to cassette tapes, the best thing they had back then, and took a tape deck to the hospital.

"Those songs just played over and over and Becky would be just lying in the bed listening. You wouldn't know if she was awake or asleep or in some kind of subconscious state. But those Mac Wiseman songs just kept playing and playing, because I knew how much she loved his music. I'm sure that the nurses and doctors, if they never heard another Mac Wiseman record, it would be too soon. We just kept right on playing them. It was a wonderful source for her, and when she did come around and began to express her thoughts and feelings and all, she just thanked me over and over for all that music that she got to lay up there and listen to. It was a wonderful gesture on Mac's part, giving us all those records."

Bill and Mac have been survivors because they adapted to changing times by combined their talents with more contemporary artists, Anderson co-writing with the likes of Steve Wariner, Skip Ewing, Jon Randall, Vince Gill and Jamey Johnson. Meanwhile, Mac's linked up with Charlie Daniels, Scott Rouse and John Prine. Both are now members of the Country Music Hall of Fame, though Bill preceded Mac by a *baker's dozen* years.

Bill and Mac haven't yet collaborated in the studio, but Anderson added: "Man, would I love that! I'd never thought about it before, but I'd sure enjoy doing it. You know I went over to Mac's house when I was doing the *Bill Anderson Visits With The Legends* shows on XM Radio. John Prine came over, too, and we sat up the microphones right in Mac's living room. We had an incredible hour. We got the guitars and he and John are such fans of each other; each so great in his own right. What a remarkable show that was. I didn't want to leave. I just wanted to stay and enjoy the rest of the day with them. That was some pretty neat stuff."

Anderson added enthusiastically, "Let me tell you my favorite Mac Wiseman story: We were booked on a show in Worcester, Massachusetts, and Patsy Cline was also on the same show. This was just about the time 'I Fall to Pieces' had come out and before she had her big surge, though people were beginning to know who Patsy was. Well, Mac had invited me to drive up with him in his car, and I told him I'd help pay for the gas. Now we were driving from Nashville to Worcester, before interstate highways, if you can believe that. Not all of us yet had buses.

"Early in the morning, just as the sun was coming up about 5:30 or 6, I'm in the backseat sleeping and he had told me before I went to sleep, I'm going to get off the main road a little bit to go to my sister's house. She lives somewhere close by and is going to cook breakfast for us. Great, I thought, that sounds wonderful.

"So I got in the backseat to sleep and when I awoke, the sun's coming up and I notice we're stopped, so I figure we're at Mac's sister's house. So I looked up and instead of seeing Mac's sister, I saw a big old ugly state trooper with his head stuck in the window, talking to Mac. Well, evidently Mac had been going over the speed limit. This trooper had pulled us over and was going to take Mac to the justice of the peace. It was obviously a speed-trap type thing.

"Mac said to me, 'You just stay here with the car. This won't take long. I'll be right back. The place is just up the street.' So there I was sitting in Mac's car in the center of Virginia somewhere by myself.

"In about an hour, he came back and I heard conversation. Mac had gone to the Justice of the Peace and so I asked how much did it cost? He said it was twenty-six dollars, and Mac was mad, he was just burned up! Twenty-six dollars was twenty-six dollars. Mac was angry about the whole thing. Then this patrolman, who had been so gruff throughout the whole thing, came back up to Mac and said, 'Hey Mac, I'm a big fan of yours and before I go, have you got any albums with you that you can give me?' Mac looked at him and said, 'Yes sir, I've got a whole trunk full. How many do you want? They're twenty-six dollars a piece!'"

Mac enjoys hometown visit with brother Kennie, sisters Virginia and Naomi and her husband John.

215

23 'Just Doin' My Time'... With a Worried Mind

"It won't be long, just a few more days
I'll settle down and quit my rowdy ways Lord, Lord
With that gal of mine, with that gal of mine
She'll be waitin' for me when I've done my time..."

"I had played the Geateau show (an annual festival outside Montreal) on a Friday, along with Waylon Jennings, and Kitty and Johnnie (Wright) were booked for the following night, and came in early with their troupe to do the Montreal show. Well, I was beat after the show, so I headed right back to the hotel, and went up to my room and fell asleep immediately," relates Mac.

"What woke me up was I heard some commotion and a key turning in the lock. I jumped up cussing and hollering, thinking it might be someone trying to break into my room. Turned out it was merely the desk clerk and Bobby Wright trying to get into the room. Booker Brian Edwards had booked him and me into the same room for different dates. But, Bobby told me later that I frightened them, as well, because they didn't know if I had a gun or not, and they didn't even stop to apologize! Months later, Bobby [who had co-starred on ABC-TV's popular sitcom *McHale's Navy* with Ernest Borgnine and Tim Conway] told me about that incident."

Throughout the 1980s, Mac hit the festival circuit as much as he chose to. In 1980 alone, Mac played fifty-seven music festivals, but still found time to do a week in Calgary, Alberta, Canada, from March 11-15 (delayed a week due to Mom's death); an Easter gig at the Wembley International Country Music Festival in London, April 6; also a special concert at Western Carolina College in Cullowhee, North Carolina (renewing his friendship with then-Professor Wade Macy), April 12. Mac spent the Fourth of July in Kingston, Ontario. After his show in Cranston, Rhode Island, he fulfilled gigs at Gilley's and Johnny Lee's own club in Pasadena, Texas, during October.

Wiseman headlined a special concert at the Smithsonian Institute in Washington, D.C., November 16, which was sold out in advance of his arrival: "That booking came to me personally. There was no intermediary booker that I can recall." [Incidentally, during August 2012, Mac was interviewed in his home by an archivist, intent on taping Wiseman's words, for America's historic Library of Congress.]

In the 1980s, nine albums were released on Mac, though none on a major label. Among his charted singles were covers of the Fleetwood Mac song "Never Goin' Back Again," the Kingston Trio success "Scotch and Soda" and the duet with iconic Woody Herman, "My Blue Heaven."

Come 1981, Mac worked forty-five bluegrass festivals, besides additional bookings, including Ball State University in Muncie, Indiana, January 1. He had a week's engagement at the Crossroads Hotel in Calgary, Alberta, March 18-22, and the following month - April 19-26, Wiseman traveled through some 10 countries to play shows in London, Stockholm, Rotterdam, Paris, Frankfurt and Zurich, sharing the bill with then-heavyweights Brenda Lee, Jerry Lee Lewis, Tammy Wynette, Don Gibson, George Jones and Melba Montgomery.

The latter two had been duet partners prior to George's celebrated teaming with Tammy, who had divorced Jones before this overseas tour. George and Melba enjoyed such hits as "We Must Have Been Out Of Our Minds" (number three, 1963). Rumor has it, Melba rejected his earlier marriage proposal.

"I remember Melba and I chaperoned George during that whole damn tour, trying to make sure he did his shows. After he got back from that tour, he turned himself into rehab... We'd played two nights in Paris where I earned five encores, which had Brenda and Tammy coming out of their trailer dressing rooms to see what it was all about - and I only had a little rock band backing me. But they were really attuned to my music, and played it straight. We did the whole show in a huge tent."

Mac says he spent Easter that year in Zurich: "Some of these guys said they knew some good spots to eat at, so we drove all through that city, but never did even get a lunch. We couldn't get in anywhere, as they were all closed. It was a total bust, so we went back to the hotel where we did manage to get a snack."

Come July 4th (and 5th) Mac was participating at Gilley's Picnic in Pasadena, followed by gigs in Marseilles, Illinois, and Meriden, Connecticut, before playing Crandon, Wisconsin, July 31: "That was a huge festival at an Indian reservation with a high, high fence surrounding it. So the law couldn't come on the premises where hippies were having a high old time, some passing out. A number of them stayed a week to avoid the cops waiting outside to run them in on drug charges.

"Tony Conway booked that date. That was the only place I ever played where I had to encore every damn song. It was located in Northeastern Wisconsin, almost up to Sault Sainte Marie. They booked me every year for a while. You know Benny Martin was very popular up there, as he would tear their butts up performing!"

On one tour, Mac played five concerts in five different states in five days, but points out what made it possible was traveling via airplane. The gigs were: Council Bluffs, Iowa, September 4; Salem, Virginia, September 5; Indiana, Pennsylvania, September 6; Logan, Ohio, September 7; and the Washington, D.C. area, September 8, 1981. "Mainly, I would use pick-up bands back then."

On October 25, 1981, Mac opened a show at Madison Square Garden in New York City, for Charley Pride and Alabama, which was televised and shown twice on network TV: "Charley was also emcee or host, but was in his cups somewhat and in the camera close-ups his eyes showed red. I mean he did a good job, but they avoided (beaming) those close-ups on him. You know Charley told me he was also part Indian, and that he was everything but white. He was funny.

"That proved a very successful booking for us, and it was sponsored by Stetson Hats. They even gave me a courtesy Stetson with my name on it. That was something I would've treasured, except some S.O.B. stole it out of my dressing room. Marge was with me and we were staying just across the street. Well, I'd finished my early part of the show and decided to watch Alabama from the wings, and left my Stetson on the dressing table. Whoever took it, probably wore it right outside, so that nobody would notice them leaving with it.

"For that concert, I arranged for my real estate agent, my attorney and my farm machinery guy to come up to New York for the Madison Square Garden gig, which Rudy Kallicut had booked. At our hotel, we were sitting at the bar having drinks. Well, there was this old guy sitting at the counter next to me, who drank my drinks a couple times. I looked at

Graves Mountain festival with Charlie Waller.

my empty glass and knew that I didn't drink them. So, the next round I caught him swiping my drink, and boy I chewed his ass out good. Then to top it off, when we got ready to leave, he jumped into our cab ahead of us and stole our ride!

"Well, we caught a cab down to a place called Rosie O'Grady's, quite a large nightspot right down in the heart of the Big Apple. I just wanted to unwind and have a drink, but my attorney went up to the bandstand to tell them I was there. Turned out it was a group from Ireland, who had played backup for me over there. How ironic is that? So there we were having a reunion on stage in New York City."

Kallicut, incidentally, was at one time called "the world's largest country promoter," handling Opry stars and other big acts for venues both here and abroad, including Asia and Europe. Reportedly, Kallicut promoted "the world's largest country indoor variety show" at the Pontiac Silverdome near Detroit, but Mac wasn't on that bill.

"He was booking the Lansdowne Auditorium situated between Washington, D.C. and Baltimore, however, and I played a rodeo there for five successive dates. I think I was the only music person booked - it was a time back when John Denver was at his peak of popularity and he also played that venue. That was a huge place and there was this little platform at the end of the arena where I was, and when and if they had any delay (in the rodeo), I would do a song. Sometimes that would be only a single song and I was there a week, but got paid regardless. That felt like the longest week I ever did... Later, I was booked there for a big bluegrass festival along with guys like Doc Watson, Ralph Stanley and Jim & Jesse - I mean it was a big package show - for a couple days at Lansdowne."

In 1982, Mac performed at fifty-one music festivals, including additional gigs in Fairbanks, Kenai and Anchorage, Alaska, May 7-9; Carlisle, Ontario, June 4-5; back in time for Bill Monroe's Bean Blossom Festival in Indiana, June 17; and Stanhope, New Jersey on August 20-21. Mac also did two guest spots on TNN, and spent November 12-13 shooting *Fire On The Mountain*, and December 10 did Ralph Emery's TBS show *Nashville Alive!*

Following the session with Merle Travis in late 1982, Mac went back into the studio to record again, this time ten tracks, which he produced himself. Released in 1983 as "If Teardrops Were Pennies," on Wise Records, it was also included in a Columbia Special Projects set. Carl Butler (the "Don't Let Me Cross Over" hit-

218

maker) is credited with writing "If Teardrops Were Pennies," initially a 1951 Top Ten single for Carl Smith, but reportedly came from the pen of prolific songwriter Arthur Q. Smith, who we mentioned swapped songs to pay his bar bill.

Ironically, two decades later when Mac struck a deal with the Canadian-based Madacy distributors, the ". . . Pennies" collection was revised as Music Mill's "Maple On the Hill" (November 20, 2001).

In 1983, Mac cut back to thirty-three music festivals, though he increased his TV guest shots, notably the *25th Anniversary of CMA* Special in Washington, D.C. March 16; TNN's *Yesteryear in Nashville* (a chat show with Archie Campbell), May 9; *Nashville Now* (with Ralph Emery), May 10; *Hee Haw* (with Roy Clark & Buck Owens), October 13; and back to Canada for CBC's *Sun Country Show* in Edmonton, Alberta, October 17-18 (with host Tommy Hunter).

Scott and Dad on tour.

Meanwhile, Mac volunteered time behind the scenes for the non-profit ROPE organization, dedicated to helping musicians in need. He was one of ROPE's 1983 charter members recruited by founding father Gordon Terry. The Alabama fiddler, who played for such notable bandleaders as Bill Monroe, Johnny Cash and Merle Haggard, felt industry members needed a reason to get together other than a funeral. So he conceived the idea for an organization in which trade members could socialize, while also chipping in to aid less fortunate folk.

Leslie Elliott and steel guitarist husband Ron Elliott were among those who helped get ROPE going. Ron was its first vice president and Leslie appointed its secretary. Currently she's ROPE executive director, but there's a little story behind all that. Leslie had grown disillusioned with the way ROPE was initially being run: "I mean Gordon as president was rather belligerent, saying nothing could be done unless he OK'd it. I was secretary four years, doing everything like putting shows together, and was looking for ways to cut costs. They were paying out six thousand dollars just for lighting, when it could be done for half that. Him and Frank Mull got together and rented a limousine to pick Gordon up in Pulaski, Tennessee, where he lived some seventy miles south of Nashville, to bring him to our awards show. So I got out of it.

"It was Mac's fault I'm doing the ROPE thing today," chuckles Leslie. "I was working for Ray Pennington at Step One Records in February 1998, when Mac and Charlie Dick came and asked me to come back. Mac, Ray and Joe Taylor were pretty upset when their annual ROPE banquet didn't make any money (despite donated talent), and the next year made two dollars and ninety-eight cents. A whole series of checks were unaccounted for and they had spent like six hundred dollars just to get the tickets printed.

"Well, I agreed to help them and the first year we made several thousand dollars on the banquet and they were amazed," she continues. "I believe in saving, including on the printing which was costing so much. I designed everything myself saving lots of money. Like I had 400 pieces printed for fifty-seven dollars, but they didn't do anything like that. I do that kind of stuff for ROPE. Mac was a good president (serving five terms) and today Marty Martel's also a wonderful president (whose term has since ended)."

Half way through the decade, Mac enjoyed a musical reunion-of-sorts with Bill Monroe, thanks to producer Emory Gordy, Jr., who invited him to record "Travelin' This Lonesome Road" with the "Father of Bluegrass." Bassist Gordy, who had toured with such pop notables as Neil Diamond, Elvis Presley and John Denver, later wed singer Patty Loveless. He was producing the MCA album "Bill Monroe & Stars of the Bluegrass Hall of Fame," released in 1985.

It was late 1985, when 1970s' outlaw Tompall Glaser produced Mac's MCA-Dot Master Series album "Once More With Feeling," also titled abroad as "Mac Wiseman" (1986). It was produced at Glaser's studio, and featured guest instrumental fills by John Hartford playing banjo and guitar. The title tune, co-written by Kris Kristofferson and Shel Silverstein, became a 1970 #2 *Billboard* record for Jerry Lee Lewis. Besides that title track, songs on Mac's album were songs relatively new to him: "Old Country Songs," "Lean On Me," "How Lonely Can You Get," "Countin' Pennies," "Ramblin' Round," "Rose With No Thorns," "Now That You Have Me, You Don't Want Me" and "I'd Do It All Over Again." One particular tune - "You're the Best of All the Leading Brands" - became a Wiseman fan favorite, and enjoyed ample airplay.

"At one time, MCA was releasing albums by some thirty veteran artists, and I was part of one of those releases on their subsidiary MCA-Dot. The only reason I agreed to go into the project, was that they weren't releasing seven or eight albums at a time. It was also understood that they wouldn't release any singles from any of those albums for obvious reasons, because if they did it for one, they'd have to do it for all of them. In our conversation prior to the session, Tompall said, 'I'll help you get some material together,' but when he didn't bring anything in, finally I said, 'You haven't brought me any songs,' and he said 'That's because you mentioned so damn many good ones, I didn't need to.' I think one of the cuts, 'Countin' Pennies,' written by bluegrass artist Mike Jackson, is a hit, and I'd like to put it on another album one of these days. It would probably go today (2011), as the hard times are affecting so many people."

"Tompall was fine to work with, though we did a lot of late sessions. Usually afterwards, we'd go out to get a bite to eat… He told me, 'You just don't know what your taking that job with Dot did for us entertainers. It gave us the idea we could do that, too.' That was flattering, as I didn't know anybody was paying much attention." Tompall also cut an LP in the MCA-Dot series. Others who did were Dave & Sugar, Buck Trent, Boxcar Willie, Sonny James, Jan Howard, Billy Walker, Asleep At The Wheel, George Hamilton IV, Charlie Walker, Margo Smith, Jeanne Pruett, Jimmy C. Newman, Justin Tubb, Ferlin Husky, Hank Thompson and Red Steagall.

Regarding that MCA-Dot Masters project, in November 1986 *Billboard* quoted Jimmy Bowen, then MCA president: "MCA-Dot is a preservation and development

220

label. We set about the first year in preservation because it hadn't been done in country music. There were thirty country artists who still worked and were still viable in certain parts of the entertainment industry, who felt they could still sell fifteen thousand albums."

As a result, those whose discs didn't were dropped, explained Bowen: "The bottom line, the product margin in the record industry, hasn't been good for the past year-and-a-half when these albums came out. They were hurt by that. Sales just weren't there. To be fair, our distribution set up in the mainstream record business may not be able to reach that consumer. We couldn't sell some things, and I see them go on to sell a million."

By 1987, Mac was down to about seventy-five shows annually, from a peak of about three hundred in the 1950s.

"I'm enjoying it more than ever now," he told AP's Joe Edwards in December 1986. "I can call my shots and not have to be available every time the phone rings. At the end of the season, I get a little road weary. I'm home five or six weeks, and I get the itch to go out again... I sing in the same keys I did forty years ago. But if I can't, I drop them down to where I do them comfortably."

During a late 1987 interview for *Country Scene* magazine in Nashville, Mac disclosed, "I can still average sales from sixty-to-sixty-five thousand dollars a year in records and tapes. I feel very fortunate. It has been an interesting career and I've enjoyed it. I've worn a number of different hats, and done just about everything."

That was also the year Wiseman was inducted into the Society For the Preservation of Blue Grass Music Association's Preservation Hall of Greats. The organization is the brainchild of Chuck Stearman, who heads the organization and is its festival promoter. It started out as an awards show in Chuck's home state of Missouri in 1974. The event was moved to Nashville in 1984, under Stearman's guidance, and their first International Band Championship commenced that year in conjunction with the tenth anniversary of the SPBGMA Bluegrass Music Awards show.

"Now he opened a lot of doors for acts like The Country Gentlemen and Martha & Eddie Adcock, who began to play the festival, which did help a lot of smaller groups in the Midwest, as it became the place to be, and it became so crowded, you couldn't find a parking space out there," explains Mac. "At the same time, its operation put a lot of the other Midwest festivals out of business. Being a non-profit operation out there in Missouri, I didn't make a move to support him in any way, and he had approached me many times about playing. I was always busy during that period, and I was also booked when it came time to present my award (induction into SPBGMA's Preservation Hall of Greats, Class of 1987, along with fellow veterans Doc Watson and Charlie Waller).

"It was supposed to be a showcase around town. But if you worked the gigs out there you got awards and a place in his book, his magazine, for the annual awards show and such. Now some chose to do all that, like the Lewis Family, and that's fine, but I was sorry to see the other festivals close down," adds Mac.

Mac had long been a buddy to fellow inductee Doc Watson, who resided where he was born Arthel Lane Watson on March 3, 1923, near Deep Gap, North Carolina. He and wife Rosa Lee had two children Eddy Merle in 1949, and Nancy Ellen in 1951. Sadly, Doc's son, named after Eddy Arnold and Merle Travis, died following a tragic accident, after his tractor rolled down a steep hillside on his farm, October 23, 1985. He was thirty-six years old, and had suffered polio at age six, which for two months paralyzed his legs from the waist down. Fortunately through therapy and bicycle exercises, Merle regained the use of his legs and reduced the subsequent limp somewhat. Still, he continued to encounter pain, prompted by that initial hip and joint damage throughout the remainder of his life, prompting the taking of pain-killing drugs.

In 1988, Doc launched Merle-Fest, sponsored by Wilkes Community College in Wilkesboro, North Carolina, that still attracts major names from both bluegrass and country annually,.

According to Mac, "The first one we did out of respect to Doc, and we all donated our services, including Chet Atkins, Grandpa Jones, his wife Ramona and quite a few others. We all played at our own expense, but the understanding was that if it became successful, we'd come back again at our usual fee. They made so much they built a pavilion in Merle's honor the second year.

"I've played a number of gigs with Doc, a great guitarist. One was a folk festival in San Francisco, about a year before Merle died, where they had the Hell's Angels (motorcycle gang) as our security. That promoter was sharp as hell. The word was out that the Hell's Angels were planning to come and break up the festival, so the promoter decided it would be wise to hire them as their security guards. That worked out fine. They walked around there, and some of them were quite open about being gay. I mean they would walk around holding hands and kissing one another, but nobody dared to confront them about it. A sign warned patrons, 'No dogs or intoxicating drinks in the seating area.' Now I looked down on the crowd after I was introduced and all these dudes were sitting on their blankets with their dogs and jugs of wine… "

Yet another name act Mac shared a bill with was an unlikely co-star for a country balladeer: "In the mid-1980s, I did a show over in North Carolina for some sort of little old convention at a hotel, and most people in the area knew me, so when I came on they raised a big ruckus. I heard later Frank Sinatra, Jr., got pissed. He wouldn't even look at me and if he had to, just offered dirty looks. Just like his Daddy did, he had his own entourage following him around. A few of the promoters laughed and one told me, 'I guess you showed his ass!' But that wasn't my intent. I was just doing what I do, entertaining."

Sinatra, Jr., suffers the same situation affecting numerous second-generation artists, standing in the shadow of a more famous figure. He has become a skilled arranger, bandleader and vocalist. Unlike sister Nancy, however, Junior has yet to chart a single on *Billboard's* weekly lists.

Nancy "with the smiling face," as Frank once sang in his little girl's honor, was far more familiar with country music than baby brother. Her mainline producer was none other than Lee Hazlewood, who wrote her biggest hit "These Boots Are Made For Walkin'," and produced most of her records, including her cover of the Johnny Cash-June Carter hit "Jackson," on which Lee also sings. Additionally, Nancy joined Mel Tillis for a duets album "Mel & Nancy" (1981), which spawned country chart singles "Texas Cowboy Night," "Play Me Or Trade Me" and "Where Would I Be?" She was wed briefly to pop singer Tommy Sands, once a client to Colonel Tom Parker.

When Martin Haerle requested another CMH album from the "Voice With a Heart," Billy Troy served as Wiseman's co-producer. Troy was the son of former Country Boys' picker Buck Graves. The CMH sessions were conducted in 1989 at Home Place Studio in Nashville. The twenty-two songs were a mixed bag, though all were of vintage origins, such as "Doin' My Time," "Don't Let Your Deal Go Down" and "Lost At the River." Many of these had been popularized earlier by Wiseman associates.

This collection was released as "Grassroots To Bluegrass," on April 6, 1990, qualifying it to be nominated for NARAS' Best Bluegrass Album Grammy award, Mac's first nomination. The following is a review in part from *Entertainment Express* magazine, following the double album's 1990 release:

"'Grassroots to Bluegrass - A Very Special Album' is a decidedly different presentation. It showcases the Virginia mountain minstrel's tasty vocals on a variety of old-timey numbers, including country, folk, gospel and bluegrass. In its liner notes, Mac and Middle Tennessee University historian Paul F. Wells explained some background on the vintage tunes... 'How nice to again hear such classics as 'Wait For the Light To Shine,' 'I'm Just Here To Get My Baby Out of Jail,' 'I'm Using My Bible For a Road Map' and 'Doin' My Time' especially as sung by Mac... Besides vocals, Wiseman excels as a string musician, performing rhythm guitar for this outing.'

"The singer scores high marks, too, on the Johnnie & Jack hit 'Cryin' Heart Blues.' The very rarely heard 'Poor Ellen Smith,' which Mac says he first listened to when backing Molly O'Day, registers a strong reading by the master. Wiseman does equally well on the Carter Family success 'Sailor On the Deep Blue Sea,' Acuff's 'Streamlined Cannonball' and the Bailes Brothers' song 'Dust On the Bible,' a big record for Kitty Wells.

"This treasury of classics, co-produced by Mac and Billy Troy, essayed by one of the finest tenors in country music, proves a real collectors' item. It also earned Mac his one and only Grammy Award nomination in 1990."

CMH's boss Martin C. Haerle died on September 4, 1990. He'd earned respect for his efforts to showcase classic country and bluegrass music of the legends on his independent label. Wiseman had emphasized that "Grassroots To Bluegrass" was some fifteen years in the making, noting: "The theme of the CD is that it traces the evolution of old-time music from the late 1920s, songs first recorded by the Carter Family, Jimmie Rodgers, Riley Puckett and pays tribute to the pioneers up until the 1950s, when the old-time music took on the terminology of bluegrass."

Further, as Mac pointed out, "I couldn't be more pleased with the timing of this nomination. I am especially happy that critics and fans alike have recognized the heart and soul that the late Martin Haerle put into this effort. I only wish that he could have lived to share in this great honor accorded us by the NARAS voters."

In 1990, Mac was also invited to record with fellow artists like Lynn Anderson, Kix Brooks, T. Graham Brown, Vince Gill, Highway 101, Johnny Rodriguez, Dan Seals and Pam Tillis as a vocal group, Tomorrow's World, in honor of Earth Day. The song also titled "Tomorrow's World," co-written by Pam Tillis and Kix Brooks, charted *Billboard* number seventy-four, one week only, May 5, 1990.

As Mac told WSM announcer Eddie Stubbs, "It's been my philosophy, if the business is healthy, I'll get me a little piece of it, and if it isn't, nobody wins. I've

223

always worked overall to do everything I can to contribute to the business, as well as to myself personally with that philosophy."

Being one of the founders of the CMA, Mac could see parallels to that organization and the attempt to inaugurate the International Bluegrass Music Association (IBMA), a quarter century later: "One of the first things we did was to go to the higher echelon of advertising agencies to make them aware that they were using country music to sell their products, citing the Don Gibsons, Jim Reeves

Vince Gill and Mac sang together for 'Tomorrow's World' benefit.

and crossover artists (like) Ray Charles, though William Morris (public relations agency) didn't consider them country music, but just the popular music of the day that they could sell merchandise with, you know. Tex Ritter, who was our diplomat of the whole (CMA) organization, went to New York City for a banquet, inviting all the ad agencies including William Morris.

"I got a Tennessee Walking Horse for him as a door prize," continues Mac. "I swear I did, and he just turned a lot of heads by pointing out that they were using country music, but that was just one of the things we did. Then we'd go to various cities like Houston to have our board meetings for a couple days, and actually we put on a tremendous sales pitch in every one of those markets we went into; but, at the same time, all the board members had to pay their way. I went to London a couple times, just so they'd have a forum, and it wasn't convenient, I'll tell you that, but I went.

"I just want to point out on behalf of the artists, and not being too negative as I may have been a little earlier, but the reason in both cases, there had been an attempt to start a DJ organization and some of the people in it, well it was one of those cases where everyone was Chiefs and no Indians, and some of the money had been misappropriated. They finally dissolved it. People like Connie B. Gay were in it, but his integrity made him get out of it, if you follow me.

"So, that was one reason that the artists didn't trust it; they'd heard about the bad side of this, thinking they're just trying to start another money scam. The same thing happened with the IBMA, and I was one of the doubters on that. I never joined that first round they made, where they had headquarters in Kentucky and some lady was the head of it. That was one reason artists were hesitant to come aboard, thinking a bunch of good ol' boys were gathering and gonna want initiation fees and stuff like that -- and they're not gonna do nothing for us! That's all I've got to say... but I did think in their defense, I needed to add that, so it wouldn't look like the artists were just ignorant, which they aren't. But they were pretty cagey about getting their feet wet again."

Mac, of course, is a member and supporter of IBMA, a respected trade organization promoting bluegrass. Formed in 1985, its first headquarters was established in Owensboro, Kentucky. In 1988, IBMA launched a bluegrass museum in partnership with the city's River Park Center. It was in 1990 that IBMA kicked off its *World of Bluegrass*, a combination trade show convention and awards gala.

During 1997, the annual program was shifted to Louisville; however, IBMA relocated its offices to Nashville in 2003. Just recently, the annual meet was switched to Raleigh, North Carolina, though not necessarily permanently.

Bill Monroe, along with Flatt & Scruggs, became charter members of IBMA's Hall of Honor in 1991; followed by the Stanley Brothers and Reno & Smiley in 1992; with Mac Wiseman and Jim & Jesse as its 1993 recipients. That put Mac among the first five pioneer acts voted into the Hall of Honor. [Following the move to Music City, the legends category revised its name from Hall of Honor to Bluegrass Music Hall of Fame.]

"I was honored to be included or rather inducted into the Hall, at a time when I'm still very much in the ballgame, that is recording and getting out there to entertain the fans," Wiseman said. The crowd went wild on hearing him being included.

"When they called my name, Jimmy Martin walked out. I didn't think that was too professional," recalls Mac, who in 1949 worked with Martin, then one of Monroe's Blue Grass Boys. "He was sure glad to see me go, because he took my job when I left Bill."

In 1995, when *The Nashville Musician* called the self-styled "King of Bluegrass" to ask how he felt being named to the Bluegrass Hall of Honor, Jimmy snapped at the editor, "It's about goddamn time!" He meant it.

Although a lone ranger, Mac was also a team player: "I never tried to steal the spotlight, but I pulled my weight in order to get the attention I thought I deserved, when it came my turn."

He acknowledges deriving great satisfaction working behind the scenes: "We have to put something back. Otherwise, we rape the industry, the way plantation owners ravished the fertile land of the South. They kept growing cotton, without fertilizing and when the land became so poor that it took ten acres to produce what one acre had previously produced, they just cultivated as much land as it took to fulfill their greedy needs. I wouldn't want to see our industry that depleted."

Maxine and Dad with 1993 IBMA
Hall of Honor awards.

24 Groovegrass Boyz...
'Salty Dog Blues'

"Standin' on the corner, with the low down blues
Great big hole in the bottom of my shoes
Honey, let me be your Salty Dog...
Let me be your Salty Dog
Or I won't be your man at all
Honey, let me be your Salty Dog..."

"If today's industry leaders are to continue to enjoy the boom in country's popularity, they need to gain greater insight into the roots and history of this musical genre. And if Nashville is to be deserving of its reputation as a music center, the people now on the scene must learn to look out for their own," maintains Reunion Of Professional Entertainers (ROPE) Chairman of the Board Mac Wiseman.

As noted earlier, this was one of the reasons for founding ROPE. Some seventy artists lamented that the only time performers seemed to get together was at funerals or weddings, and felt it was time to organize their own club where they could fraternize. ROPE was chartered by show business comrades as a non-profit organization, not only to socialize, but more importantly aid and assist members in times of need, whether financial stress, serious illness or death.

For starters, a death, health and welfare program - a trust fund - was initiated to benefit members and their survivors. In 1988, ROPE inaugurated an awards show to raise funds and to honor its own, mainly the veterans, who mostly are ignored by contemporary award programs, such as the Country Music Association, Academy of Country Music, and the all-genre Grammys bestowed annually by the National Academy of Recordings Arts & Sciences.

Gordon Terry, a key founder or instigator, if you will, assumed ROPE's presidency at the start. He held onto that position for a decade until Mac was voted president, a post he held for five consecutive terms. All the while, he was on ROPE's Board of Directors, and during his tenure as President, the group began participation in the annual Fan Fair, now known as the CMA Music Festival, to create a greater awareness of the organization. This included opening membership to outsiders, a la Friends of ROPE - a non-voting element - and even partnered with CMA in a mission to create a retirement center for show business veterans, by utilizing ROPE's non-profit corporate status. Former MCA executive Katie Gillon coordinated this project with The Crescendo Music Community Fund, partnering with CMA, Opry Trust Fund, Academy of Country Music's Bill Boyd Memorial Fund and ROPE.

Opry member Justin Tubb, then ROPE vice president, lamented the lack of media coverage for its functions: "I'm appalled at the almost total lack of mention for ROPE, whose main goals are simply to help fellow entertainers in need and, hopefully, someday build a retirement home or community for retired entertainers in need of a place to live out their golden years. While all ages are eligible to join ROPE, most of our members have been in the business for 25-45 years or more - the ones the new super powers' of country music seem determined to put out to pasture or completely ignore - with exception of one or two a year who are inducted into the CMA Country Music Hall of Fame. But there are many, many others who will never make the Hall who contributed much to our music and need to be remembered and never forgotten.

"That's why the Golden ROPE Awards were started... but they seem to be one of the best-kept secrets in country music," stressed Tubb (in 1993). "This past Sunday night at the Opryland Hotel, the fifth annual awards banquet was held with awards presented in four categories for lifetime achievement in country music... For those who missed the 'big' story, awards were given to the surviving members of the families of Patsy Cline, Hawkshaw Hawkins, Cowboy Copas and Randy Hughes.... ROPE needs all the help we can get from the local media. We could also use some help from some of the 'new tradition,' who might need ROPE sooner than they think!"

Although *The Tennessean* newspaper usually allotted a small space to the resulting awards for a time, in recent times they are again generally ignored. Seldom do other media sources report the awards, determined by vote of the ROPE membership. (In fairness to the media, it's not always a fair barometer of contemporary popularity, since many of the winning artists don't even have current records and some no longer tour.)

Mac was awarded Golden ROPE Awards in the Artist, Business and Songwriting categories. At the time of this writing, ROPE's still going strong, though establishing a retirement home is in limbo, as the CMA seemingly drags its feet on this project. Mac coordinated CMA's utilizing ROPE's non-profit status, supposedly to establish a retirement home. Still no word yet on the country music home being built for the sick or elderly, since he stepped out of the picture.

Wiseman's Golden ROPE award; and Golden Voice radio statuette.

227

Despite such behind-the-scenes efforts, Wiseman continued to entertain fans. He remained one of the more popular American artists north of the border, as well. A 1986 tour remains memorable to him: "One time Irving Oil sponsored a festival in the Maritime on which I was booked with younger artists such as k. d. lang, the Forrester Sisters and a well-known Canadian fiddler when we played New Brunswick and Nova Scotia. You know k.d. is a helluva entertainer, though she dressed like a guy, complete with brogans, and even jumped off stage and got up on a rail at the old racetrack we were playing, walking around the stadium, all the while singing. Brian Edwards had promoted that show very well, on radio and TV, and the Irving stations advertised if you bought a specified number of gallons of gas you'd get a free ticket to the concert.

"At the same show, as I was on stage doing my act, I noticed paramedics coming down to the front row near the stage - though I kept on singing, rather than alerting the audience to the problem - to assist an old man. Well, as it turned out, he had been ailing and his family brought him to the concert to see me, and you know he literally died right out there in front of the stage. They told me later that he'd insisted on coming to see me one more time. Irving also hired me to go on a bill with Buck Graves, Kenny Baker, Ruth McLain's Family Band (from Berea, Kentucky) at the Opryland Hotel, and I was asked to pull the band together for the convention of U.S. dealers."

Mac also had an invitation from the cast of the CBS-TV series *In The Heat Of The Night* to record a CD "Christmas Time's A'Comin'." Reportedly this tied in with a storyline developed by director Arthur Penn and star Carroll O'Connor with co-star Denise Nicholas. Nicholas, in real life was involved in the American Civil Rights Movement, and on the show played a southern councilwoman who has an interracial romance with the town Sheriff Bill Gillespie (O'Connor, who ironically in a previous TV incarnation was the bigoted Archie Bunker of *All In The Family*), the series hero. The sister of civil rights activist Nicholas became a murder victim, ten years earlier. She felt the show might help bring some closure to her and the family.

Alan (Bubba) Autry and Randall Franks, who played deputies on the series, co-produced the album as a fundraiser to combat drug abuse, inviting veteran artists to lend their talents to the project, including Mac, Kitty Wells, Johnnie Wright, Bobby Wright, Pee Wee King, Jim & Jesse, Doug Dillard, Buck Graves, Chubby Wise, Ralph Stanley, Jimmy Martin, Buddy Spicher, The Whites, Little Jimmy Dickens, Jerry Douglas, Pig Robbins and The Lewis Family. It was released by Sonlite Records & MGM/UA in 1991, and proved a popular seller with fans of country and the series.

Nearly a year later, Mac lost another of his heroes and the industry lost its fabled "King of Country Music" as Roy Acuff died November 23, 1992, at age eighty-nine. Wiseman recalls: "Roy Acuff, a few months before he died, invited me to his dressing room backstage at the Opry, and wanted me to sing some of the old songs he loved that I'd recorded. He sat there in his recliner and his eyes shut, listened and when he knew the words would sing along. Finally, someone came to say, 'Roy, we gotta do the next show.' Roy stood up to excuse himself, thanked me and shook my hand, slipping me a hundred dollar bill. I said, 'Roy, I wasn't doing it to be paid.' He said, 'I know, but I want you to have it.' So I had him autograph the bill and have it to this day. He was funny about that request, thinking it was illegal to write on money from the U.S. Treasury, but he did sign it for me."

By the late 1980s, Branson, Missouri, became a hot ticket destination, especially for families, giving Nashville a run for its money as a country music mecca. In 1985, romance novelist Janet Dailey and husband Bill bought the Hee Haw Theatre, renaming it Country Music World, spotlighting vibrant violinist-showman Shoji Tabuchi, who hailed from Osaka, Japan, a big Roy Acuff fan, as its headliner. The couple flew a plane load of Nashville media to Branson on an introductory flight. It was the beginning of a surge for the Ozark Mountain site, where artists like Boxcar Willie and Mel Tillis established competing theaters.

One of country's music biggest draws established his Willie Nelson Ozark Theatre in Branson, then invited another major star, Merle Haggard, to work with him for prime time engagements. To round out their schedule, both agreed on inviting Mac Wiseman to entertain the breakfast crowd.

"Mornings With Mac" became an extremely popular attraction from its spring through October 31, 1992 booking. Strategically situated across the street from the Cracker Barrel family restaurant, Mac was a welcome magnet following a hearty breakfast, thanks to tickets priced at twelve dollars, though enterprising tourists could easily find three dollars-off coupons in area hotels, restaurants and stores. (Little did Mac dream he and Merle would tackle a duet CD, some twenty years down the road.)

In November 1992, banjoist Larry Perkins invited Mac to do a vocal guest spot (and as arranger) for Pinecastle Records' "A Touch Of the Past," also featuring artists such as John Hartford, Alison Krauss, Del and Rob McCoury, Earl Scruggs and the Osborne Brothers, recorded at Studio 19 in Nashville.

Willie had obviously appreciated Mac taking on the responsibility of the morning show, because he was quick to accept an offer to headline a ROPE benefit Mac promoted at the Ryman Auditorium in August 1994, to aid fellow members in need. Yet another superstar Kenny Rogers was also persuaded by Mac to headline a ROPE benefit held at Nashville's former Starwood Amphitheater, and he'd also lured iconic Cherokee Cowboy Ray Price from Texas. ROPE shows had not previously enjoyed such huge crowds for their benefits, boosting the organization's Trust Fund.

Mac remembers, too, a TV special he did at an Iowa Public Broadcast Station (PBS) for Bob Everhart: "That was done in the studio with Bob. It occurred right after we closed in Branson . . . we drove up there and then back to Nashville, driving through Iowa, Illinois and Indiana, and I never saw so damn many cornfields in my life."

Another Bluegrass venture saw Mac Wiseman being engaged to provide voice-over for the acclaimed "High Lonesome - The Story of Bluegrass Music," a film documentary directed and scripted by Rachel Liebling, and released in April 1994. Rachel was a student of noted documentarian Ken Burns, and Mac's early training in radio no doubt aided him in pulling off this prestigious assignment.

The New York Times' film critic Janet Maslin had only favorable comments, citing such genre heroes as Bill Monroe, Ralph Stanley and Mac Wiseman. In one paragraph she recalled Mac's voice-over statement, *"Some called it folk music, with overdrive,"* adding *"The film's images recall the Appalachia of Walker Evans (photographer) and James Agee (author). But if the images that Ms. Liebling has found are less studied and mournful, maybe Bluegrass itself is a factor. Even when dealing with sad subjects, this is music to make the spirit soar."*

Also in 1994, Mac was asked to perform as part of *Martha White Bluegrass Nights* at the Ryman Auditorium, scheduled June 14 - August 30. Mac shared the stage with pals Jim & Jesse on July 26, while other headliners in the series included Bill Monroe, Alison Krauss, Marty Stuart, Bela Fleck, Del McCoury, Ricky Skaggs, the Osborne Brothers, and Ralph Stanley. Indeed, he was hailed as a Bluegrass pioneer once more.

More than a year later, Wiseman was also invited to participate in a six-hour TBS documentary series, *America's Music: Roots of Country*, beamed in 1996. Directed by Tom Neff, who co-wrote the script with journalist Robert K. Oermann, their Emmy-nominated effort was narrated by Kris Kristofferson. Mac was well represented when it came to television or films, having been a longtime member of the American Federation of Television & Radio Artists (AFTRA), ever since his California days.

"I joined AFTRA in 1957, when I moved out to the West Coast, as I was starting to do television out there, and at the time you had to be a resident six months before you got your card; however, you could work while you were waiting on your card. I still belong to AFTRA because for one thing they have a better scale than the American Federation of Musicians (AFM)."

As Mac was in his sixth decade as an artist, a seventieth birthday salute was slated a bit late on August 25, 1995 in Waynesboro, Virginia, at the local fairgrounds. The Wiseman family all showed up, he grins: "Of course, my birthday's May 23, but this was the more convenient time."

Throughout much of his career, Wiseman found a respite from the stress of the music business by taking time out to fish and hunt with friends from within the industry and apart from it.

Mac and Dr. Ken Smith take a hunter's break in S.C.

As noted earlier, Mac enjoyed fishing with co-workers such as Lee Moore of WSVA-Harrisonburg, as well as Ferlin Husky - or was it his alter ego *Simon Crum*? - Dr. Ken Smith, and Lyle West, way up in Alaska.

West is Wiseman's senior fishing friend. Although this hardy soul hailed originally from South Dakota, he's been part of the Alaska terrain since 1943, back when Mac was about to graduate from high school.

On the music side, Lyle West was a lover of bluegrass: "I've been over that (Al-Can) highway sixty-eight times driving to Nashville, which is about five thousand miles from here. Over in Norris, Tennessee, John Rice Irwin has his *Tennessee Homecoming* celebration in the fall (at the Appalachia Museum), and I've gone to it for probably twenty years, though I've missed it a couple times. I hope to make it this year if I can (2011).

"Now I first met Mac at a music festival in Spruce Pines, North Carolina, in 1973, and we became good friends. I knew a woman, Mrs. Baird, who was booking the Alaska State Fair, so I put in a good word for him with her, and they brought him up. I think that was in 1975, anyway it seemed like it was the year after he had that big operation (stomach bypass surgery)."

Mac has fond memories of visiting with Lyle at his home near Homer: "We also went to Valdez hoping to rent a boat for fishing, but when we got there, all the boats were rented, An elderly gentleman, however, had a boat all to himself. Well, he saw we couldn't rent one, so he invited Lyle and I to go out with him. I thought that was very generous of him.

"When we came back into the boat dock after fishing, we went into a bar-restaurant... Next thing we knew, some fellow came in and said, 'You had better go kill that fish you caught. The way it's flopping in the boat, it'll beat the bottom out of it.' The old gent got up, went outside and with his pistol shot the fish, then told us, 'I guess that'll stop his flopping,' but later when we all went out to go home, he found his boat had sunk! The bullet went through the fish and shot a hole in the bottom of his boat!"

Lyle, a carpenter by trade remembers Mac inviting him to spend some time with his family in Nashville: "Yes, I spent two or three Christmas holidays in Nashville, in the mid-1980s."

Mac remembers Lyle did some carpentry work while visiting, which he so appreciated. The Alaskan laughs about the time he tried interesting friend Mrs. Baird in booking Mac: "She hadn't heard too much about Mac and his talent, so I had a bunch of tapes I'd made from the festivals, and he would send me new records he made. So I invited her out and played some of Mac's music. We had the windows open, as it was summer and I had a pretty good sound system, so the music carried. Now this

Lyle West and a whopper of a fish in Alaska.

was fairly virgin country I homesteaded, about twelve miles from town, so there were quite a few bears hanging around. The bears knew I raised hogs and they liked fresh pork. When we looked out the window, we saw the bears, but this one sort of hung around as though it liked hearing Mac singing. As soon as I took Mac's music off to play somebody else, the bear took off. It only liked Mac's voice. I told Mac about that . . . You know I treasure my friendship with Mac."

Mac's made many such friends over the years.

"When it came to hunting, I went to Texas, Georgia and also Charleston, South Carolina. I'd go there every year the day after Christmas to Jack's Island, a plantation in the suburbs of Charleston. My friend there was Dr. Ken Smith, who owned his own clinic. The house we stayed in when I first went down there had a big cannonball hole in it... We'd hunt ducks in the a.m. and quail in the afternoon. I did quite well with all of them. Ken and I met when he attended festivals where I performed. I think the first time was in Gatlinburg, Tennessee. He became a wonderful friend and made very liberal donations to ROPE. We'd room together and everything, when I went to Charleston.

"They had a good clubhouse and an excellent black cook. Cy, the guy who owned it all, was a good friend to former President Richard Nixon. 'Doc' would lease us a condo and that's where we stayed. Now Cy had duck blinds on his property and they'd take me out in a boat to shoot the ducks, then they'd come back and get me. We hunted ducks and quail in Georgia, too.

"Down in Texas, we hunted with a guy who ran the Country Club in Dallas. There was me, Chubby Wise and the local Game Warden. You know doves are the stupidest birds in the world. One time we were in the field of a bunch of small sunflowers... "

Seeing the undersized sunflowers prompted Mac to ask, "Where did you get the seeds for small sunflowers?," thinking he'd like to grow some back home. "But he said because of the dry weather down there, that's as big as they grow."

Mac and Georgia hunting pals nab their quota of ducks (and then some).

Regarding the dove hunt, Mac adds, "We'd shoot at them in one tree and they'd fly over to another. Then you'd shoot at them there and they'd fly right back to the tree we fired on first. Sometimes I'd shoot my doves from the front seat of a jeep, so I didn't have to walk all over with my bad leg. When we quit hunting that first afternoon, we took the several hundred birds we bagged to the edge of the field and pulled the breast out of them to carry back. Our game warden friend suggested he take all of the dove breasts back to Dallas, where we were staying, in his vehicle. That way, he reasoned, if he got stopped, we would all chip in to help pay any fine. Otherwise, if we got stopped carrying the breasts in separate cars there would be multiple fines." (He didn't get stopped.)

Throughout the 1980s, Mac recorded; hit the festival circuit as much as he chose to; worked behind the scenes with ROPE; was inducted into the SPBGMA's Hall of Greats in 1987; and in 1993, came his Bluegrass Hall of Honor induction.

After garnering his Grammy nomination for best bluegrass album - "From Grassroots To Bluegrass" - he performed on the Grammy-nominated, multi-artist "Christmas On The Mountain" featuring Mac's self-penned "Christmas Memories" in 2002; and Charlie Daniels' "Songs From The Longleaf Pines" in 2005, both produced by the innovative Scott Rouse.

Rouse, one of Wiseman's true champions, revitalized the veteran's career via various fun-filled GrooveGrass Boyz recordings. His daddy Jim had long been a big Mac fan. Adds Mac, "I met Scott at Doc Watson's MerleFest. They'd go over every year to that festival. It was Scott's thing to 'babysit' Doc. I mean, lead him around and be sure he's taken care of. Well, when I got back, Scott called to say, 'I've got this idea, this bluegrass bit.' So we go into the studio together and did 'Salty Dog' with that wild beat he arranged. He said, 'Let's get Del McCoury and his band,' so Del and his boys came in on it and I thought they'd die laughing. They felt Scott was maybe pulling their leg, but before it was over, they were getting into it pretty good."

Their efforts resulted in Rouse's "Country Macarena," also featuring Doc Watson and hip-hop musician Bootsy Collins, spending three weeks on the *Billboard* charts in 1996, and even enjoyed a little pop action and went to seven on their Bubbling Under chart in 1996. "Some people thought that was my son Scott on there, and they said Mac's son sure sounds like his dad," Wiseman laughs.

Albums Rouse produced on his newly-assembled group were 1997's "The GrooveGrass Boyz With Doc, Del and Mac," followed by "GrooveGrass 101," a 1998 CD, mixing it up with Doc, Jerry Douglas, funky bassist Bootsy Collins, and Del McCoury's sons Ronnie and Rob.

"The main reason," relates Rouse, "is to make bluegrass palatable for kids and dance clubs in New York and L.A., who weren't exposed to it before. They'd see that Doc, Mac and Del were on the records and maybe buy other records by them."

Rolling Stone magazine called their "GrooveGrass 101" album, "A high-concept mix of bluegrass and funk... unmoved by the grandeur of country."

"Bluegrass was the stepchild of country. It was like the hip-hop of Rhythm & Blues," relates Rouse, one of the more creative talents to hit Nashville in the 1990s. Brother Mitch Rouse is an actor-screenwriter-filmmaker, and was a cast member of Jim Belushi's *According to Jim* TV sitcom.

Rouse developed a healthy respect for bluegrass music during boyhood days, and also learned to dig rock, R&B and disco dance grooves in adolescence. Studying guitar and drums at Boston's School of Music, this *wunderkind* helped engineer the popularity of youth bands New Kids On The Block and New Edition (their success prompted Scott to drop out of school).

On the side for a change of pace, Rouse was blending bluegrass sounds into rockin' rhythms, a fusion he began producing for Boston area dance clubs. Scott soon became a champion of combining different genres, creating his GrooveGrass sound by mixing bluegrass into danceable pop rhythms: "I had the kernel of an idea, but actually I can't take credit for coining that terminology because a Boston club DJ started calling it 'Groovegrass,' which reflects a 'mash-up' (mixing) of hip-hop and bluegrass."

Subsequently, Rouse recruited pioneer bluegrass musicians Watson, McCoury and Wiseman to record with Collins, one of Scott's other musical heroes. Rouse:

"Bootsy was the very roots of modern funk [and now a member of the Rock Hall of Fame]. It's common knowledge that he took what he learned with James Brown and then George Clinton, with whom he started Parliament/Funkadelic, producing a hipper, redefined punk sound (heavily influenced by jazz and psychedelic rock)."

Scott's collection of craftsmen came together as Scott's GrooveGrass Boyz, who hit with a countrified cover of the Spanish musical hit "Macarena," recorded by a duo called Los del Rio, whose tune topped charts from Austria to The Philippines to the U.S., selling more than four million singles. Rouse's 1997 version "The Country Macarena," boasting revised lyrics, may not have been as lucrative, but it startled Doc, Del, Mac and Bootsy, as much as anyone, else by charting *Billboard*, peaking at number seventy on the Hot Country Songs chart, and remained on their lists a long time, a career plus for Mac and all concerned.

According to *Billboard's* Chet Flippo: "CMT's Chris Parr (program director) saw a definite pattern that year. 'Over the whole year there have probably been only five or so consistently selling singles on that chart without a video. One was a novelty song 'Country Macarena'... ,' Parr stated."

Working with Mac, was a delight for Scott: "He's the big dog in the room and makes you feel like a super-hero. Mac's one of the funniest people I know. He's not a one-upper, but you can't one-up him."

For a time, Rouse accepted an offer he just couldn't refuse: "Terry Herd is like THE bluegrass DJ and a friend of mine. Well, he calls to say, 'I'd like to talk to you about doing this pod-cast thing on Sirius Satellite.' I said yeah I was interested, as I'm always looking for something new and different, and I came up with this short interview format called *Five Minutes With Wichita*. I didn't want anybody to know it was me, so I talked in this really weird voice as Wichita Rutherford."

To test the waters, Scott interviewed Mac for Terry: "It was really bizarre. I thought Terry knew it was me, but he really didn't. This show got thousands of hits right off, from all over the world. It got huge. Mac's interview got over one hundred thousand downloads!"

Subsequently Scott met with Terry at the Station Inn in Nashville, though Herd didn't realize at first that Rouse was actually Wichita. Its popularity proved a time-consuming task for Scott, however, interviewing all his bluegrass cronies and a who's who of country artists, as well: "I was having to do interviews with strangers. It was weird."

Currently, Wichita's sort of lost in time: "I put it on hold because I just didn't have the time to do it anymore."

Scott's too busy building up his bank account. When he first arrived in Music City back in 1988, it was a different story, all he had were a pocketful of dreams and few contacts.

Rouse reached out to the major labels with his concept of musical "mash-ups," drawing derisive laughter from the major labels. Finally dropping by Warner Bros., someone actually listened to his ideas: "Bob Saporiti was the guy who treated me with some respect. I told him, 'Here's what's gonna happen next,' and he listened. Now the big boss, Jim Ed Norman, was always good to me, too. The trend at the time was towards country music, as the pop scene was starting to die down. I saw Randy Travis and Garth Brooks, acts like that, and thought, 'This is where it's going.' I believed you could do things being done for pop acts for country stars, as well. That had never been done before in country.

"I like to follow trends and patterns on what's happening, not just in music but in the world, from economy to fashions to music. If you follow trends, you can pretty much see what's coming. I saw country coming back, so that's why I moved to Nashville. Did you know that the gay clubs always start a trend? So in Boston we began watching what was happening there. Those club DJ's are always on the front line, and they know what's going to catch on.

"I remember saying to Warner Bros. that 'Cassettes are going out; man, don't do them anymore. Start putting your stuff on CDs'… Then I asked about letting me do this dance remix or mash-up on one of their country classics, 'Swingin',' which had been a number one for John Anderson years earlier.

"Jim Ed said, 'Are you sure?' I said, 'Yes, trust me,' and got hold of the master and took it into the studio and did it. Warner Bros. was elated, but Anderson shot it down, saying, 'Dance remixes for country will never happen!' Of course, everybody had a copy of it and the others said, 'That's what we ought to do.' A DAT tape of it got out and it caught on at local dance clubs. Before you could say 'Swingin',' every dance club in America had a copy, and it was the rage. Suddenly they all wanted dance mixes."

Mark Wright at Decca gave Scott the green light to remix their 1968 Top Forty country single "Rocky Top," the Osborne Brothers' signature song.

"I called Sonny and Bobby and told them, 'Here's what I want to do, explaining and asking, 'Do you guys mind if we do this?' Bobby and Sonny were into it and Decca released it, and today it's the longest-charting single in *Billboard's* history."

True, "Rocky Top" peaked at number two in 1996 for the Osbornes and a decade later was still charting for a whopping one hundred and fifty-two weeks. Prior to that the duo's highest charted entry had been "Once More" at thirteen in 1958. "Rocky Top" originally peaked at thirty-three in 1968 (fine for a bluegrass record) and there was even a subsequent version by the brothers with Wiseman.

Scott Rouse who hails from Louisa, Kentucky, is one of three children born to James and Marilyn Rouse. Dad, who plays guitar and was a good pal to Doc Watson, is also a renowned physician in Knoxville, a radiologist specialist. He's a big Wiseman fan. He helped Scott co-write such novelty numbers as "Here's Your Sign" for Bill Engvall and "Big Ol' Moon" for Jeff Foxworthy. Mac and Del joined Jeff for the latter track, which appeared on Foxworthy's million-selling comedy CD "Crank It Up - The Music Album" (number three, 1996).

That all came about when Warner Bros. came to Scott saying they had this nightclub comic Jeff Foxworthy under contract: "We've got this comedian selling ten-thousand discs, how do we get him to where he sells like thirty-three thousand by the end of the year?"

"I said, 'I know what to do; we'll take the live stuff and put a little song around it, something that hasn't been done before'. Someone said, 'Nah, that won't work.' I told them, 'Let me take it home with me. I'll put it together and bring it back to you. If you don't like it, you don't have to pay for it. OK?' Bob Saporiti said, 'You know what? I think it'll work. We ought to do it.' So to test the waters they put it out as a single. In the next few months, it became their biggest-selling comedy album.

So the formula became single and album, featuring name artists on the Foxworthy singles like Little Texas ('Party All Night'), Alan Jackson ('Redneck Games') and Mac and Del ('Big Ol' Moon')."

Actually, Rouse became producer of Foxworthy's efforts which include "You Might Be a Redneck If," and "Games Rednecks Play." He also signed on to produce yet another redneck comedian, Bill Engvall, whose best-selling albums include "Here's Your Sign."

Talk about a success story, Scott Rouse had only been in town some five years. They had sparked a blue collar movement for country comedy albums, but ever humble, Rouse declares, "All I did in a different way was copy what Ray Stevens had done with 'Guitarzan' and I told them to do videos, which they balked at because they were being charged half-a-million to make them. I told them to do the videos for $25,000. Well, we did quite well commercially, selling millions of those things.

"It got to the point where I couldn't produce them anymore. Do it once, it's funny, but do it twice and it's not so funny. Imagine hearing that stuff all the time! You can only take so much of redneck humor. Then they wanted to bring in bathroom jokes and I said, 'No way. We won't go into that.' Finally, I said, 'I'm outta here, I can't do this anymore.' Well, they hated me after that."

Mac's 80th birthday bash with (from left)
Scott Rouse, Ronnie and Del McCoury
in Nashville's Scoreboard Lounge.

Attesting to his good guy image, Rouse saw wise guys out there early on buying up celebrity names on the Internet at a nominal cost, and then charged a hefty fee when those same names tried to lock in their claim to their VIP name. Seeing the writing on the wall, Rouse bought up Mac Wiseman's name and subsequently helped in the procedure of establishing Mac's website.

Another project involving Mac, conceived to coincide with The Millennium, was the brainchild of CMH's David Haerle and his assistant Jim Silvers. It took the form of a compilation CD, "Three Tenors of Bluegrass," released March 7, 2000. According to its overblown liner notes: "American originals Mac Wiseman, Bobby Osborne and Jim Silvers, each a noted bluegrass singer and legend in his own right, create an unforgettable musical experience and weave a heartbreaking tapestry of love and loss in this captivating album..."

Inspired by the popularity of teaming Italian operatic tenors Plácido Domingo, José Carreras, and Luciano Pavarotti, followed by Irish tenors touring a la Finbar Wright, Anthony Kearns, and Ronan Tynan, Silvers scheduled fifteen ballads with each artist either sharing vocal slots or doing solo spots. The least known, Silvers included one duet featuring him and unbilled Herb Pedersen on "Walkin' the Dog," and four Silvers solos. Mac's participation included a single solo "I Still

Write Your Name in the Sand" and three duets: "Poison Love," "The Bluebirds Are Singing For Me" and "I'm a Stranger Here" with Osborne. Bobby fared best being on nine tracks, including "Hillbilly Fever," "Old Flames" (with Terry Eldredge of The Grascals), "Sunny Side of the Mountain," "Georgia Piney Woods," "Take Me As I Am" and "The Tragic Romance."

"That was strictly reissue stuff I cut way before," muses Mac. "This guy Silvers was put in charge of configurations, and it was a chance to put out some of his songs. I had lunch here with him twice, the first and last. I wasn't too excited about its release, but it looked alright (the packaging, that is)."

Rouse wasn't forgetting friend Wiseman. He took on producing chores for new bluegrass band Blue Highway, but also did a star-studded bluegrass holiday album - "Christmas On the Mountain" for Universal Music Group - that featured Mac vocally on four tracks, included Mac's composition "Christmas Memories," and was akin to a reunion for the GrooveGrass Boyz - Del, Doc and Mac. It also garnered a Grammy nod.

Then when Scott agreed to do a bluegrass album in 2005 on legendary southern rocker Charlie Daniels - "Songs From the Longleaf Pines," Daniels' first bluegrass-gospel CD - he learned that Charlie was also a "Big Mac" fan, and they gave the veteran a call: "We were sitting at The Palms (restaurant) in Nashville with David Corlew, Charlie's manager, and the topic came up, so I just called Mac up right from the table there and asked him to participate in the project."

 25 'Christmas Time's A Comin'... Friends Welcome!

"Can't you hear them bells ringin' ringin'?
Joy don'tcha hear them singin'?
When it's snowin' I'll be goin'
Back to my country home
Christmas time's a comin'
Christmas time's a comin'
Christmas time's a comin'
And I know I'm goin' home . . ."

"Del McCoury? I admire him greatly. He played around for years in Baltimore clubs and also worked in a sawmill, (and) in the woods as a logger to take care of his family," says Mac, adding, "His wife Jean kinda helps run the show. She calls and invites the people who come to their place. I just had a birthday card from them and she saw to it that the boys signed it as well. Now that's so thoughtful."

Kicking off the chat, Del says, "I'm so glad you're doing this book because he's worked with all the pioneers like Molly O'Day, Tex Ritter and Hank Williams. When I think of Mac, I know he was at the beginning of so many things. You know, he was with Bill Monroe, Flatt & Scruggs, and was a founding member of the CMA, then the IBMA. He's been there for all the things that are important to us in this business. I think a lot of Mac, I always have."

Delano McCoury stands as one of bluegrass music's most award-winning artists and with his band, including sons Ronnie on mandolin and Rob on banjo, augmented by Jason Carter on fiddle and Alan Bartram on bass, has earned thirty-one IBMA awards - nine times Entertainer of the Year - and boasts multiple Grammys.

"The first time I saw Mac was on TV," recalls Del. "In the 1940s, all we had was radio and the three stations you could get bluegrass in on were WSM-Nashville, WWVA-Wheeling and WRVA-Richmond. We kept turning the dial until we got one of them tuned in. Later on, we got a TV, actually a combination TV, radio and record player. The screen was only little bitty. I had three sisters and two brothers, and one sister married a fellow who put up TV aerials, and where we lived, we could pick up three stations in Baltimore.

"We kids were not supposed to stay up late and usually would go to bed when the news signed off, but one night I stayed up later and got to see Ray Davis, a DJ in Baltimore. That night he had Mac Wiseman on - that must've been about 1950 or '51 - and boy was I excited. Another thing I remember is Mac had Big Jim Williams playing mandolin. Well, I finally met Jim at Mac's eighty-fifth birthday party and that was the first time I saw him in person.

"Seems like on TV, he was singing lead on the chorus and Mac was singing tenor - and he could really sing high - then a little short guy played banjo; in retrospect, I think his name was Wayne Brown. So that was the first time I saw Mac on TV.

238

"We were raised in York County, Pennsylvania, on a farm. When I was about nine, my older brother taught me to play guitar. We never went too many places, because we had like eighteen cows to be milked, morning and evening, every day. There were no vacations. When my brother was old enough, he left the farm and got a factory job. So he could buy records and things, and he bought Mac Wiseman records.

"Mac later told me he had a deal with his label (Dot Records) where they released a new single about every six weeks. You know that's a lot of songs to put out there... The first major city near us was Baltimore. Me and my brother went up there to see Mac, expecting to see his banjo picker Donnie Bryant with him, who was so good. Instead, when we got there, a tall, skinny redheaded boy was playing banjo with him, name of J. D. Crowe. Now he's not that much older than me, so I suspect he was still in high school at the time. Of course, he wasn't all that good then, but I was impressed because he was on stage with Mac."

Wiseman recalls McCoury telling him that all he had when he got into Nashville was his instrument and a Mac Wiseman songbook he used. Del remembers thrilling to the sound of Mac's tenor singing hits like "Love Letters in the Sand," "There's a Rainbow in the Valley" or "I'll Still Write Your Name in the Sand."

"In 1965, Carlton Haney had the first bluegrass festival in Fincastle, Virginia, which I missed. Don't think I knew about it. I quit Bill Monroe in the early part of 1964, and met Carlton in 1966, and then played it with such musicians as David Grisman, who played mandolin, and Kenny Baker playing fiddle...

"Kenny Baker, myself and my brother Jerry McCoury, who was a great bass player, all backed Mac at Sunset Park in Pennsylvania. (That's the music venue started by "Uncle Roy" Waltman in 1940, about 40 miles from Philadelphia in Chester County, and continued by son Lawrence.) Lawrence's wife Hazel explained that during the 1950s, 'We told Mac that any Sunday he wasn't booked, he should come right here and play.' That was a pretty good deal for him. A lot of times, my band would back Mac after he dropped his band. I enjoyed that and from that time on, I got to know Mac better."

Mac remembers it was actually Uncle Roy who made the offer to play any Sunday he was free - "He not only was a good businessman, but a fan of mine. I remember he had a rocking chair sitting by the end of the stage and whenever I performed, he'd come out and sit to watch my show. He didn't do that very often for others. You know he was the first guy to pay Hank Williams a thousand dollars a day, which was coordinated by Jim Denny. I believe that was the first time in country music history an act was paid that much."

"Mac Wiseman has that unnatural high voice," Del continues. "Nobody sings like Mac, just as no one sang like Bill Monroe or even Lester Flatt. Mac was truly one of the pioneers and for his style of music, he was unique and had set a style way back when he began performing."

Noted historian Bill Malone has said that Mac Wiseman was the best solo singer in bluegrass.

Mac's enthusiasm for the oldtime ballads is shared by Del: "Those old storysongs are powerful. He told me that his mother used to write those songs down when she heard them on the radio. I'll bet he treasures that collection of songbooks she gave him, and it's amazing he's kept them so long. He's one of the greatest singers, you know. Mac was also one of the most business-oriented artists I knew. He'd sell anything and had a record label, booking agency, publishing, produced sessions, and even one time headed up that music show at (WWVA-) Wheeling."

Del was a bit puzzled when Scott Rouse approached him about doing the GrooveGrass Boyz project: "I don't remember what I thought, but looking back he did have some wild ideas, didn't he? Mainly, when I heard it would involve Mac and Doc, I decided to do it. You know what? We didn't rehearse anything... we sorta knew those traditional things we did, but kinda had to learn 'The Country Macarena.' Bootsy wasn't there. No, there were just Scott, Mac, Doc and my boys Rob and Ronnie in the studio. Bootsy wasn't there with us (but added later), so I never met him."

McCoury also remembers record-ing the Grammy-nominated "Christ-mas On the Mountain" CD, released in 2002 by Universal South Records, with Scott and Mac: "I think I had done one Christmas song before that, probably in the 1970s, but that was my first holiday album. I remember we did 'Blue Christ-mas,' the old Ernest Tubb hit, which El-vis also cut and 'Christmas Memories.' Ronnie and us did 'Bluegrass Christ-mas.' 'Christmas Time's a Comin' (fea-turing him, Doc and Mac) was fun. It was an interesting project."

Yet another production Del enjoyed doing was the GrooveGrass Boyz al-bum for Sugar Hill in 1998, "Del, Doc & Mac," which featured guest artists Alison Krauss and Jerry Douglas. Its baker's dozen songs included McCoury's self-penned "Beauty of My Dreams," but

Del McCoury

that's not the one that stands out in his mind: "I can still remember me, Doc and Mac singing that old song 'There's More Pretty Girls Than One.' I enjoyed doing that and singing with two of my heroes."

We remembered Del also sang along with Mac and redneck comic Foxworthy on his spoof "Big Ol' Moon," co-written with Scott and Jim Rouse, referring to exposing one's buttocks to express disagreement.

"That wasn't particularly memorable to me," chuckles McCoury. "But you know a lot of times I get requests, even for songs I wrote and I may not even re-member them anymore."

Del, an Opry cast member, laments the fact that so many of his heroes have left the scene, like Monroe and Flatt, but appreciates having Mac around yet: "I guess Earl Scruggs called Mac, 'the kid' didn't he? (Earl's a year older.) They say about seven years back when the Country Hall of Fame was paying homage to Scruggs,

Earl saw Mac and called, 'Hey Mac, pull up a couple chairs and sit down.' Oh Mac likes a good joke himself, and man, he sure can tell one!"

McCoury has become something of a storyteller himself, hosting a regular Sirius XM Satellite radio show several years: *Hand-picked With Del McCoury*. When Del won the National Heritage Medal from the National Endowment For the Arts in June 2010, it included a tax-free award of twenty-five thousand dollars. Good buddy Wiseman called to congratulate him:

"He said, 'Hey, you owe me half of five thousand, because when I got the award I only got twenty thousand dollars!' He's a hoot."

Mac was pleased Del was inducted into the IBMA Bluegrass Hall of Honor in 2011, along with sideman George Shuffler, who was lead guitarist for the Stanley Brothers.

"He's past due," insists Wiseman. "He's very well-qualified and will carry the banner for our kind of music for many years to come."

Doyle Lawson

Yet another voice heard from regarding friendship with Wiseman is that of Doyle Lawson: "I love Mac. He's such a great guy."

Lawson and his band Quicksilver, is another of bluegrass music's more successful contemporary acts. A multi-instrumentalist, Doyle's best known for his mandolin playing, and Gibson Guitar has even produced a Doyle Lawson-model Mandolin. Incidentally, there's also a Del McCoury model Gibson Guitar.

"You know I was born in Eastern Tennessee near Kingsport, but I've settled in Bristol rather than Kingsport," notes Lawson. "I was just a kid who got to hear Mac, Ralph and Carter (Stanley), and a fellow at WCYB, who was probably there for that whole thing by name of Curley King with his Tennessee Hilltoppers. I remember hearing them all live. Of course, I also listened to shows like the *Grand Ole Opry* on Saturday nights, and those programs from Knoxville.

"My dad (Leonard) worked in Kingsport with Eastman Kodak during the Korean War. Then they laid off the folks, and when the Vietnam War came along, they called him back to work. In between all that we moved to Hancock County, where dad was raised as a kid.

"When I was fourteen years old, (neighbor) Jimmy Martin came home for Christmas and one of his sisters heard me pickin' and asked would I like to come over and meet him? Oh boy... when J. D. Crowe left him in 1960 or so, I had a chance to go with Jimmy, but my parents wouldn't hear of it. So when I was eighteen, I did get the call again and that's when I hopped on a bus, went to Nashville and never looked back."

Martin's band he joined was the Sunny Mountain Boys, but they had nothing on Mac's Country Boys, he adds, "There was no mistaking their talent. Mac's voice was so great, with its authority, and that confidence and presentation of his made quite an impression on me. Then, to get to know him as I did, when he wasn't carrying his Country Boys anymore and he was traveling solo. The promoter would get some of us to accompany him, and to me that was an honor."

After his stint with Martin, Doyle went with J. D. Crowe's Kentucky Mountain Boys, which evolved into New South and in 1971 he became one of the Country Gentlemen for eight years. (Crowe, of course, had once been with Mac.)

"They really gave me a lot of freedom and a chance to produce music," recalls Doyle. "I realized early on this is a business, and one of the people I look up to in a business sense more than anyone is Mac Wiseman. I watched him close because he has a head for business and a feel for what's happening and what might take place. I mean he headed up Dot Records out in California, went to Wheeling, did the Renfro Valley festival... Mac was like a chameleon, in that he had a way of changing, but you know in some ways he never changed. I always look up to him.

"I'll never forget one time J. D. Crowe, Sonny Osborne, Dan Hays, me and Mac were at one of our periodic lunches at The Palms on Lower Broad, and I said, 'Mac, you know this business world we live in lends itself to every worldly factor that you can imagine. Too many times I think maybe the younger people don't take it seriously. When did you start thinking about it as a business?' I'll never forget, without hesitation Mac said, 'It was always a business to me.' That's why Mac was one of the people I watched. If exciting things were going to happen, if you checked close enough, there would be Mac Wiseman."

Doyle adds, "I remember when the bluegrass purists were having a fit because I had a drummer with snare and brushes. Then Mac said he was using a drummer way back in 1955. One thing I learned from Mac, if you don't want to know what he thinks, then don't ask him. He says, 'An innovator who cares about his craft shouldn't let anybody dictate to him; he'll do what he thinks is best without fear of what somebody else says.' That's why he's still one of my heroes."

Indeed Mac recorded Kris Kristofferson's "Me & Bobby McGee," because he liked it, though Bill Monroe said it wasn't bluegrass or even country. Mac muses: "But you know when I played bluegrass festivals, I had requests for that number from the fans. They'll let you know what they want."

Doyle says Mac enjoys talking shop: "We had the luncheon get-togethers, and I remember when I came to his birthday party at the Texas Troubadour Theatre, and went up to say hello. He looked surprised and said 'You came!' I told him, 'Absolutely! You'll only be eighty-five one time and I wouldn't miss it!' I went over to his house not too long ago. And to see this guy I look up to who's still enthusiastic about his music - he's producing a box-set of his past recordings - at his age working on his craft, gives me another shot of energy about my own career."

Jesse McReynolds' career kick-off with his elder brother as Jim & Jesse almost dates back to Mac's first session for Columbia in 1946: "I listened to Mac in Knoxville when he worked with Molly O'Day. We started on radio in 1947. In 1952, we recorded on Capitol for the first time. A lot happened in that time period. I just got married and then got drafted, and they sent me off to Korea. I met

Jim & Jesse and Mac in earlier days.

Charlie Louvin over there, when I think he was still Charlie Loudermilk, who worked in the post office in Korea. We got together and played a lot over there, doing things like hospital shows.

"The first show I seen Mac do was when he and Curly Seckler came close to my hometown at St. Paul, Virginia. I always remembered they had a small sound system with a little speaker and only one microphone. I think they were working out of WCYB-Bristol. I got to know Mac best when we started playing bluegrass festivals. We even backed him up... I'd be on stage and then come back out when Mac was on, just to back him. That's when we started to communicate."

Jesse and his late brother Jim McReynolds boast a proud heritage and are third generation pickers. Their granddaddy Charlie McReynolds was one of the musicians who recorded at the historic Bristol Sessions in 1927, which included Ernest Stoneman, Jimmie Rodgers and the Carter Family.

"The first time we met with Mac, he was trying to get a band together and came down to our home place, but we were trying to help our dad with the farm and had thoughts about getting our own act together. So we didn't go with him, but we were all young then and Mac was playing some real good music.

"I remember when Lester and Earl with Cedric Rainwater and Jim Shumate were with him. Boy, they had a heckuva band (Foggy Mountain Boys). It was a time when Ralph and Carter were also at WCYB. You know that's where the Foggy Mountain Boys got going good, and the people really went for them. They would do two or three shows a day at those little old schoolhouses at the time. Now we were on a smaller station, which didn't give us the coverage throughout the area as WCYB did...

"We traveled the circuit a lot, working different stations like WWVA-Wheeling, WNOX-Knoxville, WNER-Live Oak, Florida, and it was interesting doing a western show out in Kansas in 1950 (KFBI-Wichita), singing songs like 'Home On the Range' to satisfy listeners. We also did a lot of concerts in Canada, and in fact, for about five or six years, we had a festival up there in Ontario, the *Kingston Family Reunion Bluegrass* show, and Mac might've played that for us."

Jesse became best known for his cross-pickin' style of mandolin, and added an innovative split-string technique, coupled with Jim's high-lonesome vocals and smooth guitar stylings, it all blended into their distinctive bluegrass sound.

In 1964, Jim & Jesse were invited to join the WSM *Grand Ole Opry*, the same year as the Osborne Brothers. Jesse recalls, "I suggested to one guy at the Opry about putting Mac on, and don't know why they didn't invite him, as he had chart hits. We got on through Martha White (Flour, the biscuit maker), as did Flatt &

Scruggs. Martha White helped a lot of people get booked on there and a long time ago they'd sponsored the Carter Family.

"We worked quite a few things with Mac. In recent years, Mac and me have been pretty close. We recorded some tracks - thirty-four in all – old-time songs that I'd heard in my youth. That was an experience I enjoyed, and he got two albums out of it. We went into the studio here [the Germantown facility belonging to John Prine and David Ferguson] and I told Mac, 'Well, about everything I've learned through the years is on your two albums.' I had to do most all the playing, kick-offs, turn-arounds, backup and everything. There was just Mac on guitar and me. I liked working with Mac, because he does the type of songs I enjoy playing."

Strictly speaking, Mac's venture at that time was doing songs that he'd heard on the radio in the 1940s and '50s, notes McReynolds: "And his mission now is to preserve as many of those songs as he can for new generations."

Mac produced the CDs, both released October 13, 2009 on his Wise label: "Waiting For the Boys To Come Home," containing songs connected to war-time; while the second "Old Likker In a New Jug," yesteryear heart songs. Both acts - Jim & Jesse and Mac - went into the IBMA Bluegrass Hall of Honor in 1993 together. After that, they shared the spotlight during Martha White's month-long celebration at the Ryman Auditorium in July 1994.

In December 2002, the McReynolds family suffered sad losses. Twelve days after wife, Aretta June died of cancer that month, husband Jim McReynolds succumbed to the same disease. His December 31st death ended a popular brother act that began fifty-five years earlier, a record of sorts for siblings sticking together among bluegrass or country acts.

In 2008, when Wiseman was himself under the weather, he personally invited Jesse McReynolds to accept his prestigious National Heritage Fellowship Medal from the National Endowment For The Arts.

According to Jesse, "That was an unusual situation. I remember in 1997, Jim and I went to Washington to accept that same award, and for me to go back and get one for Mac was unique. I told them that not many people get up there a second time to pick up this award. We did a couple numbers in tribute to Mac. It seems like they played a track of Mac's vocals on ''Tis Sweet To Be Remembered' and 'I Wonder How the Old Folks Are At Home,' and me and my boys got on stage and played in the same key he was singing in, and as they opened the curtain we were playing and finished it up. That was nice the way they put that together, and such an honor to be a part of something that important. We were surprised that we had even been nominated for it when we were given the honor."

Jesse was less surprised to learn his long-

Mac, Scott Rouse and Jesse McReynolds.

244

time colleague ran for the Secretary-Treasurer's post at the Nashville Association of Musicians, AFM Local 25, in 1996.

"I guess we all have it in the back of our minds we want to try something else, but I don't think Mac liked it so well after he won. But he had worked other jobs behind the scenes before," recalls McReynolds. "Mac's truly one-of-a-kind and there'll probably never be another like him, although I recall on Ralph Emery's show them a-calling Mac the 'Burl Ives of Bluegrass.' But he was versatile, like doing that Gordon Lightfoot tribute, singing duets with Woody Herman, cutting a lot of country songs and straight-ahead bluegrass. We got a lot in common, I think, as we both like all kinds of music."

Friendships loom large in Mac's life, mostly a lone ranger in his lengthy career. One thing seems certain, once you become Mac's friend, unless you cross him unnecessarily, you'll be a friend for life. He even got over his little buddy Jimmy Dickens slapping his face and running away.

Mac smiles recalling in later years - but before the contemporary political party of that name - Hank Snow in the mood for company, initiated an ongoing "Tea Party" in his home. He invited friends Johnnie Wright, Johnny Russell and Mac to his so-called "Rainbow Ranch," calling to say simply, "It's about time we had a tea party!"

"He would hold it at his office in the rear of his house in Madison. We'd go out there and Hank was most cordial, as we'd talk and tell 'road stories.' Once he told us that when he heard his hero T. Texas Tyler sing, 'It just made the hairs stand up on my head… ' But Russell was taken aback by Hank's descriptive comment, being well aware that the bald 'Singing Ranger' wore toupees, and Johnny had to restrain himself from laughing out loud."

Tea Party celebrants (from left) Johnny Russell, Mac, Johnnie Wright and Hank Snow at Rainbow Ranch in Madison.

A fan of Hank's vocal style, Mac especially admired his impeccable enunciation, as well as his songwriting - "I'm Moving On," "Bluebird Island" and "Music Makin' Mama From Memphis" - and flawless guitar playing. In turn, Snow suggested WSM consider his friend Wiseman as an Opry cast regular: "I don't know who killed that suggestion."

A rowdier pal, Charlie Dick, offered a somewhat humorous take on the balladeer. A show business pro himself, Charlie's also the widower of Patsy Cline and hence known as "the keeper of the flame."

Regarding "Big Mac," Charlie adds, "Mac's just fine, and a good friend of mine as long as he behaves. We had more fun outside the industry than we did in the business. He has a fine sense of humor, a regular good old boy."

Like Wiseman, Dick's a Virginia native, "but I never was a big bluegrass fan myself. When I first heard that type of music, we called it string music. I lived in northern Virginia, up close to the West Virginia state line, out in the country. My mother kept the radio on as long as its battery would hold out. That was in the 1940s and actually I didn't know one style from the next. She could pick up stations clearly like WSVA-Harrisonburg. Mac was on that station back then. I listened to some of it, the things I liked. Mom listened all the time, until the battery wore down.

"Mac was just country to us. The music we heard in Virginia then wasn't called bluegrass, it was more raw hillbilly country without any amplifying or anything. As I got older, we started going to parks on weekends, where they had about any kind of acoustic music you could think of, some pretty smooth and some wild and crazy. I got so I liked all of it and maybe that's why I ended up in the music business."

After Dick moved to Winchester, he got to hanging around with local musicians and got more into it: "One weekend after I met Patsy, she was working a park down in Fredericksburg, and one of the other artists on the bill was Mac Wiseman (who actually promoted the show and hired Patsy). I had not yet met Mac. Well, Patsy brought along a box of fried chicken and me, I had a picnic-jug full of grapefruit juice and something else - it might've been gin (he chuckles). Now Mac was tickled to death to share Patsy's chicken, but I think he even liked my beverage better, you know having something to wash it down with.

"Also on that day, they were advertising to 'give away' a Mac Wiseman Cadillac car by means of a raffle. I thought, 'Wow! This is great!' Back then I didn't know too many people driving Caddies, especially one who was going to give it away. Then I heard it had a hundred thousand miles or more on it already, and figured Mac had driven it about all it was gonna go. But they did give it away. Meanwhile, backstage, the three of us ate, drank and visited, and we got on very well."

Good buddies Mac and Charlie Dick.

According to Mac, promoter Carlton Haney actually drove the car, a 1941 or '42 Cadillac, down from Richmond for the raffle, and a fellow from Warrenton won it, then turned around and sold it for fifteen hundred dollars, right there at the park.

Dick picks up the conversation, "I don't know that Mac's style of music was Patsy's favorite, but she listened, very intently, to all styles and what interested her about pros like Mac was their phrasing and showmanship. So she watched how they addressed an audience and picked up pointers from them. I mean she'd appeared on shows like Jimmy Dean's TV program, but she was still relatively new to performing before big crowds, so she sat back, listened and learned."

"I was around Mac a bit in Wheeling when he worked at WWVA," continues Charlie. "I'd go over with George Riddle to the *Wheeling Jamboree* a few times when Mac was running that operation. He liked doing that, but I told him he liked being where he didn't have to do nothing but sit around."

By the 1970s, Charlie worked with Starday Records, and played a part in promoting Red Sovine's milestone chart-topping recitation "Teddy Bear," which stayed number one a solid three weeks.

As Dick recalls, "You know, Moe Lytle bought the Dickerson Road studio and Starday's masters from Don Pierce. Tommy Hill, who was as good as they come, was part of that deal. One time when Tommy was on the road, Red called me and said, 'I got something I want you to hear.' He added, 'You know, somebody gave it to me awhile back and I didn't pay any attention to it, but I've just listened and like it. See what you think?' So he played the tape over the phone, asking 'What would you do if you had it?' I told Red, 'If it were me, I'd record it today.'

"Red already had that smash recitation 'Giddyup Go,' which he co-wrote with Tommy, so when Tommy got back, we all listened. But Moe was out of town and Tommy didn't do too many things without his OK; but, as I recall, we went ahead and recorded it. Well, we put it out right away and 'Teddy Bear' sold over a million records and hit number one for us (1976). Moe wasn't upset about that."

Charlie and Mac never really worked together, but Charlie joshes they became good pals socially: "He'd try to beat me out of my money all the time, but I was slicker than he was. We're both on the ROPE Executive Board and he became our president, so we got closer through that affiliation. I remember when it was time to pick a new president, after Gordon Terry, our first, stepped down. Two or three persons nominated Mac, though I don't believe he was too thrilled.

"Anyhow, Mac agreed to let his name be put in the mix, and he won. Oh, I mean we tried to get rid of him before he finished his fifth term, but he was so damn big, we couldn't carry him out the door!"

A kidder, Charlie was actually a champion of Mac's presidency: "Aw, he did a good job. A lot of times at the meetings he sat back and listened and let me conduct them. Every now and then he would toss something in and usually it was something we wanted to hear. Mac tried to resign when he got the gig with Willie and Merle in Branson, but we wanted him to stay on, knowing he wasn't indispensable and there really wasn't that much going on that we couldn't handle. He did, and now they've made me and Mac permanent board members, and we accepted with the proviso that we didn't have to attend all the meetings."

Dick doesn't recall Mac coming to his home much though: "When we had the ROPE gatherings out at StarLite (Dance Club), Mac and Marge came by my house one time and we had a few drinks, and he was soon picking, singing and grinning. As long as he's been in this business, one certainty I've found with Mac is he still enjoys singing. Anytime you hand a guitar his way, he's ready to sing. That's probably his secret for longevity, he loves what he does and it's not really like a job to him."

 'I'll Sail My Ship Alone'... Smooth Sailing

"I'll sail my ship alone, with all the dreams I own
Driftin' out across the ocean blue
I'll sail my ship alone, though all the sails are torn
And when it starts to sink, then I'll blame you..."

"Of my brothers, I've always been the more active one - a joiner. I remember I got involved in the Association of Country Entertainers (ACE)... I was on their board (and Executive Director)," recalled Vic Willis, also a cast member on WSM's *Grand Ole Opry* at the time of his remarks.

Vic Willis was a longtime friend to Mac Wiseman, more recently due to mutual involvement in ROPE. Vic also spent a dozen years as Secretary-Treasurer of the Nashville Association of Musicians (AFM Local 257).

Willis wielded a lot of power in the Local, having been an Opry performer, jingles producer, music publisher and due to Music Row friendships developed over the years. When President Jay Collins decided to step down, he hoped to continue his union association as editor of its newspaper, *The Nashville Musician*; however, much to Jay's displeasure, Vic threw his weight behind an outsider, who subsequently became the board's final choice. He was also instrumental in promoting guitarist Harold Bradley as Collins' presidential successor.

Accordionist Willis was younger brother to guitarist Guy and fiddler Skeeter Willis, who first gained renown as The Oklahoma Wranglers, notably while traveling with Eddy Arnold. Later they joined WSM's Opry as The Willis Brothers, known for their western-flavored songs. Following his brothers' deaths, Vic continued with a few different units, usually billed as The Vic Willis Trio, mainly C. W. Mitchell and Curtis Young. For a short stint, however, Vic's trio featured Lorna Greenwood on fiddle, and Kathy Shepard as guitarist, two stylish harmony vocalists who proved a real attention-getter for Vic.

Like Mac, Vic was also a great practical joker. It's worth noting that the Oklahoma Wranglers (featuring Chuck "Indian" Wright on bass) backed an unknown Hank Williams during his first recording session in Nashville, December 11, 1946, for the independent Sterling Records. A shared-session, set up by producer-songwriter Fred Rose of Acuff-Rose Music Publishing, it was for the brothers, and Alabama native Hank, whom Vic expected to hear little from in the future.

When Rose asked them to back Williams, Vic said Fred warned that Hank sang out of meter: "We hadn't been used to hearing a country singer who was as country as he was. At the end of each verse of 'Wealth Won't Save Your Soul,' Fred wanted us also to sing with Hank on the phrase, *'My friend, it won't save your poor wicked soul.'* For some reason, Hank couldn't say 'poor.' Every time he sang it, it sounded like 'purr.'

"We were cutting directly onto acetate and, of course, there was no way to splice out any mistakes. If you made any, you just had to start the song all over again. Finally Fred, who could be a little short-tempered at times, told us, 'Dammit Wranglers, sing it just like Hank does.' And you can hear it on the record like that today."

It was another eight months before Williams first charted *Billboard* with his Top Five MGM single "Move It On Over," which led the following year to his joining KWKH-Shreveport's *Louisiana Hayride*. The Willis Brothers didn't attain a Top Ten until 1964 via "Give Me 40 Acres (To Turn This Rig Around)," a trucker's anthem released on Starday Records. So apparently enunciation wasn't that important after all.

Like Wiseman, Willis was savvy behind-the-scenes and during the 1960s and 1970s "moonlighted," producing commercials for banks, beer and automobiles. His Custom Jingles proved very successful. For twelve years, Vic found himself negotiating with his Opry bosses on behalf of the pickers as Secretary-Treasurer, a post he held until his death January 15, 1995. That occurred in a one-vehicle crash on the Natchez Trace Parkway near Hohenwald, Tennessee. Vic was hoping to go the next day to Pulaski, Tennessee, with the editor to print their newspaper.

"Steady and solid as a rock describes Vic Willis," says pal Wiseman. "I recall first meeting him on package shows in the 1950s. He had a jolly, upbeat attitude about him, which he never lost through the years. Through ROPE, we had a lot of camaraderie. Years ago, I was driving down the Highway in Oklahoma (in 1993), when I saw this big sign with his name on it as his hometown (Schulter). I came back and made one helluva big deal out of it, saying I had torn it down. I razzed him about that and he just laughed. Vic always had a tremendous sense of humor and a lot of pride. I found him to be a real credit to our industry."

In an interview marking the AFM's centenary several months prior to the '96 election campaign, Mac, a former Local 257 board member, had already received his Lifetime Membership pin denoting fifty years as a union musician: "I have some very positive things to say about the musicians union. For starters, I've always been impressed with how Local 257 operates. I feel its cooperation with local musicians is largely responsible for the fact that Nashville is now a major recording center.

"George W. Cooper, Jr., may have been strict as Local 257 President (1937-1973), but he was always fair - and he had vision. He saw opportunity for Nashville to grow and kept the scale more than competitive instead of driving the rates up prohibitively, which otherwise would have driven the recording people out of town. He had a good rapport with members and the people he was dealing with (like WSM). When I was working in A&R for Dot Records, I did more business than the average member, including filing session reports for product recorded here, and I never had any problem."

Indeed Cooper opened Nashville's union doors to so-called "hillbilly" and "race" musicians who for the most part couldn't read music, once a membership requirement. Cooper's foresight brought the Opry musicians into the fold, and helped foster a thriving R&B music scene that gave rise to such notables as pianist-songwriter-producer Ted Jarrett ("Love, Love, Love"), bassist W. O. Smith (who performed with the unrelated Bessie Smith, Dizzy Gillespie), and later young Jimi Hendrix.

Mac continued, during the centenary celebration, "President Cooper was always courteous and I feel that our current President Harold Bradley is as courteous as can be. He is also willing to speak out on behalf of the musician members whenever their livelihood is threatened. I think their attitude has been beneficial to Nashville and the AFM, which I salute in this our one hundredth anniversary year."

That was before Mac surprised everyone in the fall by declaring himself a candidate. On hand for that meeting was Bill Anderson, who when nominations were being taken, arose to call on good friend Mac to run for office. Literally, you could have heard a pin drop. Nobody was more stunned than Bradley and his personal pick Randy Ford, who thought his only competition in the campaign ahead would be country drummer Willie Ackerman.

Wiseman was still recording and touring as much as he desired and had shown no sign he wanted to be a union officer, so his entry into the forthcoming campaign surprised many members and the media. According to Mac, "It has been pointed out to me by fellow members that not all segments of our Local are being represented as they would like; therefore, I feel it's time we get behind all our members and deal with any shortcomings in an organized way. I have been very fortunate in this business and I think it's important that we not only take, but give something back."

Meanwhile, interim Secretary-Treasurer Otto Bash chose to remain neutral, yet another surprise came in the person of Chet Atkins, who with Harold's brother Owen is credited as an architect of the fabled Nashville Sound that pulled country music out of its doldrums, with more sophisticated production techniques, as rock and roll emerged to rule the late 1950s. Chet heartily endorsed Mac as his personal pick for the vacancy. That was big among the 257 members.

The December ballots produced another surprise as Randy Ford finished third, behind second-place opponent Willie Ackerman, who did better than expected, though trailing Wiseman. According to the by-laws, however, Mac hadn't attained a fifty per cent lead over the competition, falling short vote-wise, prompting a run-off election between the two top vote getters. Bradley had only a token competitor and won reelection to his post on the first ballot, but apparently was not a happy camper when his choice candidate fell behind.

Ackerman, a longtime friend and admirer of Wiseman, wanted to back out, but was encouraged to proceed, with Mac's blessing. Nonetheless on January 21, 1997, Wiseman was voted Secretary-Treasurer. Interesting, too, was Kathy Shepard's election to the executive board, making her only the second female to serve, the first being Opry pianist Del Wood, who died in 1989, while a board member. In her first column as the Local's Live Engagement Services agent, Kathy wrote:

Secretary-Treasurer Wiseman, AFM 257.

250

"This is my first article for our publication. I was asked to supply a picture, so for this issue I decided to use one of me with my hero Mac Wiseman. I have loved his sweet voice for many years."

It appeared as balm for his loss, Ford was kept on by Harold, who wrote in his column: "I want to thank Wayne King [not the fabled waltz King of 'Goodnight, Sweetheart' fame] for running for the president's office of our Local and I wish more members would get involved in our union and its business. I also congratulate Mac Wiseman for winning the office of Secretary-Treasurer, and wish him good luck in conducting the business of our Local. I will be available to him to define his duties... I'm very pleased to announce that I have hired Randy Ford as my assistant. Randy is a very talented young man (he's been a member of this Local for twenty-two years), and in the three weeks he has been working here, he has already helped me in keeping the union's business up-to-date. Please introduce yourself to Randy the next time you're in the office."

Mac was still waiting on Harold to "define his duties," when two months later, he wrote: "Believe me, I'm still pretty much in the learning phase, but it's a good feeling to be able to help members with their problems and it's satisfying to sign up new recruits . . I have a lot of respect for the professionalism of most of my co-workers. In this regard, I'm sorry to see Beth Ackerman, our Music Performance Trust Fund (MPTF) coordinator (and wife of Willie), leave. She has been one to put her best foot forward in dealing with our members. Even though she's departing, Beth took time to complete the quarterly column for this issue, updating us on the Trust Fund program. We wish her good luck on her endeavors.

Musicians' union executives (from left) Weldon Myrick, Buddy Harman, Jimmy Capps, Mac, Leon Rhodes, Harold Bradley (president) and Stu Basore (1997).

"Congratulations to Kathy Shepard on her recent promotion to Business Agent in charge of Live Engagement Services Division, succeeding veteran Otto Bash. In that regard, she and I share something in common, as I, too, succeeded Mr. Bash as Secretary-Treasurer... I want to publicly thank Otto Bash for all the information and support he has shown this office newcomer."

Bash, of course, had been holding down the post until the next election period, but was also the Local's ongoing Sergeant-At-Arms, supposedly to maintain order at usually calm meetings.

Immediately after the election, Mac stated, "A sincere Thank You to all those who had enough confidence in me to cast their vote my way. It also provides me an opportunity to extend my hand in friendship to all the others, and to try and assure them that as Secretary-Treasurer, I want to represent each and every member of this Local. A very special 'Thank You' to two very special people who took the time to nominate and endorse my candidacy throughout: Mr. Bill Anderson and Mr. Chet Atkins! Most importantly as I start to serve you, I want to stress to our President Harold Bradley, a winner himself, and to the entire Local 257 staff, that I look forward to the challenge of working with them, and will do everything possible on my part to make ours the best team in the AFM."

Unbeknownst to Mac, for starters his inherited assistant Beverly Jordan appeared hostile toward her new boss, at least to fellow staffers. She stated to *The Nashville Musician* editor that Mac had no business running for the job, due to his age, adding that he could barely walk straight.

Beverly, also the office manager, was wed to banjoist Vic Jordan's son. It was explained to her that despite the handicap of having suffered polio as an infant, Mac with his afflicted leg could put many to shame with the schedule he maintained prior to being elected, and was only half-a-year older than President Bradley, whom she strongly supported.

One of Wiseman's first acts in assuming his new position was invite his predecessor to share office space, as Bash had been relegated to sitting in the Local's conference room, when not looking after the building and its grounds. Mac had publicly acknowledged upon his victory: "I will do my utmost to try and fill the very capable shoes of my predecessor, Mr. Otto Bash. He may not be aware of this, but the man who helped inspire me to the office of Secretary-Treasurer - and one who served for more than a dozen years in that job - Vic Willis, has stated that Otto Bash was (and is) one of the most loyal members this or any other union ever had."

The new office holder would need blinders not to notice the less-than-warm reception accorded him by most of the office staff, with the exception of Bash, ever the professional, stepping up to offer counsel, which Wiseman gratefully accepted: "I invited him to share my office, as he didn't really have an office at that time. So that pleased him very much. You know he was very gracious from the standpoint that if I got a phone call, and he sensed it was a business call or personal, he would immediately get up and leave the room. I knew Otto before, when he played gigs in different groups around town. Another gesture he did on my behalf was invite me to go with him to business luncheons where he introduced me very proudly to the people out there. I enjoyed that and they made me feel welcome. I have nothing but fond memories of Otto." [The drummer died May 25, 2010, at age eighty-four.]

As it happened, Mac had some performing commitments scheduled prior to seeking the union post, and brought this to Harold's attention and was granted permission to fulfill those dates. Further, he was allowed freedom to perform or record in his own off-duty time. Among the gigs he did was the annual festival in tribute to friend Stringbean Akeman, killed by cousins John A. and Marvin D. Brown in a 1973 robbery.

A 1998 recording stint for producer Scott Rouse (cited earlier) was also conducted, "Del, Doc & Mac." He and buddies McCoury and Watson collaborated to cut thirteen tunes, released by Sugar Hill Records. It was a project all enjoyed participating in, a session to remember, as Mac recalls.

One problem area that Wiseman zeroed in on as Secretary-Treasurer was the fact so many road musicians weren't being covered, at least in reference to the AFM Pension Fund. In conversations with noted session player Buddy Harman, union business agent, Mac learned studio musicians were pretty well covered since agreements had been forthcoming from those who contracted their services. Mac talked with L. D. (Rick Money) Wayne and Calvin Crawford, who lamented they weren't being properly taken care of by leaders they worked for.

"Too many times, the contractor/boss doesn't want to bother with the paperwork, so at best only token contributions are made on behalf of these hardworking musicians," stated Mac. "That boils down to the sour note that they are never fully vested (in the Union Pension). L.D. says a lot of the younger musicians tend not to worry about the future too much, so they don't request that money be contributed on their behalf.

"L.D., who picked for Randy Travis and Porter Wagoner, says he knows sidemen who would gladly pay the Pension portion just to ensure something for their own future. Under existing rules, however, the individual musician cannot contribute. It must come from an incorporated source. This is a problem area I would like to see resolved, so that individual players have some sort of security down the road."

In a summer 1997 chat with L. D. Wayne, he pointed out that not enough employers of band musicians concern themselves with contributing their share of an employee's input to the AFM Pension Fund, which would assure musicians a security blanket in their last years. Some who cared for their bandsmen were Bill Monroe, Roy Clark and Jimmy Dickens.

"I feel the union needs to make artists aware of the real need for it (paying into the Pension) for band members," stressed Wayne, who reiterated that the Pension Fund regulation states: "No contributions to the fund by individual employees are permitted."

Wiseman explained: "If you have worked in the areas of recording, jingles, the *Grand Ole Opry*, television or the symphony, you are covered by the AFM-EP Fund. The ones who seem to be getting the short end of the stick here are the road warriors, mainly because they're not allowed to contribute directly to the fund as an 'individual employee' - either their artist-employer won't fill out the paperwork on their behalf or they are just not aware of the procedure."

Crawford, then leader for Little Jimmy Dickens' band, noted: "It's also the musicians' fault for dragging their feet. Some are just plain ignorant about the fact that they can become vested in the AFM Pension Fund. A lot of young pickers don't understand the situation or may not see the real benefit since retirement seems so far away. They need to be made aware of the program." [Mac had informative pieces published in the union paper.]

It was Jimmy's wife Mona Dickens who made the appropriate changes for her husband's backup boys, who like Mac's earlier band, were called The Country Boys.

Mona noted, "Finally Calvin came to me... After we sat down and talked, I realized the importance of it. I knew that anything Jimmy could do to help his musicians further down the road, he would feel we should do that. We certainly weren't aware of it until Calvin brought it to our attention. But we didn't have any negative feelings whatsoever about doing it."

Country Music Hall of Famer Dickens saw to it that a percentage of the musicians pay be contributed directly to the Pension Fund. His musicians remained loyal, including Crawford, who worked with Dickens some 20 years. Mac maintains Jimmy hired some of the best pickers to ever hit the road.

The Opry's senior cast member Dickens acknowledged, "I've been blessed I guess by being able to recognize good talented players. I've had exceptionally good steel and fiddle men through the years. I'm also a good judge of character. I believe in treating them right... They treat me right, too. Yessir, the business has been good to me." (Dickens died January 2, 2015 at age 94.)

Mac served on the board of the CMA's steering committee to evaluate the goal of providing care for country's seniors, then helped volunteer the CMA's usage of ROPE's non-profit status in this regard. Other prospects to benefit members that Mac was keen on, included spearheading an affordable health plan for musicians, and aligning the Local with the Musicians Assistance Program (MAP), to help afflicted players recover from drug addiction.

"It's all about one musician talking to another, and it works," Mac wrote in his column, citing reed player Buddy Arnold, who'd been hooked on heroin. "Arnold is MAP's first success story. The talented trouper, who worked for the likes of Tommy Dorsey, Buddy Rich and Stan Kenton, hit rock bottom both physically and financially at age fifty-four. With inspiration of his wife Carole Fields and God, Buddy turned it all around - and then decided to help other addicts come clean. Founded by Arnold, MAP has succeeded to the extent it's received a multi-million dollar grant from the Recording Industry Association of America (RIAA) and has an enviable list of movers and shakers on its boards, including Quincy Jones, Hal David, Irving Azoff, Eric Clapton and Paul Williams."

Despite their long-time association dating back to his Dot days, when he steered a lot of business to the Bradley brothers, by recording in their quaint Music Row studio, the Quonset Hut, Mac was still waiting on Harold to "define his duties."

One incident that remains in Mac's memory occurred initially between him and his assistant: "Beverly came in my office one day and said that I owed the Local thirty-eight hundred dollars, and did I want to settle it now or what? It was supposedly for days missed at the office to go play shows, which I knew I had cleared with Harold when I was sworn in, noting I had some engagements already booked and wanted to play (having given his word to the promoters). Harold had said, 'It's OK, because I also take time off to go to England and do other dates.' My first reaction was to tell Beverly, 'I'll pay it.' But on second thought, I felt differently. I was back out front before she even got seated at her desk, telling her I was not going to pay it, and we'd just take it before the board.

"I got to checking the dates she listed that I was away, and found she had billed me for a Saturday, too, and of course the union wasn't open Saturdays. So, during a conversation with board members prior to the next board meeting, they encouraged me to bring it up, which I did.

"At the meeting, Stu Basore and Jimmy Capps both spoke up on my behalf and said it was 'unforgivable' that I had been billed after having brought it to the attention of the President from the start. Weldon Myrick, usually very soft-spoken, stood up and said, 'This is making me mad!'... I spoke towards Harold, reminding him that he had originally said it was OK. He hung his head as though he would rather have been any place but there, and Beverly and Kathy Shepard left the conference room in tears."

Headlines in the July 1998 issue of *The Nashville Musician*, however, shocked many Local 257 members: *Mac Wiseman resigns Union post*, with the over-line

Randy Ford steps in. According to the report, "Half way through his term, the veteran musician departed in order to resume morning therapy sessions for an old back injury that had flared-up again, and to pursue other commitments: 'I don't want to be a part-time Secretary-Treasurer. That wouldn't be fair to other staff or all those members who voted for me.'…"

In May, Wiseman presented his resignation letter, effective June 1, 1998, which spurred Bradley to assign Randy Ford as Acting Secretary-Treasurer for an interim period until a September special election. Ford acknowledged: "I accepted this responsibility with an understanding of the diplomacy and diligence that the position demands. I know that one of Mac Wiseman's concerns was to make the union more accessible and customer-oriented. I share that concern and will endeavor to work towards those goals."

Later, Mac spoke out addressing those who read more into the status of his health than stated: "Since resigning… rumors have been rampant as to the state of my health. While I truly appreciate the interest and concern, which many of you have expressed to me personally, let me assure the membership at large that the reports of my 'ill health' have been greatly exaggerated. True, my mobility has progressively declined over the years, due to post-polio syndrome, but this had little to do with my resignation, other than a desire to resume my therapeutic exercise program.

"I primarily came to the conclusion that the restrictions of a 9-to-4 p.m. five-days-a-week position, prevented me from pursuing other interests and projects. I'm still 'on the road' and looking forward to getting back into the studio among other things. I have enjoyed serving as your Secretary-Treasurer and hope I fulfilled your expectations during my tenure. Thank you again for your support, interest and concern. Hopefully, I'll be seeing you somewhere along the trail."

Bradley wrote in his column: "Apparently the job was too time-constraining for Mac to pursue his real love, performing as one of the most talented bluegrass artists in history. He leaves us to pursue his career, and he leaves with my best wishes and thanks for his great efforts on our behalf. The staff also wishes Mac the best. I've never met a more talented performer and a better gentleman."

Meanwhile, in July 1998, Mac was named by officials of the annual Uncle Dave Macon Days Festival as recipient of its Heritage Award, presented at Canonsburgh Village, Murfreesboro, Tennessee. Established in 1980, the first ever recipient was Macon's friend Roy Acuff. The award honors "individual artists who have made significant contributions to the continuation of the musical heritage embodied by such sterling performers as pioneer Uncle Dave Macon." This made Mac the Grand Marshal for the opening parade, as well, which involved riding in an open horse-drawn carriage, which he enjoyed. He was also glad he knew the great Uncle Dave personally.

Macon, as Mac recalled, was a colorful character whose garb was equally memorable. He usually sported a shirt with high white collar and dark tie, over which he wore a vest, its pocket boasting a gold watch matching his gold teeth, while his pants were of the pinstriped variety. Uncle Dave's ankle-high laced boots were highly buffed, and he often "fanned" his banjo with his black porkpie hat, to show how hot and smokin' his playing had been.

Yet another country original who became Mac's friend was Opry founder Judge George D. Hay, whose 2010 preservation society selected Mac Wiseman, along with fellow artists like George Strait and the late Jimmie Driftwood, to be inducted into its Hall of Fame in West Plains, Missouri, for their contributions. Unable to attend due to a busted leg, the plaque was mailed to Mac's home, where it sits prominently on the mantle, beside his Golden Voice statuette presented by Bettie Walker, Billy's wife.

Shortly after resigning as Secretary-Treasurer, Mac received some information from fellow members questioning the operation of the Music Performance Trust Fund, which engages players for special shows, such as those at nursing homes, hospitals or park concerts where no admission fees are assessed. MPTF was initiated via agreements between AFM and recording companies as part of strike settlements to get recordings back on track. Co-sponsors coordinate for such entertainment programs through the Locals, providing work for pay to selected members. Through the grapevine, Wiseman was aware that some at the union were attempting to shift the blame towards their ex-Secretary-Treasurer.

Thus, in an open letter to members, Mac pointed out, "During my service as your elected official, I conducted myself in accordance with the existing By-Laws, which served as my sole guidance, since I was never officially presented the books, documents, correspondence and other property pertaining to the responsibility as Custodian of the Seal (Secretary-Treasurer).

"It was only after action prompted by order of the distinguished members of the Board, once they became aware of the lack of transition, did the stamp or seal that contained my name as co-signer on matters of disbursement, come into my possession. Nor did I know, until I read the complete By-Laws, that by virtue of my office, I was empowered to appoint members of the Vic Willis Emergency Relief Fund Committee and upon being bonded, learned that I was also a duly-designated Fiduciary Trustee of the Funeral Benefit Fund. Tell me this country boy didn't feel important!

"But really, I took these responsibilities very serious and always conducted myself in a manner I felt was worthy of your faith in me. When I took leave of that elected office in June 1998, I believed that I was departing at a time when the budget was balanced and things appeared to be running smoothly. However, several members have brought to my attention the fact that a serious situation developed in the operation of the MPTF, and as a result my fellow musicians were not properly reimbursed for their work. That bothers me immensely.

"When I took office, the MPTF Administrator was Beth Ackerman, who was the first to extend her hand in congratulations to me after the 1996 election, despite the fact that I had defeated her candidate-husband Willie Ackerman. From my observation, she had done an excellent job with MPTF. Unfortunately, not too long after the election, she departed due to personal reasons. Her replacement was a less-experienced clerk, who seemed to be doing an OK job; otherwise, I felt her supervisor, Office Manager Beverly Jordan, wouldn't have informed me she was delegating some of her duties as Assistant To The Secretary-Treasurer to the new MPTF clerk.

"My own function was to approve payment vouchers submitted by the MPTF clerk, much as I did for the Electronic Media Services Division, conducted so efficiently by Carol Hardin. I am disheartened to learn that our members were not receiving payments when due, and sincerely regret that any delay occurred, causing hardship for them and their families. It was never brought to my attention or I would have taken action.

"AFM New York headquarters dispatched an MPTF specialist to Nashville to work diligently to correct the problem, which had been occurring since May 1998, thus bringing the reports up to date. On my behalf and yours, I thank him for his efforts. It would be a real tragedy if, due to this alleged mismanagement, the MPTF program was withdrawn from members of the fourth largest Local in North America. After all, AFM worked very hard to negotiate this valuable agreement with the record labels during the historic 1940s' strikes [overseen by James Petrillo, AFM president from 1940-'58]."

Indeed, Mac was faultless. In the aftermath, on the watch of Secretary-Treasurer Ford, a matter concerning payments due AFM by Local 257, became an embarrassment to the officers of the Nashville Association of Musicians. Effective May 6, 2003, Randy Ford submitted his resignation after having served as Secretary-Treasurer nearly five years, noting in part: "I'm sure that it comes as no surprise to you that this position is extremely demanding. As I have stated before, no one should aspire to hold it forever - it's time for another member to pick up the shovel that President Bradley told me about my first day on the job. I will be happy to assist in any way to ensure a smooth transition."

In addition to traipsing off to England to help give the CMA its quorum earlier, Mac also was receptive to visiting his nation's capital, and encouraging Congress to support some needed legislation to benefit the music scene. While in D.C., he called on West Virginia Senator Robert Byrd, a longtime country music fan and fiddle enthusiast.

"I remember sitting in his outer reception area for a decent interval, then he welcomed me into his office. But you know he had two outer offices, each with a secretary, and you had to pass through them before you got to him," grins Wiseman, adding, "After I took a seat, he came over, reached behind my chair to pull out this ancient guitar and invited me to play a few songs. He listened intently, then said, 'Alright, now what can I do for you?'… It was interesting that when I was leaving Byrd's office, I ran into our (Tennessee) Senator Jim Sasser, who knew why I was there and assured me that he would vote for us, as well."

Mac says yet another time the CMA's Jo Walker Meador was arranging a Nashville reception for Senator Byrd, "who had an album of fiddle tunes out ('Sen. Robert Byrd: Mountain Fiddler,' County Records, 1978). They were asking all the fiddlers here in town to attend, but apparently he had also requested that I be invited, so there I was with the Senator and all those fiddlers. But I felt very honored that he personally wanted me there."

During his Nashville visit, Wiseman relates with a smile, "Senator Byrd got to know Joe Meadows, and liked Joe's bluegrass fiddlin' so much that he got him a job up there in Washington [actually working in the Senator's mail and correspondence department], so they could fiddle together up in his office whenever he wasn't tied up in the Senate and wanted to relax."

27 'Step It Up And Go'...
Keep Movin' On

"Got a little girl, little and low
She used to love me but she don't no more
She gotta step it up and go - yeah, go
Can't stand pat, swear you gotta step it up and go... "

"My blindness has certainly changed the sequence of events in my life," says Ronnie Milsap. "Had I been sighted, I'd have grown up in my hometown (Robbinsville, North Carolina) in the Smokies, and worked in the sawmill or something, which would've been fine."

It seems Milsap, like Wiseman, succeeded in show business because of the impetus put on him by a handicap as an infant. Ronnie emphasizes that his blindness has not been a career handicap: "As a matter of fact, there was a time in my career that it gained me instant attention. People would say, 'Have you heard that blind guy playing over at the King Of The Road motel?' They'd reply, 'Oh yeah, that's Ronnie somebody...' But more than that, in a larger sense, my blindness has been a blessing, because it took me totally out of that old existence. It changed my destiny from that of my father who died of lung cancer, and grandfather, who lived humbly. My whole life is different today because I am blind. I know I wouldn't be doing what I'm doing today otherwise. My life, as it is, is real exciting and I wouldn't trade it for anything."

Ronnie Milsap

Milsap's success as an artist has made him an international name, whose versatile vocals have helped him chart country, gospel, pop and R&B. On *Billboard*, he has racked up thirty-five number one country singles and won numerous Grammy, CMA and Academy of Country Music awards. He and his wife Joyce began their love affair fifty years ago, and have a devoted son, Todd.

"Mac Wiseman? Oh, I love him," Ronnie replies, when called for a comment or two on his fellow Southerner. "I grew up on his music where I was born (in the shadow of the Great Smoky Mountains), then heard him on the radio in Raleigh, when I went to the state school for the blind for thirteen years."

(Little could he know at the time of our chat that he and Mac, along with their late musical friend Hank Cochran, would be inducted into the Country Music Hall of Fame at the same time in 2014.)

Ronnie shared a story concerning them both, that occurred when booked on Ralph Emery's weekly syndicated show: "The way it was, you could go sit in an afternoon and do all the talking and they put the music in later. Well, Mac Wiseman was on with me and I was so glad, because as I said, I grew up on his music. When I went out there, I had my slate and pointer [Charles Barbier's Slate & Stylus invention that enabled the blind to write] back in those days. It's difficult to learn to write Braille that way [embossing a series of dots]. There's so many cooler ways to do it now, with all the advanced technology."

Milsap continues, "So Ralph said during taping, 'And Ronnie, we're going to put the microphone down there to listen to you write this the Braille way.' Ralph likened it to 'chicken pecking.' So we get to taping show number five, and Ralph keeps on talking, then towards the end, says, 'You know Ronnie's been over here writing his Braille...' Well, by then I'd already put my slate and pointer away, but he said, 'Let's put the mic over there and listen to Ronnie write his Braille again.' So I hurry, reaching for the slate and pointer, saying, 'Oh Ralph, let me get my 'pecker' out!' Mac, who was sitting in the chair next to me, laughed so hard his chair leaned back and he fell over! Ralph laughed, too, but I thought we'd be censored! When I got home, I told Joyce, 'I made the biggest mistake! I'll never be asked back!' Ralph later said he loved it, adding, 'We've still got that incident in our archives!' Of course, I went back and even did his *Nashville Now* TV series."

Yet another of Mac's friends was Del Reeves, an Opry star whose big hits were "The Girl On the Billboard" and "The Belles of Southern Bell," and who also hailed from North Carolina. He was named Franklin Delano after President Roosevelt (who had inspired Mac), but on the marquee went by the shortened nickname "Del."

Reeves confided: "I was the youngest of eleven children and we all sang and played. I had four brothers in World War II, and when they left home, they left their old guitars lying about. I got to playing around with them and little by little learned to play. My mother used to tune the guitar for me."

According to Mac, "Del invited me to play his annual festival at his hometown of Sparta, and Big Jim Webb was his steel player and such a generous man. I was the guest-star attraction and used his band. It was a great show. To my surprise, Ralph Epperson from WPAQ-Mt. Airy came over to cover it. And do you know he told the audience how he first met me, wanting to work on his station. I was flattered that he drove that distance. Ralph told the crowd the whole incident of my coming by his house on a Sunday when he was shaving, and how he told me to come by Monday and hired me, and what a great job I did at the station. He added we stayed in touch all through the years.

Del Reeves and Mac.

259

"Would you believe WPAQ's still country. You know, I heard Ralph fell and died after hitting his head. His son still runs the station, and now owns the station in Galax, Virginia, as well.

Throughout the 1980s, Mac hit the festival circuit as much as he chose to, in addition to country bookings he accepted. It was in 1987 that he had been inducted into SPBGMA's Hall of Bluegrass Greats. That same year started Scott Rouse's experiment with his musical mixmaster, coming up with what would be GrooveGrass and called his musical congregation GrooveGrass Boyz, as noted in previous pages. Initially he revamped the Delmore Brothers' classic "Deep River Blues," into a dance mix, and its success led him to try something similar with John Anderson's pithy "Swingin'" for the same market. His biggest success in this regard was adapting the Osborne Brothers' signature song "Rocky Top," selling over one hundred thousand units, a surprise to Sonny Osborne who once told Mac he knew how many bluegrass fans were out there: fifteen thousand, the average number of discs the Osbornes usuallly sold.

Rouse's "Country Macarena" also sold more than a hundred thousand. More importantly, it was exposing new generations to the musical talents of Del, Doc and Mac. Scott remembers the time backstage when Dolly Parton met Doc Watson, an artist she much admired. She asked the blind man did he have any idea what she "looked" like? Then she took his hands and guided them all down her body from her head to her bosom and below. Doc agreed that was quite a memorable introduction.

Doc, Del and Mac's musical collaboration garnered much attention. They got noticed in such disparate national publications as *Rolling Stone* and other magazines, as well as newspapers around the country. Rouse's then-current release "GrooveGrass 101" on Reprise Records, was favorably reviewed by *The Tennessean* newspaper, in November 1998:

"My two all-time favorite baseball players are former Cubs left-fielder Billy Williams and ex-Red Sox left-fielder Ted Williams. Suffice it to say, I have a certain fondness for things from left field. In this case, left field isn't made of AstroTurf, but something called GrooveGrass, this weird mix of funk and bluegrass. No kidding. Scott Rouse, the producer-engineer, chief vocalist and dominant instrumentalist, actually recorded 'GrooveGrass 101' in 1993, before the Rednex dance novelty 'Cotton Eyed Joe' ever made it into public circulation. But this project has much of the same principles: heavy dance mixes, classic bluegrass and country tunes, goofy premise. The guy has the strange desire to build an entire song around a sample of Minnie Pearl's 'Howdy,' to apply a Sly Stone groove to a Delmore Brothers' song, and to have Parliament grad Bootsy Collins mumble something that sounds vaguely like outtakes from George Duke's 'Dukey Stick' over a souped-up version of Patsy Cline's 'Walkin' After Midnight.' How outrageous does it get? The funkadelic Collins, bluegrass veteran Doc Watson and ex-Eagle Bernie Leadon all contribute to a synthetic remake of Roy Acuff's 'Wabash Cannonball' that probably has the King of Country Music rolling over in his grave. If it all sounds weird, well, it is. Weird sometimes equals fun."

Speaking of "The King," Acuff liked to come to his bandsman Bashful Brother Oswald's private picking parties in suburban Madison, but would wait until after the crowd thinned out. Mac further recalls, "He and I would sing the saddest songs. One of the best of the 'graveyard' songs was his 'Unloved and Unclaimed' [originally written by Jim Anglin and sold to Acuff]. Its lyrics were mournful: *'She lay on a cold marble slab at the morgue/Thousands viewed her, but none knew her name/They will lay her to rest in Potter's Field tomorrow/She will lay there unloved and unclaimed...'*

Old friends reunite: Buddy Starcher, Pete Kirby and Mac.

"Now Oz (Pete Kirby) would have bottles there for the people to imbibe. He would almost get me saturated. I had a glass beside me, and he was always keeping it full. He and his wife had the best guests, people like Acuff, Chet Aktins, and some you might not expect to be there. Quite often as the party ran down, and just about all had departed, Chet and myself would be sitting there in the living room and I'd be singing some old pop song, just rambling on. If I missed a lyric, Chet would feed them to me. I was very surprised and said, 'Chet, I didn't know you knew the lyrics to these old songs.' He said, 'I had to learn the lyrics before I learned to pick 'em.' I thought that made sense."

When Mac did his shows, he was certainly not an Elvis Presley or Garth Brooks on stage with modern flash and pyrotechnics, but he was ever mindful of the fact that a lot of his songs were slow and sad. He knew he was there to entertain people, so usually he'd dish up a funny tale to hit their funny bone and give them their money's worth.

"I never did anything special before going on, but usually I'd kick off with an uptempo number and that sort of gave my voice a chance to open up... John Hartford and I had a conversation one time regarding stage techniques. I mentioned I learned very early in my career you had to work the mood of your audience. I made a practice of doing two songs back-to-back in the same key, so I wouldn't be jumping around and the audience had time to absorb the mood. The other thing John and I agreed on, we always did two songs in the same tempo. I learned that back when I first started and didn't have any real plan. But by experience, I found it was soothing to the crowd not to change tempos too soon, and so mostly I was doing two in a row in the same key and same tempo."

Among one-liners he incorporated into the act, some occurred in introducing his song, say "I Wonder How the Old Folks Are At Home," musing, "I used to wonder that, until I woke up this morning and realized I was one!"

Other zingers he might deliver to loosen up the crowd: "Times sure have changed... back in my early recording days at the height of my career, ladies would throw things on stage, like brassieres and hotel room keys. They still throw things up, but all I get any more is Support Hose or Depends."

He grins, "You'd see the old ladies snicker behind their hands."

Sometimes he even tried to imitate the characters: "I'd slip one in now and then, so I could tell by the reaction of the audience how much liberty I could take. If they weren't reacting, I just kept hitting the songs to entertain them... "

261

Mac was not above dishing up dark humor: "Never have had any success with my love life. I've been married three times and the first two didn't work, and just seemed to go down the toilet. My first wife died from eating poison mushrooms, my second wife died from a severe blow to the head, because she wouldn't eat her damn mushrooms!"

There were even hints of normally taboo topics: "This guy told his doctor, 'My wife is very forgetful. I don't know whether she's starting to get Alzheimer's or has HIV. What would you suggest I do?' After a bit of thought, doc said, 'Here's what I would do: I'd take her about 20 miles out of town and if she finds her way home, don't make love to her'..."

When queried as to whether he thought his on-stage jokes were appropriate for a biography, Wiseman retorts: "Well yes. It's a true part of my stage repertoire, and most people who attended my concerts will recognize these little pieces of humor."

Wiseman judged by a crowd's reactions which sort of joke would go over best with them, and even the aging came in for some ribbing: "A near 60-year-old woman went to a doctor for an exam. Afterwards, he told her in no uncertain terms, she was pregnant! She said, 'Oh I can't be, not at my age,' and Doc said, 'Well you are.' She asked to use the telephone, called home, and her husband answered the phone, so she said, 'You old bastard, you got me pregnant!' Her husband's reply, 'Who's calling?'..."

Mac was on a roll, May 15, 1990, when Bill Monroe invited him back into the studio, this time for a gospel set with producer Steve Buchanan, at Reflections Studio in Nashville. Mac's numbers with Bill included "What Would You Give in Exchange For Your Soul," "Cryin' Holy Unto the Lord" and "Just a Little Talk With Jesus."

"What Would You Give in Exchange For Your Soul," Mac says, was the first number Bill and brother Charlie recorded for RCA in 1935, humming and singing a verse of the gospel standard, *"What would you give in exchange for your soul/Oh, if today God should call you away/What would you give in exchange for your soul... "*

"I was very flattered by him asking me to sing that with him, and pleased to be a part of his gospel album, because when I was with him at the Opry, we featured a lot of sacred songs. In fact, at his request, I taught him several that had been very popular for me on early radio shows. You see Bill had been doing the same ones frequently and was glad to have some new songs to sing... though I don't remember every song on that session. One song in particular, titled 'I've Been Waiting,' was from the Stamps-Baxter hymnal and the notation stated it was the last words of an old lady known as Granny Solomon."

Mac enjoyed their reunion, and a couple months later received another invite, to add two more numbers with Bill, recording July 24, 1990, singing and playing rhythm guitar on "Shine, Hallelujah, Shine" and "This World Is Not My Home." Apparently Bill had been happy, too. The resulting MCA album, titled "Cryin' Holy Unto the Lord," was released later that year.

In the 1990s', Mac's music was becoming even more plentiful, including a pair of Bear Family retrospective recordings being marketed. First came the German label's "Teen-Age Hangout" in 1993, boasting multiple tracks Mac originally recorded at Dot during the late 1950s' rise of rock and roll. None of which critics raved over.

Back then, Randy Wood was attempting to cash in on the new rock popularity by having his favorite country singer try on some rockabilly songs for size, trying to appeal to the youth market. This included the title tune, the lively "Step It Up and Go" and "I Like This Kind of Music," and also covers on such cross-over hits as "The Three Bells," "Sixteen Tons" and "(Hang Down Your Head) Tom Dooley." It was a real off-the-wall offering for Mac's die-hard country and bluegrass fans.

Mac was also prominent on Bear Family's belated tribute to Lester Flatt, released in 1999, under the title "Flatt On Victor," meaning RCA, of course. That six-disc box set boasted Lester's tracks from 1964-1974, encompassing albums teaming him and Mac, among its one hundred and forty-eight tracks.

One of Mac's longtime fans last caught up with him at the 2004 Lewis Family Homecoming Bluegrass Festival in Lincolnton, Georgia, at Elijah Clark State Park. Barney Zellars, who ranks Mac right up there with blues man Blind Boy Fuller, always made it a point to attend Wiseman gigs when in the area. Barney was well versed on Mac's musical repertoire.

"Barney was always collecting anything of mine, notably records and what have you," recalls Wiseman. "I've got a license tag out in the garage I think I'll send him."

Zellars proved pretty lively at the Lewis Family Festival, prompting Mac to invite him on stage where he introduced him to the audience. He was obviously enjoying the attention, so Mac asked him to join in on a number he planned.

"It was a Southern audience and I wasn't sure what they might think, so I asked Barney if he was familiar with a song I recorded - 'Step It Up and Go' - and indeed he was," explains Wiseman. "We kicked it off and I could judge the crowd was with us, so we did an extended version of the song. Why he knew verses I wasn't even aware of and they were eating it up. Of course, it had been an earlier hit by Blind Boy Fuller (1940)."

"Got a little girl, her name is Ball/Give a little bit, she took it all/I said step it up and go-yeah, man/Can't stand pat, swear you gotta step it up and go... Me an' my baby walkin' down the street/Tellin' everybody 'bout the chief of police... Gotta step it up and go-yeah/Can't stand pat, swear you gotta step it up and go."

Mac learned he had made Barney's day: "When I was loading my vehicle up to go, I glanced over and saw him signing autographs for some of the fans. He'd become a 'star' in a minute!"

28 'Keep On The Sunny Side'... Always Upbeat

"Well, there's a dark and a troubled side of life.
There's a bright and a sunny side to...
Keep on the sunny side/Always on the sunny side,
Keep on the sunny side of life..."

"Well, I'm almost sorry now/I caught you messing around/'Cause you packed up your pickup/And boogied out of town," warbled Chet Atkins, best known for exceptional guitar playing. *"Well darling, I think you'd like to know/That I still write your name in the snow..."*

This impromptu performance occurred when Mac was participating in one of Larry Black's *Family Reunion* DVD shows. Chet Atkins was parodying "I Still Write Your Name in the Sand," and was aware friend Mac had recorded the song. Actually host Bill Anderson asked the ailing Atkins, who died a short time later in 2001, to sing, something he didn't normally do. Despite mounting health problem, Chet quietly kicked off "I Still Write Your Name in the Snow," with apologies to Buddy Starcher and Mac, as an off-color reply to a cheating gal, accompanying himself on acoustic guitar.

Atkins continued: *"Well I once had an inkling that you'd come back again/But I see now I was only tinkling in the wind/You hurt me more than you'll ever know... I write your name so beautifully/But it's hard to dot the i's and cross the t's/Do you think of me when you're feeling low/And wish that you could write my name in the snow?"*

Wiseman himself hosted Larry Black's first *Bluegrass Homecoming Reunion* DVD, recognizing the historical significance of the tapings with their spontaneous entertainment and off-the-cuff chatter.

Accompanying Mac these days to shows was daughter Maxine or son Scott, who also helped with merchandise sales: "I remember when Maxine had broken her wrist and though she was having a hard time, still wanted to go out with me, but when Scott heard that, he jumped in saying he would ride with me." Scott really seemed to enjoy it, and boy he was some salesman. He really got with it, and while someone was buying one CD, he was pitching a second one that he insisted they really needed to have."

Maxine began working for Dad during high school: "All of us traveled to Dad's shows at one time or another to help with product sales. I worked with him later regarding bookings. When flying got so expensive that it was eating into our end (of profits), I put a pencil to it and decided to do fewer dates and by upping his price a bit, he still made as much and had all the dates he could handle. After 9-11, we never flew again because for him to go through that airport security *rigamarole* was just too much for him. We had one more date scheduled down in Florida when that happened, so we ended up driving to that one. Thereafter, we did only dates that were within driving distance."

264

Mac was somewhat surprised, but pleased by his daughter's revamping of his itinerary. She worked hard on his behalf, coordinating tour dates, including handling contracts, correspondence and scheduling personal appearances of all kinds.

"People paid the higher fee without batting an eye. It made me wish I had put her in charge earlier. I was working less but still making the same money."

In 2002, Wiseman was stunned but flattered when invited to record with Americana artist David Grisman, a cult favorite as a songwriter and mandolinist. David's album was titled "Life of Sorrow."

"To an extent, we all live 'a life of sorrow.' We all experience pain, suffering, loss and disappointment - and much of our life's work becomes how we deal with it," said Grisman, in part, while talking up his CD during April 2003. "The songs in this traditional American collection share common threads of human trials and tribulations; themes of unrequited love, heartache, tragedy, incarceration and death. While some of the melodies are somber and wistful, much of this music is uplifting, despite the dire messages of the lyrics. In essence, these songs are the antidote for the sorrow they depict, and that is perhaps why they are so meaningful...

"This project is comprised of recordings, formal and informal, spanning over thirty years of picking and singing with some of my best musical friends and heroes... friends from years on the festival circuit include Bryan Bowers, the Nashville Bluegrass Band, and bluegrass patriarchs Ralph Stanley and Mac Wiseman," continued David, "To all of them I say, 'Thanks for all your great music and memories.' And may your sorrows be few."

Initially Grisman specialized in "Newgrass," despite being from Hackensack, New Jersey, not exactly a bastion of 'grass that's blue. Some twenty years younger, David admired Mac's style. No surprise there since back in the early 1990s, he decided to start up Acoustic Disc, a label with a mission of preserving and promoting acoustic or instrumental sounds. One of his consistently best-selling acts has been his own David Grisman Quintet.

"He approached me about the project he had in mind in 2002," recalls Wiseman. "I did two songs for him, and the actual session was at Cowboy Jack Clement's studio here. That same morning I did a couple songs on the Tennessee Mafia Jug Band's album - 'Barnyard Frolic' - at Jack's. Those guys include Leroy Troy, (Lonesome) Lester Armistead and his son Mike, also the

Mac jams with TN Mafia Jug pals Lonesome Lester, Mike Armistead and Leroy Troy.

act's 'schemer' that is booking coordinator, who named his first-born son Little Mac after me. Now isn't that something?"

Grisman's selections spotlighted Wiseman's vocals with his own mandolin in the forefront for "When You And I Were Young, Maggie" and "You're the Girl Of My Dreams." Yet somehow David jammed with Mac on the A.P. Carter tune "Keep On the Sunny Side (Of Life)," which Mac seemed to have forgotten. It appears on "Life Of Sorrow" as a hidden bonus track, along with "Maggie..." and "Girl Of My Dreams," all sung by Wiseman.

David, of course, is known for his jazzy "Dawg" style of picking, however, on this CD he chose to play it closer to his traditional bluegrass vest, but boasts a lot of fine studio backup from pros like Herb Pedersen, guitar; Ronnie Mc-Coury, mandolin; Bryan Bowers, autoharp; Rob McCoury, banjo; Mike Bub, bass; Del McCoury, guitar; Mark Hembree, bass; and fiddlers Stuart Duncan, Laurie Lewis and Jason Carter.

"You know I still get a royalty statement from David's management company," smiles Mac. "David was very personable. I liked him. He had me do numbers that I recorded before... As he said, I originally met him while performing around on some festivals earlier."

Wiseman never had a number one record and his Top Tens were covers, yet he became a triple-threat talent in the music industry. So it's not so surprising that fellow performers, including Johnny Cash, fascinated by his artistry, themselves became fans.

Cash found fame first on the indie Sun Records, recording with Sam Phillips. His very first charted single was "Cry, Cry, Cry," which only charted one week in November 1955.

"Johnny's booking agent called and said that their guy would like to come on tour with us and sort of open our show, which was fine with us, as he wasn't asking any real money," says Mac. "He had a record out called 'Hey, Porter' (the flipside to 'Cry, Cry, Cry') and they were trying to promote it (1955). So I can say that Johnny Cash did his first tour with me. (A year later, he charted his first number one record 'I Walk the Line' and Cash's career literally took off into the stratosphere.)"

"I hadn't talked to Johnny in ages," recalls Mac. "Then one Sunday in October (2002), I was sitting there watching television and the telephone rang. It was Johnny. He said, 'You want to come out a little while if I send my car over?' I said, 'I'd love that.' So he sent David Ferguson over and we drove out to his place in Hendersonville. He wasn't at the house. He was over across the road in his compound, where he keeps all kinds of exotic animals, and has a studio over there."

In Wiseman's world, that was a truly memorable moment, having an old pal call to renew their friendship. Five decades earlier Mac tried convincing Dot to sign the emerging rockabilly artist, but the label was hesitant about advancing Cash the ten thousand dollars he asked, so he was picked up by Columbia. When Mac was seriously ill in Los Angeles, it was Cash who sent a thousand dollar check that allowed him to check himself out of the hospital upon recovery; the pair also played Carnegie Hall and the Newport Folk Festival together.

Mac fondly remembers the first day of their final encounter on Cash's estate, "He wasn't in the studio, however, and it was a crisp autumn afternoon. They had a little fire built up outside back of the studio, out there in the woods. As it drew closer to evening and there was a chill in the air, his wife June came out and made sure Johnny had a shawl around his shoulders to protect him from the night air. She apologized to me saying, 'I hate to break this up,' then excused herself and went back inside.

"But we sat there really having a good visit. The atmosphere was great and we just sat there talking about old times and reminiscing. Johnny said, 'Do you know how I start my day every morning?' Of course, I had no idea. He said, 'I start my day listening to your 'Reveille Time In Heaven.' That just floored me! I guess it was his influence with the military, as well as his spiritual side. I was almost in shock. Hearing that, the hair was standing up on the back of my neck.

"I said, 'Mi'God, John, we oughta record that.' Johnny replied, 'Would you record that with me?' I thought he was just being nice, but I said it would be a pleasure. He sent me on back to my house. A couple weeks later he called and said, 'Are you ready to record?' He said the only reason it took that long is he'd sent a letter to his producer Rick Rubin, who owns the label American Records in California, to ask if it would be acceptable. Johnny said he didn't want to have me record it if he couldn't get it released. I thought that was just a wonderful gesture, and Johnny showed me the letter from Rick. So we did record that and a song of his I really like, 'I Still Miss Someone.' [Cash's composition was first charted as B side to his number one 'Don't Take Your Guns to Town,' and served as title to a 1998 short film featuring singer Mark Collie as Cash.]"

Mac and Johnny's first track, of course, was their mutual pick, "Reveille Time in Heaven," with its inspirational lyrics: *"When they call reveille, reveille in Heaven for my boy/He'll stand there smiling thru, as he did for the red, white and blue/He'll rest in peace up there forever more/No more fighting, like he had to do before/He's just waiting for his mother, his dad, his sis and brother/When its reveille time in Heaven for my boy."*

"Shortly after that, June died (May 15, 2003). But he called me again and asked, 'Do you want to record some more?' We did it the same way and he sent his car for me again. He'd been recording ever since June died. I hear he recorded forty-some songs. Rick had called him and said, 'I want you to record everything that you ever wanted to cut and didn't.' Rick was smart to do that. So John did Hawaiian songs, cowboy songs, western swing and just about everything.

"We went through a lot of songs together. I took some things out and he had some suggestions. On the last deal we were going through songs and nothing was ringing a bell for either one of us. Then I mentioned the song, 'Hold Fast To The Right,' and he said, 'Hey, I learned that from my Mom.' And I told him, 'By gee, that's how I learned it, too.'"

"Hold Fast To The Right," composed by Bill and Bob Brumley, is an old-time mother's song of inspiration, and it turned out that June Carter Cash once recorded it, as well: *"Kneel down to the side of your mother, my boy/You have only a moment, I know/But stay 'til I give you this parting advice/It is all that I have to bestow... Hold fast to the right, hold fast to the right/Wherever your footsteps may roam/Oh, forsake not the way of salvation, my boy/That you learned from your mother at home."*

"You know how low John sings and my voice is much higher, yet we were able to do it in the same key, but in a different range. I did mine and didn't have to modulate or anything, but was able to do it in my register, an octave higher is what I'm trying to say. It wasn't no time after that he passed away."

Mac treasures a note on which Johnny wrote some lyrics for his new duet partner to sing, Cash's "I Still Miss Someone." Actually the duo, whom some might label an odd couple, recorded in early August 2003, and shortly thereafter the fabled *Man In Black* succumbed to his diabetes-induced illness diagnosed as Shy-Drager, a form of Parkinson's disease - September 12, 2003 - nearly four months after June died. He was seventy-one, and she seventy-three.

That final session left Mac as the last artist to record with Cash. He's heard that Ferguson had mastered the cuts from the Cash-Wiseman sessions: "But we're not quite sure when they might be released (if ever)."

On February 23, 2010, Rubin's label released a portion of Johnny

Johnny jotted lyrics for Mac to his song 'I Still Miss Someone.'

Cash's home-recorded songs as "America VI: Ain't No Grave," minus his tracks with Wiseman. The label's publicity promoted that as the singer's last recordings, though apparently that's not quite factual. According to music writer James Joyner on January 14, 2010 on the Internet's *Outside the Beltway*: "'American VI: Ain't No Grave,' billed as the final installment in a series of comeback recordings overseen by producer Rick Rubin, will be released on February 26, the seventy-eighth anniversary of Cash's birth, said a spokeswoman for Rubin…'"

On the West Coast, Rick Rubin remained an avant-garde musical genius living near the beach in Malibu, and was then running Sony Music (or the old Columbia Records-Epic entity) as a co-chairman with Steve Barnett. The bearded, laid-back Rubin was a founder of Def Jam Records, a hip-hop label producing hits for moneymakers like Run-DMC, The Beastie Boys and The Red Hot Chili Peppers.

Although Rubin has also worked with such contemporary acts as Dixie Chicks and actor-singer Josh Groban, reportedly his more satisfactory accomplishment was producing the aging Cash's "comeback" albums. Cash's cover of Nine Inch Nails' "Hurt" earned him the CMA's best single and best video for 2003.

Mac remembers that Cash was aware of his vocal shortcomings, but knew how to pace himself while they were recording together in what were virtually his last days: "It was as though he were on a mission to leave as much of himself as he humanly could, if only on these virtual 'field recordings,' before his time was up. Johnny told me not to be concerned about his vocals as he could come back later and overdub his part. He didn't make a big point about it, but he wanted to assure me that might not be the one released… "

According to Rubin, Cash's illness started affecting his performances while recording his "Unchained" album project in 1995: "He wanted to be able to do more than he was physically able to do. He couldn't understand why one day he would come in and be able to sing great, and the next he would come in and not be able to catch his breath, and would have to lie down between takes. He was suffering a lot."

Mac continues, "You know Johnny didn't do a lot of duets in his career, apart from June. So I was quite pleased to record with him." [In Cash's later career, Mac was probably not aware Johnny did do those tracks with Waylon, Willie and Kris Kristofferson as The Highwaymen, and a vocal guesting with Hank Williams, Jr. Cash's daughter Rosanne also sang on his latter day cut "The Ballad of a Teenage Queen," which charted briefly.]

Buck (Uncle Josh) Graves was there when Johnny and Mac cut "Reveille Time In Heaven," noting then of Cash, "He'd just walk in a room and it was like a magnet. When that affects musicians, it's gotta be pretty strong." Buck added that Jack Clement and John Carter Cash were also there, as Johnny tried to get through the song: "John did the recitation and Mac sang. That brought your hair on end hearing that voice."

Mac took issue with Graves' recollection of Cash doing a recitation: "I don't think that's right. Perhaps old Buck had one too many. Johnny sang the song with me and was very familiar with the song. I mean he's the one who started the whole recording thing with me, based on that song. Now I don't have a copy of it to check for you. It was one of those house recordings for Rubin and I don't think Fergie has a copy of it, nor does John Carter. But I'm almost 100 per cent sure John didn't just do a recitation."

Wiseman points out that Johnny's son and his then-wife Laura Weber Cash, who Mac calls "an incredible fiddler," were at their sessions both times, though not at the fireside chat he first had with Cash, when June appeared to make sure Johnny was kept warm in the evening chill.

Mac has since learned that Laura Weber initially perfected her playing while recovering from an injury at age nine. Her carpenter-dad obtained the instrument from a violinmaker in exchange for building him a two-story deck on his house. At age seventeen, she won a national fiddling championship in Idaho. Laura later toured with such notables as Patty Loveless, James House, Pam Tillis and June Carter Cash (which is how she met her future husband).

"She is so gracious," smiles Mac, "and you know she calls me every now and then just to chat. I appreciate that."

In addition to playing fiddle on various recordings, Laura sang a duet with Larry Gatlin on the 2006 CD "Voice of the Spirit, Gospel of the South." (She and John Carter Cash have since divorced.)

Mac interjects, "I remember Larry Gatlin dropped by and listened to our play-back and made the comment, 'Mac, you're really singing good.' Then Johnny spoke up and said, 'Hey, he's singing as good as he did thirty years ago!' I felt quite flattered by their comments. But we weren't trying to be flashy or to out-do the other one. We just each did our thing and brought it together the best way we could, you know. It was the sincerity of it all that mattered."

Wiseman reflects further, "I don't know that Rick will release another posthumous collection on Johnny. He'll do what he thinks is best, and he's a very intelligent fellow. But I've already made myself a promise that they're going to play the sides I have, at my 'farewell party' whether it's released or not. What are they gonna do? Wake me up?"

David Ferguson was present throughout their session and handled the engineering. "Fergie" as he's nicknamed, relished his engineering-mixing project with Rubin for Cash's final recording sessions at his place in Hendersonville.

"During the last months of his life, Johnny was recording a lot. It was almost an everyday thing… it seemed as if playing and singing was the only thing that took his mind off his health problems… After June died, John briefly worked with their son John Carter Cash on a Carter Family tribute album, but soon afterwards we got back on the American (Records) stuff. It was hard for John to get around, so we took the recording equipment to him… I would set up the equipment and John or I would call his favorite musicians and we'd record."

Incidentally, Nashville native Ferguson had learned rudiments of his trade from Jack Clement, who produced some of Cash's finest recordings in their heyday and also Wiseman's. Fergie continued, "The whole point of the Nashville recordings was to get Johnny's vocals, the key and the tempo. Rick likes to be hands-on with the tracks, so we later took the recordings to Los Angeles. The Nashville process was to focus on recording Johnny singing with musicians he loved, and a few instrumental bits remain on the final albums… You don't take Jack Clement's playing off anything!"

Mac and Johnny at Cash's home studio
only weeks before his passing.
(Photo courtesy Laura Weber Cash)

270

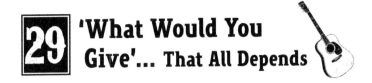

29 'What Would You Give'... That All Depends

"Brother afar from the Savior today
Risking your soul for the things that decay
Oh, if today God should call you away
What would you give in exchange for your soul..."

Wiseman was also pumped having Charlie Daniels and Rouse invite him to record for Daniels' "Songs From The Longleaf Pines" CD, which also gave Mac an opportunity to perform with Charlie at the Country Music Hall of Fame. That event captured the Charlie Daniels Band project on DVD, titled "Preachin', Prayin', Singin' - Charlie Daniels & Friends 'Live From the Country Music Hall of Fame'."

That shoot occurred on April 25, 2005, when Charlie decided to preview some songs off his new "Songs From The Longleaf Pines" by videotaping the performances. His live audience was delighted to find the guests consisted of Mac, Ricky Skaggs, The Whites, and the McCoury family band. On the DVD, Charlie's heard reflecting on the music of Mac; playing with the Earl Scruggs Review in the late 1960s; and his early days with his own contingent. Additionally, backstage chats involve the likes of Charlie, Earl and Mac.

Obviously, Mac wasn't the only guest artist on Daniels' album, as Earl, Cyndi Wheeler, Chris Thile, Skaggs and The Whites, also lent their considerable talents to the Scott Rouse-produced project, along with his GrooveGrass Boyz: Rob and Ronnie McCoury, Mike Bub, Jason Carter, Andy Hall and Tim May.

Mac was involved vocally on the tracks "I'm Working On a Building," an A. P. Carter arrangement; "The Old Account," a public domain tune; "The 23rd Psalm" (primarily a recitation); "Walking In Jerusalem," by Bill Monroe; and "What Would You Give (In Exchange For Your Soul)," written by J. H. Carr and F. J. Berry.

"As I said before, that song 'What Would You Give...' Bill told me was the first song that he and brother Charlie recorded together as the Monroe Brothers. That was before they ever heard of 'bluegrass' music," grins Wiseman. It was recorded by the Monroe brothers in Charlotte, North Carolina, February 17, 1936, though previously cut by The Prairie Ramblers, heard so effectively on Patsy Montana's 1935 million-seller "I Want To Be a Cowboy's Sweetheart." Prairie Ramblers at the time were: Floyd "Salty" Holmes, guitar; Chick Hurt, mandolin; Tex Atchison, fiddle; and "Happy Jack" Taylor, bass.

Charlie Daniels and Mac did it up just right: *"Oh, if today God should call you away/What would you give in exchange for your soul..."*

"I was glad we did that number," Mac adds, recalling that he and Daniels were once neighbors on properties owned in Wilson County. "I first bought some farm land in DeKalb County, Tennessee, with all the money I could scrape up and ran a cattle operation. I think it was seven hundred acres. When I sold it, I came down to

Lebanon, Tennessee, to purchase about two hundred acres there (adjacent to Daniels' cattle spread). We had a lot of frontal footage and city water, so it was broken up into acre lots, then started buying HUD houses and that proved successful for me, too. You see I had a good real estate man to work with.

"Our farms were adjoining, and Charlie he'd be over there working his horses on his riding range, and we'd take ours over by there, too. The fellows who handled our places actually did a lot of the work, while Charlie and I chatted, and that's when I learned how far back I went in his memory. He said his dad used to take him to see our shows all the time. I think his dad raised tobacco..."

According to Daniels, "The first music I ever played seriously was bluegrass and I developed

CD liner notes show Mac and Charlie in studio.

a deep and abiding love for this pure and honest music. Not every musician understands bluegrass; its fragile acoustical sound, its unusual phrasing and its intangible dynamics can elude the ear of the finest musicians.

"Either you 'get it' or you don't, and while I certainly don't consider myself any kind of virtuoso, I am thankful that I at least 'get it.' I have long desired and even planned to try my hand at doing a collection of bluegrass songs, and when Scott Rouse came up with the idea of coupling me with The GrooveGrass Boyz - Ronnie, Rob and Del McCoury, Jason Carter, Mike Bub, Andy Hall, Tim May, Mac Wiseman, Earl Scruggs, Ricky Skaggs, The Whites and others - to record many of my favorite old bluegrass hymns, I jumped at the opportunity. It was a joy to work with these talented bluegrass musicians, and I think the result speaks for itself."

USA Today's 2005 review of "Songs From the Longleaf Pines: A Gospel Bluegrass Collection" in part reads: "Taking literally the Psalmist's exhortation to 'play skillfully on the strings, with loud shots,' Daniels makes bluegrass that's produced like hip-hop, with the standup bass cranked way up and the other instruments so compressed they're ready to explode from the internal pressure. The rhythm swings more toward funk than Bill Monroe would have, but the music makes no apologies for its religion or tradition, with most of Del McCoury's band backing Daniels, plus great guest turns from Mac Wiseman and Earl Scruggs."

Following their collaboration, Mac checked himself into a hospital for a pacemaker to be implanted. However, he suffered some problems after the fact: "I'd just about given up hope after I went through four procedures and began to wonder if they were ever going to get this thing right."

Fortunately, the last surgery proved the charm and worked fine, and Mac was raring to go, including playing a few festivals following his recuperation from that procedure.

One person who hadn't bought a Mac Wiseman album, though his father might well have, was Dave "Mudcat" Saunders, a Roanoke County real estate developer turned best-selling author from Virginia. Mac enjoys meeting people and making new friends. Saunders certainly ranks among the more unique acquaintances he's made, ironically during the 2008 Presidential campaign, when such politicos as Hillary Rodham Clinton, Joe Biden, Chris Dodd, Dennis Kucinich and John Edwards sought the Democratic nomination that subsequently went to Barack Obama.

Mudcat happened to be a senior campaign strategist for John Edwards, who with John Kerry comprised the 2004 Democratic ticket for president and vice president, respectively, but lost to the GOP incumbents George Bush and Dick Cheney. Saunders co-wrote the satiric Simon & Schuster book "Foxes In The Henhouse: How the Republicans Stole The South And The Heartland, And What The Democrats Must Do To Run 'em Out" (New York, 2006). Campaigning, he proved more successful in supporting bids by Mark Warner to become Governor of Virginia in 2001, and former Marine Jim Webb's U.S. senatorial run in 2006. (Now Warner's also a senator, and some circles would like to see Webb seek the 2016 Presidential nomination.)

During a gathering of music folk in Nashville at which Mudcat was the guest of honor, Mac was "warned" by his hosts that the Democratic political strategist was pretty straitlaced, so no one should use the F-word in his presence. Wiseman was not aware of Saunders' previous accomplishments, but wasn't impressed by John Edwards. Nor was Mac the least bit intimidated by the younger strategist from his home state, who he learned did like music, football, fishing, hunting and NASCAR. Knowing this, Mac reasoned that Mudcat couldn't be all bad.

As the meeting progressed, someone suggested it was time to order something to eat, and Mac spoke up saying, *"I don't know about you, but I could go for a f---ing hamburger without any f---ing catsup!"* Nobody laughed any louder than Mudcat, who was tickled that Mac had his number, and he became an instant Big-Mac fan: "That dog will hunt!"

In mid-decade, Saunders had sought to bring the Democrats back into strength in Dixie, by uniting the rednecks he calls "Bubbas" with blacks that already felt their best chance for a decent future rested with Democratic leadership. In conversation with Mudcat, whose southern drawl was as pronounced as Mac's wasn't, we learned why Mudcat thought the Democrats had lost in 2004: "They can't f----ing count! That's the Democrats' problem. You don't get in the football game and punt on first down. You concede nothing. We conceded twenty states at the start then six more by Labor Day 2004 -- that's two hundred and twenty-seven electoral votes. As a result, Bush-Cheney needed only eighteen per cent of what remained of electoral votes to win."

According to a review on Saunders' book, "The ideas in 'Foxes in the Henhouse' may not all be original, but the tone of the book is pure 'Mudcat,' a breath of cow-pattied, countrified air. He and co-writer Steve Jarding (a fellow campaign adviser and Harvard University professor) had a warning for the potential come-back of the Democrats: 'Lose the 'wuss factor' and bone-up on the culture of country people -- even if it means forgetting about the women's studies professors and the gay rights activists (they'll vote for Democrats regardless, the authors argue) -- instead concentrate on broadening the base: Show rural people in the South and the heartland that, while you may not personally play the banjo, hunt deer or go to NASCAR races, you appreciate that they do. If urban areas tend to go Democrat and suburban/exurban areas go Republican, 'The swing vote is what's left, and it lives in rural America. These people have been voting Republican, but they're not really Republicans and we need to show 'em why,' says Saunders."

Regarding their joint Democratic "playbook" contribution, Mudcat joshed, "Steve wrote the book, I added the cuss words." In early 2014, Mudcat inspired Virginia state Senator Emmett Hanger to introduce a Senate Joint Commending Resolution, recognizing *Favorite Son* Mac Wiseman, who turned age eighty-nine, May 23, 2014.

David 'Mud Cat' Saunders

Mud Cat Saunders book:
'Foxes In the Henhouse.'

274

30 'The Good Times Are Ready'... Clear The Cobwebs

*"We'll buy some new shoes for the babies
We'll catch us some new fish to fry...
It'll be hallelujah in Wallins, Kentucky
After the work is all done...
It won't be long till we're rollin' in groceries
And the good times are ready to come..."*

"I just love Mac, and he's such a great singer to start with," explains singer-songwriter Leona Williams, when asked why she invited Wiseman to sing "The Good Times Are Ready To Come" for her "Grass Roots" album

"You know he's from Virginia and they have coal mines, too, and there's a line I was listening to, *'There's a coal-train in eastern Kentucky,'* and it just had a Mac Wiseman feel to it. I had to hear him sing that. I guess we have a mutual admiration society going because I'm a straight-ahead country singer and he always compliments that," adds Williams, with a chuckle.

Via portable equipment, a housebound Mac nursing a busted leg recorded with Leona from his living room. Their collaboration, "The Good Times Are Ready To Come," was co-produced by multi-instrumentalist Bruce Hoffman.

"I knew Bruce from Branson where he played fiddle for Mel Tillis," she notes. "Sometimes he would play for us – 'The Grand Ladies' - shows we did over there (alternating with fellow female singers Jean Shepard, Jan Howard, Jeannie Seely, Helen Cornelius and Barbara Fairchild). Not long after my husband Dave Kirby died, I wrote this song 'Come and See Me Sometime' in tribute to him, and Bruce got me started doing that song. Then I thought I wanted to do a whole album like that. So that's how my 'Grass Roots' album came about."

It proved biographical in that it reminded Leona of the music she did in her younger days in Missouri, where as a 15-year-old she had her own radio show "Leona Sings": "It's music like that, which I grew up with when I got to playing guitar, and loving the songs of Kitty Wells and George Jones. You know, I'm doing a CD tribute to Jones right now that I'm calling 'By George! This is Leona Williams.' With Jones having so many hits, it's hard to pick out which ones to do."

Regarding her "Grass Roots" CD, for Loveshine Records, an internet report by a reviewer known as Occasional Hope was posted August 15, 2011, citing the Leona-Mac duet: "The optimistic 'The Good Times Are Ready To Come,' sung as a duet with bluegrass veteran Mac Wiseman, is also great... with a very Depression Era feel, about a Kentucky couple looking forward to spending the proceeds of mining wages, with a new road and coal prices up: *"We'll buy some new shoes for the babies... It won't be long till we're rollin' in groceries/And the good times are ready to come..."*

Mac adds, "She told me that was her favorite track." The set marked Williams' special bluegrass bow and also boasts harmonies by her daughter Cathy Lee Coyne, son Ron Williams, the Opry's Cheryl and Sharon White, and a tribute tune to the Father of Bluegrass Bill Monroe in the one hundredth anniversary year of his birth (2011), titled "The Legend."

She laughs when told she shares her middle name - Belle - with Mac, his being Bell. While Mac didn't expect the duet with Leona to be a single, he relished the opportunity to record her song, as he highly respects Leona, both as a writer and singer. He was quite pleased by their vocal pairing upon hearing it in playback.

Two years earlier at the ROPE awards, Leona was a surprise recipient of the annual caregiver's award, named in honor of the former ROPE president - Mac Wiseman's Nightingale Award - recognizing Williams for the care she rendered her late husband Dave Kirby during his ill-fated cancer fight, and later looking after longtime friend Ferlin Husky, who died in 2011.

"I was so proud of that award, for obvious reasons," asserts Leona, who also won the 2011 top entertainer honor bestowed by ROPE. "I had a hard time believing I won that one! Amazing!"

In the fall of 2011, Mac was persuaded to drop by Larry Black's RFD network program *Larry's Country Diner* to chat with host Black and the "Sheriff" Jimmy Capps, taped October 3. Black is the genial producer who asked Wiseman to host his bluegrass family reunion video earlier. Mac ended up doing three impromptu numbers, winning a big hand from the "diners" assembled, including Ray Stevens, another scheduled guest star.

"Dad hasn't sung in four years," said Scott Wiseman, just before Mac kicked off his first number. "I'm sure he's nervous about it." Though in a wheelchair, he showed no hesitation in kicking off "The Baggage Coach Ahead," much to the delight of all in attendance. The trouper amazed backing musicians Ronnie Reno and Jimmy Capps by singing his songs in the same key as when recorded several decades earlier. The Wiseman segment beamed December 8, 2011 to RFD viewers.

Yet another collaboration with Reno, concerned some tapes in Wiseman's possession purchased from Hal Smith. Ronnie, of course, is the son of Don Reno, of the award-winning duo, Reno & Smiley, an act produced by Mac for Dot Records in the late 1950s.

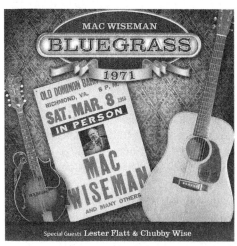

Mac's 2010 release of earlier tracks.

"Ronnie Reno is the force behind twin releases, showcasing the talents of seven Bluegrass Hall of Famers, both of which landed on *Billboard's* Bluegrass albums chart," according to an April 2010 review in *The Nashville Musician* newspaper, reprinted here in part. "The pioneers are Mac Wiseman, Lester Flatt, Chubby Wise, Reno & Smiley and the Stanley Brothers. In

276

April, 'Reno & Smiley - Bluegrass 1963' was at number nine, while 'Mac Wiseman - Bluegrass 1971' was number twelve. Both are also available as DVDs.

"Ronnie compiled performances from a 1963 TV series starring his father and Red Smiley for the Rural Rhythm Records' CD… Of the seven Hall of Famers only Mac Wiseman survives. The CD showcasing Mac comes from a Renfro Valley music festival he hosted in 1971, featuring guests Lester Flatt and Chubby Wise, plus as emcee there's an eighth behind-the-scenes Bluegrass Hall of Famer Carlton Haney.

"Mac's set kicks off with 'Wabash Cannonball,' a song that enriched Roy Acuff's career, then the bluegrass icon segues into a ballad he helped popularize 'I Wonder How the Old Folks Are At Home.' Assisting Wiseman instrumentally are Shenandoah Valley Cut-Ups' Hershel Sizemore, Billy Edwards, John Palmer and Tater Tate, plus there's input from *music-meisters* Paul Warren, Harley Gabbard, Joe Greene, Josh Graves, Roland White, Haskel McCormick, Johnny Johnson and Howdy Forrester. Incidentally, Greene, Tate and Wise perform a unique and fiery fiddle trio break on the instrumental '(Give Me) Liberty,' nestled snugly between masterful Wiseman vocal performances on 'Me & Bobby McGee' and 'Four Walls Around Me.'

"A more judicious bit of editing might've avoided Mac being cut-off on his studio version of 'The Prisoner's Song' (so popular the year he was born, 1925!). Just after Mac warbles the line *'Please meet me tonight all alone/For I have a sad story to tell you/It's a story that's never been told'* and it isn't, as it ends abruptly.

"Nonetheless, this is an important find, which was mainly recorded live in 1971, when Mac headed up the Renfro Valley Bluegrass Festival venue (in liaison with musician-publisher pal Hal Smith). It captures the vibrancy and immediacy of these talents, entertaining their fans as they did on personal appearances for several decades - and now it's all on CD… Ronnie's twin releases are on the Rural Rhythm label."

Don Reno died in 1984, at age fifty-seven, well aware of Ronnie's credits, including playing for the Osborne brothers, Merle Haggard's Strangers and winning a BMI Award for his 1978 hit song "Boogie Grass Band" recorded by Conway Twitty.

Ronnie derives as much satisfaction behind the scenes, and is aligned with Stan Hitchcock, who launched Country Music Television. Since selling CMT, Hitchcock founded cable's Blue Highways TV, working with Reno.

Mac recalls first sighting Ronnie, dressed only in a diaper, when calling on Don and his wife at home in a Dickerson Road trailer court in Nashville: "He was just playing out there in the dirt; he was all boy."

The first time Ronnie witnessed Mac in performance: "Mac appeared on Dad's TV show. Mac used to come by our TV show anytime he would come through Roanoke, because he and Dad were such good friends. Dad thought the world of Mac and I think he felt the same way towards Dad. Many times Dad wished that he and Mac had joined together as a team. He felt Mac's unique style of singing and his technique on banjo playing would have been an asset together."

Currently, Ronnie Reno's *Old-Time Music Hall*, a half-hour bluegrass program, beams in prime time Saturdays on RFD, an independent network created primarily for farm and ranch viewers. Its estimated viewership is twenty million households.

"You know Ronnie came to me for advice way back when he was deciding whether to go with Haggard's band, and I was flattered that he came to me for my input," muses Mac.

Ronnie's indeed a Mac Wiseman champion: "I think Mac is an American treasure. What's so unique about the man is his ability to take any situation and basically realize the ups and downs of it, and make the correct decisions most all the time. Mac is such a talented individual, not only in his music, but in other areas as well. I admire his business sense as much as I do his musical ability. Mac's the whole four quarters it take to make a dollar!"

In Reno's eyes, being a success on the entertainment scene requires about twenty per cent talent, while eighty per cent concerns knowledge and business acumen: "My Dad was a horrible businessman, though my mother was wonderful with a dollar. That is, Dad made a lot of money but didn't keep any of it. He just took it as it came so-to-speak. I guess that's why I admire Mac, who plans for the future and takes care of the present in a responsible manner... You always want to be successful and you take it so personally if you're not, thinking maybe you did something wrong and a lot of times that's not correct."

Reno adds: "You have to understand what the odds are and make the best of them. Oh Lord, we've all done that. Mac's been through it and has been very successful at it, though like the rest of us, he's experienced some down times."

Like Mac, Ronnie has a passion about preserving the past: "Yeah, I'm a history buff, but believe in telling the truth correctly on how it all happened. A lot of times down through the years, it gets way-laid through different people's interpretations, and though they don't mean to, in everybody's way of telling it, sometimes the story's not told correctly. However, if you have it on video and you're seeing it done, then there's no disputing who said what or what's taking place. In 1992, I did a video with Bill Monroe and had him tell the story of when the banjo player started coming with him. Bill said he offered Dad the job before Earl Scruggs got it. I had heard that information before, but to hear Bill himself tell it, then it was said and couldn't be disputed. That was so gratifying to me.

"Then to have Mac entrust me with this historic footage at his music festival meant so much to me. I said, 'Mac, I want to do it correctly. I want you to sit down and talk about it. Then we'll go back and show it. That way it's done in a documentary form and, to me, when it's done in that way, it's correct.' That's what I was trying to do with Mac's festival footage. What was fortunate for me is that Mac keeps everything in wonderful condition.

"Oh, I had to do a little work on it, but nothing compared to what I had to do with Dad's TV footage, which he kept laying out there in the barn for many years. Mac at least had his under controlled temperatures in-doors and the old two-inch reel was still in wonderful shape. That's just the way Mac does things. He crosses his t's and dots his i's.

"When I visit Mac at his house, I cherish every minute of it, because we sit and talk, we laugh and just have a wonderful time. He remembers things that I want to know and he knows that I do and he tells me. Mac's sharp as a tack and he still has a lot of life in him and is a pleasure to be around. Mac and I are talking about putting a project together which I am so excited about, where we'll do as many as four DVD's together that tell *The Mac Wiseman Story*. I am honored that he would even think of me in that capacity, to be capable enough to do it. Of course, it's going to take awhile to do that. It's not a project where you can just rush out and slap it together. It will take time, but it will be with us for a long time as well."

Mac, of course, first linked up with Rural Rhythm when it was under the leadership of Jim O'Neal, as did Reno & Smiley. Both acts enjoyed their Rural Rhythm affiliation. Mac's less sure about its current management, headed up by Sam Passamano.

"We talked about doing some recording," recalls Mac. "I believe Carl Jackson was interested in producing, but I presented my terms and have yet to hear from Sam. I'm not doing something for nothing, I've been there and done that... So now the ball's in his court."

Reno says where business is concerned Mac is known throughout the industry as fair and knowledgeable: "My dad and Mac worked well with their band-members and other artists they encountered through the years. I don't recall anybody having any feuds going with Don Reno or Mac Wiseman.

"Mac relates to an audience about as well as an artist can. He's truly an entertainer. If he doesn't have a band with him, he'll talk to the crowd and sing what they want to hear while accompanying himself on guitar. They like that just fine."

At age 89, Wiseman is a man with music still in his soul. Even younger people have made pilgrimages to his unpretentious house in the Antioch neighborhood of Nashville, just for a visit, including Reno, Prine, Anderson, Scott Rouse, Eddie Stubbs, Del McCoury, Chris Scruggs, and from Texas, the Quebe Sisters - Grace, Hulda and Sophia, and Canada, April Verch, who invited him to record.

"Mac Wiseman for me personally has been a mentor and an example in so many ways," says Dan Hays, then-IBMA executive director. "I had a great father growing up, but from that perspective I'll say Mac has been like a great 'Uncle.' I treasure my relationship with him, and that's about as succinct as I can get in this regard."

Until February 29, 2012, Hays headed up the organization that recognized Wiseman's years of making music via induction into the Bluegrass Hall of Honor in 1993.

"It was a good fit, coming after Bill Monroe and Flatt & Scruggs, whom he played for early in his career," continues Hays. "Of course, those first few years we could've probably inducted twenty-five people without too much trouble deciding who (went in)."

Attesting to his confidence in Mac, he was one of the first Dan confided in that he was planning to leave IBMA. He has great admiration for Mac, both as friend and entertainer: "Certainly as an artist for his ability to stand up on a stage to sing and play and entertain a crowd, he is in my opinion one of the masters. There are any number of classic songs that he's put his signature on and is associated with. He is simply a master and the fact that he's in the Bluegrass Hall of Honor is testament to that. Cross my fingers, I mean I know that these things don't lend themselves to lobbying, but my hope would be that someday the Country Music Hall of Fame finds sufficient reason to induct him, as well. (Indeed Hays hope finally came to pass.)

"Then there's Mac the businessman. There are certainly a lot of astute people who have artistic talents and also combine those with business skills to move things forward. But I'm also afraid we have a lot of examples where that's not the case. Mac is the exception to that and he's a person, whether running a record label or putting on an event or running promotions, who essentially knows how to take care of the business side of things; he's equally a master of that.

"Then there's just Mac as a person. You can layer over all of that and still be a kind of person that people might not like to be around, or didn't feel like there was a fellowship with that person, but I don't know anybody - and I know a lot of people certainly in the bluegrass genre and the broader entertainment world, as well - who gets to be around Mac that doesn't just cherish the opportunity to do that. Mac's the kind of person you want to be around. You feel like whether it's him walking into a room or you walking into a room where he is, that there's a kind of kinship there, and that when he smiles and that gleam in his eye looks out at you and welcomes you, you know that you've been welcomed and it's sincere."

Mac's strength was his versatility, as Dan Hays proclaimed: "He wasn't a guy who said, 'I'm a bluegrass artist and that's all I'm ever gonna be.' He pushed some boundaries, and had enough self-confidence that he wasn't worried that the traditions he was trying to portray were going to go away, just because he went and tried something new. That's what makes a pioneer a pioneer. It's somebody who's willing to venture out beyond the grass that you mowed and get into the high weeds every once in awhile."

Networking is another important tool for those seeking success in the music world, as Wiseman learned early on. Hays added, "I think that's why when Rural Rhythm Records, Blue Highway TV and Ronnie Reno form partnerships, you get a win-win out of it and everybody benefits. My sense is that we're looking at more collaboration on the business side, as well. The role of the record label, the publicist, the distributor, your agent and your management and those kinds of things, who does what, is getting blurred more and more all the time, as people have to do multiple things. Part of it might be the economy, the downsizing of the music industry... Mac has been a leader in this, and that shouldn't surprise any of us as he has said a number of times, 'Nobody's going to look out for me like I will.' The new model seems to be you have to be able to wear multiple hats. Even if you're not doing all those jobs, eventually you need to know what those other people are doing in order to guard and make sure you're taking care of your own career, not just hoping that somebody else is doing it."

These days, Mac's career and past friendships prompt moviemakers and authors coming to him for input on the likes of Bill Monroe or David Akeman for first-hand reminiscences. Noted historian John Rice Irwin called upon Mac for a segment he included in his book "A People And Their Music: The Story Behind the Story of Country Music," devoting a chapter to Wiseman's musical exploits, complete with rare photos.

"Mac was a person I admired more than anyone in the country music field," Irwin points out. "He was also the easiest person I ever interviewed. With each question, he gave me a succinct answer. Hey, his memory is remarkable and he responds as though he knew I was going to ask that particular question. So I'd say he's well-prepared."

Irwin, who founded the Museum of Appalachia in Norris, Tennessee, has also been a musician, but is not as mobile today: "I've got health problems, but I'm still getting along pretty good."

Wiseman recalls fondly, "John hosted an annual Homecoming event sponsored by his museum, and I worked it for about fifteen years. I was drawing good crowds, so he paid me pretty good. I look on him as a good friend, not only to me but to the music industry, as well."

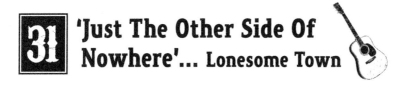

31 'Just The Other Side Of Nowhere'... Lonesome Town

"Sick of spendin' Sundays,
wishin' they were Mondays,
Sittin' in a park alone.
So give my best to anyone who's left
Who ever done me,
Any lovin' way, but wrong,
Tell them that the pride
Of just the other side of nowhere's goin' home..."

"I really admired Mac's singing, you know. He sings better than ever at 80. He really does," said John Prine. "When I close my eyes and hear his voice, it sounds like somebody ice skating smoothly across the pond. So when he expressed interest in doing this record, I didn't shy away from it. Hey, it was all I could do to keep up with him. Just sitting across the table from Mac every morning to sing with him, well, I wanted to keep on doing it five days a week, every day. That would be a perfect job to me."

John joined Mac Wiseman in bringing back little pieces of time remembered fondly, for their 2007 collection "Standard Songs For Average People," released by the independent Oh Boy! Records.

Here's Mac's recollection of the project and meeting John: "I never met John Prine until January a year ago (2006). Louise Scruggs always had a birthday party for Earl, usually the first part of January. She'd just invite tons of people and have loads of food. I asked her one time if she were sure theirs wasn't a Second Harvest food bank.

"David Ferguson, a wonderful engineer was there. He and Prine own a little studio over by the river in Nashville's Germantown. He's quite boisterous and said to me, 'John said if you don't come over there this Thursday, he'll kick your ass!' I thought, that's worth exploring. So I went over, met him and had a good conversation.

"After a bit - Fergie's pretty crazy, he had a band come over and had taken a Kris Kristofferson song he knew ['Just The Other Side of Nowhere'] and sang it and had them put down tracks behind him. Fergie said, 'Why don't you and John try this?' They took Fergie's voice out and we sat right there across the table and put the earphones on and it came out pretty damn good. Kristofferson heard it and was pretty knocked out by it. I'd never heard it before, but it's a helluva song, called something like 'Old Lonesome On The Other Side Of Town's Coming Home.' I did some harmony on the chorus and we just kicked it around a bit."

Mac had earlier recorded Kristofferson's early classic "Me & Bobby Mc-Gee," to good effect, and was surprised to hear himself called "one of the heroes" by Kris Kristofferson. Regarding their vocalizing on the Kristofferson ballad, Mac continues, "Nothing was said about John doing anything further. A few weeks later, I got a call and was told 'John's wondering if you'd be interested in doing an album?' So that's what we did. There wasn't any discord whatsoever. We alternated verses, alternated lines, no friction at all..."

Prine, young enough to be Mac's son, nonetheless had been entertaining audiences more than thirty-five years. Among John's more memorable creations are "Angel From Montgomery," "Paradise" and "I Just Want To Dance With You." Prine earned his first Grammy (1991) for "The Missing Years," which featured legendary co-performers Bruce Springsteen, Bonnie Raitt, Tom Petty, Phil Everly and John Mellencamp; and another (2006) Grammy for his solo effort, "Fair & Square."

Teaming with Wiseman seemed to indicate indeed that opposites do attract.

"Oh sure," Prine chuckles. "There was a seed planted long ago by Jack Clement, who mentioned he thought that me and Mac might try to do something together sometime. We kind of rolled it around there and I thought, 'Man, I'd love to,' but I didn't know if Mac knew me from Adam. It turned out that Mac liked some of my stuff, and I sure liked his music."

No doubt nudging the effort along was Ferguson, who with Prine owns The Butcher Shoppe recording studio. "Do you know David Ferguson?," asks Prine. "Well, Fergie (who co-produced) kind of tricked us. He found that Kristofferson song 'Just the Other Side of Nowhere' on a record, cut his voice out and invited me and Mac down to the studio and cut it in a key where it wouldn't be too rough for either one of us to sing, just to check our voices. Some people's voices are good and you might think that they are like-minded singers who could sing together; but sometimes your voice just doesn't go with another's. Somehow ours seems to complement each other."

Ferguson had suggested Mac drop by the studio to meet John. Soon he had them jammin' together. Once Ferguson blended their vocals on the Kristofferson number, he felt they were a good combination.

"I wouldn't have thought so either, but it seemed to work," continues Prine. "We were encouraged, both Mac and I, by listening to it."

That lesser-known Kristofferson tune fit John like a glove, and Mac was equally impressed with it. Several years later in an in-

Mac and John Prine meet about album.

terview with *The Tennessean* newspaper's Peter Cooper, Kris confided his feelings about Wiseman and in particular Mac's earlier recording of "Me & Bobby McGee."

"Mac is one of the heroes. Having Mac cut 'Me & Bobby McGee' was one of the highlights of my life. When I was young, he had a hit song on 'Love Letters in the Sand' and I just loved that. Maybe someone tried to put him in that bluegrass box, but he is so much more than that. Mac's is a great, great voice."

Prine delights in pointing out he and Mac shared a liking for the same songs: "Originally, Mac and I came up with most of the songs. We just each made a list, regardless of how old or how new the song was or how well known or not well known it was. Then about a month later, we sat at Mac's house, and I think we both had a list of about fifteen songs and it turned out seven of the songs were the same on both lists.

"I mean out of hundreds-of-thousands of songs to pick from and to come down to that, it's amazing! We then started paring it down and when we got into the studio and we'd sing something that you'd think would work, like 'Sing Me Back Home,' and if it wasn't happening right away the first couple of times we did it, we'd just go on to the next song. Heck, we had all these songs sitting there, so we'd just go on to the next number."

The duo caressed such evergreen ballads as the rockabilly classic "I Forgot To Remember To Forget"; a tale with a twist, "Saginaw, Michigan"; and the poignant "Blue Side of Lonesome."

Each had special songs that appealed to them for different reasons. Prine leaned towards nostalgia: "Yes, the gospel stuff - 'In the Garden,' 'The Old Rugged Cross' - were the songs that I had heard from my mom and my grandmother, and those I could do with a guitar and vocals. I half way knew them, at least a verse and chorus already. That's why I suggested them. They were very popular songs, so we both were familiar with them."

According to John, "Mac brought Al Dexter's 'Pistol Packin' Mama' in, and I had heard the song but I was more familiar with Bing Crosby's version. Mac told me how long it had been at the top of the charts by Al Dexter and everything. Hey, he's a walking encyclopedia of music. He knows the songs. He not only knew who made them hits, but probably traveled a couple hundred miles in a car with them. He's got lots of stories about those people, so it was an adventure, besides making a record."

John especially remembered cutting the Dexter ditty, "We were both in a playful mood that day and we'd certainly done a lot of ballads, because we both love ballads, so we were kind of anxious to chop her into bits and do something a little upbeat. Tim O'Brien (guitar) and Ronnie McCoury (mandolin) and Mike Bub (bass) were playing on it, and everything just kind of fell in line. I thought it came out pretty good, too. Les Armistead did the harmony on it, sort of knocking it up another notch for me."

The duo also did Crosby's 1932 pop hit "Where The Blue of The Night (Meets the Gold of the Day)," based on "Tit-Willow" from the Gilbert & Sullivan operetta "The Mikado." Mac recalls listening to it as a boy, "When I was about nine or ten years old, working out in the garden, my mother would call out to me to take a break when she knew it was time for Bing Crosby's show. He was on for fifteen minutes back then, and I'd sit under the tree while she turned the radio up loud, so I could hear him through the open window. That's how I first heard it."

As Mac remembered, John went out of the studio, then came back with a set of lyrics to ". . . Blue of The Night," handing them to him, "I was so glad he did." Another song they both chose was "The Death of Floyd Collins," a hit for Vernon Dalhart twenty years before Prine was born. It's the oldest secular song on their album, adds Mac, "I think the reason John was fairly acquainted with it was because at one time Billy Bob Thornton thought about making a movie out of it. Wouldn't that have been something?"

One song Mac wasn't too keen on covering was Tom T. Hall's "(Old Dogs, Children and) Watermelon Wine," explaining, "I wasn't jittery about doing it, but had misgivings about whether I could do it justice. Tom T. didn't leave a damn thing out when he did it. But I think it came off OK."

Prine agreed, and indicated the reason he pushed for Hall's song, "I just had to hear him sing that line *'I was sitting in Miami, pouring blended whiskey down'*..." Another standout for John was Leon Payne's "The Blue Side of Lonesome," a 1966 posthumous number one single for Jim Reeves.

"That was a favorite of mine. I was always partial to Jim Reeves' version of that. I spend my summers over in Galway. My wife's Irish (Fiona Whelan) and we got a little house over there in Ireland. I don't know how many times me and my friends closed this pub down, singing 'The Blue Side of Lonesome.' So that was kind of a good record for me."

Mac also loves the song, but notes that writer Leon Payne's bluesy ballad borrows its melody from the 1890s' temperance tune "Little Blossom," which he sings a bit of to show its likeness: "It's exactly the same."

A second Payne song selected for the CD was his number one "I Love You Because," also hitting way back to Ernest Tubb and Clyde Moody. Mac says, "I knew Leon Payne. He was blind. I met him here. You know, he was doing dinner theater-type shows back in the Ozarks, even before they were doing them in Branson. I know because Lonzo & Oscar got booked over there. Leon was quite humble, but very sure of himself, much like Doc Watson. They can hear a song and really feel them."

Another "duplication" on their separate lists of suggested songs was Ernest Tubb's "Blue-Eyed Elaine," the first record Tubb cut for Decca in Houston, on April 4, 1940. Tubb's tune was soon covered by Hollywood cowboy Gene Autry. That proved Prine himself is something of a music scholar, as the song was recorded six years before his birth. Another Tubb hit "Don't Be Ashamed of Your Age" (a 1950 duet with Red Foley) was solely on Wiseman's list: "That was a fun song to do."

Prine became aware early on that the studio musicians got an extra charge out of playing these golden oldies: "They all seemed to love them. They really did. We kinda cut the tracks mostly live, but we gave everybody their day in court. We'd bring Kenny Malone back in. You know, Kenny can always spend a day with his percussion kit, going over stuff and getting it just right. Chuck Cochran loved playing piano on this and he added so much to it. I found that those guys really enjoyed playing the old songs."

Obviously for John, it also represented a welcome breather from having to write an album's worth of songs for a particular project: "You're right. It's always a mixed emotion thing for me recording new stuff of mine. I'm usually half in love with it and half not, and always wondering about it, whether it's going to work for somebody else and is it working for me? But these were all songs I knew I loved. I was just trying my best to tell the story as opposed to like introducing new songs... So I was just concentrating on telling the story and trying to sing them from my heart."

Having whipped cancer, John's just happy to still be on the scene and thankful that his captivating whiskey baritone survived it all. Even in younger days, neither he nor Mac were ever considered teen idol types, but their talents gained them major feminine followings, which no doubt inspired their performances.

Regarding his effort with Wiseman: "I want it to get out there to a lot of people. It was just a delight working with him and I'd like people to hear it."

John Prine

285

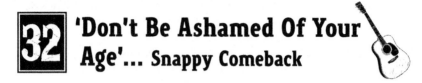 32 'Don't Be Ashamed Of Your Age'... Snappy Comeback

"Don't mind the grey in your hair
Just think of the fun you had puttin' it there
And as for that old book of time
Boy, you never skipped a page
So don't be ashamed of your age..."

After having recorded fourteen songs together for their album, Mac and John still had another shared event ahead. Both were playing the newly constructed Schermerhorn Symphony Center in downtown Nashville during December 2007, and that was to be Mac's final official live public performance concert.

Meanwhile, a variety of CD reviews marked the premiere musical pairing of John and Mac. Reviewer Ted Drozdowski's (May 22, 2007) take on the CD was upbeat: "When two buddies get together to sing and pick their favorite songs, the results are not always fit for public consumption. But when the pals are John Prine and Mac Wiseman, it's a different story. Prine is the author of 'Angel From Montgomery' and 'Dear Abby'; Wiseman is a 60-year veteran bluegrass and country multi-instrumentalist. As for the songs, they're a mix of standards ('The Old Rugged Cross'), weepers (Tom T. Hall's 'Watermelon Wine' and 'Blue Side of Lonesome'), and playful tales ('Pistol Packin' Mama' and 'Don't Be Ashamed of Your Age') - numbers that come from the country and folk traditions, and a wide variety of authors. What they have in common are the kind of storylines and imagery found in Prine's own work - which is why his piney-woods voice wraps around the lyrics so well. Wiseman's age is audible in his singing, and yet his weathered warble pairs well with Prine's drawling timbre. This duo delivers every song with the effortlessness that comes with, well, practice - and true affection for their material. Which makes this disc the rare back-porch picking party that's worth attending."

According to Louis Skorecki, a thirty-year music writer in Paris, France, he rendered it a five-star rating: "The songs are perfect, the treatment is ever so soft, conservative in the best sense of the word, and I've been listening to this sweet-sounding CD non-stop for months, which is the best criterion of quality isn't it? It'll wear well, as all deceptively simple records always do. Buy it, listen to it, music lives on forever with this kind of respect for tradition."

The now-defunct *No Depression* magazine carried comments by John Milward (May 2007): "John Prine and Mac Wiseman are not average people, and the songs they've chosen for this low-key collection are hardly standard. Prine is famous for a superior catalog of songs with lyrics that boast a wry sensibility and emotional acuity. Wiseman, who turns eighty-two in May, is known for the mellow tenor voice, which first gained notice in the 1940s, when he sang with Flatt & Scruggs and Bill Monroe. For decades, he's been a mainstay on the bluegrass festival circuit. The songs are certainly first-rate, with copyrights from Ernest Tubb ('Blue-Eyed Elaine'), Bill Anderson ('Saginaw, Michigan') and Kris Kristofferson ('Just the Other Side of Nowhere')... 'Don't Be Ashamed Of Your Age,' a snappy shuffle might as well be the collection's unofficial theme song, though nothing emphasized the disc's old-fashioned values better than 'Old Cape Cod,' a 1957 Patti Page hit that's wrapped in the schmaltzy singing of the *Grand Ole Opry's* Carol Lee Singers. Add a couple of traditional gospel numbers, 'In the Garden' and 'Old Rugged Cross,' and you've got an amiable picking party that evokes placid Sunday picnics more than rowdy Saturday nights. And while the results are pleasant enough, one can't help but wish somebody had spiked the punchbowl."

Hearing Prine and Wiseman duet on the frisky Red Foley-Ernest Tubb Top Ten from fifty-seven years earlier, "Don't Be Ashamed Of Your Age," was a highlight of their collaborative effort and fitting since John had already turned sixty, though still twenty-one years Mac's junior. In fact, when the Cindy Walker-Bob Wills' hit was recorded by the Decca duo Foley and Tubb, Prine was four years old:

"Listen, Mr. Smith, Mr. Brown/Don't let your age get you down/Life ain't begun until you're forty, son/That's when you really start to go to town... Don't wish that you were a lad/Why, boy, you've lost more gals than they've ever had/And, listen, you've graduated from that ol' sucker stage/So don't be ashamed of your age, brother... Don't be ashamed of your age."

On November 30, WSM conducted a Prine-Wiseman pre-concert plug at The Station Inn, billed as a "Breakfast With Bill Cody" reward for steady listeners. Cody, a member of the DJ Hall of Fame, as of this writing is still the station's morning drive-time host.

"We were seated inside at a table when it was decided we should do the 'live' broadcast on stage, which presented a problem for me as I was in a wheelchair," notes Mac. "But a couple brawny guys stepped up to lift me and my chair right up on stage like I was a lightweight. The set-up was that Cody would chat with both of us and then play some songs; however, he got so absorbed in talking with John and playing his songs that I was left out. So when they took a commercial break, I asked, *'What the f--- am I doing here?'* Well Bill said something like WSM didn't have much Mac Wiseman in the record library, which was really bullshit, as I was a frequent guest of Eddie Stubbs, who plays my records a lot."

Incidentally, the event also recognized the eighty-second birthday of WSM, which first aired November 28, in the year of Mac's birth, with old-timer Uncle Jimmy Thompson playing fiddle songs. Richard Weintraut was one of the guest listeners at Station Inn: "Mac Wiseman was there and told great stories of touring with Hank Williams, Jim Reeves, Flatt & Scruggs and many more. The only sad part of the show was that he announced that he had chosen his appearance with John Prine... to be his last official performance, and that he was going to retire. I think this will be a very special concert. John and Mac stayed long after the show, talking to people, signing autographs... I got to talk to both of them for just a moment, and got my 'WSM place-mat' signed by both'."

On that eventful Sunday night, December 16, 2007, Mac was the opening act for the Symphony Center gig, just across the street from the Country Music Hall of Fame. Accompanying Mac in concert were David Ferguson, bass; Jason Carter on fiddle, and Ronnie McCoury, mandolin - musicians who made the star quite comfortable in an unusual setting for him.

"You know when Ronnie was just old enough to sit up, his mother Jean took a picture of him sitting on my lap. I think that was at Watermelon Park in Berryville, Virginia. Well, believe it or don't, when Ronnie got married and began having kids, he had pictures made of each one sitting on my lap. I remember that he had two boys fairly close together, and had hoped for a girl and finally got one. I thought it was interesting that they named her Emma, as that was my second wife's name."

Mac felt it appropriate having Fergie, who engineered "Standard Songs... ," there for the finale, having played a part in his sessions with both Cash and Prine. They kicked off their portion with Acuff's old standard "Wabash Cannonball," followed by such classic country ballads as "That Silver-Haired Daddy of Mine," "The Prisoner's Song," "Wreck of the Old '97," "Bringing Mary Home" and Mac's Top Fiver "Jimmy Brown The Newsboy." Of course, time with Mac wouldn't be complete without his inspiring signature song "'Tis Sweet To Be Remembered."

Wiseman was in top form, and even shared some crowd-pleasing jokes with patrons, most notably his rib-tickling "Repaint!... And thin no more!" He'd announced it would be his final concert. "I apologize for not standing, but a person could get a lot older waiting for me to get up," said the wheelchair-bound entertainer.

As Mac's act seemingly came to a close, Prine appeared on stage to reprise their album tracks like "Don't Be Ashamed Of Your Age," "Blue Side of Lonesome" and "Pistol Packin' Mama" together.

Following an intermission, Prine reappeared for his set, opening with "Spanish Pipe Dream." He was backed that evening by Dave Jacques on bass; Jason Wilber on guitar; and guest guitarist Pat McLaughlin. Prine's selections played included "Six O'Clock News," "The Great Compromise," "Souvenirs," "Daddy's Little Pumpkin" and naturally enough, "Paradise."

As bittersweet as it may have sounded to Mac's fans, even then he didn't plan to quit working entirely and made a guest appearance a few months later with bluegrass buddies Jesse McReynolds and Curly Seckler at Station Inn.

"You know John Prine came to the show, and due to audience response came up on stage to perform impromptu, and was a crowd favorite," Mac adds thoughtfully. "We even made a DVD of that night's performance... It's so rewarding at this time

Bluegrass legends Everett Lilly, Jesse McReynolds and Curly Seckler.

in my life, the twilight years so-to-speak, to be invited to record with the Charlie Daniels and John Prines in the business and, of course, with Johnny Cash, as well."

Mac's serious about staying off the road, and for the most part really doesn't plan to resume performing again: "Been there, done that." He adds, "Yes, I've turned down a number of things, including

Charlie Daniels calling me to come on the Opry with him. While I appreciate that, I plan to stick with my announcement to retire. There was also an invite to participate in Bill Monroe's hundredth anniversary celebration in Owensboro that I had to decline. I think you have to be as smart about retiring as you do about promoting your career while you're still active."

Although Mac broke his femur while attempting to step up into the kitchen from the garage in October 2009, he was coming along fine when he welcomed in the New Year. Unfortunately, Mac suffered a second fall, again in his kitchen during January 2010, breaking the same leg. This hindered his mobility even more, but he can move about the house with the aid of a rollator, a walker on wheels, albeit slowly and carefully.

Despite such setbacks, a cheerful Mac remains active behind the scenes, and even negotiated with CMH Records' David Haerle to lease the original masters to several of his albums for a box set, done right from his easy chair. Mac planned its art design and liner notes, coordinated the manufacturing of a one hundred and fifty-three-track CD for fall 2011 release on Wise Records. Noted engineer John Eberle assisted Mac, who notes, "He's about the best in town."

The albums reproduced included his Grammy-nominated "From Grass Roots To Bluegrass," "The Clayton McMichen Story," "Mac Wiseman Sings Gordon Lightfoot," "Songs That Made the Jukebox Play," ". . . Most Requested" and "Country Music Memories." Mac has put them on the market at a suggested blue-collar cost-conscious price tag of forty-nine dollars and ninety-eight cents.

Additionally Mac prepped his own webpage to make it easier for fans to find his works: www.macwiseman.com... as well as a Facebook blog - https://www.facebook.com/pages/Mac-Wiseman/218121821580408 - and he's continued recording, confiding, "I have a list of about two-hundred songs I'd like to record before it's all over. You see I sat down one day with a legal pad and just jotted down all the ones I'd like to see preserved."

Mac's are among the Smithsonian Institution's classic American recordings. Listening to this Octogenarian sing, it's easy to tell why he's still at it, simply because he can. Indeed, Mac has the breath and stamina yet to sustain hard-to-reach notes, just as "The Voice With a Heart" did on those earlier CMH recordings he revived. Nor has he lost any of the feeling he incorporates into a song, harking back to days when he was "singing hungry," that is, putting his whole heart into the music.

Currently, two ambitious box sets produced in Germany by Bear Family Records, still sell worldwide, thanks to the Internet and continuing interest in the voice Bill Monroe called the strongest he ever had in his band. "'Tis Sweet To Be Remembered," a 2003 release boasting six CDs, a seventy-six-page booklet by Eddie Stubbs and the late Charles Wolfe, features one hundred and sixty-four songs recorded between 1951 and 1964, selling on *Amazon.com* at two hundred and thirty six dollars, at this writin; while its 2006 sequel "On Susan's Floor," with four CDs, a booklet by Colin Escott, features one hundred and fourteen tracks recorded between 1965-1979, with a list price of one hundred and forty-nine dollars on *Amazon.com.*

Ronnie Reno and Mac put out (2012) a three-DVD set with a single CD, titled "Legacy: Mac Wiseman - An American Treasure." According to Reno it boasts a documentary with footage from a 1978 PBS-TV Special produced in Richmond, Virginia; Mac guesting on the *Hank Thompson Show* in Tulsa, Oklahoma; a concert appearance on the 1980 *Alabama Jubilee*; and a Wiseman interview with Archie Campbell. Both Thompson and Campbell have since left the scene, as sadly have so many of Wiseman's peers.

GrooveGrass Boyz co-star Doc Watson died May 29, 2012.

All of his heroes are gone. A tinge of sadness blurs Mac's eyes, as the beloved godfather of bluegrass (or at the very least its favorite uncle) recalls friends and associates lost just since starting his biography, including Ferlin Husky, Charlie Louvin, Doc Williams, Speedy Krise, Carlton Haney, Wilma Lee Cooper, Kenny Baker, Marshall Grant, Liz Anderson, Billy Grammer, Charlie Collins, Earl Scruggs, Doc Watson, Johnnie Wright, Kitty Wells, George Jones, Slim Whitman, Ray Price, Don Light, Jimmy C. Newman, George Hamilton IV, Jimmy Dickens, Jim Ed Brown and, of course, his mentor, Randy Wood. Sounds like a lead-in to the old Eddie Dean song "I Dreamed of a Hillbilly Heaven," which Mac's friend Tex Ritter also recited and sang so well. Incidentally, on March 10, 2011, Mac's second wife Emma died, only hours after marking her ninety-first birthday. His first wife, Alberta Forbus Marshall, eighty-five, died on August 16, 2013.

"I've known some wonderful people in my time, and I still value all those friendships I made throughout my life... My greatest hope is that I will be able to keep my health to the extent that I'm not bedfast or a burden to my family. Meanwhile, I wonder how can I get all the things done I hope to do before it's all over? But as they say, what will be, will be."

In September 2012, Ronnie Reno called to say Merle Haggard wanted to set up a session with Mac. That led to an October 23-24 studio session for them at Starstruck Studios, owned by Reba McEntire, located in the heart of Music Row. A third session was slated October 29, but Merle canceled, says Mac, "Merle has dental implants and they're giving him fits... we can handle it electronically between Bakersfield and Nashville. We've done thirteen songs for this CD."

Finally, Reno slated a June 24, 2013 session at Hilltop Studio in Madison. Among the tracks heard on our studio visit were "Jimmy Brown The Newsboy," "Bringing Mary Home," "I'll Be All Smiles Tonight," "Love Letters in the Sand," "Wonder How the Old Folks Are At Home," "If Teardrops Were Pennies," "High On a Hilltop" and "'Tis Sweet To Be Remembered." Reno co-produced, with Steve Chandler engineering. Session players included Carl Jackson, guitar; Aubrey Haynie, fiddle; Ben Isaacs, bass; Rob Ickes, Dobro; and Andy Leftwich, mandolin and fiddle.

290

Incidentally, Mac was pleased that their duet collaboration attracted such studio visitors as Prine, Ferguson, Del McCoury, Frank Mull, Al Bunetta, Peter Cooper, Dan Tyminski and Alison Krauss. Some say Alison, along with The Isaacs and Vince Gill, added some shimmering harmony for selected tracks, while Carl Jackson covered tenor harmonies.

Mac murmured, "Dan Tyminski used to lead a band up in New England that backed me on my shows up there before he came onto the national scene. You know during a break in my session with Merle, he leaned into my ear to tell me he had asked Alison to marry him and they just got engaged. I felt honored that he would share that with me when the news hadn't yet been given outside of their families."

Reports indicated The Hag was negotiating with Rural Rhythm, Rounder and Broken Bow Records to determine the best fit for his next album. Reno and Wiseman awaited his final verdict. (Finally he agreed to a special marketing edition released by the Cracker Barrel restaurant chain, May 12, 2015.)

On November 6, 2012, Mac added guest vocals to Canadian newcomer April Verch's CD "Bright Like Gold," on the songs "The Only One," which reportedly she wrote with him in mind, and the Sylvia Trace inspirational "My Home in the Sky." Verch, an outstanding fiddler, vocalist and step-dancer, Tweeted November 4: "Today is another day of mixing! Tomorrow Sammy Shelor joins us in the studio; and Tuesday, Mac Wiseman. Beautiful individual, amazing life"

Out of the blue, we got a call in February 2014, from Virginia State Senator Emmett Hanger, a District Twenty-Four Mount Solon Republican, seeking background career data, noting he was co-sponsoring a Joint Commendation Resolution to honor native son Malcolm Bell Wiseman. Coordinating with Hanger's legislative aide Holly Herman, we fulfilled their informational needs, so that SR-131 was introduced in the Senate a year later by fellow Senator Ralph Smith (R-Roanoke), and passed in February 2015, commending Mac Wiseman.

During early 2014, Mac was also invited to guest on a new Larry Black *Bluegrass Family Reunion*, co-hosted by Bill Anderson and Ricky Skaggs, during which he sang "I'll Be All Smiles Tonight," which he had recorded before, and beamed on the RFD network. There were also invitations to do guest shots on the new albums of Laura Cash and Jett Williams, recently widowed by the death of hubby Keith Adkinson. Documentarian Ken Burns' crew visited Wiseman on April 9, 2014, for an interview relevant to an historic country music program being produced for the PBS TV network.

A young Hank Cochran.

All My Memories Fit For Print

On April 22, 2014, Mac attended an announcement to the media by CMA board member Kix Brooks at the Country Music Hall of Fame, citing the newest artists being voted into that august institution. As we know, Wiseman shared the honor with Ronnie Milsap and the late Hank Cochran, both of whom he enjoyed friendships with through the years.

"All these distinguished Southerners overcame serious hardship before finding the opportunity to hone their talents to professional levels and make the inspired country music that has led to this moment," noted Kyle Young, executive director of the Country Music Hall of Fame & Museum. "Their indelible mark has earned them country music's highest honor, membership in the Country Music Hall of Fame."

Cochran, who passed away in 2010 from cancer, had supplied hits to each of his fellow recipients, notably Milsap's March 11, 1989 number one "Don't You Ever Get Tired of Hurting Me," and Mac's only Capitol Records *Billboard* charting, "Your Best Friend and Me," topping out at number twelve in 1963.

Mac's friend Bobby Bare made the presentation for Cochran, acknowledged by Hank's widow Suzi, while young artist Hunter Hayes did the honors for his hero Milsap. Jo Walker-Meador, who served as the new CMA's only full-time staffer, while Mac was a founding board member in 1958, welcomed Wiseman into the Country Music Hall of Fame. Jo, affectionately known as "The Iron Lady of Country Music," became the trade organization's longest-serving CEO (1962-1991), until her retirement, and has been a Country Music Hall of Famer herself since 1995.

Although Mac had seniority over her and so many of those inducted earlier, he wasn't one to show any bitterness over being overlooked despite earlier nominations. Nonetheless, he managed an understandable bit of grousing after the milestone announcement, musing that he'd about given up on ever being inducted.

"I anticipated and hoped for it a long time," Mac told the assemblage, adding humbly, "This is the biggest thing that ever happened to me in my seventy-odd years. Being in the same categories with all the greats over the years, I'm just really flattered."

Mainly he was satisfied at being recognized finally as an equal in country music.

"Being a founding member of the CMA, I have always been proud of my role in helping make country music popular," he reiterated. "Being inducted into the Country Music Hall of Fame is the icing on the cake and certainly a highlight of my career."

Sarah Trahern, CMA's current CEO, proclaimed in part, "Mac is a revered figure in the world of Bluegrass and a founding board member of the CMA," afterwards confiding to Mac that her father regarded him as a favorite singer, and as a youngster she accompanied dad to Wiseman concerts.

Shortly after this gathering, a surprised Mac was approached to record yet another album, this time for the indie Wrinkled Records. The label, launched by Sandy Knox, with Katie Gillon as its executive director, is home to artists like B. J. Thomas and Jimbeau Hinson. Knox is a noted songwriter, having supplied major hits to Reba McEntire, notably "Does He Love You" and "Why Haven't I Heard From You?"

Since it's been in business awhile, Mac smiled, knowing the label wasn't named with him in mind, but Sandy had her reasons: "Wrinkled Records was originally started in 1997. As a songwriter, I decided to do a CD on my own called 'Pushing Forty, Never Married, No Kids.' At the time I was thirty-eight years old and my attorney gave me grief about putting my age in the title. When it came time

292

to name the label in order to publish the record, I named it Wrinkled Records, just a little bit more of a dig."

Mac was then only acquainted with Katie, who while associated with the CMA, coordinated with Mac, then Local 257's Secretary-Treasurer, to offer health insurance to musicians at a reasonable rate. They also combined to assist the CMA in making plans to establish a home for future music retirees during their twilight years, a program projected on a non-profit basis.

Assigned to co-produce Mac's session for Wrinkled were musicians Peter Cooper (also a broadcaster and reporter for the local daily newspaper *The Tennessean*) and Thomm Jutz, a German-born classical guitarist (who toured with Mary Gauthier and Nanci Griffith) and songwriter ("Across America"), co-writing with notables like Griffith and Kim Richey.

After visiting Wiseman's home and discovering the handwritten songbooks lovingly created and compiled by Mac's mother during his boyhood, the producers hit on the idea of recording a folk-style CD, titled along the lines of "Mac Wiseman: Songs From My Mother's Hand." Since she had penned the lyrics while hearing the songs performed on radio, the jewel case would include pictures of her, her farmer-husband and young Mac, as well as her kitchen table and vintage notebooks.

On June 11, 2014, Mac laid down the tracks at Hilltop, with Jimmy Capps and Thomm Jutz playing acoustic guitars: "I sang twelve songs all on that day. Mostly, I sang them in a lower key to fit the folk style." Among these were nostalgic nods to classics such as "Blue Ridge Mountain Blues," "Answer To Weeping Willow," "I Heard My Mother Call My Name In Prayer," "Answer To The Great Speckled Bird" and his paternal grandmother's favorite, "Will There Be Any Stars In My Crown." He also was on hand at Jutz's *TJ Tunes* place for overdubbing June 12, and though Mac didn't attend, Grandpa and Ramona Jones' daughter Alisa Jones Wall played the hammered dulcimer on June 16, furnishing yet another unique sound to their mix. Added to the session overall were such sterling players as mandolinist Sierra Hull, bassist Mark Fain, harpist Jelly Roll Johnson and multi-instrumentalist Justin Moses.

"Thomm has quite a neat little studio himself," grins Wiseman, pointing out Deutschland's expatriate had produced such stars as Nanci Griffith ("The Loving Kind"). Mac made himself available later in June for a series of chats at SiriusXM Studios in the Bridgestone Arena Tower, and also did a vocal cameo with the Opry's newly-inducted Old Crow Medicine Show band there, sharing the microphone on the Grandpa Jones' classic "Old Rattler," as introduced by singer-host Elizabeth Cook.

They sang, complete with barking hound sounds, *Rattler was a good old dog, as blind as he could be/But every night at suppertime, I believe that dog could see... Here Rattler here, here Rattler here/Call old Rattler from the barn, here Rattler here.*

Cooper confided that Mac's CD was really quite impressive, thinking maybe it might even qualify for a best folk album Grammy. In retrospect, the artist must've set some sort of record for a country singer recording a studio album at age eighty-nine. Nonetheless, just the fact he recorded his first session in 1946, and this set in 2014, some sixty-eight years later, suggests a record of sorts for a solo singer.

Meantime, the CD's release date was September 23, 2014, only days before his *Grand Ole Opry* guesting, where he performed a trio of tunes (when normally guests are allotted time for two): "Blue Ridge Mountain Blues," "I Heard My Mother Call My Name In Prayer," and his signature song "'Tis Sweet To Be Remembered."

"That was quite a memorable time. I had fifteen minutes all to myself out there on stage," explains Wiseman, adding, "They gave me standing ovations, and Vince (Gill) came out and joined me on my last number. Now wasn't that nice?"

An October 21, 2014 concert at the Franklin Theatre in nearby Franklin, Tennessee, sold out weeks before the gig. Advertised as "Mac Wiseman: Stories & Songs," *Nashville Scene* magazine's Jon Weisberger wrote, "Wiseman's got plenty of both stories and songs, thanks to a career that ranges from playing on some of Hank Williams' first songwriting cuts to his brand new 'Songs From My Mother's Hand.' His resume includes stints as an A&R man, a founding member of the CMA and much more. Album co-producer Peter Cooper will elicit stories via onstage conversations while handling guitar duties with co-producer Thomm Jutz and a cool acoustic band (Mark Fain on bass, Casey Campbell on mandolin and fiddler Shad Cobb) on nearly an album's worth of songs. 'The Voice With a Heart' still has plenty of it, and plenty of smooth vocal moves, too – and though he's 89, Wiseman's a practiced raconteur with a good memory and a crafty wit. This is a don't miss taste of history, with some mighty fine music besides."

Mac's mom wrote song lyrics in composition books for him.

33 'Bittersweet, But Wonderful'... Carpe Diem

"I was standing by my window
On one cold and cloudy day
When I saw that hearse come rolling
For to carry my mother away ...
Will the circle be unbroken
By and by, Lord, by and by
There's a better home a-waiting
In the sky, Lord, in the sky..."

A trio of good-time friends, the Class of 2014, were officially inducted into the Country Music Hall of Fame, October 26, 2014, though one was no longer on the scene. Hank Cochran, who died in 2010, was a posthumous inductee, but coincidentally had supplied song hits to his surviving celebrants: Ronnie Milsap and Mac Wiseman.

Cochran's "Don't You Ever Get Tired (of Hurting Me)" became number one for Milsap in March 1989, while the songwriter's earlier effort "Your Best Friend And Me," gave Wiseman his last major *Billboard* singles charting in 1963.

Acording to Bobby Bare, "Hank was like a heat-seeking missile. If he had a song for you, you might as well go ahead and cut it, because he was relentless and nine times out of ten, it would be a hit."

In a star-studded night of testimonials and musical performances of songs closely associated with the honorees, museum director Kyle Young affirmed their election into the prestigious Hall of Fame. During the annual Medallion ceremony, fellow Hall of Famers Bare, Brenda Lee and Jo Walker Meador made the actual presentations for Cochran, Milsap and Wiseman, respectively. It was only the second such event conducted in the newly expanded museum's eight-hundred-seat CMA Theatre.

Arriving earlier at the end of the symbolic red carpet, we were met by Mac's son Randy, inquiring, "When am I going to get to read my father's biography?" After four years working on the project, and witnessing the subject's refusal to sign contracts, the answer forthcoming was, "Well, your Dad might best be called a 'control enthusiast,' and that, in part, accounts for the publishing delay." Without hesitation, Randy retorts, "I was wondering where I got that from?"

Citing Randy, Sheila and Maxine, Mac mused, "Well, I got one child from each of my marriages here tonight." He could also look out on faces of such folk as Bill Anderson, John Prine, Thomm Jutz, Rose Lee Maphis, Ronnie Reno, Peter Cooper, Eddie Stubbs, Jan Howard, David McCormick, Stonewall Jackson, Les Leverett, Jerry Bradley, Donna and Patsy Stoneman, Doris Trott, Gloria Boyd, all rooting him on.

"Mac Wiseman has one of the great voices in American musical history," said Young. "He is known as 'The Voice With a Heart,' and it's hard to imagine a more accurate nickname."

A strutting Charlie Daniels stepped up to render his spirited version of Mac's Top Five single "Jimmy Brown The Newsboy," sans his familiar fiddle, but adding a unique Charlie Daniels' dance to the tune. "He's been a hero of mine since I learned my first three chords. Tonight Mac Wiseman, you *The Man!*"

Maxine cheerfully concluded, "Charlie kinda rocked out on 'Jimmy Brown,' huh?"

Jim Lauderdale, an Americana alternative music favorite, sang "Goin' Like Wildfire," another much-requested Wiseman number, adding, "I started listening to him when I was a kid, and I think he's one of the greatest singers we've ever had. I love the way he has bridged a gap between bluegrass and country music."

Country Hall of Famer Vince Gill, who weeks earlier had appeared on the Opry with Wiseman, sang Mac's signature song "'Tis Sweet To Be Remembered," as only another upper range tenor can do so astonishingly well. Vince called it "a great song," and singing it, on behalf of "a great man."

Artists sharing the stage for this festive evening also included Martina McBride, Gene Watson, Alison Krauss, Hunter Hayes and Sam Moore. Backing the assorted performances was a band of Nashville's finest musicians, led by John Hobbs, keyboards; and including Steve Gibson, guitar; Michael Rhodes, bass; Deanie Richardson, mandolin and fiddle; Eddie Bayers, drums; Paul Franklin, steel guitar; Biff Watson, guitar; Jeff White, guitar and vocals; and Mac's good friend Laura Weber Cash, fiddle and vocals. Joining them for Milsap's songs, was Mark Douthit on saxophone.

"You know The Old Crow boys wrote me a full-page letter saying they would be in The Netherlands, apologizing for missing my Medallion ceremony at the Country Music Hall of Fame," explained Wiseman, off stage. "Now that was so thoughtful of them. They are an amazing act."

Long-time friend Jo Walker Meador, now ninety, stepping up to slip the Medallion around her associate's neck, recalled the birth of the Country Music Association itself, with Mac serving as a founding father: "He had ideas and suggestions that made the organization become what it is today. He was such a great help to me."

Of course, in 1958, Jo was the new unit's only full-time staffer and admittedly not that familiar with country music and its heritage. In Mac, she found just the one to enlighten her on the traditions and culture of the country genre. Ultimately, she became its CEO, watching the format's coverage grow from about a hundred full-time stations to nearly twenty-five hundred upon her retirement.

In accepting the Medallion and its significance of membership in the Country Music Hall of Fame, a humbled Wiseman acknowledged, "I've looked forward to it so long. Having been part of the original foundation of the CMA to start with, and to see the great strides it's made, is most encouraging. I'm just elated."

Cochran's widow Suzi called Hank's belated induction "bittersweet, but wonderful. He would have been very proud." Hank's former wife Jeannie Seely was in attendance, along with her current husband Gene Ward, former attorney for Hall of Famers' Ernest Tubb, Lefty Frizzell, Webb Pierce and Faron Young. Not so incidentally, Seely earned a 1966 Grammy, singing Cochran's classic "Don't Touch Me."

Reba McEntire, originally slated to present Milsap's medal, instead attended her father's funeral. Filling in at the last minute. Lee's tribute to the singer - sightless since infancy - could have just as easily applied to Mac, a polio survivor, or Hank, who spent much of his childhood in an orphanage. "Thank you for helping the world to see a little more clearly what can be achieved, when no obstacle is too great to overcome in life," were Brenda's heartfelt words of praise.

Citing the career importance of associates, Milsap singled out such stalwarts as manager Jack Johnson, music publisher Tom Collins, RCA label chief Jerry Bradley, producer Rob Galbraith, session player Charlie McCoy, artist-friend Charley Pride, and, of course, his wife Joyce, who through the years helped guide him professionally.

"Thank you so much for having me in the Country Music Hall of Fame. It's a true honor," Milsap stated for one and all. Upon conclusion, Ronnie unexpectedly ordered his accompanist to take him to the piano, where he began pounding the keys in a boogie version of "Will The Circle Be Unbroken," the customary closer for the annual Medallion ceremony. Mac, taken aback by the switch in style, started "scatting" the song, before the assemblage of performers and Hall of Fame elite began singing in earnest: *Will the circle be unbroken/By and by, Lord, by and by/ There's a better home a-waiting/In the sky, Lord, in the sky."*

Mac felt right at home, sharing the stage with the night's performers, as well as Hall of Famers such as Emmylou Harris, Bud Wendell, Alabama's Don Owen, The Jordanaire's Ray Walker, Harold Bradley, Charlie McCoy, Charley Pride, Bobby Bare, Jo Walker Meador, Bill Anderson, all joined for the first time by the Bethlehem United Methodist Church Chancel Choir (led by musical director Joe Smyth).

It proved a night to remember for all concerned; Carpe diem, a Latin term for seize the day.

On February 8, 2015, Mac appeared with Rhonda Vincent (voted into the 2014 Class of Bluegrass Preservation Hall of Greats) during the forty-first annual Society For The Preservation of Bluegrass Music of America's (SPBGMA) awards gala, at the Sheraton Music City Hotel, Nashville. (Mac was inducted in 1987, along with Doc Watson and Charlie Waller.)

We asked what happened to Mac's vow to remain retired, to which Wiseman simply reasoned, "Well, they offered me a cool two thousand dollars. How could I say no?"

Mac's knowing eyes still twinkled, while pondering a fitting epitaph for his life story, then intoned: "I'd merely say, he did the very best he could, and always treated others the way he wanted to be treated."

Maybe he should just Tweet one and all, "Yes, *'Tis Sweet To Be Remembered,' remembered, yes remembered...* " Meanwhile, as Mac celebrates his ninetieth birthday, he's just learned he will be a great-great grandfather for the first time, courtesy daughter Linda's lineage, and following that birth, yet another great-great grandbaby's on its way. How sweet it is indeed!

Contributing Author – Walt Trott

Walt Trott is a Nashville-based writer, editor and publisher, who specializes in music, and has reviewed movies, recordings, concerts and reported extensively on the entertainment scene several years in Europe (*Stars & Stripes* daily newspaper & *Variety*); New England (Portland ME *Press Herald, & Variety*); Midwest (*Capital Times*, WI, & *Variety*); and in Music City for such publications as *Country Sounds, Nashville Enquirer, Country Scene, Entertainment Express* and served some twenty years as editor of the AFM newspaper *The Nashville Musician*, and Canada's *Country Music News*, and continues his monthly news to *Country Music People* in the UK. He has written books on veteran artists Johnnie & Jack, Kitty Wells, Martha Carson, and furnished more than fifty bios for Oxford University Press' "The Encyclopedia of Country Music." Additionally, Trott has written extensive liner notes for albums on artists such as The Browns, Connie Smith, Sonny James, Martha Carson, Johnnie & Jack, Red Sovine, Ginny Peters, Dick Curless and Kitty Wells, and DVDs on Jim Reeves, Ray Price & Faron Young for Gannaway Productions' *Classic Country* series. Among his honors are the USO Council President's Certificate of Distinction, Paris 1973; ARSC Award for Excellence in Country Music Research ("The Johnnie & Jack Story" 1992); ROPE International Media Award, 2008; and the Charlie Lamb Lifetime Award for Excellence in Country Music Journalism, 2010. He is currently at work on a Conway Twitty book.

MAC WISEMAN - SESSION DISCOGRAPHY

MOLLY O'DAY's Columbia Records session @ WBBM radio station, 410 N. Michigan Av., Chicago, IL, Dec. 14, 1946. Personnel: Molly O'Day [Lois LaVerne Davis] vocals, banjo & guitar; Lynn Davis, vocal/guitar; George (Speedy) Krise, dobro; Cecil (Skeets) Williamson, fiddle; Malcolm B. Wiseman, standup bass; Uncle Art [Arthur Edward] Satherley, producer. Songs: Tramp On the Street, When God Comes and Gathers His Jewels, The Black Sheep Returned to the Fold, Put My Rubber Doll Away, Drunken Driver, Tear-Stained Letter, Beneath the Lonely Mound of Clay and Six More Miles (To the Graveyard). First single, Tramp On the Street b/w Put My Rubber Doll Away, released July 14, 1947. Later albums include "The Unforgettable Molly O'Day" (Harmony Records) June 1963.

LESTER FLATT, EARL SCRUGGS & THE FOGGY MOUNTAIN BOYS, a Mercury Records session @ Radio Station WROL, 524 S. Gay St., Knoxville, TN, November 1948. Personnel: Lester Raymond Flatt, vocals, guitar; Earl Eugene Scruggs, banjo; James (Jim) Shumate, fiddle; Malcolm Wiseman, vocals, rhythm guitar; and Howard (Cedric Rainwater) Watts, bass; (Robert) Murray Nash, producer. Songs: God Loves His Children, I'm Going To Make Heaven My Home, We'll Meet Again Sweetheart and My Cabin in Caroline. First gospel single, God Loves His Children b/w I'm Going to Make Heaven My Home, released Jan. 31, 1949. "Original Sound of Lester Flatt & Earl Scruggs," album released in March 1963.

BILL MONROE & THE BLUE GRASS BOYS recorded a Columbia session @ Castle Studios, Tulane Hotel, 206 8th Ave. N., Nashville, Oct. 22, 1949. Personnel: Bill (William Smith) Monroe, vocals, mandolin; Mac Wiseman, vocals, rhythm guitar; Chubby (Robert Russell) Wise, fiddle; Rudy Lyle, banjo; Jack Thompson, bass; Art Satherley, producer. Songs: Can't You Hear Me Callin', Travelin' This Lonesome Road, Blue Grass Stomp, and The Girl in the Blue Velvet Band. First single, Blue Grass Stomp (instrumental) b/w Girl in the Blue Velvet Band, released Dec. 19, 1949. "Bill Monroe & His Blue Grass Boys" album released July 27, 1953. This marked Bill's first session in Nashville.

MAC WISEMAN and The Country Boys session recorded @ Radio station WCYB, Bristol, TN, 1950 (regulars on the station's *Farm & Fun Time* program), featuring Mac Wiseman, vocals and guitar; Ted Mullins, mandolin; Joe Medford, banjo; Don Davis, bass; Ralph Mayo, fiddle; Wiseman, producer. Songs: From the Manger To The Cross, A Broken Heart To Mend, and Grey Eagle (instrumental). Released as Rebel Records EP, "Live Again! WCYB-Bristol Farm & Fun Time," 1988.

MAC WISEMAN recorded Dot Records session @ Radio Station KWKH, 509 Market St., Shreveport, LA, May 23, 1951. Personnel: Mac Wiseman, vocals and guitar; Ted Mullins, mandolin; Joe Medford, banjo; Don Davis, bass; Ralph Mayo, fiddle; Bob Sullivan, producer. Songs: Tis Sweet To Be Remembered, Little White Church, I'm a Stranger, and Are You Coming Back To Me. First single, Tis Sweet To Be Remembered b/w Are You Coming Back To Me, released Nov. 26, 1951. Later, "Tis Sweet To Be Remembered" Dot album released Sept. 14, 1957, a compilation of singles recorded previously.

MAC WISEMAN recorded Dot session @ Radio Station WHIN, 1625 Hwy 109, Gallatin, TN, January 1952. Personnel: Mac Wiseman, vocals and rhythm guitar; Rollin (Oscar) Sullivan, mandolin/rhythm guitar; David (Stringbean) Akeman, banjo; Tommy Jackson, fiddle; Ernie Newton, bass; Randy Wood, producer. Songs: I'll Still Write Your Name In the

299

Sand, Four Walls Around Me, Georgia Waltz, and Dreaming Of a Little Cabin. Single on I'll Still Write Your Name in the Sand b/w Four Walls Around Me, released March 2, 1952.

MAC WISEMAN did Dot session @ Radio Station WHIN, Gallatin, TN, April 1952. Personnel: Mac Wiseman, vocals and guitar; Jimmy Williams, mandolin; Ernie Newton, bass; Russell Vass, banjo; Tommy Jackson, fiddle; and Randy Wood, producer. Songs: You're the Girl Of My Dreams, Six More Miles, I Wonder How the Old Folks Are At Home, and Going To See My Baby. First single from session, I Wonder How the Old Folks Are At Home b/w You're the Girl Of My Dreams, released in August 1952.

MAC WISEMAN recorded Dot session, WHIN-Gallatin, July 1952. Personnel: Mac Wiseman, vocals and guitar; Jimmy Williams, vocals and mandolin; Ed Amos, banjo; Tommy Jackson, fiddle; Ernie Newton, bass; and Randy Wood, producer. Songs: It's Goodbye and So Long To You, The Fire In My Heart, Waiting For the Boys, By the Side of the Road. First session song released was By the Side Of the Road b/w Waiting For the Boys, October 1952.

MAC WISEMAN cut Dot session @ Castle Studios, Nashville, November 1952. Personnel: Mac Wiseman, vocals and guitar; Ed Amos, banjo; Rollin Sullivan, mandolin; Ernie Newton, bass; Tommy Jackson, fiddle; Randy Wood, producer. Songs: Shackles and Chains, Goin' Like Wildfire, You're Sweeter Than the Honey, Don't Let Your Sweet Love Die. First session song released was Shackles and Chains b/w Goin' Like Wildfire, Jan. 5, 1953. (Also featured on Dot's "Songs Of the Hills," Mac's first EP, 1955.)

MAC WISEMAN made Dot session @ Castle Studios, Nashville, March 1953. Personnel: Mac Wiseman, vocals and guitar; (Thomas) Grady Martin, rhythm guitar; (Walter) Hank Garland, mandolin; Wayne Brown Lyle, banjo; Ernie Newton, bass; twin fiddles featuring Tommy Jackson and Dale Potter; Randy Wood, producer. Songs: Crazy Blues, You'd Better Wake Up, When I Get the Money Made, and Rainbow In the Valley. First session single: Crazy Blues b/w Rainbow In the Valley, released May 11, 1953.

MAC WISEMAN did Dot session @ Castle Studios, May 1953. Personnel: Mac Wiseman, vocals and guitar; Grady Martin, rhythm guitar; Hank Garland, mandolin; Joe Zinkan, bass; Jackie Phelps, banjo; Tommy Jackson and Dale Potter, twin fiddles, and Randy Wood, producer. Songs: I'd Rather Die Young, Remembering, My Little Home in Tennessee and Let Me Borrow Your Heart (Just For Tonight). First session single was Remembering b/w Let Me Borrow Your Heart, released Sept. 21, 1953. (Featured also on Dot LP "Keep On the Sunny Side," released December 1960.)

MAC WISEMAN recorded Dot session @ Castle Studios, Nashville, October 1953. Personnel: Mac Wiseman, vocals and guitar; Ernie Newton, bass; Chubby Collier, mandolin and fiddle; Tommy Jackson, fiddle; Allen Shelton, banjo; Randy Wood, producer. Songs: Love Letters In the Sand, I Haven't Got the Right To Love You, Keep On the Sunny Side, Dreams Of Mother and Home, Reveille in Heaven, The Waltz You Saved For Me, and Paradise Valley. First single off session was Love Letters In the Sand b/w The Waltz You Saved For Me, released March 1, 1954.

MAC WISEMAN cut a Dot session @ Castle Studios, Nashville, January 1954. Personnel: Mac Wiseman, vocals and guitar; Ernie Newton, bass; Hank Garland, mandolin; Allen Shelton, banjo; Tommy Jackson and Dale Potter, fiddles; Randy Wood, producer. Songs: I Saw Your Face in the Moon, You Can't Judge a Book By Its Cover, I Love You Best

Of All, and Wabash Cannonball. First single off session was I Saw Your Face in the Moon b/w You Can't Judge a Book By Its Cover, released June 14, 1954.

MAC WISEMAN recorded Dot double session @ Castle Studios, Nashville, September 1954. Personnel: Mac Wiseman, vocals and guitar; Ernie Newton, bass; Don Hoaglin, mandolin; Donnie Bryant, banjo; Tommy Jackson and Dale Potter, fiddles; and Randy Wood, producer. Songs at first session: Don't Blame It On Me, I Didn't Know, The Little Old Church in the Valley. Songs at follow-up session, same date: When The Roses Bloom Again, Wabash Cannonball, Fireball Mail, Darlin' How Could You Forget So Soon, I'm Drifting Back To Dreamland, and Smilin' Through. First session single was Don't Blame It On Me b/w I Didn't Know, released Nov. 1, 1954.

MAC WISEMAN cut Dot-approved session @ WARL radio, Arlington, VA, 1954, recorded during *Town & Country Time* program, featuring Connie B. Gay, emcee, and Mac Wiseman on vocals and rhythm guitar. Songs: You Can't Judge a Book By Its Cover, and I Saw Your Face In The Moon.

MAC WISEMAN recorded Dot session @ Castle Studios, Nashville, February 1955. Personnel: Mac Wiseman, vocals and guitar; Hank Garland, lead guitar; Grady Martin, guitar; Ernie Newton, bass; Donnie Bryant, banjo; Tommy Jackson and Dale Potter, fiddles; and Randy Wood, producer. Songs: The Ballad of Davy Crockett, and Danger, Heartbreak Ahead. Both were paired as a single, released Feb. 21, 1955, with the A side, "The Ballad of Davy Crockett," charting *Billboard,* the trade weekly, May 28, 1955, peaking in Top 10.

MAC WISEMAN recorded Dot session @ Castle Studios, Nashville, April 1955. Personnel: Mac Wiseman, vocals and guitar; Ernie Newton, bass; Benny Williams, mandolin; Jackie Phelps, banjo; Curtis Lee and Tommy Vaden, fiddles; and Randy Wood, producer. Song: Mac recorded one number, The Kentuckian Song, released in the U.S. and in the United Kingdom during August 1955.

MAC WISEMAN cut Dot session @ Castle Studios, Nashville, in October 1955. Personnel: Mac Wiseman, vocals and guitar; Johnnie Maddox, keyboards; Tommy Jackson, fiddle; and Beasley Smith producing. Songs: I Hear You Knockin', and Camptown Races. A single was released on these Oct. 17, 1955.

MAC WISEMAN recorded Dot session @ Castle Studios, Nashville, December 1955. Personnel: Mac Wiseman, vocals and guitar; Chet Atkins, lead guitar; Donnie Bryant, banjo; Ernie Newton, bass; Tommy Jackson and Dale Potter, fiddles; and Randy Wood producing. Songs: Dark As a Dungeon, I Want To Be Loved, These Hands, and I'm Eatin' High On the Hog. First session single was These Hands b/w I'm Eatin' High On the Hog, released Jan. 2, 1956.

MAC WISEMAN did Dot session @ Castle Studios, Nashville, on April 4, 1956. Personnel: Mac Wiseman, vocals and guitar; Bob Moore, bass; other orchestral members unknown; and Billy Vaughn, Dot A&R chief, producer. Songs: The Meanest Blues in the World b/w Be Good Baby, released as a single, April 7, 1956.

MAC WISEMAN cut Dot session @ Radio Recorders studio, 7000 Santa Monica Blvd., Hollywood, CA, on Aug. 17, 1956. Personnel: Mac Wiseman, vocals and guitar; Barney Kessel, guitar; Larry Breen, bass; Alvin Stoller, drums; Jack Marshall, guitar; Milton (Shorty) Rogers, piano; and Billy Vaughn, producer. Songs: I'm Waiting For Ships (That

Never Come In), One Mint Julep, and Hey, Mister Bluesman. Vaughn combined I'm Waiting For Ships That Never Come In with One Mint Julep as a single, released Aug. 22, 1956. (Martha Carson's composition Hey Mister Bluesman went unissued until Bear Family in Germany released it on lease in 1977, on that label's compilation album "Country Meets Rock & Roll, Volume 2.")

MAC WISEMAN did Dot session @ Radio Recorders, Hollywood, CA, on Jan. 31 1957. Personnel: Mac Wiseman, vocals and guitar; Barney Kessel, guitar; Larry Breen, bass; Dick Shanahan, drums; Jack Marshall, guitar; The Jack Halloran Singers, chorus (featuring Bill Kanady, Bob Tebow and Bill Cole); and Billy Vaughn, producer. Songs: Step It Up and Go (arranged by Wiseman), Sundown, and Gone. Session song issued as a single was Step It Up and Go b/w Sundown, released on Feb. 6, 1957.

MAC WISEMAN cut this Dot session @ Radio Recorders, Hollywood, April 12, 1957. Personnel: Mac Wiseman, vocals/guitar; Joe Maphis, lead guitar; Shorty Rogers, piano; Larry Breen, bass; Howard Roberts, guitar; Milton Holland, drums; and Billy Vaughn was producer. Songs: Teen-Age Hangout, Because We're Young, and Shame, Shame, Shame. Vaughn released single Because We're Young, April 29, 1957.

MAC WISEMAN cut this Dot session @ Radio Recorders, Hollywood, on Aug. 20, 1957. Personnel: Mac Wiseman, vocals and guitar; Tony Rizzi, guitar; Howard Roberts, guitar; Shorty Rogers, piano; Mack Bennett, bass; Dick Shanahan, drums; The Jack Halloran Singers, harmony; and Billy Vaughn, producer. Songs: I'll Still Write Your Name In the Sand, and Tis Sweet To Be Remembered. The revised songs were released as a single on Aug. 26, 1957.

MAC WISEMAN recorded this Dot session @ Radio Recorders, Hollywood, on June 12, 1957. Personnel: Mac Wiseman, vocals and guitar; featuring The Jack Halloran Singers; produced by Billy Vaughn, recording A Promise Of Things To Come, and Thinkin' About You, released as a July 1, 1958 single.

MAC WISEMAN recorded this sole song at Dot session @ Radio Recorders, during October 1957. Personnel: Mac Wiseman, vocals and guitar; cutting the W. Lee O'Daniel ballad Put Me in Your Pocket, released as a single on March 11, 1958.

MAC WISEMAN recorded the Dot session @ Gold Star Recording Studio, 6252 Santa Monica Blvd., Hollywood, on Feb. 21 1958. Personnel: Mac Wiseman, vocals/guitar; Joe Maphis, lead guitar; Jimmy Pruett, piano; Pee Wee Adams, bass; (Enos) Skeets McDonald, bass; and Billy Vaughn, producer. Song: When the Work's All Done This Fall, apparently an album filler.

MAC WISEMAN recorded multiple Dot sessions @ Bradley Film & Recording Studio, Jan. 22-23 and Jan. 26, 1959. Personnel: Mac Wiseman, vocals/guitar; Joe Zinkan, bass; and Mac, producer. Songs: Beside The Still Waters, How Great Thou Art, Just a Closer Walk With Thee, Standing Somewhere in the Shadows, When God Dips His Love in My Heart, Hold Fast To The Right, Did You Stop to Pray This Morning, Whispering Hope, Will There Be Any Stars in My Crown, Does Jesus Care, Each Ring Of The Hammer, and It Is No Secret. These tracks were recorded for Mac's gospel album, "Beside The Still Waters," released Feb. 12, 1959; however, the label did release an initial single - Each Ring Of The Hammer b/w Did You Stop To Pray This Morning – on March 16, 1959.

MAC WISEMAN recorded this Dot session @ Bradley Film & Recording Studio, Nashville, March 23, 1959. Personnel: Mac Wiseman, vocal; Chet Atkins, rhythm guitar; Ray Edenton, electric guitar/banjo; Joe Zinkan, bass; Morris Palmer, drums; and The Jordanaires, harmony vocals; and Wiseman, producer. Songs: Jimmy Brown The Newsboy, Driftwood On the River, When It's Lamp Lighting Time in the Valley, Little Moses, The Baggage Coach Ahead, The Girl In The Blue Velvet Band, Barbara Allen, I've Got No Use For the Women, The Wreck Of The Old '97, Just Tell Him That You Saw Me, The Preacher and The Bear, and The Wildwood Flower. First single off the session was Jimmy Brown the Newsboy b/w I've Got No Use For the Women, released April 24, 1959, and it proved to be Mac's biggest chart record, first hitting the *Billboard* country chart Aug. 10, and peaked Oct. 26 in the Top Five, charting a total 20 weeks. Randy Wood wasted no time following it up with an album, "Great Folk Ballads," released Aug. 18, 1959.

MAC WISEMAN recorded a special recruiting aid for the U. S. Air Force's public service program *Country Music Time,* in Nashville during 1959, pickin' and singin' Wabash Cannonball, Driftwood On the River and the inspirational number Hold Fast To The Right.

MAC WISEMAN did yet another series of songs for the U.S. Army's *Country Style USA* TV show's season three, recorded in 1959 in Nashville. Sgt. Tom Daniels served as M.C., while Mac sang and played rhythm guitar, adding harmony vocals was Helen McCoy, all under the production hand of Harold Bradley. Songs: Tis Sweet To Be Remembered; Love Letters In the Sand; Keep On the Sunny Side; Goin' Like Wildfire; Shackles And Chains, Blue Doll, Each Ring Of The Hammer, Preacher And The Bear, I'm Drifting Back To Dreamland, The Wildwood Flower, and Stay All Night, Stay a Little Longer, theme.

MAC WISEMAN recorded Dot sessions @ RCA Victor Studio, 1610 Hawkins St., Nashville, on March 14-15, 1960. Personnel: Mac Wiseman, vocals/guitar; Hank Garland, lead guitar; Ray Edenton, rhythm guitar; Pig Robbins, piano; Joe Zinkan, standup bass; Buddy Harman, drums; Harold Bradley, tic-tac bass; The Jordanaires, harmony; and Wiseman, producer. Songs: The Ballad of Davy Crockett, Darling Nellie Gray, The Old Lamplighter, (Hang Down Your Head) Tom Dooley, Old Shep, He's Got the Whole World in His Hands, 16 Tons, The Fool, El Paso, Running Bear, I'm Movin' On, and The Three Bells.

MAC WISEMAN's Dot follow-up album sessions recorded @ Bradley Film & Recording Studio, on May 31, 1960, and June 6, 1960. Personnel: Mac Wiseman, vocals/guitar; Hank Garland, lead guitar; Ray Edenton, rhythm guitar; Pig Robbins, piano; Joe Zinkan, standup bass; Buddy Harman, drums; Harold Bradley, tic-tac bass; The Jordanaires, harmony vocals; and Wiseman, producer. Songs: There's A Star-Spangled Banner Waving Somewhere, Let The Lower Lights Be Burning, and In The Sweet Bye And Bye. A single, There's A Star-Spangled Banner Waving Somewhere b/w Darling Nellie Gray, was released June 9 1960, followed by Dot's folk LP "Mac Wiseman Sings 12 Great Hits," released July 6, 1960. (Dot later included selections in LP, "Mac Wiseman Sings Best-Loved Gospel Hymns," released in June 1961.)

MAC WISEMAN returned to record for the U.S. Army telecast *Country Style U.S.A.* in Nashville, during 1960, backed by Billy Grammer, harmony vocals; Pig Robbins, piano; and Joe Zinkan, bass. Sgt. Tom Shaw was M.C., while Harold Bradley produced. Songs: There's A Star-Spangled Banner Waving Somewhere, Darling Nellie Gray, Bonaparte's Retreat, In The Sweet Bye And Bye, and Stay All Night, Stay a Little Longer.

MAC WISEMAN recorded Dot session @ Bradley Studio, Nashville, on June 13, 1960. Personnel: Mac Wiseman, vocals/guitar; Floyd Cramer, piano; Farris Coursey, drums; Joe Zinkan, bass; The Jordanaires, harmony; and Wiseman, producer. Songs: I Heard My Mother Call My Name in Prayer, Lord I'm Coming Home, Where Is My Boy Tonight, If I Could Hear My Mother Pray Again, Bringing In The Sheaves, and Shall We Gather At the River.

MAC WISEMAN recorded Dot session @ Bradley Studio on Sept. 17, 1960. Personnel: Mac Wiseman, vocals/guitar; Marvin Hughes, piano; Farris Coursey, drums; Joe Zinkan, bass; Earl Scruggs, banjo; Tommy Jackson and Tommy Vaden, fiddles; Ray Edenton, rhythm guitar; and Wiseman, producer. Songs: I Like This Kind of Music, Now That You Have Me, I'm The Talk of The Town, and Glad Rags. First single off the session, Now That You Have Me b/w Glad Rags, released Sept. 26,1960.

MAC WISEMAN recorded a Dot session @ Bradley Studio, during February 1961. Personnel: Mac Wiseman, vocals/guitar; Benny Williams, banjo; and Papa John Gordy's Dixieland Band; with Beasley Smith as producer. Songs: The Prisoner's Song, and There'll Be No Teardrops Tonight.

MAC WISEMAN recorded this Dot session @ Bradley Studio on March 4, 1961. Personnel: Mac Wiseman, vocals/guitar; Hank Garland, lead guitar; Pig Robbins, piano/organ; Joe Zinkan, bass; Buddy Harman, drums; The Jordanaires, harmony; and Wiseman, producer. Songs: Tell Mother I'll Be There, The Beautiful Garden of Prayer, Beautiful Isle of Somewhere, and Peace In The Valley. (These tracks were later on Canaan Records' "Shenandoah Valley Memories," released in the United Kingdom, August 1977.)

MAC WISEMAN conducted a Capitol Records session @ Bradley Studio, on Dec. 20, 1961. Personnel: Mac Wiseman, vocals/guitar; Joe Zinkan, bass; Ray Edenton, rhythm guitar; Benny Williams, mandolin; Joe Drumright, banjo; Chubby Wise and Buddy Spicher, fiddles; Ken Nelson, A&R chief, produced. Songs: Footprints In The Snow, Just Outside, Pistol Packin' Preacher, and What's Gonna Happen To Me? Capitol released Footprints in the Snow b/w Just Outside on Feb. 3, 1962. (Later, Capitol subsidiary label Hilltop included these tracks on its "Mac Wiseman" LP in 1967.)

MAC WISEMAN recorded a Capitol session @ Bradley Film & Recording Studio, on Jan. 17, 1962. Personnel: Mac Wiseman, vocals/guitar; Ray Edenton, bass and tple; Joe Zinkan, standup bass; Buddy Harman, drums; Joe Drumright, banjo; Chubby Wise and Buddy Spicher, fiddles; and Marvin Hughes, producer. Songs: The Ballad Of The Little Pine Box, When The Snowflakes Fall, I'll Remember You Love in My Prayers, and Free From The Old Chain Gang. These tracks were on Capitol's LP "Bluegrass Favorites," released Oct. 20, 1962.

MAC WISEMAN did these Capitol sessions, recorded at Columbia Recording Studio, 804 16th Avenue S., Nashville, on Feb. 9 and 12, 1962. Personnel: Mac Wiseman, vocals/guitar; Joe Zinkan, bass; Ray Edenton, guitar; Benny Williams, vocals/mandolin; Joe Drumright, banjo; Buddy Spicher and Tommy Vaden, fiddles; Buddy Harman, drums; and Marvin Hughes, pianist-producer. Songs: Two More Years, Bluegrass Fiesta, Cotton Fields, Sing Little Birdie, Are You Missing Me, Freight Train, Have a Drink On Me, and Just a Strand From a Yellow Curl.

MAC WISEMAN recorded a Capitol session at Columbia Studio, Nashville, on Sept. 24, 1962. Personnel: Mac Wiseman, vocals/guitar; Joe Zinkan, bass; Buck Trent, banjo; Ray

Edenton, guitar; Buddy Harman, drums; Cecil Brower, fiddle; Maybelle Carter, autoharp/ vocals; Millie Kirkham, Gordon Stoker, Ray Walker, Neal Matthews, harmony; Ken Nelson, producer. Songs: Tis Sweet To Be Remembered, Wildfire, and I Like Good Bluegrass Music. Nelson released I Like Good Bluegrass Music b/w Wildfire as a single on Jan. 12, 1963.

MAC WISEMAN in 1963 elected to perform again for the Armed Forces Radio & TV Service, singing the songs Wildfire and I Like Good Bluegrass Music.

MAC WISEMAN recorded a Capitol session at Columbia Recording Studio, Nashville, on April 12, 1963. Personnel: Mac Wiseman, vocals/guitar; Grady Martin, bass guitar; Ray Edenton, guitar; Junior Huskey, string bass; Buddy Harman, drums; Joe Drumright, banjo; Lew (Childre) Houston, dobro; Benny Williams, mandolin; and Marvin Hughes, producer. Songs: The Scene Of The Crime, Your Best Friend and Me, What a Waste of Good Corn Likker, and When the Moon Comes Over the Mountain. Capitol released the single "Your Best Friend and Me (b/w When the Moon Comes Over the Mountain) on July 20, 1963, a radio hit that charted eight weeks on *Billboard*, starting Sept. 21, peaking at #12 on Oct. 26, 1963.

MAC WISEMAN & The Country Boys recorded "live" at the Newport Folk Festival in Rhode Island, from July 26-28, 1963.   Songs covered included I Wonder How the Old Folks Are At Home, Love Letters In the Sand and Footprints In the Snow. Vanguard Records released these in the album "Country Music & Bluegrass At Newport," on May 9, 1964.

MAC WISEMAN recorded at Columbia Studio, Nashville, a double session, on Feb. 13, 1964. Personnel: Mac Wiseman, vocals/guitar; Ray Edenton (12-string) guitar; Lew Houston, dobro; Donnie Bryant, banjo; (Grover) Shorty Lavender and Tommy Jackson, fiddles; (Charles Ray) Charlie McCoy, harmonica; Joe Zinkan, bass; Buddy Harman, drums; and Marvin Hughes, pianist-producer. Songs: Mother Knows Best, Old Pair Of Shoes, The Mole, If I Could Live That Way, Heads You Win (Tails I Lose), Bluegrass Music's Really Gone To Town, Dark Hollow, and Brother Joe. First single off the Capitol Records' session: Old Pair of Shoes b/w Heads You Win (Tails I Lose), released Aug. 29, 1964.

MAC WISEMAN returned to Columbia Studio, on Valentine's Day, Feb. 14, 1964, adding Marion Worth to the line-up for a duet on Katie Waits For Me. Additional songs cut: Sweet Summer's Gone Away, Brush It Off (It's All in Your Mind), and They're All Going Home But Me. On July 29, 2003, Music Mill Records released these previously unissued tracks as part of Mac Wiseman's album "Lost Session."

MAC WISEMAN recorded at the RCA Victor-Canada Studio in Montreal, Quebec, during July 1965. Personnel: Mac Wiseman, vocals; Ronald McMinn, lead guitar; Lloyd Grant, banjo; Don O'Neil, mandolin; Ward Allen, fiddle; Papa Joe Brown, standup bass; with Wiseman and George Taylor co-producing. Songs: Bringing Mary Home, Maple Sugar Sweetheart, Legend Of The Irish Rebel, Ghost of Bras D'Or, Prince Edward Island Is Heaven For Me, What a Waste of Good Corn Likker, My Nova Scotia Home, When It's Apple Blossom Time in Annapolis Valley, My Molly Bawn, Pistol Packin' Preacher, Atlantic Lullaby, My Cape Breton Home. Canada's subsidiary label Sparton released the first single, The Legend Of The Irish Rebel b/w The Ghost Of Bras D'Or, in December 1965 in Canada. Released Stateside under Mac's new Wise Records banner, the 1965 album was titled "Mac Wiseman At The Toronto Horseshoe Club" (though it wasn't recorded there, but sponsored by the club's owner). A U.S. single, Bringing Mary Home b/w Maple Sugar Sweetheart, was released in June 1966.

MAC WISEMAN recorded for Rural Rhythm Records at a studio in Akron, OH, during April 1966. Personnel included Mac Wiseman, vocals/rhythm guitar; Rudy Thacker, guitar; Peggy Peterson, dobro; others unknown; all produced by Lee Sutton. Songs: Wreck Of The Old '97, Little Mohee, Corinne Corinna, I'm Sittin' On Top Of The World, How Many Biscuits Can You Eat, When They Ring Them Golden Bells, I Saw Your Face In The Moon, I'll Be All Smiles Tonight, Mary Of The Wild Moor, Just Over In Gloryland, The Waltz You Saved For Me, My Grandfather's Clock, The Rovin' Gambler, Little Blossom, There's More Pretty Girls Than One, Sourwood Mountain, Black Sheep, Bringing In The Georgia Mail, Turkey In the Straw, Little Pal, A Picture From Life's Other Side, Midnight Special, Tramp On The Street and Precious Memories. These resulted in a Rural Rhythm double LP, "Mac Wiseman Sings Old-Time Country Favorites," released in 1966.

MAC WISEMAN recorded independently for Dot Records at Columbia Studio, Nashville, May 1, 1966. Personnel: Unknown. Bonnie Guitar (Buckingham) produced this session in liaison with Wiseman. Songs: The Letter That Never Came, The Wreck Of The C&O Number Five, Black Sheep, Legend Of The Haunted Woods, Put My Little Shoes Away, The Letter Edged In Black, The Ballad Of The Lawson Family, The East Bound Train, My Mother's Old Sunbonnet, May I Sleep In Your Barn Tonight Mister, and Molly Bawn. Under a subsidiary label, Hamilton Records, "Songs Of The Dear Old Days," was released in 1966.

MAC WISEMAN recorded another bluegrass album for Dot at Columbia Studio, in May 1966. Personnel: Mac Wiseman, vocals/guitar; (Robert) Bobby Osborne, mandolin/ vocals; (Roland) Sonny Osborne, banjo; Tommy Jackson, fiddle; Joe Zinkan, bass; Willie Ackerman, drums; Wiseman self-produced. Songs: Midnight Special, We Live In Two Different Worlds, The Tragic Romance, I'll Be All Smiles Tonight, This Is Where I Came In, You're The Best Of All The Leading Brands, Don't Make Me Go To Bed And I'll Be Good, The Bluebirds Are Singing For Me, New Black Suit, How Lonely Can You Get, Darling Little Joe, A Million, Million Girls, Since The Day You Went Away. Dot released the subsequent double LP, "Mac Wiseman Bluegrass," on Aug. 22, 1966.

MAC WISEMAN again recorded independently for Dot at Columbia Studio, Nashville in May 1966. Personnel: Mac Wiseman, vocals/guitar; Bob Moore, bass; Kelso Herston, guitar; (Roddis) Pete Drake, steel guitar; Pig Robbins, piano; Buddy Harman, drums; and Bonnie Guitar producing. Songs: Little Bird, White Silver Sands, Just a Baby's Prayer At Twilight, When It's Springtime In The Rockies, You're the Only Star In My Blue Heaven, A Maiden's Prayer, At Rainbow's End, This Is Where I Came In, Lonely City Park, Me and Your Memory, The Isle of Capri, Forever And Ever. First single off session, White Silver Sands b/w Just a Baby's Prayer At Twilight, released July 9, 1966. Dot's album "Mac Wiseman – A Master At Work" was released Aug. 22, 1966.

MAC WISEMAN recorded at Cowboy Jack Clement's home studio, 3102 Belmont Blvd., Nashville, May 3, 1968. Personnel: Mac Wiseman, vocals; other musicians unknown; co-produced by Jack Henderson and Jack Clement. Songs: Got Leavin' On Her Mind, and She Simply Left. MGM Records released Got Leavin' On Her Mind b/w She Simply Left, Sept. 21, 1968, and the single charted starting Nov. 9, seven weeks, stalling at #54 on *Billboard's* country chart.

MAC WISEMAN recorded at Jack Clement's studio on June 29, 1969, as produced by Cowboy Jack, for presentation to RCA Records. Song: The Things You Have Turned To. RCA released The Things You Have Turned To, July 28, 1970, to radio.

MAC WISEMAN recorded at Jack Clement's studio, on Oct. 1, 1969. Cowboy Jack produced the session. Songs: Johnny's Cash and Charley's Pride b/w Put My Little Shoes Away. The resulting RCA single was released later in October 1969. Johnny's Cash and Charley's Pride entered *Billboard's* country chart Dec 6, 1969, peaking at #38 during its nine weeks' charting.

MAC WISEMAN, signed to RCA, recorded at the RCA Victor Studio, 800 17th Avenue South, Nashville, on Feb. 2-5 1970. Personnel: Mac Wiseman, vocals; Billy Grammer, guitar; Lloyd Green and Ben Keith (Schaeufele), steel guitars; Kenny Buttrey, drums; Billy Sanford, bass guitar; Pig Robbins and Jerry Smith, piano; Williams Irwin, organ; Junior Huskey, string bass; Buddy Spicher and Johnny Gimble, fiddles; Bobby Thompson, banjo/ guitar; and Cowboy Jack Clement produced. Songs: Crystal Chandelier; All I Have To Offer You Is Me; Wrinkled, Crinkled, Wadded Dollar Bill; Ring of Fire; Me and Bobby McGee; The Ballad Of A Teenage Queen; Guess Things Happen That Way; The Day The World Stood Still; The Easy Part's Over; Big River; and The Little Folks. RCA released the single Me & Bobby McGee b/w Ring of Fire on March 14, 1970, followed by the Wiseman-Clement concept LP "Johnnie's Cash & Charlie's (sic) Pride," which boasted a mix of acoustic and electric instruments, as well as a Hawaiian steel guitar.

MAC WISEMAN recorded at RCA Studio, Nashville, on Jan. 28, 1971 (with over-dubs Feb. 5 and March 10). Personnel: Mac Wiseman, vocals; Jack Clement, guitar; Billy Grammer, guitar; Buck (Josh) Graves, dobro; Jerry Byrd, steel guitar; Ben Keith, steel guitar/ dobro; Henry Strzelecki, bass; Pig Robbins, piano; Williams Irvin, organ; Junior Huskey, bass; Willie Ackerman, drums; Jack Clement, producer. Song: Sweet Sadness. RCA single, Sweet Sadness, released July 6, 1971.

LESTER FLATT & MAC WISEMAN recorded together at RCA Studio, Nashville, March 15-17, 1971. Personnel: Mac Wiseman, vocals; Lester Flatt, vocals; Howard Johnson, guitar; Josh Graves, dobro; Vic Jordan and Haskel McCormick, banjos; Roland White, mandolin; Paul Warren and Howdy Forrester, fiddles; Pig Robbins, piano; English Jake Tullock, string bass; Jerry Carrigan, drums; Jack Clement and Bob Ferguson, co-producers. Songs: We'll Meet Again Sweetheart, The Bluebirds Are Singing For Me, How Lonely Can You Get, Will You Be Loving Another Man, Sweetheart You Done Me Wrong, Homestead On the Farm, Now That You Have Me, Jimmy Brown The Newsboy, I'll Never Love Another, Your Love Is Like a Flower, You're The Best Of All The Leading Brands, and Special. RCA initially released Will You Be Loving Another Man b/w Jimmy Brown The Newsboy, on May 1, 1971. Their album, "Lester 'N' Mac" was released in June 1971. Incidentally, their joint effort, "Lester 'N' Mac," became the first Bluegrass album to make *Billboard* magazine's Top 100 list.

MAC WISEMAN recorded "live" promoting his Renfro Valley Bluegrass Festival at the historic Renfro Valley Barn Dance, Old U.S. Hwy 25, Mount Vernon, KY, in 1971. Personnel: Mac Wiseman, vocals/guitar; Lester Flatt, vocals/guitar; Harley Gabbard and Josh Graves, dobros; Haskel McCormick and Billy Edwards, banjos; Roland White, Herschel Sizemore and John Palmer, mandolins; Chubby Wise, Howdy Forrester, Paul Warren, Tater Tate, and Joe Greene, fiddles; Shenandoah Valley Cut-Ups; and Carlton Haney, emcee. Songs: Wabash Cannonball, Homestead On The Farm, Me & Bobby McGee, Give Me Liberty, Four Walls Around Me, I'll Still Writer Your Name In the Sand, The Bluebirds Are Singing For Me, Sweetheart You Done Me Wrong, I'll Be All Smiles Tonight, Will You Be Loving Another Man, Are You Washed In the Blood, Jimmy Brown The Newsboy, and The Prisoner's Song. Mac also addressed the crowd with a History Of Bluegrass Music, and Carlton Haney publicly interviewed both Wiseman and Flatt. Rural Rhythm Records, coordinating with producer Ronnie Reno, released a CD "Mac Wiseman – Bluegrass 1971" on March 30, 2010, which charted *Billboard* in April, peaking at #12. (Reno also released their set as a DVD on Blue Highways in 2010.)

LESTER FLATT & MAC WISEMAN reunited to record at RCA Studio on Oct. 19-20, 1971. Personnel: Lester Flatt, vocals; Mac Wiseman, vocals; Howard Johnson, guitar; Josh Graves, dobro; Haskel McCormick, banjo; Roland White, mandolin; Howdy Forrester and Paul Warren, fiddles; Pig Robbins, piano; Jerry Carrigan, drums; Don Smith, bass; Bob Ferguson and Jack Clement, co-produced. Clement's subsequent sessions featured players Chuck Cochran, piano; Joe Allen, string bass; Danny Flowers, harmonica; and James Isbell, drums, for over-dubbing. Songs: I'll Stay Around, Salty Dog Blues, Just a Strand From a Yellow Curl, Mama and Daddy's Little Girl, Blue Ridge Mountain Home, Me And Your Memory, Waiting For The Boys To Come Home, On The Southbound, I'm Waiting To Hear You Call Me Darling, Are You Coming Back To Me, When You Are Lonely, You Can't Trust a Friend Anymore, I'll Still Write Your Name in The Sand, I'd Rather Live By The Side Of The Road, and Sing Little Birdie. First single off these sessions was Salty Dog Blues b/w Mama and Daddy's Little Girl, released Feb 26, 1972.

MAC WISEMAN recorded at RCA Studio, on May 18, 1972 for a solo project. Personnel: Mac Wiseman, vocals; Joe Allen bass; Bob McDill, guitar; Lloyd Green, steel guitar; James Colvard, bass/guitar; Allen Reynolds, guitar; Chuck Cochran, piano; James Isbell, drums; Buddy Spicher, fiddle; Allen Reynolds and Bob McDill co-produced. Songs: Colours, Song Of The Wildwood, At The Crossing, Let Time Be Your Friend, and On Susan's Floor. RCA's first single from the session - On Susan's Floor b/w Song Of The Wildwood - released July 17, 1972.

MAC WISEMAN recorded at RCA Studio, Nashville, on Sept. 27, 1972. Personnel: Mac Wiseman, vocals; Claude Phelps, guitar; Eddie Adcock, banjo; Josh Graves, dobro; Buddy Spicher, fiddle; Joe Allen, bass; Kenny Malone, drums; Allen Reynolds and Bob McDill co-produced. Songs: Let's All Go Down To The River, Sunny Side Of The Mountain, and Eight More Miles To Louisville.

MAC WISEMAN at RCA Studio, Nashville, on Nov. 8, 1972. Personnel: Mac Wiseman, vocals; Claude Phelps, guitar; Bobby Thompson, guitar/banjo; Josh Graves, dobro; Buddy Spicher, fiddle; Joe Allen, bass; Kenny Malone, drums; Bob McDill and Allen Reynolds co-produced. Songs: Keep On The Sunny Side, Will The Circle Be Unbroken, The Tragic Romance, It Rains Just The Same in Missouri, The City Of New Orleans, and Catfish John. RCA released It Rains Just the Same in Missouri b/w Keep On The Sunny Side, as a single on Nov. 17, 1973.

MAC WISEMAN back in RCA Studios on June 20, 1973, to record a single song. Personnel: Mac Wiseman, vocals; Reggie Young, guitar; James Colvard, guitar; Bobby Thompson, banjo; Chuck Cochran, piano; Jackie Phelps, guitar; Steve Shaffer, bass; James Isbell, drums; Buddy Spicher, fiddle; and Jack Clement produced. Song: You Can't Go In The Red Playin' Bluegrass. An over-dub session on June 25, 1973, recalled Chuck Cochran, Bobby Thompson and Steve Shaffer, to play additional parts.

LESTER FLATT & MAC WISEMAN returned to the RCA Studio, Nashville, on July 5, 1973. Personnel: Lester Flatt, vocals/guitar; Mac Wiseman, vocals/guitar; Ray Edenton, guitar; Charlie Nixon, dobro; Josh Graves, resonator guitar; Haskel McCormick, banjo; Roland White and Marty Stuart, mandolins; Paul Warren and Howdy Forrester, fiddles; Jerry Carrigan and Robby Osborne, drums; Johnny Johnson and Don Smith, basses; Jimmy Riddle, harmonica; and Bob Ferguson and Jack Clement co-producers. Songs: Over The Hill To The Poor House, Blue Ridge Mountain Home, When My Blue Moon Turns To Gold Again, The Girl I Love Don't Pay Me No Mind, I'll Go Steppin' Too, There Are More Pretty Girls Than One, Ain't Nobody Gonna Miss Me (When I'm Gone), I'm a Stranger in This World, Tis Sweet To Be Remembered, and Waiting For The Boys To Come Home. RCA's follow-up Flatt & Wiseman album was titled "Over The Hills To The Poorhouse," released in 1973.

MAC WISEMAN recorded at RCA Studio, on March 13, 1974. Personnel: Mac Wiseman, vocals; Dave Kirby, guitar; Leon Rhodes, bass; Bobby Thompson, guitar; Stu Basore, steel guitar; Johnny Gimble, fiddle; Bunky Keels, piano; Joe Allen, bass; Larrie Londin, drums; and Ray Pennington, producer. Songs: It Comes and Goes, The Dixie Hummer, and I've Got To Catch That Train. RCA released It Comes And Goes b/w I've Got To Catch That Train as a single May 11, 1974.

MAC WISEMAN recorded an independent session at Gusto Recording Studio, 3557 Dickerson Road, suburban Madison, TN, in 1974. Personnel: Mac Wiseman, vocals/rhythm guitar; Marty Stuart, mandolin; Bobby Thompson, banjo; Kenny Ingram, banjo; Buddy Spicher, fiddle; Josh Graves, dobro; Junior Huskey, bass; and Wiseman produced. Songs: Jimmy Brown The Newsboy, Goin' Like Wildfire, I Saw Your Face In The Moon, I Still Write Your Name In The Sand, Barbara Allen, The Prisoner's Song, Sweeter Than The Flowers, Johnny's Cash And Charley's Pride, 18 Wheels A-Hummin', Wabash Cannonball, Don't Make Me Go To Be And I'll Be Good, Put My Little Shoes Away, I Wonder How The Old Folks Are At Home, I Haven't Seen Mary In Years, The Waltz You Saved For Me, Where Is My Boy Tonight, I Heard My Mother Call My Name In Prayer, Poison Love, Love Letters In the Sand, Bringing Mary Home, She's Got Leavin' On Her Mind, Tis Sweet To Be Remembered, Rocky Top, My Baby's Gone, Your Best Friend and Me, Home Sweet Home, Christmas Time's A-Comin', and The Girl In The Blue Velvet Band. Starday Records leased some tracks to produce its "16 Greatest Bluegrass Hits," released in 1977, while Gusto's album "20 Bluegrass Originals," was issued in 1978.

MAC WISEMAN with The Shenandoah Cut-Ups recorded at Jewel Recording Studio, 1594 Kinney Ave., Cincinnati, OH, in 1975. Personnel: Mac Wiseman, vocals/rhythm guitar; Tommy Boyd, dobro; Billy Edwards, banjo; Buddy Griffin, fiddle/autoharp; Tater Tate, fiddle; Jeff Terflinger, mandolin; John Palmer, string bass; and co-produced by Fred Bartenstein and Lou Ukelson. Songs: Crazy Blues, Knoxville Girl, I Haven't Got the Right To Love You, Goin' To See My Baby, Footprints In The Snow, The Little White Church, Georgia Waltz, Don't Let Your Sweet Love Die, When The Roses Bloom Again, The Black Sheep, Let Me Borrow Your Heart, What a Waste of Good Corn Likker, The Letter Edged in Black, Fireball Mail, Reveille Time in Heaven, The Girl Of My Dreams, Fire In My Heart, Shackles and Chains, Hills Of Roane County, You Can't Judge a Book (By Its Cover), Mary Of The Wild Moor, Each Ring Of The Hammer, My Little Home In Tennessee, and Four Walls Around Me. Vetco Records released its "New Traditions, Volume I" and "New Traditions, Volume II" double albums during 1975.

MAC WISEMAN, after signing with CMH Records, recorded at the Arthur Smith Studio, 5457 Old Monroe Road, Charlotte, NC, in 1976. Personnel: Mac Wiseman, vocals/rhythm guitar; Arthur Smith, guitar/dobro/fiddle/mandolin; Clay Smith, rhythm guitar; Tater Tate, fiddle; Billy Edwards, banjo; John Palmer, bass; David Brakefield, drums; and Arthur (Guitar Boogie) Smith produced. Songs: Little Blossom, Love Letters In the Sand,

I've Got No Use For The Women, Dark Hollow, The Wreck of the Old '97, May I Sleep In Your Barn Tonight Mister, Ballad Of The Lawson Family, Bringing Mary Home, The Girl In The Blue Velvet Band, I Wonder How The Old Folks Are At Home, Jimmy Brown The Newsboy, I'll Be All Smiles Tonight, Remembering, The Little Box Of Pine, These Hands, The Baggage Coach Ahead, Tis Sweet To Be Remembered, I'll Still Write Your Name In The Sand, Dreaming Of a Little Cabin, and Six More Miles. CMH released its set "The Mac Wiseman Story" in 1976.

MAC WISEMAN recorded again at the Arthur Smith Studio in Charlotte, also in 1976, for CMH. Personnel: Mac Wiseman, vocals/rhythm guitar; Arthur Smith, guitar/dobro/ fiddle/mandolin; Clay Smith, rhythm guitar; Tater Tate, fiddle; Billy Edwards, banjo; John Palmer, bass; David Brakefield, drums; Arthur Smith again produced. Songs: I'll Sail My Ship Alone, Don't Be Angry, The Green Light, All For the Love Of a Girl, My Baby's Gone, I Wonder Where You Are Tonight, I Love You a Thousand Ways, Flesh and Blood, Me & Bobby McGee, Mother The Queen Of My Heart, They'll Never Take Her Love From Me. CMH's Mac Wiseman LP "Country Music Memories" was issued in late 1976.

MAC WISEMAN was not expecting this "live" reproduction being recorded during a concert in Nova Scotia, Canada, Dec. 12, 1976. Performing with Wiseman were pick-up musicians Vic Mullen, Eva Fogarty, Ralph Vidito, and Dale Wood, while Wendell E. Simm credited himself as producer. Songs: Dueling Banjos, Wabash Cannonball, I Wonder How The Old Folks Are At Home, Me And Bobby McGee, The Prisoner's Song, They'll Never Take Her Love From Me, Jimmy Brown The Newsboy, Footprints In The Snow, Catfish John, Put My Little Shoes Away, Eight More Miles To Louisville, Keep On the Sunny Side, and Will The Circle Be Unbroken. A label ID'd as Country Road issued this Canadian LP in 1982.

MAC WISEMAN recorded at Arthur Smith Studio, Charlotte, in 1977. Personnel: Mac Wiseman, vocals/rhythm guitar; Arthur Smith, dobro/mandolin/fiddle; Clay Smith, acoustic guitar; Eddie Adcock, banjo; Jim Buchanan, fiddle; Rob Thorne, drums; Arthur Smith served as producer. Songs: Cotton Jenny, Rainy Day People, Summertime Dream, For Loving Me, Steel Rail Blues, Ribbon Of Darkness, The House You Live In, Early Morning Rain, Old Dan's Records, and Sundown. This fulfilled CMH's Martin Haerle's wish for a Gordon Lightfoot tribute, released as "Mac Wiseman Sings Gordon Lightfoot" on Nov. 15, 1977.

MAC WISEMAN recorded at Arthur Smith Studio, Charlotte, probably early in 1982, though no date given. Apart from Mac Wiseman on vocals and rhythm guitar, and no doubt Arthur and Clay Smith supplying back up, no other players are cited. Produced by Arthur Smith. Songs: In The Pines, Did She Mention My Name, The House Of The Rising Sun, and Ida Red. CMH issued "Mac Wiseman Bluegrass – Greatest Bluegrass Hits," on Nov. 12, 1982; while tracks were incorporated by CMH in its collection "The Great Stars Of Bluegrass Music: 30 Spectacular Performances," also released in 1982.

MAC WISEMAN recorded at Arthur Smith Studio in 1977, a single track, on Albert Brumley's classic Dreaming Of A Little Cabin, which Mac originally cut in 1952. CMH included this Smith-produced gem in its "Country Gospel Collection," released in 1978.

MAC WISEMAN recorded at Ironside Recording Studio in Nashville, during December 1977, with producer Bob Millsap for Churchill Records. No information on musicians. Songs: Never Goin' Back Again, and Goodbye Mexico Rose. Churchill released these as a single in February 1978, and it charted *Billboard's* country chart on March 18, 1978, stalling at #78.

MAC WISEMAN returned to Ironside Studio in late 1978. Bob Millsap produced a trio of tunes, though names of the participating players are unknown. Songs: Dancing Bear, Scotch And Soda, and Me And The Boys. Churchill's single - Scotch And Soda (b/w Dancing Bear) - spent three weeks on *Billboard's* chart, starting July 7, 1979, peaking at #88. Me And The Boys went unissued.

WOODY HERMAN and MAC WISEMAN were teamed for a session at The Wax Works, a Nashville studio, in January 1979. Both artists blended their vocals on the old Gene Austin chestnut My Blue Heaven b/w (a combined) If I Could Be With You, and It Must Be True, released by Churchill as a single in March 1979. Produced by Bob Millsap, their single charted *Billboard* on May 12, 1979, holding steady four weeks, peaking at #69.

MAC WISEMAN recorded a final Churchill session at Ironside Studio, also in January 1979, and again a produced by Bob Millsap. These solo performances consisted of Two Hundred Dollars, and 45's-And-8x10's, ballads that went unissued (until Bear Family Records reprised them for Wiseman retrospectives).

THE OSBORNE BROTHERS & MAC WISEMAN joined forces for CMH, recording at the Hilltop Recording Studio, 902 Due West Ave., Madison TN, on Jan. 31, and Feb. 1, 1979. Personnel: Bobby Osborne, vocals, mandolin; Sonny Osborne, vocals and banjo, Mac Wiseman, vocals and guitar; Ray Edenton, guitar; Josh Graves and Jerry Douglas, dobros; Benny Birchfield, harmony and tenor guitar; Wynn Osborne, banjo; Blaine Sprouse and Buddy Spicher, fiddles; Jimmy Brock, string bass; and Robby Osborne, drums; Sonny Osborne, produced the sessions. Songs: Keep On The Sunny Side, Old Brush Arbors, Mountain Fever, Tis Sweet To Be Remembered, and I've Always Wanted To Sing in Renfro Valley. These songs and others recorded later comprised the CMH compilation "The Essential Bluegrass Album – Osborne Brothers & Mac Wiseman," released Aug. 1, 1979.

OSBORNE BROTHERS & MAC WISEMAN blended their talents again at Hilltop Studio, on March 15, 1979. Personnel: Mac Wiseman, vocals/rhythm guitar; Bobby Osborne, vocals/mandolin; Sonny Osborne, vocals/banjo; Benny Birchfield, vocals/tenor guitar; Ray Edenton, guitar; Josh Graves and Jerry Douglas, dobros; Wynn Osborne, banjo; Blaine Sprouse and Buddy Spicher, fiddles; Robby Osborne, drums; Jimmy Brock, string bass; Sonny Osborne produced. Songs: Family Bible, Poison Love, Take Me Back To Renfro Valley, Shenandoah Waltz, Pins and Needles, The Bluebirds Are Singing For Me. Don't Let Your Sweet Love Die, and Travelin' This Lonesome Road.

OSBORNE BROTHERS & MAC WISEMAN recorded for CMH Records at Hiltop Studio, on April 19, 1979. Personnel: Mac Wiseman, vocals/rhythm guitar; Bobby Osborne, vocals/mandolin; Sonny Osborne, vocals/banjo; Benny Birchfield, vocals/tenor guitar; Ray Edenton, guitar; Josh Graves and Jerry Douglas, dobros; Wynn Osborne, banjo; Blaine Sprouse and Buddy Spicher, fiddles; Robby Osborne, drums; Jimmy Brock, string bass; and Sonny Osborne produced. Songs: You're The Girl Of My Dreams, It's Goodbye And So Long To You, I'll Still Write Your Name in The Sand, Are You Coming Back To Me, and I Wonder How The Old Folks Are At Home.

OSBORNE BROTHERS & MAC WISEMAN conduct a CMH session at Hilltop Studio, on April 25, 1979. Personnel: Mac Wiseman, vocals/rhythm guitar; Bobby Osborne, vocals/mandolin; Sonny Osborne, vocals/banjo; Benny Birchfield, vocals/tenor guitar; Ray Edenton, guitar; Josh Graves and Jerry Douglas, dobros; Wynn Osborne, banjo; Blaine Sprouse and Buddy Spicher, fiddles; Robby Osborne, drums; Jimmy Brock, string bass; and

Sonny Osborne produced. Songs: Midnight Flyer, Shackles And Chains, and I'm A Stranger Here. A CMH single, Shackles And Chains b/w Midnight Flyer, charted *Billboard's* country chart Oct. 13, 1979, lasting three weeks on the list, then dropping off at #95.

OSBORNE BROS. & MAC WISEMAN reteamed for CMH at Hilltop Studio on May 8, 1979. Personnel: Mac Wiseman, vocals/rhythm guitar; Bobby Osborne, vocals/mandolin; Sonny Osborne, vocals/banjo; Benny Birchfield, vocals/tenor guitar; Ray Edenton, guitar; Josh Graves and Jerry Douglas, dobros; Wynn Osborne, banjo; Blaine Sprouse and Buddy Spicher, fiddles; Robby Osborne, drums; Jimmy Brock, string bass; and Sonny Osborne producing. Songs: Four Walls Around Me, Mother Maybelle (song tribute), and Little White Church. CMH's album "The World's Greatest Bluegrass Bands: 32 Great Performances, Volume 2," was released in 1979, incorporating Osborne/Wiseman collaborations.

MAC WISEMAN visited Dallas, Texas, to recruit Western Swing artist-musicians for a CMH concept album saluting that uniquely Lone Star State music style. He recorded Oct. 16-18, 1979 at Sumet-Bernet- Sound Studios, utilizing the engineering guidance of Bob Sullivan. Personnel: Mac Wiseman, vocals/rhythm guitar; Johnny Gimble, fiddle/mandolin; Jim Belken, fiddle; Will T. Briggs Jr., saxophone; Eldon Shamblin, lead guitar; Dick Gimble, bass; Curly Hollingsworth, keyboards; Bill Mounce, drums; Herb Remington, steel guitar; Bill Stone, trumpet; Johnny Gimble and Wiseman were co-producers. Songs: Bubbles In My Beer, Slippin' Around, I Wish I Had Never Seen Sunshine, Home in San Antone, My Mary, No Letter Today, Yesterday's Girl, Love Letters In the Sand, I Love You Because, Time Changes Everything, Worried Mind, Drivin' Nails In My Coffin, It Makes No Difference Now, Waltz Across Texas, Divorce Me C.O.D., Born To Lose, I Wonder How The Old Folks Are At Home, The Wild Side of Life, Oklahoma Hills, (Remember Me) I'm The One Who Loves You, Live And Let Live, and One Has My Name. CMH's masterful double album, "Songs That Made The Juke Box Play," was released Feb. 1, 1980.

MAC WISEMAN & CHUBBY WISE collaborated for a project at Gilley's, 1135 South Lamar, Dallas, TX, in 1982. Personnel: Mac Wiseman, vocals/rhythm guitar; Chubby Wise, fiddle; Herb Remington, steel guitar; Curly Hollingsworth, piano; Johnny Gimble, fiddle; and Johnny Gimble also served as producer. Songs: Give Me My Smokies & The Tennessee Waltz, The Maiden's Prayer, The Waltz You Saved For Me, The Wreck of the Old '97, The Prisoner's Song, Carroll County Blues; Put My Little Shoes Away, I Wonder How The Old Folks Are At Home, Footprints In The Snow, Shackles And Chains, The Wabash Cannonball, Driftwood On The River, Catfish John, Lee Highway, Faded Love, Westphalia Waltz, It Rains Just the Same In Missouri, Liberty, Mary Linda, Pretty Little Widder, Kind Of Love, Cacklin' Hen, and How Great Thou Art. The cuts comprised the Gilley Records' album "Mac Wiseman & Chubby Wise," released Oct. 5, 1982. (Mac later re-released these Dec. 4, 2001, on his own Wise Records' CD "Mac Wiseman & Chubby Wise.")

MERLE TRAVIS' CMH concept double LP, "The Clayton McMichen Story," was produced at John Wagner Productions Studio in Albuquerque, New Mexico, in 1982. Personnel included Merle Travis, vocals and guitars; Mac Wiseman, vocals and rhythm guitar; Joe Maphis, vocals and lead guitar; Jackson D. Kane, bass; and Red Herron, fiddle. Songs: Give The Fiddler a Dram, In The Pines, Fire On The Mountain, Fifty Years ago Waltz, Hell Broke Loose in Georgia, Trouble In Mind, McMichen's Reel, Peach Pickin' Time In Georgia, Limehouse Blues, The Convict And The Rose, Carroll County Blues, The House Of The Rising Sun, Dreamy Georgiana Moon, I'm Looking Over a Four-Leaf Clover, Ida Red, Waitin' For The Robert E. Lee, Rock Jenny Rock, Arkansas Traveler, Bile 'Dem Cabbage Down, In The Blue Hills Of Virginia, Back To Old Smoky Mountain, Darktown Strutters'

Ball, Sweet Georgia Brown, They Cut Down The Old Pine Tree, Goodnight Waltz, Farewell Blues, and Sweet Bunch of Daisies. CMH released "The Clayton McMichen Story" album in 1982. (It was released Sept. 9, 1988 in cassette form by CMH, and in CD format in "The Mac Wiseman Story," via Wise Records, on Feb. 14, 2012.)

MAC WISEMAN songs released by Columbia Records' Special Products in affiliation with Music Mill and Madacy Music. Selections: If Teardrops Were Pennies, Don't Make Me Go To Bed (And I'll Be Good), You Are My Sunshine, The Mansion On the Hill, Let's Say Goodbye Like We Said Hello, Maple On the Hill, A Picture From Life's Other Side, Tramp On The Street, Remembering, and Blues In My Mind. Released as Columbia Special Products set "If Teardrops Were Pennies" in 1983.

MAC WISEMAN recorded for MCA-Dot Records, probably during late 1985 in Nashville. Producer: Tompall Glaser. Songs: Once More With Feeling, Old Country Songs, Lean On Me, How Lonely Can You Get, Countin' Pennies, You're The Best Of All The Leading Brands, Ramblin' Round, A Rose With No Thorns, Now That You Have Me (You Don't Want Me), and I'll Do It All Over Again. These were for the album "Mac Wiseman," released by MCA-Dot in 1986.

MAC WISEMAN recorded for CMH at Home Place Studio, Nashville, in 1989. Personnel: Mac Wiseman, vocals/rhythm guitar; Jim Campbell, fiddle; Jesse McReynolds, mandolin; The Masters: Kenny Baker, fiddle; Josh Graves, dobro; Eddie Adcock, banjo/guitar; and The Masterettes: Martha Adcock, rhythm guitar; and Missy Raines, string bass; co-produced by Mac Wiseman and Billy Troy. Songs: Don't Let Your Deal Go Down, Train 45, The Little Rosewood Casket, Poor Ellen Smith, Kentucky, Salty Dog Blues, Dust On The Bible, Cryin' Heart Blues, Old Camp Meeting Time, It's Mighty Dark To Travel, Streamlined Cannonball, Red Rocking Chair, Doin' My Time, I'm Just Here To Get My Baby Out Of Jail, Wait For the Light To Shine, The Lonely Mound of Clay, Short Life of Trouble, I'm Using My Bible For a Road Map, Don't Give Your Heart To a Rambler, How Mountain Girls Can Love, Sailor On the Deep Blue Sea, and Light At The River. The CD set was released as "Grassroots To Bluegrass," on April 6, 1990. Subsequently, it earned Mac Wiseman his first Grammy nomination for best album of the year.

MAC WISEMAN recorded a follow-up session for CMH in early 1990, utilizing many of the same musicians. Songs: I'm On My Way Home, Roll In My Sweet Baby's Arms, The Last Letter, and I Love You So Much It Hurts.

MAC WISEMAN recorded tracks for a holiday album in 1994, in Nashville. Songs: Up On The House Top, It Came Upon a Midnight Clear, Silent Night, Go Tell It On The Mountain, Away In a Manger, We Wish You a Merry Christmas, The First Noel, and oddly enough Too-Ra-Loo-Ra-Loo-Ral (That's An Irish Lullaby). No information on personnel engaged for this session. An independent firm, Power Pak, issued "Number One Christmas," during the Yule season 1994. (Apparently selected tracks were part of a True Value Hardware presentation *True Value Happy Holidays, Volume 36,* released in 2001.)

DEL McCOURY, DOC WATSON & MAC WISEMAN were featured as The GrooveGrass Boyz for a Sugar Hill recording in Nashville during 1998. The main men: Del McCoury, vocals/guitar; (Arthel) Doc Watson, vocals/guitar; Mac Wiseman, vocals/rhythm guitar; Scott Rouse, producer. Songs: Little Green Valley, Old Account, Speak To Me Little Darlin', There's a New Moon Over My Shoulder, Beauty Of My Dreams, I'll Sail My Ship Alone, When a Soldier Knocks (And Finds Nobody Home), Live and Let Live, I've Endured,

Talk Of the Town, Black Mountain Rag, I Wonder Where You Are Tonight, and More Pretty Girls Than One. This Sugar Hill album "Del, Doc & Mac" was released Oct. 20, 1998.

THE GROOVEGRASS BOYZ (DEL McCOURY, DOC WATSON & MAC WISE-MAN), featuring Del McCoury's Band, assembled in 1998 in Nashville for a holiday album. Personnel: Del McCoury, vocals/guitar; Doc Watson, vocals/acoustic guitar; Mac Wiseman, vocals/rhythm guitar; Cyndi Wheeler, vocals; Tim O'Brien, vocals/multi-instrumentals; Sonny Osborne, vocals; Bobby Osborne, vocals; Ronnie McCoury, vocals/mandolin; Jason Carter, fiddle; Mike Bub, bass; Rob McCoury, banjo; Jerry Douglas, dobro; Scott Rouse, vocals/guitar; Terry Eldredge, guitar; Gene Wooten, dobro; and Scott Rouse, producer. Songs (featuring Mac): Our 12 Days of Christmas, Bluegrass Christmas, Christmas Time's A-Comin', Silent Night, Christmas Memories (written by Mac Wiseman). Released on the album "Christmas On The Mountain – A Bluegrass Christmas," distributed by Universal South Records during fall 2002.

MAC WISEMAN's Wise label recorded a series of songs for Madacy/Music Mills sessions in Nashville, 2001. Personnel: Mac Wiseman, vocals/guitar; Mark Casstevens, acoustic guitar; Tom Brumley, steel guitar; Eddie Adcock, banjo; Josh Graves, dobro; Buddy Spicher, fiddle; Jack Jackson, bass; Eddie Bayers, drums; Charlie McCoy, harmonica; Mac Wiseman, producer. Songs: The Great Speckled Bird, Mom And Dad's Waltz, Travelin' Blues, Have I Told You Lately That I Love You, Wedding Bells, The Letter Edged In Black, When God Dips His Love In My Heart, The Old Spinning Wheel, That Silver-Haired Daddy Of Mine, The Last Letter, The Wreck Of The Old '97, I'd Trade All Of My Tomorrows, Rockin' Alone In An Old Rocking Chair, No One Will Ever Know, There's a Little Pine Log Cabin, The Prisoner's Song, Just Because, Let's Live A Little (Before We Say Goodbye), Filipino Baby, and Silver Threads And Golden Needles. These were part and parcel of the Music Mill release "Letter Edged In Black," on Oct. 23, 2001; and "Just Because," also on Oct. 23, 2001. (Madacy released them as "Best Of Bluegrass" in Canada Feb. 1, 2004, and "The Heart Of a Legend" on Sept. 24, 2002.)

MAC WISEMAN recorded at Home Place Studio, Nashville, during 2001. Personnel: Mac Wiseman, vocals/rhythm guitar; Beecher Ray (Brother Oswald) Kirby, dobro; Charlie Collins, guitar; Eddie Stubbs, fiddle; Jesse McReynolds, mandolin; Kent Blanton, bass; Mac Wiseman, producer. Songs: Mother's Mansion Is Higher Than Mine, Precious Memories, Remember Me, The Things That Might Have Been, Precious Jewel, When You And I Were Young Maggie, Little Pal, The Great Judgment Morning, A Sweet Bunch of Daisies, May Darling Nellie Gray, and Carry Me Back To The Mountains. Wise Records' album "Mac Wiseman Shares 'Precious Memories' With Brother Oswald," was released Dec. 4, 2001.

MAC WISEMAN recorded "live" with The Lewis Family in Nashville during 2001. Personnel: Mac Wiseman, vocals/guitar; Little Roy Lewis, harmony vocal; Polly Lewis, vocals; Travis Lewis, harmony vocals; Lewis Phillips, harmony vocals; and Mac Wiseman, producer. CD Introduction by Mac Wiseman. Songs: Tis Sweet To Be Remembered, Jimmy Brown The Newsboy, The Prisoner's Song, The Wreck of The Old '97, I'll Be All Smiles Tonight, The Letter Edged in Black, That Silver-Haired Daddy of Mine, Old Shep, Beagle Hound Story (spoken), Footprints In The Snow, The Little White Church, I Wonder How The Old Folks Are At Home, Catfish John, Love Letters In The Sand, The Carnegie Hall Story (spoken), I'd Rather Live By The Side Of The Road, Keep On The Sunny Side, and Will The Circle Be Unbroken. A Wise Records release, "Mac Wiseman With His Guitar – First Recorded 'Live' Concert,' issued Dec. 4, 2001.

JOHN PRINE & MAC WISEMAN recorded at The Butcher Shoppe, a studio in Nashville's Germantown neighborhood, during Fall 2006 for Oh Boy Records. Personnel: John Prine, vocals/guitar/steel guitar; Mac Wiseman, vocals/rhythm guitar; Pat McLaughlin, guitars/mandolin/ukulele/harmonica; Cowboy Jack Clement, guitar/dobro; Tim O'Brien, guitar/banjo; Jamie Hartford, electric guitar; Lloyd Green, steel guitar; Ronnie McCoury, mandolin; Stuart Duncan, fiddle; Joey Miskulin, accordion; Chuck Cochran, electric piano; Mike Bub and David Jacques, bass; Kenneth Blevins, snare drums/percussion; Pat McInerney and Kenny Malone, drums; The Carol Lee Singers; and John Prine and David Ferguson, co-producers. Songs: Blue-Eyed Elaine; Don't Be Ashamed Of Your Age; Pistol Packin' Mama; I Forgot To Remember To Forget; I Love You Because; Saginaw, Michigan; Old Dogs, Children & Watermelon Wine; Old Cape Cod; The Death of Floyd Collins; The Blue Side of Lonesome; In The Garden; Just The Other Side of Nowhere; The Old Rugged Cross; and Where The Blue Of The Night (Meets The Gold Of The Day). Oh Boy Records released the resulting duets album "Standard Songs For Average People" on April 24, 2007.

MAC WISEMAN recorded tunes for release on his own Wise Records label in Nashville during 2009. Mac Wiseman, vocals/guitar/producer; Jesse McReynolds, vocals/mandolin. Songs: I Was Seeing Nellie Home, I'm Thinking Tonight Of My Blue Eyes, Send Me Your Address From Heaven, Comin' Home Some Ole Day, Be Nobody's Darling But Mine, What Is Home Without Love, My Two Sweethearts, Lonesome Roving Gambler, Darling Little Joe, Sailing on Golden River, Ballad Of The Haunted Woods, Philadelphia Lawyer, When The Work's All Done This Fall, Listen You Drunken Drivers, Old Likker In A New Jug, and Please Carry Me Back To The Mountains. Released as the album "Old Likker In A New Jug," on Oct. 13, 2009.

MAC WISEMAN recorded the following 14 songs during 2009 in Nashville. Self-produced by Wiseman, who supplied vocals and guitar, while Jesse McReynolds furnished vocals and mandolin. Songs: Waiting For The Boys To Come Home, My Mary Dear, When It's Reveille Time In Heaven, Let's Thank God For the U.S.A., One Of The Boys In Blue, Silver Dew On The Bluegrass Tonight, I Wonder How The Old Folks Are At Home, Put Me In Your Pocket, Soldier's Last Letter, There's A Star-Spangled Banner Waving Somewhere, The Ballad Of The Irish Rebel, Filipino Baby, (Think Of Me) Each Night At Nine, and Rainbow At Midnight. Wise Records' album "Waiting For The Boys To Come Home" was released on Oct. 13, 2009.

MERLE HAGGARD & MAC WISEMAN recorded at StarStruck Studio on Music Row, Nashville, Oct. 23-24, 2012, for an independent duet session. (Additional overdub session June 24, 2013 at Hilltop Studio, Madison, TN.) Personnel: Merle Haggard, vocals/guitar; Mac Wiseman, vocals/guitar; Carl Jackson, guitar; Aubrey Haynie, fiddle; Ben Isaacs, bass; Rob Ickes, dobro; Andy Leftwich, mandolin/fiddle; Alison Krauss, vocal harmony; Ronnie Reno and Merle Haggard, co-producers. Wiseman songs include Jimmy Brown The Newsboy, I'll Be All Smiles Tonight, I Wonder How The Old Folks Are At Home, Bringing Mary Home, High On A Hilltop, Love Letters In The Sand, and 'Tis Sweet To Be Remembered. (Album initially released by Cracker Barrel, May 19, 2015, under the title "Timeless.")

MAC WISEMAN recorded at Hilltop Recording Studio in Madison on June 11, 2014, for the independent Wrinkled Records of Nashville; with overdubbing accomplished at TJ Tunes, Nashville, June 12, 2014. Personnel: Mac Wiseman, vocals; Thomm Jutz, guitars; Jimmy Capps, guitar/dobro; Sierra Hull, mandolin; Mark Fain, bass; Lisa Jones Wall, hammered dulcimer; Justin Moses, bass/dobro/fiddle/harmony; Jelly Roll Johnson, harp; Peter Cooper,

Lindsay Hayes and Eric Brace, harmony vocals; Thomm Jutz and Peter Cooper, co-producers. Songs: Blue Ridge Mountain Blues, The Wreck Of Number Nine, You're A Flower (Blooming In The Wildwood), Old Rattler, When It's Lamp Lighting Time In The Valley, Answer To Weeping Willow, The Eastbound Train, Answer To Great Speckled Bird, I Heard My Mother Call My Name In Prayer, Little Rosewood Casket, and Will There Be Any Stars In My Crown. The album "Songs From My Mother's Hand" was released September 23, 2014.

ONE SHOTS AND VARIOUS GUEST APPEARANCES ON OTHER ARTIST OR ALL-STAR RECORDING STINTS

Through the years, Mac Wiseman has performed/guested on numerous artists records, really too many to provide a perfect compilation; however, below are some of the more memorable sessions he has participated in during his many decades as an artist.

BILL MONROE & His Blue Grass Boys performed with MAC WISEMAN & DON RENO during Carlton Haney's Bluegrass Festival, at Cantrell's Horse Farm, Fincastle, VA, on Sept. 5, 1965. Featured at Haney's Bluegrass Festival were Bill Monroe, vocals and mandolin; Mac Wiseman, vocals and rhythm guitar; and Don Reno, vocals and banjo, all recorded "live." Songs: When He Reached Down His Hand For Me, When The Moon Comes Over The Mountain, The Baggage Coach Ahead, and Jimmy Brown The Newsboy. Folkways Records released the collaboration on "Bill Monroe & His Blue Grass Boys 'Live' Duet Recording, 1956-1969, Off The Record, Volume 1," Sept. 24, 1993.

JOHN HARTFORD & MAC WISEMAN. In late 1975, while recording at Soundshop Studio, 1307 Division St., Nashville, John invited Mac to join him for a few cameo appearances, to provide both lead and harmony vocals. Other Personnel: John Hartford, vocals and banjo; James Colvard, guitar; Dale Sellers, guitar; Sam Bush, vocals and mandolin; Buddy Emmons, dobro/steel guitar; Benny Martin, fiddle; David Briggs, piano; Junior Huskey, bass; Dalton Dillingham, bass; Kenny Malone, drums; and Mike Melford produced. Songs on which Wiseman collaborated included the novelty number Granny Won'tcha Smoke Some Marijuana, In Tall Buildings and a medley of Somewhere My Love and We'll Meet Again Sweetheart. Flying Fish released Hartford's "Nobody Knows What You Do" album in 1976.

THE OSBORNE BROTHERS' Opryland album, produced at the theme park's Theatre By The Lake, Oct. , 1981, featured Mac Wiseman as guest artist, furnishing vocals and rhythm guitar for such selections as Remembering and I'd Rather Live By The Side Of The Road. The 11-song set was distributed by RCA Records, initially via the label's "Bluegrass Spectacular" album, as released April 10, 1982.

BILL MONROE & MAC WISEMAN paired up at Sound Stage Studio, 10 Music Circle S., Nashville, on May 6, 1985. Personnel: Bill Monroe, vocals/mandolin; Mac Wiseman, vocals/guitar; Wayne Lewis, guitar; Blake Williams, banjo; Glen Duncan, fiddle; Tater Tate, string bass; Emory Gordy, Jr., producer, MCA Records. Song: Travelin' Down This Lonesome Road. This track incorporated into MCA album "Bill Monroe & Stars Of The Bluegrass Hall of Fame," released in 1985.

BILL MONROE invited Mac Wiseman to Reflections Studio, 2741 Larmon Drive, Nashville, to record a song on May 15, 1990. Bill Monroe, vocals/mandolin; Mac Wiseman, vocals/guitar; Tom Ewing, guitar; Blake Williams, vocals/banjo; Tater Tate, vocals/fiddle;

Billy Rose, bass; and Steve Buchanan produced. Song: What Would You Give In Exchange For Your Soul. (It went unissued by MCA Records.)

BILL MONROE similarly invited Mac Wiseman back to Reflections Studio, on July 24, 1990, to cut additional tracks, with the same line-up of musicians as on the previous May 15, 1990 session. This time Mac contributed his talents to Shine Hallelujah Shine, This World Is Not My Home, and Cryin' Holy Unto The Lord. MCA released "Cryin' Holy Unto The Lord as a single in 1990.

MAC WISEMAN joined members of the NBC-TV series *In The Heat Of The Night* to record a benefit album of holiday songs, joining an all-star roster of country music acts, including Kitty Wells, Johnnie Wright, Bobby Wright, Jim & Jesse McReynolds, Ralph Stanley, Chubby Wise, Jimmy Martin, Doug Dillard, Josh Graves, and The Lewis Family. Co-produced by series actors Alan Autry and Randall Franks, the project was designed to combat drug addiction, a topic close to series star Carroll O'Connor's heart, as his actor-son Hugh (who played Lonnie on the show) suffered from this since age 16, when diagnosed with Hodgkin's Disease. Hugh survived the cancer with chemotherapy and subsequent surgeries, but became addicted to the drugs prescribed for pain, and later took his own life, after tiring of rehabilitation programs. Mac appeared on the album's title track, and added a recitation, to the Sonlite CD, "Christmas Time's A-Comin'," also issued by MGM/UA in 1991.

BILL MONROE & His Blue Grass Boys performed with MAC WISEMAN & DON RENO during Carlton Haney's Bluegrass Festival, at Cantrell's Horse Farm   Fincastle, VA, on Sept. 5, 1965. Featured were Bill Monroe, vocals and mandolin; Mac Wiseman, vocals and rhythm guitar; and Don Reno, vocals and banjo, all recorded "live." Songs: When He Reached Down His Hand For Me, When The Moon Comes Over The Mountain, The Baggage Coach Ahead, and Jimmy Brown The Newsboy. Folkways Records released the collaboration on "Bill Monroe & His Blue Grass Boys 'Live' Duet Recording, 1956-1969, Off The Record, Volume 1," Sept. 24, 1993.

BILL HARRELL & MAC WISEMAN teamed in the spring of 1995, for a Rebel Records scheduled song, Are You Coming Back To Me, as part of a Harrell-produced disc, "Bill Harrell... And Friends," released July 28, 1995.

JEFF FOXWORTHY & MAC WISEMAN & DEL McCOURY joined forces for a comedy cut, Big Ol' Moon, co-produced in 1996, by Scott Rouse & Doug Grau. It was included on Jeff Foxworthy's Warner Bros. album "Crank It Up," also released in 1996, ranking number three on the *Billboard* chart.

MAC WISEMAN, JIM SILVERS & BOBBY OSBORNE featured on a CMH compilation, pulled together by Jim Silvers during late 1999. Personnel (in part): Mac Wiseman, vocals/rhythm guitar; Jim Silvers, vocals/guitar; Bobby Osborne, vocals/mandolin; Herb Pedersen, banjo; Terry Eldredge, bass; various producers including Arthur Smith. Songs: Cannonball Yodel, Poison Love, Hillbilly Fever, I'll Still Write Your Name In The Sand, Walkin' The Dog, Old Flames, Sunny Side Of The Mountain, The Bluebirds Are Singing For Me, Fraulein, Georgia Piney Woods, I'm A Stranger Here, Take Me As I Am, Medicine Springs, Tragic Romance, and Katie Daly. Released as a CMH album "The Three Tenors of Bluegrass," March 7, 2000.

MAC WISEMAN in October 2002 and during 2003, was invited by Johnny Cash to record some selections at Cash's home studio in Hendersonville, TN. Mac was the last person to record with The Man In Black in August 2003, when they sang "I Still Miss Someone," just a couple weeks before Cash passed on Sept. 12, 2003. These were acoustic sessions in which selected people occasionally participated, notably Cowboy Jack Clement, Josh Graves, Laura Weber Cash and her then-husband John Carter Cash, and engineer David Ferguson. Two others Mac recalls doing with Johnny were "When It's Reveille Time in Heaven" and "Hold Fast To The Right." None have yet been released, but are in the possession of Johnny's producer Rick Rubin.

DAVID GRISMAN & MAC WISEMAN. Having mandolinist-pianist David Grisman invite Mac to record with him was certainly a surprise, as Grisman, 20 years' Wiseman's junior, had earlier performed with such disparate players as the Grateful Dead's Jerry Garcia and jazz-fusion violinist Stephane Grappelli. Grisman, a Hackensack, NJ, native, founded his own jazz-fusioned form of bluegrass tagged "Dawg" music, after a nickname Garcia gave him. For Grisman's 16-song set he wanted Mac to join him on a trio of tunes: When You And I Were Young Maggie, Girl Of My Dreams, and a bonus number Keep On The Sunny Side (Of Life). Others joining Grisman for this project included Stuart Duncan, fiddle; Harriet Rose, bass; Artie Rose, guitar; Ralph Rinzler, mandolin; John Nagy, guitar; John Hartford, banjo; Pat Enright, guitar; Alan O'Bryant, banjo; Herb Pedersen, guitar; The Del McCoury Band; Ralph Stanley & His Clinch Mountain Boys; Bryan Bowers, vocals; David Grisman, vocals/mandolin/producer. The album, "Life Of Sorrow," was released Aug. 14, 2003.

CHARLIE DANIELS and The Charlie Daniels Band recorded at the Groove Grass Factory in Nashville, early in 2005. Personnel: Charlie Daniels, vocals/fiddle; Mac Wiseman, vocals/recitation; Cyndi Wheeler, vocals; Ricky Skaggs, vocals; The Whites (Sharon, Buck & Cheryl), harmony vocals; Tim May, guitar; Andy Hall, dobro; Jason Carter, fiddle; Earl Scruggs, banjo; Chris Thile and Ronnie McCoury, mandolins; Rob McCoury, banjo; Michael Bub, bass; and Scott Rouse, producer. Songs (with Mac): Walkin' In Jerusalem (Just Like John), I'm Working On a Building, Keep On The Sunny Side, The Old Account, What Would You Give (In Exchange For Your Soul), and The 23rd Psalm (recitation). This Blue Hat album, "Songs From The Longleaf Pines" (Daniels' very first Bluegrass recordings), was released March 22, 2005. MAC WISEMAN performed a single song in a session at the Cash Cabin Studio in Hendersonville, TN, in 2006. Personnel: Bryan Sutton, acoustic guitar; Jesse McReynolds, mandolin; Mark Fain, string bass; and John Carter Cash, producer. Song: By The Side Of The Road. It became part of a Dualtone Records set, "Voice Of The Spirit – The Gospel Of The South," released in 2006.

LEONA WILLIAMS & MAC WISEMAN. One of the more recent guestings found Mac performing a Depression era ballad (written by Leona) - Are The Good Times Really Over - for Williams' album, "Grassroots." Utilizing remote recording equipment, Leona invited him to record right in his living room, as coordinated by album producer Bruce Hoffman, and engineer Nick Hoffman (of Alexis Sound Studio, Nashville), early in 2011. Personnel: Leona Williams, vocals/guitar; Mac Wiseman, vocals/guitar; David Bird, guitar; Beverly Dillard, banjo; Irl Hees, bass; Dean Holman, dobro; Steve Bush, banjo; Cathy Lee Coyne and Ron Williams, vocal harmony. The "Grassroots" CD was released by Leona's label Loveshine Records, mid-way in 2011.

"ROCKIN' HILLBILLY, Volume 6," Cactus Records, UK 2011. A 32-track compilation disc featuring Mac Wiseman on the cover, along with a cartoonish depiction of square dancers. Sub-titled "32 Wise-Ass Cuts From the Hills." Mac sings "I'm Eatin' High On the Hog."

APRIL VERCH & MAC WISEMAN. Yet another guest spot found Mac Wiseman recording Oct. 6, 2012, with Canadian talent April Verch on a song she wrote specifically with him in mind: The Only One. It was accomplished via remote recording at his home, along with a second song, My Home In The Sky. Personnel: April Verch, vocals/fiddle; Mac Wiseman, vocals; Cody Walters, vocals/bass/banjo; Hayes Griffin, guitars/vocals; Josh Goforth, mandolin; Bruce Molsky, fiddle/vocals; Sammy Shelor, banjo; Matthew Smith, dobro/steel guitar; Verch, Walters, Griffin and Chris Rosser, co-produced. The songs recorded by Wiseman and Verch appear on her Slab Town Records' 20-song CD "Bright Like Gold," released April 1, 2013.

Regarding Mac Wiseman produced product as A&R country executive producer for Dot Records:

Unfortunately we don't have all the necessary data on the numerous sessions Mac Wiseman produced or co-produced on other artists during his tenure as Dot Records' A&R executive producer in the late 1950s and early 1960s (and even later production chores apart from Dot). We did discover some of the sessions, as noted below; however, Wiseman produced an array of artists on the Dot label, including Cowboy Copas, Tommy Jackson, Leroy Van Dyke, Reno & Smiley, Bill Harrell, Howard Crockett, Jimmy C. Newman, and Bonnie Guitar.

DON RENO & RED SMILEY recorded Dot session @ Bradley Film & Recording Studio, 804 16th Ave. S., Nashville, April 15, 1957, marking Mac's first production as Dot's Country A&R chief. Personnel: Don Reno, tenor vocals and banjo; (Arthur) Red Smiley, baritone vocals and rhythm guitar; Hank Garland, lead guitar; Mack Magaha, fiddle; Benny Martin, fiddle; Gordon Terry, sound effects; John Palmer, bass; and Wiseman, vocals and producer. Songs: Sawing On the Strings, Sweethearts in Heaven, One Teardrop And One Step Away, Unforgivable You. First single off session was Sweethearts in Heaven b/w Sawing On the Strings, released June 3, 1957. (In January '63, Dot released the Reno & Smiley LP "Bluegrass Hits.")

HOWARD CROCKETT cut Dot session conducted @ Bradley Studio, Nashville, on April 1957. Personnel: Howard Elton Crockett (Hausey), vocals; Cecil McCullough, lead guitar; Grady Martin, rhythm guitar; Floyd Cramer, piano; Bob Moore, bass; (Murrey) Buddy Harman, drums; The Jordanaires featuring Neal Matthews, Hoyt Hawkins, Gordon Stoker and Ray Walker, harmony; Mac Wiseman, producer. Howard Crockett, primarily a hit songwriter ("Whispering Pines," "Honky Tonk Man"), signed as an artist-in-development. Songs: I'm Gonna Try Again, Where Did My Baby Go, You've Got Me Lyin', and If You'll Let Me, all of which he wrote. A Dot single, released June 24, 1957, You've Got Me Lyin' was b/w If You'll Let Me. (Mac's tracks on Crockett were included on a Bear Family compilation LP, titled "Howard Crockett: Out Of Bounds," released Nov. 12, 2007.)

DON RENO & RED SMILEY recorded Dot session @ RCA Victor Studio, Methodist Television, Radio & Film Commission, 1525 McGavock St., Nashville, on Aug. 5, 1957. Personnel: Don Reno, vocal and banjo; Red Smiley, vocal and guitar; Hank Garland, lead guitar; Mack Magaha, fiddle; Benny Martin, fiddle; John Palmer, bass; Mac Wiseman, producer, also on rhythm guitar. Songs: Howdy Neighbor Howdy, Banjo Medley, One More Hill, Kiss Me One More Time, Where Did Our Young Years Go, Cotton-Eyed Joe, Dark Waters, and Your Love Is Dying. First session single Where Did Our Young Years Go was b/w Cotton-Eyed Joe, released Sept. 20, 1957.

HOWARD CROCKETT recorded this Dot session @ Bradley Film & Recording Studio, Nashville, during January 1958. Personnel: Howard Crockett, vocals; Cecil McCullough, lead guitar; Grady Martin, rhythm guitar; Buddy Harman, drums; Floyd Cramer, piano; Bob Moore, bass; unknown on backing vocals; Mac Wiseman, producer. Songs: Branded, and Night Rider, released as a single on Feb. 10, 1958.

DON RENO & BILL HARRELL with The Tennessee Cut-Ups were recorded in Akron, OH, during February 1967. Personnel: Don Reno, vocals/banjo; Bill Harrell, vocals/guitar; Ronnie Reno, mandolin; George Shuffler, bass; co-produced by Wiseman and Lee Sutton. Songs: Under the Double Eagle (instrumental), I'm a Man Of Constant Sorrow, Long Journey Home, Red Rockin' Chair (instrumental), Hot Corn (Cold Corn), Gotta Travel On, Little Pal, Nine Pound Hammer, I Don't Love Nobody, Poor Ellen Smith, Limehouse Blues, Molly and Tenbrooks, Whitehouse Blues, Dill Pickle Rag, Keep On The Sunny Side, Worried Man Blues, Great Speckled Bird, When The Roses Bloom Again, and Footprints In The Snow. Rural Rhythm Records released "Don Reno & Bill Harrell With The Tennessee Cut-Ups: 20 Bluegrass Favorites," in 1967.

Discography courtesy Mac Wiseman, Dick Grant and Walt Trott.

THE INDEX

Carter, A. P., 53, 266
Carter Family, 22, 117, 118, 183, 223, 243, 244
Carter, Janette, 132
Carter, Jason, 238, 266, 271, 272, 287, 314, 318
Carter, June (Smith-Cash), 130, 139, 140, 202, 222, 266-270
Carter, Maybelle, vi, 48, 84, 124, 126, 127, 130, 202, 305, 312
Carter, Wilf (Montana Slim), 24, 135
Case, Blackie, 209
Cash Cabin Studio, 318
Cash, John Carter, 269, 270, 317, 318
Cash, Johnny, iii, vi, viii, ix, 93, 105, 106, 111, 113, 122, 123, 125-127, 130, 137, 139, 140, 143, 148, 181, 200, 202, 204, 219, 222, 266, 268, 288, 317, 318
Cash, Laura (Weber), iii, xi, 269, 270, 296, 318
Cash, Rosanne, 269
Cash, Vivian, 130
Casper, Dave, 136
Cassell, Pete, 58
Castle Studios, 82, 93, 99, 110, 299-301
CBS Network, 59, 83, 84, 181,
CBS-TV, 132, 181, 228
Chandler, Jeff, 122
Chandler, Steve, 290
Chapman, Kelly, 32
Charles, Ray, 113, 187, 224
Chellman, Chuck, 115
Cheney, Dick, 273
Churchill Records, 197, 199, 201, 310, 311
Clapton, Eric, 254
Clark, Dick, 124
Clark, Herb, 91
Clark, Petula, 188
Clark, Roy, 85, 95, 129, 143, 197, 219, 253
Clement, Frank (Governor), 150
Clement, (Cowboy) Jack, iii, vi, viii, xi, 111, 143-146, 150, 151, 153, 154, 184, 191, 265, 269, 270, 306-309, 315, 318
Clements, Zeke, 142
Clifford, Gordon, 199
Clifton, Bill, 187, 188
Clinch Mountain Clan, 138, 185
Cline, Miss (teacher), 24
Cline, Patsy, iii, viii, 41, 85, 86, 129, 204, 214, 227, 245, 246, 260
Clinton, George, 234

Clinton, Hillary (Rodham), 273
CMH Records, vii, 193, 196, 201-204, 208, 223, 289, 309-313, 317
Coben, Cy, 144
Cobb, Shad, 294
Cochran, Charles (Chuck), 153, 154, 284, 308, 315
Cochran, Hank, 129, 147, 259, 291, 292, 295, 296
Cochran, Suzi, 296
Cody, Betty, 136
Cody, Bill (WSM), 287
Coe, David Allan, 88
Coiner, Malcolm, 5
Colbert, Claudette, 27
Cole, Bill, 302
Cole, Grady, 48
Cole, Hazel, 48
Cole, Lee, 83, 84
Collier, Chubby, 78, 84, 98, 300
Collins, Bootsy, vii, ix, 233, 260
Collins, Charlie, 172, 290, 314
Collins, Floyd, 37, 38, 284, 315, 329
Collins, Jay, 248
Collins, Judy, 128
Collins, Larrie, 105
Collins, Lorrie, 105
Collins, Tom, 297
Collins, Tommy, 137, 204
Columbia Records, 49, 54, 90, 124, 145, 213, 268, 299, 313
Colvard, James, 308, 316
Compton, Sonny, 193
Conn, Mervyn, 185-187, 193, 194
Conway, Tim, 216
Conway, Tony, 217
Cook, Elizabeth, 293
Cooley, Spade, 103
Coolidge, Calvin (President), 5
Coon Creek Girls, The, 146
Cooper, Carol Lee, 17, 185, 287, 315
Cooper, George C., Jr., 249, 250
Cooper, Peter, vii, x, xi, 222, 283, 293-295, 315, 316
Cooper, Stoney, 17, 84, 119, 138, 182, 185
Cooper, Wilma Lee (Leary), 17, 84, 119, 138, 182, 185
Coots, J. Fred, 82
Copas, Cowboy (Lloyd), ix, 63, 66, 81, 106, 129, 227, 319
Corbin, Dr. Marvin, 122

Lewis, Laurie, 266
Lewis, Polly, 92, 167, 314
Lewis, (Little) Roy, 91, 167, 314
Lewis, Smiley, 93
Lewis, Travis, 314
Lewis, Wayne, 316
Liebling, Rachel, 229
Liggins, Joe, 80
Light, Don, xi, 151, 184, 189, 290
Lightfoot, Gordon, 128, 196, 245, 289, 310
Lilly Brothers, The, 95
Lilly, Everett, 288
Lincoln, Abraham (President), 43
Lindeman, Edith, 90
Linneman, Jack (Hoss), 201
Locklin, Hank, 109, 117, 204
Logan, Horace, 69
Londin, Larrie, 309
Long, Hubert, 69, 116, 137, 164, 186
Long, Shorty, 80
Lonzo & Oscar, 63, 75, 80, 83, 284
Loudermilk, Charlie, 243
Louisiana Hayride, 60, 67, 161, 249
Louvin Brothers, 52
Louvin, Charlie, 52, 82, 243, 290
Louvin, Ira, 52
Loveless, Patty, 220, 269
Loveshine Records, 275, 318
Lowery, Bill, 115
Lulu Belle & Scotty (Wiseman), 39, 117,
    146, 149
Lutz, Gabby, 142, 211
Lyle, Rudy, 1, 299
Lynn, Loretta, 181
Lynn, Vera, 37
Lytle, Moe, 191, 192, 247

Mabley, Moms, 127
Mac & Bob, 74, 75
MacArthur, Douglas (General), 42
Macey, Wade (Professor), 84
Mack, Warner, 144
Macon, Uncle Dave, vi, viii, 17, 39, 63, 64,
    76, 255
Madacy Music, 219, 313, 314
Madden, Fred, 126
Maddox Brothers, The, 77, 101
Maddox, Johnnie, 301
Maddox, Johnny, 80
Maddox, Rose, 204
Madison Square Garden, viii, 217, 218

Magaha, Mack, 175, 319
Maiden, Preacher, 12
Main, Marjorie, 131
Mainer, J. E., 1
Mainer's Mountaineers, 1
Malone, Bill C. (Professor), 196
Malone, Kenny, 284, 308, 315, 316
Mandel, Steve, 195
Mandrell, Barbara, 143, 187
Mank, Chaw, 136
Manuel, Dean, 135
Maphis, Joe, 17, 84, 105, 111, 195, 202,
    208, 302, 312
Maphis, Rose Lee, 295
Marciano, Rocky, 83
Marshall, Jack, 101, 102, 301, 302
Marshall, Alberta Forbus, 290
Marshall, Esther, 156
Marshall, Toby, 60
Martel, Marty, 220
Martha White Show, 56, 230, 243, 244
Martin, Benny, 147, 217, 316, 319
Martin, Dean, vii, 188
Martin, Grady, 17, 46, 82, 89, 98, 119, 130,
    300, 301, 305, 319
Martin, Jimmy, vi, 63, 148, 149, 225, 228,
    241, 242, 317
Martin, Tommy (Parrish), 197
Martindale, Wink, 118
Matthews, Neal, 305, 319
Matthews, Vince, 144, 181
Mauldin, Bessie Lee, 61
May, Tim, 271, 272, 318
Mayo, Ralph, 66, 67, 69, 71, 299
MCA, 154, 190, 220, 226, 262, 313, 316,
    317
McAlpin, Vic, 116, 164
McAuliffe, Leon, 105, 130
McBride, Martina, 296
McCall, Bill, 107, 113
McCall, Darrell, 204
McCall, Mona, 204
McCausland, Henry, 27, 28
McConnell, Jim, 164
McConnell, Margaret, 32
McCormack, John, 136
McCormick, David, 178, 205, 295
McCormick, Haskel, 277, 307, 308
McCoury, Del, vii-ix, xi, 88, 229, 230, 233,
    236, 238-241, 252, 266, 272, 279, 291,
    313, 314, 318,

Nash, Murray, 56, 108, 299
Nashville Musician newspaper, ix, xi, 225,
   248, 252, 254, 276, 298
Nashville Now, TV show, 219, 259
Nashville Sound, The, 46, 102, 250
Nathan, Syd, 66
National Barn Dance, WLS, 39, 65, 74, 146
NBC, 59, 63, 188, 317
Neese, Chuck, 184
Neff, Tom, 230
Nelson, Ken, viii, xi, 102, 105, 109, 116,
   121-123, 134, 164, 304, 305
Nelson, Ricky, 105
Nelson, Willie, 147, 175, 184, 229
Nesbitt, Eddie, 111
Nesbitt, George, 73
New Lost City Ramblers, The, 139
Newman, Jimmy C., ix, xi, 67, 105, 108,
   109, 220, 290, 319
Newport Folk Festival, viii, 79, 128, 139,
   140, 266, 305
Newton, Ernie, 75, 77, 89, 93, 299-301
Nixon, Charles, 308
Nixon, Richard (President), 11, 232
Noack, Eddie, 93
Nobles, Gene, 80
Nolan, Bob, 27, 39
Norman, Jim Ed, 234

O'Brien, Tim, 283, 314, 315
O'Bryant, Alan, 318
O'Connor, Carroll, 228
O'Connor, Hugh, 317
O'Daniel, W. Lee, 110, 131, 302
O'Day, Molly, vi, viii, 48-51, 59, 61, 81,
   99, 111, 126, 147, 223, 238, 299
Oermann, Robert, 230
Old Dominion Barn Dance, 46, 83, 84, 86,
   87, 99, 147
O'Malley, D. J., 111
O'Neal, Uncle Jim, 138, 279
O'Neil, Don, 305
Opryland Park, 92, 192, 204, 316
Orbison, Roy, 191
Osborne, Bobby, xi, 104, 139, 141, 192,
   201, 203-205, 236, 237, 306, 311, 312,
   314, 317
Osborne Brothers, The, vii, 92, 117, 192,
   195, 201-204, 229, 230, 235, 243, 260,
   277, 311, 312
Osborne, Jerry, 128

Osborne, Robby, 201, 309, 311, 312
Osborne, Sonny (Roland), 141, 192, 201,
   242, 260, 306, 311, 312, 314
Osborne, Wynn, 201, 311, 312
Overstreet, Tommy, 143, 199
Owen, Fuzzy, 105
Owens, Bonnie, 204
Owens, Buck, 104, 105, 129, 137, 204, 219
Owens, Don, 77, 95, 98, 137, 138
Owens, Jim, 181, 212

Page, Patti, 287
Paisley, Brad, 138
Palmer, John, 277, 307, 309, 310, 319
Palmer, Morris, 303
Pamper Music, 129, 146, 147
Paramount Music, 80, 107, 143
Parker, Fess, 89, 90
Parker, Tom (Colonel), 91, 222
Parr, Chris, 234
Parton, Dolly, 141, 194, 260
Paul, Dorothy, 188
Paul, Les, 75
Pavarotti, Luciano, 236
Payne, Leon, 284
Pedersen, Herb, 236, 266, 317, 318
Peebles, Hap, 164
Peer, Ralph, 38
Pellettieri, Vito, 59
Pennington, Ray, 191, 219, 309
Penny, Hank, 58
Pepper, Jack, 32
Perkins, Carl, 204
Perkins, Larry, 229
Perryman, Lloyd, 27
Perryman, Tom, 115
Peter, Paul & Mary, 124
Peterson, Peggy, 138, 306
Petrillo, James, 257
Petty, Richard, 166
Petty, Tom, 282
Phelps, Claude, 308
Phelps, Jackie, 83, 300, 301, 308
Phillips, Lewis, 314
Phillips, Red, 17
Phillips, Stu, 142, 172
Piaf, Edith, 111
Pierce, Don, 192, 194, 195, 247
Pierce, Webb, viii, 67, 69, 111, 181, 204,
   206, 296
Poole, Charlie, 17, 208

CPSIA information can be obtained
at www.ICGtesting.com
Printed in the USA
LVOW04s1437140516

488278LV00013B/135/P